D0024759

The God of the Old Testament

The God of the Old Testament

ENCOUNTERING THE DIVINE
IN CHRISTIAN SCRIPTURE

R. W. L. Moberly

Baker Academic
a division of Baker Publishing Group
Grand Rapids, Michigan

Published by Baker Academic
a division of Baker Publishing Group
PO Box 6287, Grand Rapids, MI 49516-6287
www.bakeracademic.com

Printed in the United States of America

Library of Congress Cataloging-in-Publication Data
Names: Moberly, R. W. L., author.
Title: The God of the Old Testament : encountering the divine in Christian Scripture / R. W. L. Moberly.
Description: Grand Rapids, Michigan : Baker Academic, a division of Baker Publishing Group, 2020. | Includes bibliographical references and index.
Identifiers: LCCN 2020018331 | ISBN 9781540962997 (cloth)
Subjects: LCSH: God—Biblical teaching. | Bible. Old Testament—Criticism, interpretation, etc. | God (Christianity)
Classification: LCC BS1192.6 .M637 2020 | DDC 221.6—dc23
LC record available at https://lccn.loc.gov/2020018331

20 21 22 23 24 25 26 7 6 5 4 3 2 1

To Richard Briggs

In friendship, and with gratitude
for many years of drinking coffee
and talking about the interpretation
of Scripture

And in memory of Kesolenuo Suokhrie

Assistant professor of Old Testament theology
at Oriental Theological Seminary, Langham scholar,
and doctoral student at Durham University,
whose service on earth was cut short
in the time of the COVID-19 pandemic

Contents

Preface

In the course of the academic year 2019–2020, on six consecutive Wednesdays in January to March 2020, it has been my privilege to deliver the Hulsean Lectures at Cambridge University. This is the book of those lectures.

The relationship between book and lectures is not entirely straightforward. The six chapters here correspond to the six lectures delivered, but each chapter is much longer than each lecture. It is not that the lectures have been worked up into a book. Rather, the material has been written as a book, with the lectures in mind. Each draft chapter was pared down so as to produce a second text of a suitable length for a lecture, and was then revised in light of the lecture and responses to it.

I appreciate that some readers might have preferred the more succinct presentation of the lectures to be their enduring form in print! However, for better or worse, I decided that a fuller form of argument would better help clarify the often-problematic interrelationship of Old Testament interpretation with the disciplines of the secular academy and with the priorities of Christian life and thought.

For the record, and in case some might be interested in what could be alternative titles for the chapters of this book, the titles of the lectures were (1) "God, Wisdom, and the World"; (2) "The Voice from the Fire"; (3) "God and the Twilight of the Gods"; (4) "Divine Favoring and Hard Choices"; (5) "Monotheism and Its Teasing Logic"; and (6) "Stability and Danger in the City of God."

Most of the work for the book and lectures was done in the course of a research leave in the academic year 2018–2019, and I am grateful to my colleagues in the Durham department of theology and religion for taking over my regular responsibilities of administration and undergraduate teaching during that time. As ever, I did not travel for my research (though I enjoyed a fruitful week of lecturing and library browsing at the hospitable École Biblique et Archéologique in Jerusalem), but savored the context of my office on Palace

Green. I am grateful also to Brandon Hurlbert, my diligent research assistant, who made numerous library trips for me and helped with various tasks.

My time in Cambridge while I was delivering the lectures was a delight. My thanks to Peter Harland and Jane Wallace for their efficient organization and hospitable welcome. Colleagues wined and dined me generously. Happily, it was possible to complete the lecture series just before the coronavirus restrictions became operative.

I have benefited greatly from the insights of friends who read all the chapters in draft. Lunchtime discussions with David Day helped with reshapings, especially in the introduction. Julie Woods improved my sentences and saved me from some improprieties. Over coffee, Richard Briggs contributed many points both of detail and structure. Patrick Morrow offered stimulating reflections, many of which have become part of my text. Members of the Durham Old Testament research seminar, and also on one occasion the theology research seminar, sat through dry runs of the lectures and gave much incisive feedback. Particular mention must be made of Chris Insole for sharpening my focus in chapter 1, of Rory Balfour for helping me see more clearly what I shouldn't be arguing in chapter 4, and of Andrew Mein for helping me out of a hole in an initially confused version of chapter 6. Nathan MacDonald and Brent Strawn also contributed to individual chapters.

I owe a particular debt of gratitude to Jim Kinney and his colleagues at Baker Academic, who have been willing to produce the book on a tight schedule. This meant that the book (whose manuscript I delivered late) could reflect input from my lectures in January to March and still be published by the beginning of November to meet the deadline for the periodic review of university research sponsored by the British Government, REF 2021. As with my previous two books, the process of publishing with Baker Academic has enhanced the end result. Jim's ability to envisage a book as a whole, and to see what needs to be done to shape it accordingly, is second to none. Tim West is the meticulous and thoughtful copyeditor an author hopes to have: I think that my sentences and paragraphs are clear and well structured—until Tim points out how they are not! Between them, Jim and Tim have significantly improved this book.

If there are still deficiencies and defects in the book, I can only say that there would have been many more without the input of all these friends and colleagues.

Finally, my wife, Jenny, has put up with my ups and downs that have accompanied the writing, has been patient with my moans about what often felt like endless distractions during my research leave, and has helped with fluent translations of German. I owe her so much. She has helped make the writing of the book possible.

Abbreviations

AB	Anchor Bible
ABD	*Anchor Bible Dictionary*. Edited by David Noel Freedman. 6 vols. New York: Doubleday, 1992.
ACCSOT	Ancient Christian Commentary on Scripture: Old Testament
A.J.	Josephus, *Antiquitates judaicae* (*Jewish Antiquities*)
ANET	*Ancient Near Eastern Texts Relating to the Old Testament*. With Supplement. Edited by James B. Pritchard. 3rd ed. Princeton: Princeton University Press, 1969.
AOTC	Abingdon Old Testament Commentaries
AT	author's translation
ATR	*Anglican Theological Review*
ATSAT	Arbeiten zu Text und Sprache im Alten Testament
AYB	The Anchor Yale Bible
BBC	Blackwell Bible Commentaries
BBRS	Bulletin for Biblical Research Supplements
BCOTWP	Baker Commentary on the Old Testament Wisdom and Psalms
BDB	Brown, Francis, S. R. Driver, and Charles A. Briggs. *A Hebrew and English Lexicon of the Old Testament*.
BHQ	*Biblia Hebraica Quinta*. Edited by Adrian Schenker et al. Stuttgart: Deutsche Bibelgesellschaft, 2004–.
BHS	*Biblia Hebraica Stuttgartensia*. Edited by Karl Elliger and Wilhelm Rudolph. Stuttgart: Deutsche Bibelgesellschaft, 1983.
BTCB	Brazos Theological Commentary on the Bible
BZ	*Biblische Zeitschrift*
BZAW	Beihefte zur Zeitschrift für die alttestamentliche Wissenschaft
ca.	*circa*, about
CBC	Cambridge Bible Commentary
CC	Continental Commentaries
CCT	Challenges in Contemporary Theology
CEB	Common English Bible

ch(s).	chapter(s)
CSCD	Cambridge Studies in Christian Doctrine
CTS	Calvin Translation Society
DNEB	Die Neue Echter Bibel
Eng.	English
esp.	especially
ET	English translation
ETS	Erfurter Theologische Studien
FAT	Forschungen zum Alten Testament
Gk.	Greek
GKC	*Gesenius' Hebrew Grammar*. Edited by Emil Kautzsch. Translated by Arthur E. Cowley. 2nd ed. Oxford: Clarendon, 1910.
HAT	Handbuch zum Alten Testament
HCOT	Historical Commentary on the Old Testament
Heb.	Hebrew
HTKAT	Herders Theologischer Kommentar zum Alten Testament
HTR	*Harvard Theological Review*
HUCA	*Hebrew Union College Annual*
IBCTP	Interpretation: A Bible Commentary for Teaching and Preaching
ICC	International Critical Commentary
IEJ	*Israel Exploration Journal*
JBL	*Journal of Biblical Literature*
JEC	*Journal of Ecumenical Studies*
JM	Joüon, Paul, and Takamitsu Muraoka. *A Grammar of Biblical Hebrew*. Subsidia Biblica 27. Rome: Editrice Pontificio Istituto Biblico, 2003.
JNSL	*Journal of Northwest Semitic Languages*
JSNTSS	Journal for the Study of the New Testament Supplement Series
JSOT	*Journal for the Study of the Old Testament*
JSOTSS	Journal for the Study of the Old Testament Supplement Series
JSS	*Journal of Semitic Studies*
JTI	*Journal of Theological Interpretation*
JTIS	Journal of Theological Interpretation Supplements
JTS	*Journal of Theological Studies*
KJV	King James Version
LBS	Library of Biblical Studies
LCL	Loeb Classical Library
LHBOTS	Library of Hebrew Bible/Old Testament Studies
lit.	literally
LXX	Septuagint
MT	Masoretic Text
NCamBC	New Cambridge Bible Commentary
NCB	New Century Bible
NCBC	New Century Bible Commentary
NEAEHL	*The New Encyclopedia of Archaeological Excavations in the Holy Land*. Edited by Ephraim Stern. 4 vols. Jerusalem: Israel Exploration Society and Carta; New York: Simon & Schuster, 1993.
NEB	New English Bible

NETS	*A New English Translation of the Septuagint*. Edited by Albert Pietersma and Benjamin G. Wright. New York and Oxford: Oxford University Press, 2007.
NIB	*The New Interpreter's Bible*. Edited by Leander E. Keck. 12 vols. Nashville: Abingdon, 1994–2004.
NIBC	New International Biblical Commentary
NIV	New International Version
NJPS	*Tanakh: The Holy Scriptures: The New JPS Translation according to the Traditional Hebrew Text*
NRT	*Nouvelle Revue Théologique*
NT	New Testament
OBO	Orbis Biblicus et Orientalis
OT	Old Testament
OTL	Old Testament Library
OTM	Oxford Theological Monographs
OTR	Old Testament Readings
OTS	Oudtestamentische Studiën
OTT	Old Testament Theology
PG	Patrologia Graeca [= *Patrologiae Cursus Completus: Series Graeca*]. Edited by J.-P. Migne. 161 vols. Paris: Migne, 1857–86.
RB	*Revue biblique*
REB	Revised English Bible
RSV	Revised Standard Version
SB	Stuttgarter Bibelstudien
SBLMS	Society of Biblical Literature Monograph Series
SBLSCS	Society of Biblical Literature Septuagint and Cognate Studies
SC	Sources chrétiennes
SCS	Septuagint Commentary Series
SEThV	Salzburger Exegetische Theologische Vorträge
SHBC	Smyth & Helwys Bible Commentary
SJSJ	Supplements to the Journal for the Study of Judaism
SJT	*Scottish Journal of Theology*
SS	Semeia Studies
STI	Studies in Theological Interpretation
TDOT	*Theological Dictionary of the Old Testament*. Edited by G. Johannes Botterweck and Helmer Ringgren. Translated by John T. Willis et al. 15 vols. Grand Rapids: Eerdmans, 1974–2006.
TECC	Theological Explorations for the Church Catholic
TNAC	The New American Commentary
TOTC	Tyndale Old Testament Commentaries
TynBul	*Tyndale Bulletin*
UCOP	University of Cambridge Oriental Publications
VT	*Vetus Testamentum*
VTSup	Supplements to Vetus Testamentum
WBC	Word Biblical Commentary
WUNT	Wissenschaftliche Untersuchungen zum Neuen Testament
ZAW	*Zeitschrift für die alttestamentliche Wissenschaft*

Introduction

This is a book about God. In it I seek to set out aspects of what might be called a doctrine or "grammar" of God that is present in the scriptures of ancient Israel—in other words, ground rules for appropriate speech and action in relation to the Lord, the God of Abraham and of Israel. I will offer close readings of selected passages in these scriptures, which antedate both Judaism and Christianity yet have been preserved, received, and appropriated within each of those faiths. Although my own frame of reference is Christian, and the readings overall have a clear Christian inflection, I hope that much of the theological grammar I set out will resonate within a Jewish as well as a Christian frame of reference.

This concern with God needs one basic clarification from the outset. In the Bible, and in the Jewish and Christian faiths, an understanding of God is inseparable from an understanding of what it means to be human. This can be difficult to appreciate in the contemporary world, at least in Europe and the US, where there has been a general move away from the Christian faith and culture that once prevailed. For many people, to cease to believe in God is essentially to do some intellectual spring-cleaning, to cross off the list of worthwhile mental contents the possible reality of a putative invisible entity which never made any real difference to anything anyway, at least in the public realm of everyday secular life (whatever private consolations some might find).

In fact, however, to cease to believe in God, as the Bible and Christian faith understand God, is to usher in major change, over time, as to how everything and everyone is viewed and related to in practice (though many facets of Christian faith continue to have influence when transposed into secular thought, where the Christian dimension may have become invisible except to those alert to the history of ideas). To see our understandings of God and of humanity and of the world as inseparable is not to concede to the suspicion that all talk and thought of God is nothing but a coded account of human priorities. It is, rather, to recognize the multidimensional nature of reality and of human understanding. Thus, in the studies that follow, where God is the central concern, much of the discussion will not focus on God all the time, because many things have to be considered to make the biblical conception of God meaningful for thought and life.

Overall, I am seeking to articulate facets of the Old Testament's own prime creedal affirmation and hope, as articulated by the psalmist: "Know that the LORD is God" (*dĕʿū kī yhwh hūʾ ʾĕlōhīm*, Ps. 100:3)—which is followed, as a matter of apparent implicit logic, by a framing of what it means to be human in terms of basic identity and relationality: "It is he that made us, and we are his."[1] I offer an account of at least some of what is involved in coming to such an acknowledgment and knowledge of God on the part of those who would read Israel's scriptures as Scripture for today.[2]

In no way do I seek to be comprehensive in the six chapters that follow. For example, I offer no discussion of the affirmation of humanity as created "in the image of God" (Gen. 1:26–27). Rather, I focus on selected significant and representative voices within the biblical witness that speak specifically about the nature of God. I recognize that the selection of passages and the sequence in which they are presented may seem prima facie rather puzzling. The presentation corresponds neither to the sequential order of the biblical canon (even though each section of the Hebrew canon—the Law, the Prophets, and the Writings—is represented by two chapters) nor to a likely developmental sequence of Israel's religious thought in terms of a history of ideas. However, it is often noted that the Bible's own presentation of its theological content does not correspond to the patterns and categories of postbiblical Christian theology. This remains the case whether one reads the material in canonical sequence or whether one reads it rearranged into a putative developmental sequence; in each case, the structuring concerns have their own distinctive logic. So the logic of this presentation is a contingent logic which weaves a particular theological pattern (about which more will be said in the epilogue),

1. The alternative reading, "and not we ourselves," makes a nonreductive point about being human, akin to that in Deut. 8:2–3, 17–18.

2. I have no particular concern either to prioritize or to avoid famous "problem passages" about God. The most obviously problematic passage that I discuss here is Gen. 4, with its inscrutable God. Elsewhere I have discussed God's command to Abraham to sacrifice Isaac (Gen. 22), Israel's obligation to practice *ḥerem* on the non-Israelite inhabitants of Canaan (Deut. 7), and God's commission to a lying spirit to deceive King Ahab so that he dies in battle (1 Kings 22). See, respectively, my *Theology of the Book of Genesis*, 179–99; "Election and the Transformation of *Ḥērem*"; and "Does God Lie to His Prophets?"

with recognition that the theological grammar of Israel's scriptures could be portrayed otherwise.

Some Issues of Approach and Method

General Considerations for Reading as Scripture

In general terms, I offer worked examples of how the scriptures of ancient Israel may be read as Scripture, the Old Testament of the Christian church today. Theoretical discussions of hermeneutical issues have their place, and I will touch on them along the way. But the proof of the theoretical pudding is in its practical eating. One must be able to offer good (intellectually satisfying and existentially engaging) readings of the biblical text if any general proposal about the viability of reading Israel's scriptures as Christian Scripture is to make headway.

I here presuppose and build on earlier work, not least my *Old Testament Theology* and *The Bible in a Disenchanted Age*. In these I frame the whole discussion of theology and the Old Testament with reference to the importance of hermeneutical decisions about how one reads, focused on the notion of *reading as Scripture*.[3] I also suggest a heuristic typology of three prime approaches to reading the Bible—as ancient history, as cultural classic, and as holy Scripture. Of course, approaches to the Bible as ancient history, as cultural classic, and as holy Scripture are not incompatible with each other, and often in practice they overlap and are combined. Nonetheless, differences and divergences can be significant.

Two basic hermeneutical points need to be recognized. First, *how* we read and use the biblical text depends on *why* we read and use the text; that is, appropriate method is related to purpose and interest. Second, there is a legitimate and healthy diversity of possible purposes and interests in reading the biblical text, and so a diversity of appropriate methods and approaches. What I am trying to articulate in this book is not *the* way of interpreting Israel's scriptures but *a* way, albeit a way that I hope will have significant resonance and traction for those whose concern is to understand Israel's scriptures specifically as Christian Scripture.

3. The inevitability of making hermeneutical judgments and decisions, even on the part of those who may not think in these terms, is engagingly set out by John D. Caputo in *Hermeneutics: Facts and Interpretation in the Age of Information*. Caputo remarks, for example, that "the great breakthrough of the modern world—and it was hermeneutic all the way down—was the discovery of a new way of *reading* the world *as* a book *written* in the language of mathematics" (236).

Let me offer a summary outline of some of the key elements of what I understand to be involved in approaching Israel's scriptures as Christian Scripture, starting with two core aspects.

On the one hand, there are certain preunderstandings and expectations related to the privileged status of the ancient textual compilation, the biblical canon, as a repository of enduring wisdom and truth in relation to God, humanity, and the world. Christian faith, following the lead of Jewish faith, ascribes to the collected canonical documents special significance for the knowledge of God, knowledge that is both intellectual (*savoir*) and relational (*connaître*). At the heart of this is the conviction (with whatever qualifications) that the deity of whom the biblical writers speak is not like Zeus or Marduk—ancient deities now essentially of interest only to students of ancient history and literature and no longer options for living faith—but rather is the one God, the living God, the Creator and Redeemer, in relation to whom people can still trust, be accountable, and live in hope. This conviction (with whatever differences and nuances) is constitutive of both Judaism and Christianity (and also, though distinctly, of Islam).

On the other hand, it follows that what the biblical writers say about God and humanity is best understood—when the material is read as Scripture—not only through rigorous philological and historical work on the documents in their ancient contexts of origin but also through entering into the life and thought of Jewish or Christian faith, where there is a long history of seeking to articulate what is necessary for biblical God-language to be authentic and meaningful. Sadly, it is all too easy for God-language to become vacuous, confused, stale, manipulative, or self-deceptive. To inhabit the Jewish or Christian tradition offers possibilities (though no guarantees) for the disciplined learning of how best to understand and realize in practice that of which the biblical writers speak. Thus, the reading of Israel's scriptures as Scripture is accompanied, in one way or another, by community, identity, practices, and disciplines which do not accompany other works of ancient history or of classic cultural status. Christians characteristically locate the study of the Old Testament alongside the study of the New Testament, the church fathers, and the historic and continuing thought and life of Christianity, while Jews characteristically locate the study of the Bible/Tanakh alongside the study of the Mishnah, the Talmud, the Midrashim, and the historic and continuing thought and life of Judaism.

I take these basic understandings to be common ground between Jews and Christians. They merit spelling out at the outset insofar as they are ever less shared, and are increasingly contested, within wider Western culture, where a secular logic would construe the study of the biblical documents otherwise. The recognition of ancient Israel's scriptures as being canonical—that is, as belonging within a particular bounded and privileged collection of enduring vitality—becomes at best a facet of the documents' history irrelevant to the determination of their "real meaning," even if their canonicity is significant for their role within Jewish and Christian contexts. Thus, the study of those documents which became the Jewish and Christian Bibles might be appropriately located either somewhere within a history of ancient Near Eastern and Mediterranean religions (i.e., reading them as ancient history) or within some form of cultural studies or literary studies (i.e., reading them as cultural classics).

Beyond these basic understandings, however, there are endless divergences both among and between Jews and Christians as to how best to study the biblical documents and how best to bring a Jewish or Christian frame of reference to bear upon the study.

Particular Aspects of Reading as Scripture

In the world of biblical scholarship there is a widespread consensus that theological work in relation to the Old Testament should primarily take some form or another of a history of ideas, with a history of literature as a necessary corollary of the history of ideas, as dating and sequencing the documents becomes all-important for a history of ideas; otherwise the ideas cannot be contextualized and arranged appropriately.[4] Such work is indeed indispensable, and all students of Israel's scriptures can profit from it. Nonetheless, I am here seeking to move beyond a history-of-ideas approach to an alternative approach that seeks to be both analytic and synthetic in fresh ways, and that I call "reading as Scripture."

I will briefly set out some salient features of reading as Scripture in order to locate it, in a preliminary and indicative way, within wider contemporary debates.[5] A summary programmatic statement is: I propose to read *the received form* of the biblical text with *a second naiveté* in a mode of *full imaginative seriousness* that probes *the subject matter* and recognizes its *recontextualization into plural contexts* in relation to which I bring to bear *a text-hermeneutic and reader-hermeneutic* and also utilize a *rule of faith*.

Focusing on *the received form* of the biblical text means that one's reading is based not on a putative, and necessarily hypothetical, earlier form of

4. An argument to this effect is, for example, the conclusion of James Barr's wide-ranging survey of the field, *The Concept of Biblical Theology*.

5. I offer some account of contemporary debates about theology and the OT in "Theological Approaches to the Old Testament" and in "Theological Interpretation, Second Naiveté, and the Rediscovery of the Old Testament."

the text (although such readings can often have great heuristic significance)[6] but rather on that form of the text that is available to all readers, scholarly and popular, Jewish and Christian alike. Such a focus enables one's reading to benefit from the study of poetics in recent literary work, and also to be responsive to possible theological concerns that informed the shaping of the text into its received form. It also facilitates a rejoining of conversation with premodern readers, whose interpretations are based on reading the text in its received form.

■ I am, of course, passing over a number of potentially complex issues about the nature of Israel's scriptures in Jewish and Christian frames of reference. The canonical sequence varies between Jewish and Christian canons, and the variations are likely related to differing overall construals. There have been differing decisions as to which books constitute the canonical collection, decisions reflected both in the contents of ancient codices and in the liturgical practice of different church traditions. There are divergences at a text-critical level. The material has functioned authoritatively in differing languages (e.g., Hebrew, Greek, Syriac, Latin, sixteenth-century German, seventeenth-century English). So the "received form" of the biblical text is an abstract formulation which needs to be used with care. Nonetheless, the recognition of gray areas and diversity is not incompatible with the recognition of certain family likenesses within Jewish and Christian receptions of Israel's scriptures, and pragmatic interpretive decisions to "get on with it" can usefully be made with full recognition of rough edges and loose ends that remain. ■

The notion of a *second naiveté* has been fruitfully introduced into biblical study by Paul Ricoeur and adopted by many. It is related to his famous sentence, "Beyond the desert of criticism, we wish to be called again."[7] Scholarly analyses, while legitimate and necessary, can become arid or locked into their own scholasticisms. A second naiveté can enable readers to reengage the biblical documents as Scripture—as a privileged place that is potentially generative of a transformative encounter with God—without abandoning scholarly integrity. To be meaningful, a second naiveté must be located downwind of the insights of modern learning; scholarly reading needs to have traveled through the desert and to have learned from its time there in order to reach a *beyond* where other concerns also can flourish (and where one may perhaps return to one's point of departure and, in T. S. Eliot's memorable words, "know it for the first time").

6. For example, there is still real value in the older essays on the kerygma of J, E, D, and P, even if pentateuchal criticism has changed enormously since they were written. These essays are conveniently available in Brueggemann and Wolff, *Vitality of Old Testament Traditions*. Alternatively, there can be real value in conducting a thought experiment of reading a text both with and without material that is likely to be redactional. For examples, see the reading of the flood narrative in my *Theology of the Book of Genesis*, 102–20, or the reading of the portrayals of Judah and Saul in Sykora, *The Unfavored*.

7. Ricoeur, *Symbolism of Evil*, 349.

A key ingredient in a second naiveté is to read with *full imaginative seriousness*. This means entering into the world of the biblical text with at least the same imaginative engagement with which one would enter into a Shakespearean play, a great novel or movie, or even just one's favorite TV show. Much biblical scholarship has devoted more of its imaginative thinking to the possible context of origin of the material, the world behind the text (How did this material arise? What issues within the life of ancient Israel/Judah were being addressed?), than to the world within the text in its own right. Yet the content and images and symbolism of the world within the text offer existential possibilities for those who open themselves to it. Dismayingly, the recognition that the received form of the biblical text may arise out of a possibly complex history, and that its world is "constructed," often functions reductively and dismissively to diminish engagement with that world ("It's the reflex of an ancient dispute"; "It's a combination of conflicting viewpoints"). Yet the knowledge that a movie is entirely constructed out of scripts, actors, artificial sets, special effects, and so on usually makes no difference to whether or not one is imaginatively gripped by it; what matters is whether it is well done and genuinely engages existential realities. In a similar way (whatever the differences between modern movies and novels and the Bible), it is meaningful to acknowledge the biblical text's possibly complex origins and yet still exercise a second naiveté by reading it with full imaginative seriousness.

To speak of *the subject matter* of the text is to enter into a perennial concern to understand that of which Scripture speaks—supremely, God, humanity, and the world in the light of God. Older debates about scriptural subject matter, which tended to focus on the Latin term *res*, were given a renewed sharpness in the twentieth century by Karl Barth and Rudolf Bultmann with their long-running discussion about how best to engage the *Sache* of the biblical text.[8] For present purposes, I do not wish to theorize the issue, beyond the observation already made: that an understanding of God necessarily affects one's understanding of what it means to be human in this world. This also entails that, if the treatment of the subject matter is to go beyond paraphrase, there should be some moral and theological literacy on the part of the interpreter—hence the classic location of the study of the Old Testament in the context of other elements of Christian faith. My focus will be on selected fruits of Israel's learned discernment of God over time that have been preserved canonically and are significant for Christian faith.

8. Amidst the extensive literature, a useful window onto the debate is Bromiley, *Karl Barth / Rudolf Bultmann: Letters, 1922–1966*.

Recontextualization in plural contexts presents particular challenges. The seemingly simple adage "Don't take a passage out of context" or "Always interpret in context" is unusually complex for biblical documents, as one can always ask, "Which context?" and "Whose context?" In all likelihood, no document that is now part of the biblical canon was written to be part of the canon; or, put differently, no text that is biblical was written to be biblical.[9] The documents were written for whatever context(s) in the life of ancient Israel they were written for—on which modern scholarship has shed considerable light, though much remains conjectural. The redactional framing of the documents, their preservation beyond their contexts of origin, and their relocation into a collection alongside other documents (whose authors may not have envisaged their work keeping such company) create a new context.[10] This new context is "canonical" and "literary" and "intertextual," and its whole is more than the sum of its parts. Israel's scriptures as a distinct collection are then received and recontextualized again within the continuing life of both Judaism and Christianity, with constant liturgical use, study, and teaching in many forms. The scriptures of Judaism and Christianity have also affected the wider cultures within which they have been located. One might thus distinguish, very broadly speaking, between at least five different contexts, or resonance chambers, within which the biblical content can be heard: the context of origin, the context within the canon, the context of Judaism, the context of Christianity, and the context of historic and contemporary cultures. The primary focus of this book is on the second and fourth of these resonance chambers (biblical Israel and a Christian context), though with an eye also, in varying degrees, on the first, third, and fifth (world of origin, Jewish context, broad cultural context). In general terms, however, the question of how best to do justice to and appropriately interrelate all these contexts is probably the greatest and, as yet, least-worked-out challenge facing those who would interpret Israel's scriptures as Christian Scripture. It should be clear that there will never be just one way of doing it.

The adoption of *a text-hermeneutic and reader-hermeneutic* is in significant ways a corollary of recontextualization.[11] Unsurprisingly, much biblical

9. Here, as elsewhere, I am passing over certain possible caveats and qualifications in favor of a broad-brush picture.

10. In all likelihood, many texts may have been recontextualized several times over. This seems especially apparent in the Psalter, where there are signs of various earlier psalm collections that preceded the present collection, and where the addition of psalm headings has again reoriented construal.

11. This paragraph utilizes a terminology which may be unfamiliar to those not versed in recent discussions of hermeneutics, and it may sound abstractly theoretical. I hope, however, that the meaning may become clearer through my specific readings of the biblical text. A robust

scholarship has prioritized an author-hermeneutic—that is, a concern to know who wrote the document, and why, in relation to its context of origin. The value of this is obvious, and I utilize it myself. Yet insofar as use in context is constitutive of meaning, a change of context can bring a change of meaning. A text-hermeneutic considers the semantic potential of the words of the text and recognizes that they may be open to more than one valid construal, according to context. A reader-hermeneutic recognizes the importance of the context of the reader: the particular preunderstandings and knowledge and interests and questions that an interpreter brings to bear, all of which make a difference to reading. Thus, the exercise of a text- and reader-hermeneutic is integral to reading as Scripture.

■ The relationship between an author-hermeneutic (where "author" includes "redactor") and a text- and reader-hermeneutic is more subtle and intertwined than is sometimes realized. Generally speaking, the more persuasive an interpretive proposal that arises from text- and reader-hermeneutics ("This makes good sense to me"), the greater the possibility that it can be argued to be a matter of author-hermeneutics ("This is what the writer really meant"). Given the consistent lack of evidence for the identities and motivations of the authors and editors of the documents of the OT beyond what can be inferred from the texts themselves, it is arguable that what interpreters present as an author-hermeneutic is in fact generally a plausible text- and reader-hermeneutic that is articulated in a disciplined, historically oriented mode, however it is formally presented. ■

A *rule of faith* is a notion which is marginal if one's primary concern is to understand the biblical material in relation to its world of origin, but which comes into its own when the canonical and ecclesial contexts become significant. A rule of faith can be understood in various ways. My own preference is to use the term loosely to refer to "a sense of how things go"—that is, as a set of interrelated moral and theological judgments as to the kind of sense that does, or does not, resonate within a biblical and Christian frame of reference.[12] Different Christian traditions have each developed their distinctive rules of faith—judgments that come naturally to a Roman Catholic may not come equally naturally to a Baptist, and vice versa—even though there is a family likeness to them all. The scholar's sense of "how things go" will necessarily be refracted through an awareness of what was meaningful in the ancient world (insofar as this can be discerned), though even here, judgments about meaning in the past will not be unrelated to judgments about meaning in the

account of how the relationship between text, author, and reader might well be reenvisaged for the purposes of Christian theology is found in Martin, *Biblical Truths*, e.g., 1–37.

12. There is an interesting recent discussion in Bell, *Ruled Reading and Biblical Criticism*.

present.[13] In a different idiom, the issues here are an important dimension of biblical literacy, a facility for handling Scripture with some insight in relation to those purposes for which it has been preserved and has been important to countless people down the ages.

More could be said. But I hope that enough has been said to give the reader a sense of the frame of reference and the perspectives which are operative in the readings of the biblical text that follow. Perhaps the note on which to finish these methodological reflections, however, is to emphasize that close reading is integral to every chapter, in a way that I hope may make the engagement with the biblical text of potential interest to anyone concerned with Israel's scriptures, whether or not they are concerned to read them as Scripture.

Memorandum to the Reader

Finally, by way of introduction, I outline here some of my conventions in writing, an awareness of which should help facilitate reading.

Throughout the book I refer to the "reader" of the biblical text. I recognize that this is potentially anachronistic and/or inappropriate, since throughout history a huge number of people have encountered the biblical text as hearers. There have been hearers both in ancient Israel and the ancient world generally, where it is unclear how widespread literacy was, and in the liturgical life of both the Jewish and the Christian faiths down the ages, where those present in synagogue or church have heard the biblical text being read aloud and interpreted in the context of worship. I originally wrote "reader/hearer" but then decided that this was cumbersome. So "reader" is a convenient shorthand, without prejudice to the importance of aural reception of the biblical text, both past and present.

When referring to the Old Testament in descriptive historical perspective, I use the term "Israel's scriptures," as distinct from when I am approaching the material as "Scripture." While I appreciate the value of having a term for the material that does not imply or privilege a particular religious perspective, as do both "Old Testament" (for Christians) and "Tanakh" (for Jews), I am unpersuaded by the scholarly consensus that "Hebrew Bible" is an appropriate religiously neutral term. It privileges a Jewish meaning of "Bible" over a Christian one, it overlooks those portions written in Aramaic, and it

13. Fine short accounts of the necessary dialectic between present and past for an understanding of the past include Bultmann, "Is Exegesis without Presuppositions Possible?"; and Lash, "What Might Martyrdom Mean?"

elides the fact that most likely a majority of readers of the material, already in the ancient world, read it in Greek rather than Hebrew. "Israel's scriptures" recognizes the historical fact that these were the documents to emerge from Israel's history ("Israel's") in such a way that they became a distinct collection of religiously oriented writings ("scriptures"), but is without prejudice to the question of their historic and continuing authoritative role (Scripture / Old Testament / Tanakh) for Christians and Jews.

In each chapter there are some passages in a smaller font (as already twice in this introduction). These serve three purposes, which sometimes overlap. Some note issues of contemporary scholarly debate, on which brief comment is offered without substantive engagement, if such engagement is not needed for the argument. Some discuss questions of Hebrew language or idiom which are more substantive than is appropriate for a footnote. Some offer various kinds of theological reflections. I hope that readers may find these interesting, according to their own interests. In all cases, however, the main argument can be read without reference to these small-font sections; the text which follows the small-font sections directly resumes the discussion which precedes.

I do not presuppose a knowledge of Hebrew on the part of the reader, though I hope that the not-infrequent discussions of Hebrew idiom and usage may help the Hebrew-less reader to see its value for studying the Old Testament (and perhaps encourage them to start learning it!). My system of transliteration aims to be user-friendly and generally eschews diacritical marks, with the exception of using *ḥ* to indicate a hard "h," as in Lo*ch* Ness, and also retaining markers of the quiescent letters *aleph* (ʾ) and *ayin* (ʿ). Otherwise, I indicate long vowels and vowel letters with a macron (ā), and very short vowels (vocal *shewa*) with a breve (ă). Those who know Hebrew may quite properly prefer diacritics, but they can manage without; those without Hebrew often find them off-putting.

I work from the Hebrew text of Israel's scriptures in *Biblia Hebraica Stuttgartensia* (though with an occasional eye to *Biblia Hebraica Quinta*, where it is available), and from the Greek text in Rahlfs's *Septuaginta* (with an eye to other more recent editions also). I usually cite the English translation provided by the NRSV. Where I think the NRSV is problematic I have substituted my own preferred wording, indicated with dotted underlining (e.g., faithfully [for *ʾāmōn* in Prov. 8:30]) to alert the reader. In a footnote or a small-font section I give a reason for my preferred rendering.

Finally, I capitalize pronouns and possessive adjectives when they refer to God: thus "He," "His." Such usage is of course open to question. It may be held to transgress the academic convention that an interpreter's religious outlook should not be on display in scholarly writing. It may also be considered objectionable in a cultural context where issues of gender have a high profile. Nonetheless, I retain this gendered language in capitalized form for two reasons. On the one hand, such capitalization is a time-honored reverential practice on the part of both Jews and Christians that can have renewed significance in the not-very-reverentially-inclined culture of today. On the other hand, the capitalization implicitly presupposes and gestures towards the classic theological understanding that God is beyond gender as we understand it and that the biblical writers' own gendered usage is to be understood in a qualified way when the Bible is read as Scripture.

1

The Wise God

The Depths of Creation in Proverbs 8

Christians who regret the marginalization of theology in contemporary Western culture may be tempted to look back to earlier periods when things were different. For example, Abraham Lincoln's Second Inaugural Address of March 1865, in which he probed the meaning of the Civil War as it was ending, must surely rank as one of the most searching theological reflections in any major political context,[1] in a mode that would be hard to imagine in a serious political speech today.[2] If one looks further back in time, to late antiquity, there is a notorious example of public theology in a much-cited passage by Gregory of Nyssa, who depicts remarkable theological discourse on the streets of Constantinople at a time of ferment in ca. 380:

> All of city life is full of it—the alleyways, the marketplaces, the streets, the crossroads, clothes sellers, money changers, food merchants. If you ask someone for change, he holds forth to you about the Begotten and the Unbegotten. If

1. Lincoln had a complex and somewhat oblique relationship with Christian faith and theology. An illuminating account is Allen C. Guelzo's *Abraham Lincoln: Redeemer President*, with a discussion of the Second Inaugural on pp. 409–21.

2. One friend at my first Hulsean lecture agreed with the point but wryly observed, "Unfortunately, it is not entirely coincidental that he was assassinated within days." It is sobering to ponder the distance between Lincoln's "With malice toward none, with charity for all, with firmness in the right as God gives us to see the right" and Booth's "Sic semper tyrannis" ("That's what tyrants should always get").

> you ask about the price of bread, the answer is that "the Father is greater, and the Son inferior." If you ask whether your bath is ready, someone declares that "the Son was made out of nothing."[3]

Gregory himself is singularly unimpressed by all this. He comments that he does not know whether to call this sorry state of affairs "inflammation of the brain or madness," and he sees the people of Constantinople as being like the Athenians of Paul's day, fascinated by novelties and speaking ignorantly. It may be, however, that Gregory's objection is not only that there is a lot of theology out on the streets on the lips of the unlearned, but also that it is bad theology. Constantinople during the previous generation had been an Arian city, unreceptive to the Nicene theology to which Gregory was committed. If the theology being bandied about had differed, so also might have Gregory's estimation. All of which is perhaps a reminder that those of us who seek a revival of theological literacy in our culture may need to be just a little careful what we wish for.

I choose this scene from the late fourth century because one of the significant, driving factors in the fourth-century debate about the nature of Jesus in relation to God the Father had to do with the implications of Proverbs 8:22–31, an Old Testament passage about wisdom. Here personified Wisdom says, "The LORD created me, beginning of His way."[4] Because the New Testament appropriates this language of Wisdom for articulating the significance of Jesus, especially in John 1:1–5 and Colossians 1:15–20, an unchallenged consensus had developed by the fourth century that this voice speaking in Proverbs 8 is the preincarnate Christ. Thus, Proverbs 8 speaks of the role of Christ in relation to God the Father in the work of creation. However, the language of "creating" and "beginning" raised the possibility that, although the speaker of Proverbs 8:22 existed prior to all the familiar created order, there might yet have been a time antecedent to the creation of this speaker when God was without Wisdom / the preincarnate Son. To use the fourth-century language: Was or was not Jesus the Son eternal? Was there a time (or even a "time before time") "when the Son was not"?

This ancient debate is well documented,[5] and I have no desire to add to it here. Nonetheless, it is a striking example of how an Old Testament passage can have enduring implications for the task of understanding God and the

3. *Oration on the Deity of the Son and the Holy Spirit* (PG 46:557, my translation). Disappointingly, there appears to be no recent English edition of this treatise.

4. This is a word-for-word rendering of the Hebrew.

5. An excellent starting point is Young, "Proverbs 8 in Interpretation." An interesting recent attempt to reengage the issues is Collett, "Place to Stand."

world within a Christian frame of reference. I aim here to explore in a different way how possible enduring implications of Proverbs 8 might be articulated in relation to contested issues in our own day.

Initially, I hope it will be helpful to stand back from these larger implications and consider Proverbs 8:22–31 within its Old Testament frame of reference.

Introduction to Wisdom in Proverbs

The keynote of the book of Proverbs, which is either the climax of its prologue or a freestanding principle after the prologue, is this:

> The fear of the LORD is the beginning of knowledge;
> fools despise wisdom [*ḥokmāh*] and instruction. (Prov. 1:7)

The thought of the first line is better known in the form in which it occurs a little later:

> The fear of the LORD is the beginning of wisdom [*ḥokmāh*],
> and the knowledge of the Holy One is insight. (Prov. 9:10)

Proverbs regularly uses "wisdom" and "knowledge" as synonyms, and nothing hangs on their interchange. However, "wisdom" comes to the fore for most readers. This is partly because of its striking personification in Proverbs 1–9, partly because of its use in the "Where shall wisdom be found?" poem in Job 28, and partly because of a biblical reception history in which the importance of the Greek term for wisdom, *sophia* (used in the LXX),[6] helped give priority to its nearest Hebrew equivalent, *ḥokmāh*. So, for convenience, I will consistently use "wisdom" in preference to "knowledge."

What is this wisdom that is held out as a desirable goal for human life? The Old Testament does not specifically define it.[7] Nonetheless, a reading of

6. I am aware of rich and deep reflection on *sophia* in the literature of the Orthodox Church. I regret that I lack the space and competence to do justice to it here.

7. Technically, this is incorrect, as Job 28:28 is definitional in form: "The fear of the LORD, that is wisdom." However, although that definition is substantive and important (and probably no OT writer would have disagreed with it), it relates specifically to the context of Job. There the question about wisdom is how to handle seemingly random, and certainly undeserved, disaster and affliction such as Job suffered; it is not about wisdom for everyday life in general, as in Proverbs. "Wisdom" in Job 28 has a more specific focus than it has in Proverbs. See my "Where Is Wisdom?" (*Old Testament Theology*, 243–77).

Proverbs rapidly makes clear that wisdom is a quality that is inherently intellectual, ethical, and practical; it develops moral character and enables one to understand and cope with the world and the possibilities of everyday life.[8] Its opposite is folly, which brings blinkers and distorted vision and always threatens to shipwreck life.

■ The notion of wisdom lends itself to discussions that can range widely and fruitfully in other literature of the ancient world.[9] Scholars have often, for example, compared *ḥokmāh* with the concept of *ma'at* in Egypt, where *Ma'at* is the goddess of truth/justice. The comparison can be suggestive for a history of ideas in neighboring ancient cultures, even if conjectures about how *Ma'at* may or may not relate to the personification of wisdom in Prov. 8 remain conjectures. There are also significant parallels with Aristotle's concept of practical reason (*phronēsis*). The present discussion will focus on wisdom in the Christian canon and a contemporary Western context, without prejudice to the value of notions and practices of wisdom in other contexts. ■

How Should "The Fear of the Lord Is the Beginning of Wisdom" Be Understood?

What, then, is the meaning of "the fear of the Lord is the beginning of wisdom"? In particular, what is the meaning of "beginning" in "beginning of wisdom"? This has been much discussed, with many interpreters arguing that it means "chief part" or "best part." Although such a qualitative meaning makes good sense, it is more likely that the meaning is primarily temporal (the one comes before the other) and directional (this is the way/road to set off in, and stay in, to get to the desired destination). The term for "beginning" in 1:7, *rē'shīt*, can sometimes have a qualitative sense,[10] but the parallel term in 9:10, *tĕḥillāh*, is consistently temporal.[11] Moreover, the pedagogic purpose of Proverbs is to teach people—especially the young—the correct way to orient themselves in life, which makes a keynote of "Start here" and "Go this way" especially appropriate.[12]

8. Wisdom can also be understood more broadly elsewhere in the OT. For example, it is said of Solomon, the prime biblical paradigm of wisdom (though at the end he also embodies folly—a reminder to take nothing for granted), that, in addition to proverbs and songs, "he would speak of trees, from the cedar that is in the Lebanon to the hyssop that grows in the wall; he would speak of animals, and birds, and reptiles, and fish" (1 Kings 5:13 [ET 4:33]). Wisdom here includes knowledge of the natural world.

9. A stimulating recent account is Legaspi, *Wisdom in Classical and Biblical Tradition*.

10. E.g., Gad "chose the best [*rē'shīt*] for himself" (Deut. 33:21).

11. See the discussion in Fox, *Proverbs 1–9*, 67–68.

12. Stuart Weeks has queried the usual understanding of Prov. 1:7 and 9:10 with the argument that "the fear of YHWH is something that one gains from wisdom and knowledge, not *vice versa*" (*Instruction and Imagery in Proverbs 1–9*, 118). This receives a constructive and restrained critique

The notion that a right response to God (fear of the LORD)[13] leads to a deeper grasp of living and handling the world well (wisdom) requires careful consideration. Despite its intrinsic importance, it can easily be construed crudely and/or dismissively. On the one hand, it can be taken as little more than a trite aspiration of piety which does not really understand what it takes to flourish in "the real world." But the fact that faith (to use a Christian equivalent for "fear of the LORD") is not the only thing needed in life does not rule out that it may nonetheless be the most important thing, that which can underpin and enable all else. On the other hand, the principle can be debased into an essentially self-serving piece of guidance or instruction, the notion that piety/faith will make you wealthy and successful (a "prosperity gospel," in some form or other)—an outlook that is strongly challenged in the books of Job and Jeremiah as well as in many psalms.

Over against such misreadings, it is salutary to ponder Gerhard von Rad's account of this principle:

> There is no knowledge which does not, before long, throw the one who seeks the knowledge back upon the question of his self-knowledge and his self-understanding. Even Israel did not give herself uncritically to her drive for knowledge, but went on to ask the question about the possibility of and the authority for knowledge. She made intellect itself the object of her knowledge. The thesis that all human knowledge comes back to the question about commitment to God is a statement of penetrating perspicacity. It has, of course, been so worn by centuries of Christian teaching that it has to be seen anew in all its provocative pungency. In the most concise phraseology it encompasses a wide range of intellectual content and can itself be understood only as the result of a long process of thought. It contains in a nutshell the whole Israelite theory of knowledge. . . . Faith does not—as is popularly believed today—hinder knowledge; on the contrary, it is what liberates knowledge, enables it really to come to the point and indicates to it its proper place in the sphere of varied, human activity. In Israel, the intellect never freed itself from or became independent of the foundation of its whole existence, that is its commitment to Yahweh.[14]

The challenge today, however, is not only that a worn principle needs fresh grasping. The challenge is also to understand and grasp the possibilities of

---

from Zoltan Schwab in "Is Fear of the LORD the Source of Wisdom or Vice Versa?" I find persuasive the arguments for "fear of the LORD" as the *way* to wisdom. However, Proverbs also states that the fear of the LORD can be the fruit of wisdom (2:1–5), and the nature of the subject matter is such that there is necessarily a reciprocal mutuality between "fear of the LORD" and "wisdom."

13. "Fear of God / the LORD" in the OT is the prime term for right human responsiveness to God and is not a matter of emotional fear or fright. For further discussion, see ch. 3, pp. 108–9.

14. Von Rad, *Wisdom in Israel*, 67–68.

the contemporary postmodern context, in which some of the limitations of modernity have become apparent.[15] In particular, today there are new ways of reengaging premodern insights which were often set aside, or sometimes rubbished, in an Enlightenment-influenced intellectual world in which the natural sciences were given a dominant position as the model of desirable and usable knowledge, and also the means of attaining it.

Wisdom against Folly

The keynote principle that "the fear of the LORD" orients one to the desirable goal of wisdom does not, however, mean that this desirable goal is easy to attain. In the distinctive formulation of Proverbs, this is because of the ubiquitous and superficially attractive nature of wisdom's opposite, folly. Ways of life that initially appear attractive can in fact be deeply destructive, but it is not immediately self-evident that this is so. One needs to learn to tell the difference between wisdom and folly.

Proverbs seeks to make the issue more engaging through dramatization. That is, both wisdom and folly are personified as women who are actively at work, calling to people (especially young males) and inviting them to respond. Folly in particular receives a dual personification, appearing sometimes as a "strange woman" (*zārāh*) who is sexually enticing, and sometimes straightforwardly as a woman of stupidity (*kěsīlūt*)—though not for that reason unattractive. The opening section of Proverbs, Proverbs 1–9, which frames all the individual proverbs that follow, concludes with appeals by both Wisdom (9:1–6) and Folly (9:13–18) in which, strikingly, the invitation of each is identical: "You that are simple, turn in here" (9:4, 16). To hear the call does not of itself enable one to know whether to accept it. One needs discernment, which the book of Proverbs as a whole seeks to enable people to develop.[16]

Wisdom and Folly as Female

For some contemporary readers, the portrayal of wisdom and folly as women raises clear problems of sexism and stereotyping. As Kathleen O'Connor, for

15. The term "postmodern" (like "modern") is contestable, but little hangs on whatever terminology is preferred to indicate the issues at stake. The literature here is endless. A work of prime importance for "reading the signs of the times" and indicating something of the overall challenge is Lash, *The Beginning and the End of 'Religion.'* I have offered a preliminary account of how one might rethink the practices of biblical interpretation in *The Bible in a Disenchanted Age*.

16. A fine recent account of the formational vision of Proverbs is Stewart, *Poetic Ethics in Proverbs*.

example, puts it, "Feminist suspicion is completely appropriate. Both Wisdom Woman and Stranger Woman are male creations that project onto women all that is good and bad in human nature. As stereotypes they harm women by failing to represent them as human beings, and they also misrepresent men by portraying them as helpless victims of preying females."[17] But such difficulties, while real, need not be the determinative factor. A symbol can be bigger and more resonant and more serviceable than a suspicious reading may allow. As O'Connor herself goes on to say, "Personified wisdom transcends her patriarchal origins precisely because she is not representative of historical women, nor is she ultimately subordinated to YHWH; she is a symbol of God. Whereas Strange Woman dies a literary death, never reappearing in the texts after Proverbs 9, Wisdom takes on a life of her own, developing in biblical tradition, becoming increasingly identified with God, and standing as God in the world (Sirach 24, Wisdom of Solomon 7–9)."[18]

Serious use of the imagination enables one to enter constructively into perspectives from which one can learn substantively without needing to appropriate or replicate them entirely. Those who uphold republican forms of government, for example, can still be deeply moved by, and appropriate insights from, stories or plays in which monarchy is central and integral, such as Shakespeare's *Macbeth* or *King Lear*.

Even if the original context of Proverbs envisages instruction specifically to young men, the material in its canonical role as Scripture addresses all—male and female, young and old, and every generation down the ages. While a plain textual sense remains apparent, the extended context of canonical address encourages a metaphorical rereading of the allure of attractive women for young men: the genuinely attractive and the speciously attractive can take many forms, and everyone needs to be alert to respond wisely and not to go astray. However, in contexts where feelings about gendered language and imagery are strong, such imaginative moves will be less accessible to some than to others.

A Reading of Proverbs 8 as a Whole

The most extended personification of folly and wisdom comes in chapters 7 and 8. In 7:5–27 there is an elaborate picture of a "strange woman" who aggressively but patiently accosts and seduces a simple and unwary young

17. O'Connor, "Wisdom Literature and Experience of the Divine," 188.
18. O'Connor, "Wisdom Literature and Experience of the Divine," 189.

man—and the final word of this protracted scenario is "death." In contrast to this we encounter personified Wisdom in chapter 8, another prolonged scenario which ends on the note of "life."[19]

Proverbs 8 introduces Wisdom thus:

> [1] Does not wisdom [*ḥokmāh*] call,
> and does not understanding raise her voice?
> [2] On the heights, beside the way,
> at the crossroads she takes her stand;
> [3] beside the gates in front of the town,
> at the entrance of the portals she cries out:
> [4] "To you, O people, I call,
> and my cry is to all that live.
> [5] O simple ones, learn prudence;
> acquire intelligence, you who lack it."

Five points may briefly be noted. First, Wisdom takes the initiative in calling out to people. The implication is that she is actively seeking, as well as there to be found. Second, Wisdom is located not in the temple precincts but in everyday life. This is not to deny that Wisdom may also be found in the temple precincts.[20] But the point is that Wisdom is involved in regular, everyday life and so is not restricted to any specifically religious sphere. Third, whether her location in verses 2 and 3 is countryside and town or just different areas within a town (the wording allows either reading), the point is that she is wherever people travel or gather. Fourth, the poet is not interested in the mundane means by which Wisdom's call is mediated—something that happens, what someone says—for the point appears to be that any feature of daily life can mediate Wisdom's call. Fifth, her summons is unrestricted; it is for everyone who is alive (v. 4). As Michael Fox puts it, "The scene and events are atemporal: Wisdom addresses mankind in all cities, inside and outside the city walls, . . . repeatedly and forever. Her city represents every city."[21] Or one might paraphrase, in a different idiom, by saying that attaining wisdom is an intrinsic challenge for all human life in this world.

19. Since life and death, as outcomes of response to Wisdom, are also outcomes of response to God elsewhere in the biblical canon, there is a certain obvious sense in which Wisdom represents God. This can lead to questions about the significance of female imagery in relation to God, questions substantively discussed by, for example, Claudia V. Camp in *Wisdom and the Feminine in the Book of Proverbs* and Elizabeth A. Johnson in *She Who Is: The Mystery of God in Feminist Theological Discourse*.

20. The ascription of Proverbs to Solomon, who also built the temple, encourages the reader of the canonical text to understand wisdom and the temple in complementary ways.

21. Fox, *Proverbs 1–9*, 267.

Wisdom emphasizes the moral character of her reality, which also makes a difference to how what she says is apprehended:

> [6] Hear, for I will speak noble things,
> and from my lips will come what is right;
> [7] for my mouth will utter truth;
> wickedness is an abomination to my lips.
> [8] All the words of my mouth are righteous;
> there is nothing twisted or crooked in them.
> [9] They are all straight to one who understands
> and right to those who find knowledge.

She then underlines her value in comparison to other things on which humans regularly set their hearts and which they labor to gain:

> [10] Take my instruction instead of silver,
> and knowledge rather than choice gold;
> [11] for wisdom is better than jewels,
> and all that you may desire cannot compare with her.[22]

The reality that she represents is one at odds with human self-seeking and corruption:

> [12] I, wisdom, live with prudence,
> and I attain knowledge and discretion.
> [13] The fear of the LORD is hatred of evil.
> Pride and arrogance and the way of evil
> and perverted speech I hate.

Further, wisdom is what those with power need in order to fulfill their responsibilities well:

> [14] I have good advice and sound wisdom;
> I have insight, I have strength.
> [15] By me kings reign,
> and rulers decree what is just;
> [16] by me rulers rule,
> and nobles, all who govern rightly.

22. It is surprising that Wisdom here refers to herself in the third person. Robert Hayward has suggested to me that this could be a proverb which Wisdom quotes on her own behalf.

Wisdom returns to her intrinsic value, this time to stress that the reward she gives to those who love her and have her are great:

> [17] I love those who love me,
> and those who seek me diligently find me.
> [18] Riches and honor are with me,
> enduring wealth and prosperity.
> [19] My fruit is better than gold, even fine gold,
> and my yield than choice silver.

The terms of this reward, wealth and prosperity, have an obvious material sense. Yet an earlier passage, Proverbs 2, has already stressed the moral reward that comes from wisdom, and the material and the moral should be held together rather than set against each other.[23] Put differently, when this poetic language is read not only in the wider context of Proverbs but also of the canon as a whole, it readily resonates in metaphorical mode, somewhat like Jesus' reference to "treasures in heaven" (Matt. 6:20; i.e., being rich in relation to God). However, a sense of a flourishing life in mundane and material terms remains clear.

Moreover, lest one should indeed be tempted to construe Wisdom's reward in a narrowly self-serving way ("You should get wisdom, for then you'll get rich"), Wisdom reiterates the promise of reward in the context of the intrinsically moral nature of her being—and thus also implicitly, by extension, the moral qualities necessary for those who love and find her:

> [20] I walk in the way of righteousness,
> along the paths of justice,
> [21] endowing with wealth those who love me,
> and filling their treasuries.

In other words, Wisdom is intrinsically bound up with a moral way of living. Thus, her reward is not primarily an extraneous reward ("Do this, and you will get lots of money"), though that may indeed be included, but rather the fruit that naturally grows from a healthy root ("Do this, and you will become a better and better-off person").

Against this background, we come to the most famous part of the poem. Wisdom now gives a further reason—something deep, underpinning all else—why her call should be trusted and heeded:

23. There is a helpful discussion of this issue in Loader, *Proverbs 1–9*, 340.

[22] The LORD created [*qānāh*] me at the beginning [*rē'shīt*] of his work,
the first of his acts of long ago.
[23] Ages ago I was set up,
at the first, before the beginning of the earth.

Before there was anything else, there was Wisdom. Before God made the world, He first ensured that Wisdom was there. This priority of Wisdom to all else is spelled out in a series of images that are resonant of ancient Israel's conception of the world:

[24] When there were no depths I was brought forth,
when there were no springs abounding with water.
[25] Before the mountains had been shaped,
before the hills, I was brought forth—
[26] when he had not yet made earth and fields,
or the world's first bits of soil.

Precisely how God "brought forth" Wisdom is clearly of no interest to the poet. All that matters is that Wisdom's beginning preceded all else, both the watery expanse of which the world was initially constituted (cf. Gen. 1:2) and the solid elements of mountains and land. Whatever basic elements of the created order can be named, Wisdom was there before them.

[27] When he established the heavens, I was there—
when he drew a circle on the face of the deep,
[28] when he made firm the skies above,
when he established the fountains of the deep,
[29] when he assigned to the sea its limit
(so that the waters might not transgress his command),
when he marked out the foundations of the earth.[24]

Thus, when God acted in creation—making the heavens, constraining the deep, and setting the land in place—Wisdom, quite simply, was present: "I was there" (v. 27). Precisely *how* Wisdom was involved in God's actions we

24. I have modified the NRSV in four ways: using a dash at the end of v. 27a, putting parentheses around the middle clause of v. 29 (as it is clearly parenthetical within the sequence of six "when" clauses), deleting the comma at the end of v. 29a, and adding a full stop at the end of v. 29. This is to capture the unity of the section, which is constructed around the six uses of "when"—which renders six consecutive uses of the Hebrew preposition *bĕ* followed each time by a verb in the infinitive construct as a verbal noun ("in his establishing")—together with the keynote at the outset, "I was there."

are not told. Her role must be inferred by the poetic imagination and by any other indications that are provided.

> [30] And I am at his side faithfully [*ʾāmōn*],[25]
> and I am[26] daily his delight,
> rejoicing before him always,
> [31] rejoicing in his inhabited world
> and delighting in the human race.

There are two translational/interpretive difficulties here.[27] First, does this section continue the account of creation from verses 27–29, still speaking of Wisdom at creation: "then I was beside him" (as NRSV)? Or does it move from creation, a context about which Wisdom has already said, "I was there" (v. 27), to the present and the proximity of Wisdom to the LORD in the here and now: "and I am at his side" (my preferred rendering)? The Hebrew can be read either way,[28] but I consider the flow of the poem to be better on this second reading, where there is a move from before creation (vv. 22–26), to creation (vv. 27–29), to the regular created order (vv. 30–31) in relation to Wisdom.

The second difficulty is the sense of the term *ʾāmōn*, which depicts how Wisdom is/was beside God. The Hebrew root *aleph-mem-nun* usually has a sense of being constant or faithful, and the form here appears to be a noun that is used adverbially with the sense "faithfully."[29]

■ There is an enormous history of interpretive debate focused on *ʾāmōn*. Strikingly, the ancient midrashic reading of Genesis, Genesis Rabbah, begins its interpretation of *bĕrēʾshīt* in Gen. 1:1 with the assumption that the key to understanding God's creative work is the use of *ʾāmōn* in Prov. 8:30. The midrashist offers five different possibilities for construing *ʾāmōn*—which, interestingly, do not include "faithfully."[30]

In my judgment, however, not too much hangs on the interpretive choice for *ʾāmōn*. Other than the option preferred here, there are two main alternatives that predominate in

25. NRSV: "then I was beside him, like a master worker."

26. NRSV: "was."

27. In my handling of the philology of this text I essentially follow the fine study by my colleague Stuart Weeks—"The Context and Meaning of Proverbs 8:30a"—who reads the Hebrew with a sharp eye and cogent logic that I find fully persuasive. I do not follow him, however, on the interpretation of Wisdom in relation to creation. There is constructive use of Weeks's philology also in the wide-ranging theological interpretation of Daniel Treier, *Proverbs and Ecclesiastes*, 44–57.

28. The verb *vāʾehyeh* illustrates well the frequent difficulty of determining tense with Hebrew verbs, as the form does not indicate tense as such and can equally be either "and I am" or "and I was." I doubt that it is a worthwhile move to find here, with the *vav* prefixed, a resonance with the *ʾehyeh* of Exod. 3:14.

29. In terms of Hebrew idiom it is not problematic for a noun to function adverbially.

30. See Freedman, *Midrash Rabbah: Genesis I*, 1.

the literature. One is that *ʾāmōn* means "artisan / craftsman / master worker," and thus it depicts Wisdom as an active participant in God's work of creation. However, if one reads Prov. 8 in conjunction with Prov. 3:19 ("The LORD by wisdom founded the earth"), as I think one should,[31] the notion of Wisdom's participation in creation is clear anyway. The other possibility is that *ʾāmōn* means "little child / nursling" and thus apparently depicts Wisdom's joyful play in God's presence, with implications for the joy that Wisdom brings to humans. However, the notion of joy and delight is clear anyway, through the repeated uses of *shaʿăshūʿīm* ("delight," 8:30b, 31b) and *mĕsaḥeqet* ("rejoicing," 8:30c, 31a). If the key notions associated with these other renderings of *ʾāmōn* are already clear in the text, the importance of trying to resolve the precise sense of *ʾāmōn* can surely be lessened.[32] ■

Wisdom is a constant and reliable presence with God. Moreover, she is a figure of joy: God delights in her, and she delights in both God and the world.[33] A natural implication for humans is that with wisdom comes joy, joy in both God and the world. In the light of all this, Wisdom issues a final appeal:

> [32] "And now, my children, listen to me:
> happy are those who keep my ways.
> [33] Hear instruction and be wise,
> and do not neglect it.
> [34] Happy is the one who listens to me,
> watching daily at my gates,
> waiting beside my doors.
> [35] For whoever finds me finds life
> and obtains favor from the LORD;
> [36] but those who miss me injure themselves;
> all who hate me love death."

For the reader, there is a decision to be made. There are two choices with respect to Wisdom and her moral corollaries, choices that relate to people's deepest orientations in life: what they love (v. 17) and what they hate (v. 36). People are to seek and embrace wisdom, for in so doing they will attain life—in a metaphorical sense akin to that of the declaration of the father of the prodigal son, "This your brother was dead, and is alive; he was lost, and

31. See below, 27n37.

32. Robert Hayward has interestingly suggested in conversation that the poet may have deliberately chosen a Hebrew word that can be vocalized in different ways so as to convey a sense of the limits of language in relation to divine mystery.

33. Intriguing imaginative possibilities as to the specific forms that "delight" might take are offered by Othmar Keel, *Die Weisheit spielt vor Gott*, esp. 46–62, in terms of Egyptian iconography. The most famous artistic depiction of Wisdom—in Michelangelo's portrayal of God creating Adam, on the ceiling of the Sistine Chapel—shows solely her proximity to God, by His side and under His left arm, not her joy.

is found" (Luke 15:32 RSV). Life—not just existence, but *life as it should be*—is the corollary of gaining wisdom. The alternative is death, in a similar metaphorical sense, in which the wellspring is poisoned, the fruit is withered, and the end is bleak.

A Fuller Reading of Proverbs 8:22–31

What Does Wisdom's Presence at Creation Entail?

If this reading captures the overall movement and sense of the poem, we can return to the question of the significance of its most debated and contested section, verses 22–31. Biblical scholars who have sought to understand the likely meaning of the text in its context of origin have regularly suggested that less is at stake than many interpreters, beginning already in antiquity, have proposed. Kathleen O'Connor, for example, says that Wisdom is personified in Proverbs 8:22–31 "to establish Wisdom's antiquity and authority rather than to explore God's creative deeds."[34] Stuart Weeks claims that "their [8:22–31] principal purpose, in the context of the poem as a whole, is to affirm Wisdom's reliability, not to furnish a precise cosmological account of her nature."[35] These undeveloped binary alternatives, however, do not exhaust the interpretive options.

To begin with, we should take note of another passage about creation earlier in Proverbs:

> [19] The LORD by wisdom [*bĕḥokmāh*] founded the earth;
> by understanding he established the heavens;
> [20] by his knowledge the deeps broke open,
> and the clouds drop down the dew. (Prov. 3:19–20)

The language here is similar to that in 8:22–31.[36] In this context the sense of "by wisdom/understanding" may be adverbial: "wisely." But since an adverbial sense intrinsically says something about *how* God created, it is no stretch

34. O'Connor, "Wisdom Literature and Experience of the Divine," 186.

35. Weeks, "Context and Meaning of Proverbs 8:30a," 436.

36. For example, each passage uses the verb *kūn* for the creation of the heavens (Prov. 3:19b; 8:27a) together with the imagery of the "deep/deeps/depth(s)" (*tĕhōm/tĕhōmōt*, 3:20; 8:24, 27, 28) as intrinsic to the initial creation. In each passage the first word is the divine name YHWH, who is subject of the verb that follows, even though most commonly in Hebrew the verb precedes the subject (as in Gen. 1:1). There is comparable language and conceptuality also in Ps. 104:24: "O LORD, how manifold are your works! / In wisdom [*bĕḥokmāh*] you have made them all; / the earth is full of your creatures."

to read Wisdom here as being in some way *instrumental* in God's work of creation. In 8:22–31 Wisdom's *presence* in creation is depicted, but with no mention of her instrumentality, as in 3:19–20. The most natural move with these two poetic passages about creation, in close proximity within a distinct literary unit (Prov. 1–9), is to combine them and read the one in light of the other.[37] Thus, the Wisdom who is present when God creates should be seen as in some way God's agent in that act of creating: God creates in/by/with/through Wisdom.[38]

How best should such language be understood? I suggest that it has less to do with factual knowledge about the world, as we conceive it today, than it does with the conceptual and existential frame of reference within which the world is best handled and understood.

To be sure, the Wisdom poem indeed depicts the nature of the world as it was then thought to be: waters, earth, and sky, with supporting pillars/foundations in between, comparable to ancient Near Eastern conceptions generally.[39] This is of essentially historical interest in light of a better scientific understanding of the world. A poet writing today would presumably write differently (though both a poet and an astronomer today can still readily speak of the sun "going down"). It does not follow, however, that better empirical knowledge requires a different conceptual and existential frame of reference.

If Wisdom is God's agent in creating the world, this is best understood as illuminating not only the antiquity of Wisdom but also the world that is made thereby. For example, ancient Jewish thought makes a number of moves in relation to an understanding of God, which Richard Bauckham summarizes thus: "It is God's wisdom that orders creation for its well-being, God's wisdom that can be perceived in the good order of the natural creation, God's wisdom that ordains good ways of human living in the world, and God's wisdom that, beyond the disruption of creation's good by evil, purposes the ultimate well-being, the shalom, the peace of the whole creation."[40] These are all meaningful elements in a living theological tradition that is rooted in the biblical text.

37. The question of how 3:19–20 relates to 8:22–31 in terms of tradition history, authorship, and redaction has been extensively discussed. See, e.g., Lenzi, "Proverbs 8:22–31," esp. 694–96. The results are meager, as we lack evidence and so do not know. All we have is the received text of Proverbs, with no surviving antecedents; though of course the ancient versions of Proverbs can sometimes give clues concerning issues of tradition and redaction.

38. The Hebrew preposition *bĕ* in 3:19–20 can have all these senses. The LXX of 3:19–20 twice uses the preposition *en*, which is a natural equivalent to *bĕ*, and once uses an instrumental dative (though there is some manuscript variation).

39. See, e.g., Cornelius, "Visual Representations of the World."

40. Bauckham, "Where Is Wisdom to Be Found?," 132.

Nonetheless, I suggest that, in terms of its wording and context, the angle of vision of 8:22–31 is oriented less towards God as such than towards what it means for humans when they acquire wisdom. That is, a corollary of the world being made through wisdom is that wisdom is in some way an intrinsic or inherent or immanent (it is hard to find the *mot juste*) dimension of the world. In terms of the portrayal of Wisdom in Proverbs 8 overall, this understanding is fully in tune with the note the poet sounds at the outset (vv. 1–5). Wherever people are, Wisdom is present and is calling out to them; she is somehow *there*, everywhere in the world. A further implication is that those who learn to love wisdom are in some way engaging with the true nature of the world, with reality as it is, and conforming themselves to it. If we then turn to Proverbs' keynote, "the fear of the LORD is the beginning of wisdom," we can see that the book's concern is not just to direct people to a good handling of life and its challenges but to clarify that such good handling is a matter of being in tune with the way the world really is.[41]

Perhaps surprisingly, the specifics of how one should live wisely are not spelled out in Proverbs 1–9, as the recurrent emphasis is on shunning the allure of the "strange woman" and instead choosing Wisdom. But this is partly because chapters 1–9 introduce and frame the specific proverbs that follow in chapter 10 onwards, and these proverbs do provide the content for wise living. It is also partly because, in all likelihood, chapters 1–9 arose in a context where the importance of torah, especially as articulated in Deuteronomy, is an accepted component of the worldview.[42] That is, both torah and the proverbs give content to the notion of what it means to live wisely in terms of walking in God's way.

In any case, there is a consistent use of moral and religious terms that points in a clear direction. The way of wisdom is intrinsically moral and God-oriented; it is possible and close at hand (like the word of torah in Deut. 30:14); and it is for all and is not reserved for the elite or privileged or well educated.

Was There a Time When Wisdom "Was Not"?

What else might appropriately be inferred from Proverbs 8:22–31? We noted at the outset the famous fourth-century Christian debates about Proverbs 8:22,

41. On the puzzling and unexplained presence of folly in a world made through wisdom, see below, p. 45.

42. See Weeks, *Early Israelite Wisdom*, ch. 5; and Weeks, *Instruction and Imagery in Proverbs 1–9*, ch. 6. The point that Weeks argues in historical and authorial terms can also be made more broadly in a different mode, in literary and canonical terms: for the reader of the canonical collection of Israel's scriptures, Mosaic torah sets the context within which other parts of the collection are read.

in which the well-established Christian understanding of Jesus as personified Wisdom meant that a christological referent for 8:22 was shared by all parties, by Arius and Athanasius alike, however they argued its implications. The key question became: If the speaker of 8:22, understood to be Christ, was "created" by God, does this mean that there was a time when the speaker "was not"? Much attention was focused on the verb "created"—primarily the Greek *ktizō* rather than the Hebrew *qānāh*, as most church fathers read the Old Testament in the Greek of the Septuagint—and what it did or did not imply for its speaker's origin. In semantic terms, the precise sense of the Hebrew verb cannot be resolved; interpretive decisions depend on context, both immediate and canonical.[43] I doubt that one can improve on James Loader's observation that "the choice of *qānāh* with its polyvalence produced an aura of suggestive significance, causing controversies that would last for centuries."[44]

For the moment I want to remain with reading Proverbs 8 in its original, pre-Christian frame of reference. If we stay in this frame of reference, does the poem entail that there was a time when Wisdom "was not," and if so, what might follow from this? Interestingly, although most commentators do not ask this question, Michael Fox, the author of a major contemporary commentary on Proverbs, does. He starts, like most others, with the question of how best to translate the verb *qānāh* in 8:22. He observes that "since ancient times, interpreters have been divided as to whether *qanah* denotes *acquisition* (and thus possession) or *creation*." However, he regards this semantic debate as largely beside the point. Rather, he observes, "God acquired/created wisdom as the first of his deeds. Wisdom 'was born' (vv 24, 25) at that time. She did not exist from eternity. *Wisdom is therefore an accidental attribute of godhead, not an essential or inherent one*."[45] In other words, there was a time (or a "time" before that time which is a corollary of the created order) when Wisdom "was not," which has substantive implications for the nature of God. Indeed, Fox goes on to elaborate his point more fully:

> Though the author may not realize it, the underlying assumption is that prior to creation God was in stasis, his power only potential. He brought his power to actuality by acquiring wisdom. He acquired wisdom by creating it, drawing

43. Within Proverbs, probably the best analogy to the use of *qānāh* in 8:22 is in 4:5, 7, "Get/acquire [*qĕnēh*] wisdom," where wisdom is the object of *qānāh*, as in 8:22, and is clearly already in existence. However, the language of being "brought forth" / "born" in 8:24–25 may tip the balance in favor of "create" in the immediate context of the poem. This would be analogous to the use of *qānāh* in Gen. 14:19, where Melchizedek blesses Abram by "the Creator of [*qōnēh*] heaven and earth."

44. Loader, *Proverbs 1–9*, 348.

45. Fox, *Proverbs 1–9*, 279 (emphasis added).

> it from within, from the infinite potential for being that is inherent in Godhead. There is nowhere else he could have gotten it. That is why God's acquiring (*qnh*; 8:22) wisdom is figured in terms of giving birth (*ḥll*; v 24).[46]

The resonances here with fourth-century debates and the implications of the contention that there was a time when the Son "was not" are remarkable. But how should this reading be evaluated? On the one hand, there is a sense in which its logic holds. To contend that there was a time when Wisdom "was not," prior to her being acquired/created by God, is to articulate a consistent outworking of the possible implications of the scenario. On the other hand, the all-important phrase, which Fox uses but does not linger on, is "though the author may not realize it." This brings us back to the key question: What are, and are not, appropriate inferences to draw from poetry of this nature? What draws out well the implications of the text, and what mishandles them? Essentially, one has to evaluate any proposal as and when it is made. Here I can but register my conviction that Fox is taking a logic, one that is indeed present but that is in all likelihood unconscious and unintended, and *unduly pressing it against the grain of the poetry*. It is surely a little misleading to present the logic of the scenario as an "underlying assumption," as such assumptions relate most naturally to authorial intentions rather than to an unintended logic or implication in the words used. The poet in Proverbs 8 is concerned to establish that Wisdom existed prior to all else that God created and was with God as He created; this articulates the intrinsic relationship between God and wisdom and creation. Nothing indicates that the author was also interested in the possible implications of his scenario in terms of what it might mean for God that there was a time when Wisdom "was not"—even if this is the strict logic of his scenario, if pushed.

So why does Fox add the caveat "though the author may not realize it"? I presume it is because, as a scholar deeply immersed in the thought-world of Proverbs, he would accept the contention that the author of Proverbs 1–9 is extremely unlikely to have conjectured that there was a time when "God was in stasis, his power only potential," and also was not wise; nor would the author have welcomed such a conjecture if presented with it as a corollary of his own words. If, however, that contention be allowed, why is it a good idea nonetheless to press the intrinsic logic of the poetic scenario in the way Fox does?[47] When an imaginative scenario may have unintended logical implications, would it not be better for a good interpreter to stay with the flow of

46. Fox, *Proverbs 1–9*, 294.

47. One might also ask what wisdom would really mean "before" God's activity in creation (unless one recasts the discussion in a trinitarian frame of reference).

the poet's thought and to rule out strict logic as a wooden and inappropriate handling of the material?[48]

In short, even if the poem logically allows for a time when Wisdom "was not," one would surely be unattuned to its poetry to try to attend to that time and to say what its theological implications might be.

The Incarnation of Lady Wisdom

While we are still within the book of Proverbs itself, one final passage to note is the acrostic poem with which the book concludes,[49] the portrait of a "capable wife" (*'ēshet ḥayil*) in Proverbs 31:10–31.[50] This poem can be taken at face value as a striking portrayal of an ideal woman of the ancient world. Nonetheless, its location at the conclusion of a book that has prominently featured the feminine personification of Wisdom raises the question of how (if at all) the woman of this poem might relate to Wisdom.[51] To put it bluntly, is it appropriate to read her as an embodiment or instantiation of Wisdom? Is it not a natural move, in the context of Proverbs, to read this concluding poem metaphorically in relation to the book's earlier content? If one asks the question "What might Wisdom look like if she actually took on human form?" then a ready answer could surely be, "She might well look rather like the capable wife (*'ēshet ḥayil*)." The capable wife has deeply desirable qualities: her husband trusts in her, her whole family praises her, and she displays the fundamental quality of "fear of the LORD" (Prov. 31:11, 28, 30). In addition, she is constantly and resiliently and wisely at work for good in the home and the wider community. Does she not display in an exemplary way what wisdom in practice could look like?

48. This whole discussion can be an interesting case study of the interrelationship of author-, text-, and reader-hermeneutics.

49. There are numerous technical questions about the origin and composition of this poem and its relationship to the rest of the book which will be passed over here.

50. Translations of *'ēshet ḥayil* vary greatly because of the difficulty of deciding the best nuance for *ḥayil*, especially with reference to a woman. Its second element, *ḥayil*—which is hard to translate but carries a range of meanings such as "strength, wealth, worth, ability"—is almost always predicated of men. The common Hebrew idioms are *'îsh/'anshē-ḥayil* and *ben/bĕnē-ḥayil*, "man/men of strength"; *gibbōr ḥayil*, "strong warrior"; and *sārē ḥayil*, "commanders of the army." See, e.g., Eising, "*Chayil*," for an account of its usage.

51. A strong affirmation of the interrelatedness of Prov. 8 with the "capable wife" is offered by Christine Yoder, *Wisdom as a Woman of Substance*. Her argument relates the texts to their possible context of origin in the Persian period but does not reflect on their role in canonical context.

If it is appropriate to construe the capable wife as an embodiment of Wisdom, then a further move is also possible.[52] The phrase *ʾēshet ḥayil* is uncommon. It is used of women only three times in Israel's scriptures. Most famous is the use in Proverbs 31:10, though there is a comparable instance earlier in 12:4: "A good wife [*ʾēshet ḥayil*] is the crown of her husband." Its only other appearance is in the encounter between Ruth and Boaz at the Bethlehem threshing floor (Ruth 3:6–18). Ruth in her need asks Boaz to act as next-of-kin (*gōʾēl*) for her (v. 9). Boaz initially commends Ruth's quality of loyalty (*ḥesed*): "May you be blessed by the LORD, my daughter; this last instance of your loyalty is better than the first; you have not gone after young men, whether poor or rich" (v. 10). He then refers to her public reputation: "And now, my daughter, do not be afraid, I will do for you all that you ask, for all the assembly of my people know that you are a worthy woman [*ʾēshet ḥayil*]" (v. 11).

Ruth has not had opportunity to do most of the things that the *ʾēshet ḥayil* of Proverbs 31 does. But in her more limited sphere of action as an impoverished young widow, she has shown consistent and self-giving loyalty to her mother-in-law, Naomi, which has led her also to embrace Israel's God (Ruth 1:16–17). Boaz notes these aspects of Ruth's character and behavior in their first conversation (2:11–12), and he responds with his own generosity. It is fully in keeping with the tenor of the story that Boaz initially characterizes Ruth, first, as demonstrating *ḥesed*, a quality which is integral to the LORD's own gracious character and actions in His self-revelation at Sinai (Exod. 34:6b, 7a), and then, second, as an *ʾēshet ḥayil*, which in context means a woman of character and integrity. Given the link between moral integrity and wisdom in Proverbs, one can also appropriately see Ruth as displaying wisdom in her handling of her difficult situation, even if the specific term *ḥokmāh* is not used. Thus, if one were to ask what the ideal woman of wisdom in Proverbs 31 might look like in a more limited and mundane everyday context, a ready answer could be that she might well look rather like Ruth.

A linkage between Proverbs 31 and Ruth is also suggested by the arrangement of the Hebrew canon. Although the contents of the third part of the Hebrew canon, the Writings, have appeared in a number of different sequences down the centuries, one very common sequence found in standard contemporary Hebrew Bibles places Ruth directly after Proverbs. As Chris Seitz, who has written suggestively on the interpretive potential of the arrangement of the documents in the Hebrew canon, nicely puts it, "Proverbs ends by extolling

52. For a fuller account of this recognition, see Dell, "Didactic Intertextuality," esp. 103–4, 112.

the virtuous woman, and Ruth follows to give a stellar example (compare the *eset-hayil* of Prov 31:10 with Boaz's commendation in Ruth 3:11). . . . Reading the poem [of Prov. 31] and reading Ruth in the light of it makes for a marvelous surprise like the surprise of the book itself."[53] Thus, linking Proverbs 31 and the book of Ruth, in which Ruth implicitly exemplifies wisdom, is suggested both by specific wording and by literary-canonical context.

In summary, our discussion of wisdom in Proverbs 1–9 has traversed a number of distinct yet interrelated issues, both lofty and mundane. The book's concern with wisdom is sounded in the keynote that "the fear of the LORD is the beginning of wisdom." This is a seemingly simple-sounding principle that in fact represents a profound epistemology in terms of what best enables a person to understand how to live well. Desirable as wisdom is, however, the gaining of wisdom is not straightforward; folly, on the surface, is equally as attractive and appealing as wisdom. There is thus a necessary struggle of the will to discern and embrace wisdom. The issues at stake are heightened by Wisdom's account of herself as present with God both when the world was made and in the ongoing created order. This means that becoming wise is a matter not just of becoming successful and/or wealthy and/or powerful but rather of being attuned to the nature of reality—what one might call the deep rhythm of the world. And that deep rhythm of the world is a reflection and mediation of its Creator. Yet such possibly dizzying notions are also firmly brought down to earth with pictures of what the wisdom of creation might look like in everyday life, in the capable wife or the virtuous Moabite woman Ruth.

Wisdom and Christ in the New Testament

I noted briefly at the outset that in antiquity Proverbs 8:22 became associated with other texts. Conceptually, it was a natural move in a developing Jewish frame of reference to link primordial Wisdom with God's gift of Torah to Israel, as memorably set out by Ben Sira in his "Praise of Wisdom" (Sirach 24). Within Israel's scriptures, Genesis 1:1 became a prime intertextual linkage.[54] The verbal connection between these texts was the common use of *rēʾshīt*. The conceptual linkage was the appropriateness of the thought that the wisdom

53. Seitz, *Elder Testament*, 125, 170.

54. A fine account of how this conceptual linkage was shared in late antiquity by both Jews and Christians, albeit with differences over whether the referent of *rēʾshīt* was Torah or the preincarnate Christ, is Alexander, "'In the Beginning.'" The linkage probably goes back at least to Philo, though his own usage is distinctive (see Cohen, *Philo's Scriptures*, 160–63, 223–27).

that accompanied the LORD at creation in Proverbs 8, and is said to be the agent of creation in Proverbs 3:19, should therefore also be seen as the agent of creation in Genesis 1, where God creates *bĕ*—"in" or "by"—*rēʾshīt*, with *rēʾshīt* now construed as wisdom.[55]

In the New Testament, the conceptuality of both Proverbs 8 and Genesis 1 informs the thought of the Prologue of John's Gospel, especially its opening verses:

> [1]In the beginning was the Word, and the Word was with God, and the Word was God. [2]He was in the beginning with God. [3]All things came into being through him, and without him not one thing came into being. (John 1:1–3)

Most obviously, "In the beginning was the Word" strongly resonates with Genesis 1:1,[56] indicating that John is retelling the Genesis creation account with reference to the Word which becomes flesh in Jesus Christ. The specification that the Word "was in the beginning with God" strongly resonates with the depiction of Wisdom as being "with God" at the beginning of creation.[57] Likewise, the notion that "all things came into being through him" strongly resonates with the portrayal of Wisdom as the one by/through whose agency creation came about.[58] John appropriates the language and conceptuality of Proverbs 8 and Genesis 1 to depict the full significance of the Word. That agent of creation which Proverbs speaks of as Wisdom is now to be understood as the Word which becomes flesh in Jesus Christ.

■ Although the Johannine Prologue is the best-known NT account of the preincarnate Christ as the agent of creation, it is by no means the sole account. The other prime passage is in Colossians:

> [15]He [Christ] is the image of the invisible God, the firstborn of all creation; [16]*for in him all things in heaven and on earth were created*, things visible and invisible, whether thrones or dominions or rulers or powers—*all things have been created through him*

55. This is an interesting example of how intertextual resonances can enable constructive thought on the basis of the semantic potential of the biblical text, where recontextualization and intertextuality shift interpretive weight away from an author-oriented hermeneutic towards a text- and reader-oriented hermeneutic.

56. John's Greek *en archē* follows the Septuagint of Gen. 1:1 and uses the same form, without a definite article, as the Hebrew *bĕrēʾshīt*. In Prov. 8:23, Wisdom similarly speaks of being established *en archē*.

57. John's unusual preposition for "with," *pros*, is not used in Prov. 8 LXX, which instead uses *sun* (*sumparēmēn autō*, 8:27) and *para* (*ēmēn parʾ autō*, 8:30). However, there is no clear difference of meaning in the different prepositions.

58. John's preposition *dia*, "through," is not present in Prov. 3:19, which simply uses an instrumental dative, *tē sophiā*, but the thought is similar.

> and for him. [17]He himself is before all things, and in him all things hold together. (Col. 1:15–17, emphasis added)

It is likely that the basis of this passage, as of John's Prologue, is an in-depth exegetical engagement with Israel's scriptures.[59] Christ is identified with Wisdom in Proverbs, and the usage of *rēʾshīt* in both Prov. 8:22 and Gen. 1:1 is being utilized to articulate an account of the preincarnate Christ as the agent of creation. A comparable understanding is also evident elsewhere in the NT:

> For us there is only one God, the Father, from whom all things have come into being and for whom we live, and only one Lord, Jesus Christ, *through whom all things have come into being and through whom we live.*[60] (1 Cor. 8:6 AT)

> [1]Long ago God spoke to our ancestors in many and various ways by the prophets, [2]but in these last days he has spoken to us by a Son, whom he appointed heir of all things, *through whom he also created the worlds.* (Heb. 1:1–2, emphasis added) ■

I argued for Proverbs 8 that "a corollary of the world being made through wisdom is that wisdom is in some way an intrinsic or inherent or immanent . . . dimension of the world," and also that "those who learn to love wisdom are in some way engaging with the true nature of the world, with reality as it is, and conforming themselves to it."[61] When John appropriates this language and conceptuality to portray the Word who became flesh, it means that the reality of God as seen in Jesus is in some way an intrinsic or inherent or immanent dimension of the world. It also means that those who come to have faith in Jesus are not just adopting a possibly sectarian stance (even though sociologically there would have been a clear element of this for Christians in the first three centuries, as there is also for many Christians in contemporary contexts). They are also in some way engaging with the true nature of the world and conforming themselves to it.

Modern Accounts of a World without Meaning

I would now like to address a particular, and deep, difficulty with this whole mode of understanding. Put simply, even if the above reading of the meaning of Proverbs 8 and John 1 be entirely granted, how can it be of interest

59. A classic modern account is Burney, "Christ as the *Archē* of Creation."

60. The Greek text of 8:6 as a whole is difficult to translate, as it is strong on prepositions but has no verbs. I offer my own translation to try to clarify the likely sense that the text speaks both of creation in the past and of created and redeemed life in the present.

61. Above, p. 28.

or significance other than as a possibly interesting item in the history of ideas? The fact that people in antiquity thought thus need be no guide to how people today should think. The nature of the world (and the universe) today is known through the natural sciences; and the natural sciences do not find "wisdom" or "Christ"—any more than "God"—to be in any sense a constituent element within the world.[62] All talk, therefore, of "discovering" or "encountering" wisdom or Christ as immanent within the world must in fact be a subjective projection of our own aspirations onto the world—a world which can indeed be viewed thus, but which is not in its own intrinsic reality thus. Our moral and spiritual aspirations may say much about *us*, but they say nothing about the empirical world apart from us. In a contemporary context, it is all too easy to see the accounts in Proverbs 8 and John 1 as a kind of primitive science, a "creationism"—accounts of the "how" of creation that compete with, and have in fact been rendered null and void by, the insights of the natural sciences.

If, however, one draws on the ancient distinction between physics and metaphysics (a distinction first specifically articulated by Aristotle), it becomes possible to see things differently. In contemporary terms, it becomes possible to see the concern of the language in both Proverbs and John to be *grammatical* or *conceptual* rather than *empirical* or *scientific*. To simplify greatly: empirical and scientific approaches engage with all the particular things that are there to be known, while grammatical and conceptual approaches engage with the overall understandings and the structuring categories by which we know the particular things and also condition what we do with them. If there are different kinds of conceptuality and discourse, then they need not necessarily be in competition with one another, for their natures and purposes are distinct. They may, however, come together in an *existential* human reality, which is not at all easy to conceptualize and depict. At any rate, I propose to pursue this general line of thinking, as it readily connects with significant contemporary debates.

I choose two contemporary thinkers, John Gray and Thomas Nagel, neither of whom adhere to the Christian (or any other) faith. They represent an intellectual and cultural world which no longer believes in God (though

62. We may note the occasional tendency of scientists such as Einstein or Stephen Hawking to reach for terms such as "God" or "mind of God" when trying to express what would be entailed by a core expression of physics so "simple" and "elegant" that it explains everything. But while the sense of awe and wonder that is intrinsic to such usage is derived from the Bible and the living faiths rooted in it, the meaning of the terms is far removed from that of Jewish or Christian understanding, illustrating the problem of secular language attempting to express something of ultimate significance. None of this, of course, denies that some natural scientists do believe in God as Creator.

religious language and artifacts may still have aesthetic and psychological significance). As such, they would be dismissive of the idea that Proverbs 8 and John 1 have any enduring truth. Nonetheless, they are creative thinkers who like to raise hard questions precisely about generally received wisdom in a contemporary culture that has conceptually dismissed and pragmatically marginalized the insights of Christian (and other) faith. I am not concerned to locate them within a modern history of thought;[63] I only attend to them as contemporary thinkers.

John Gray on a World without Meaning

First is John Gray, whose thought I will consider in relation to his short and deliciously iconoclastic book *The Soul of the Marionette*. Gray contends that secular notions of freedom and progress are unwarranted prolongations of a Christian worldview that is no longer held: "The monotheistic faith that history has meaning continues to shape the modern way of thinking even after monotheism itself has been rejected."[64] With typical provocation, Gray holds that contemporary mainstream secular thought represents the triumph of Gnosticism:

> Many people today hold to a Gnostic view of things without realizing the fact. Believing that human beings can be fully understood in the terms of scientific materialism, they reject any idea of free will. But they cannot give up hope of being masters of their destiny. So they have come to believe that science will somehow enable the human mind to escape the limitations that shape its natural condition. Throughout much of the world, and particularly in western countries, the Gnostic faith that knowledge can give humans a freedom no other creature can possess has become the predominant religion.[65]

With further provocation, Gray suggests that serious study of the Aztecs, who were notorious for their extensive practice of human sacrifice, can be illuminating for a better understanding of ourselves today: "Humans kill one another—and in some cases themselves—for many reasons, but none is more human than the attempt to make sense of their lives. More than loss of life, they fear loss of meaning."[66]

63. One friend suggested significant resonance with Nietzsche and Kant for Gray and Nagel, respectively.

64. Gray, *Soul of the Marionette*, 160. Compare the following: "Secular thinking is shaped by forgotten or repressed religion" (15).

65. Gray, *Soul of the Marionette*, 9.

66. Gray, *Soul of the Marionette*, 87.

Over against modern attempts to find meaning, Gray proposes a chastened recognition of how precarious our situation is and how little we know: "Human beings act, certainly. But none of them knows why they act as they do. There is a scattering of facts, which can be known and reported. Beyond these facts are the stories that are told. . . . The stories we tell ourselves are like the messages that appear on Ouija boards. If we are authors of our lives, it is only in retrospect."[67] Acceptance of this recognition, however, brings the only real freedom that there is:

> Accepting the fact of unknowing makes possible an inner freedom very different from that pursued by Gnostics. If you have this negative capability, you will not want a higher form of consciousness; your ordinary mind will give you all you need. Rather than trying to impose sense on your life, you will be content to let meaning come and go. Instead of becoming an unfaltering puppet, you will make your way in the stumbling human world.[68]

The question of how one might arrive at Gray's position, other than by being persuaded by his argument, is perhaps indicated by a passage where he speaks of what determines people's overall understandings:

> How we come to have the world-views we do is an interesting question. No doubt reason plays a part, but human needs for meaning and purpose are usually more important. At times personal taste may be what decides the issue. There is nothing to say that, when all the work of reason is done, only one view of the world will remain. There may be many that fit everything that can be known. In that case you might as well choose the view of the world you find most interesting or beautiful. Adopting a world-view is more like selecting a painting to furnish a room than testing a scientific theory. The test is how it fits with your life.[69]

Gray's position commands respect. Indeed, one might make a case that key elements of it, especially the concern to accept unknowing and simply "make your way in the stumbling human world," have a certain affinity with the proposals of Ecclesiastes (Qoheleth) in the biblical canon. Nonetheless, it is worth noting that Gray's basic premise—that there is no meaning to life—is never as such either analyzed or subjected to scrutiny. The force of Gray's critique bears on those who unwittingly perpetuate elements of a discarded monotheistic worldview; he takes the discarding as a given.

67. Gray, *Soul of the Marionette*, 136–37.
68. Gray, *Soul of the Marionette*, 165.
69. Gray, *Soul of the Marionette*, 150.

There can be a certain attraction (at least for some people) in an unrestrained, shoulder-shrugging skepticism which treats all human desires and attempts to find meaning as an exercise that is congenial but at root self-deceptive. However, both as a point of logic and as a matter of intuition, Gray's skepticism does not in fact rule out the possibility that one story, or one family of stories, might merit a status that is different from other stories—though how one can make such a case appropriately and without special pleading is hardly straightforward.

Thomas Nagel on a World without Meaning

Thomas Nagel is another distinctive voice. Somewhat like Gray, Nagel critiques generally accepted contemporary wisdom, though the moves he makes differ from those of Gray.[70]

Nagel's starting premise is the same as Gray's. The understanding of the world and the universe that has developed in modernity through the natural sciences cannot accommodate the sense of meaning that characterized earlier religious worldviews: "The universe revealed by chemistry and physics, however beautiful and awe-inspiring, is meaningless, in the radical sense that it is incapable of meaning. That is, natural science, as most commonly understood, presents the world and our existence as something to which the religious impulse has no application."[71]

Nagel, however, is more sympathetic to the issues raised by a religious outlook than are many other philosophers. He identifies a religious outlook as "the idea that there is some kind of all-encompassing mind or spiritual principle in addition to the minds of individual human beings and other creatures—and that this mind or spirit is the foundation of the existence of the universe, of the natural order, of value, and of our existence, nature, and purpose." The religious question about how to bring one's life into appropriate relation with the universe is not an expression of curiosity: "It is rather a question of attitude: Is there a way to live in harmony with the universe, and not just in it?"[72] Nagel's concern is not to renew a religious outlook. Instead, he wants to take the religious outlook seriously, as expressing a deep and widespread human concern, and to propose a secular alternative.[73]

70. I will draw on two of Nagel's writings, his essay "Secular Philosophy and the Religious Temperament" and his monograph *Mind and Cosmos*.

71. Nagel, "Secular Philosophy and the Religious Temperament," 8.

72. Nagel, "Secular Philosophy and the Religious Temperament," 5.

73. "What, if anything, does secular philosophy have to put in the place of religion?" (Nagel, "Secular Philosophy and the Religious Temperament," 4).

Nagel's own preferred approach is that "there is a nonaccidental fit between us and the world order: In other words, the natural order is such that, over time, it generates beings that are both part of it and able to understand it." Such a view "does not postulate intention or purpose behind one's existence and relation to the universe," but rather sees human life as "the product of natural teleology."[74] He seeks to offer an account "that make[s] mind, meaning, and value as fundamental as matter and space-time in an account of what there is," and his "guiding conviction is that mind is not just an afterthought or an accident or an add-on, but a basic aspect of nature."[75] Although Nagel hopes that this contention may be true, he is nonetheless aware of its fragile status. It is entirely possible to reject it, even though "a sense of the absurd may be what we are left with."[76]

Although ideally I would set out Nagel's interesting account more fully, I will focus specifically on the way he portrays any kind of religious alternative to his proposal. For the language he uses is revealing of what he takes that religious alternative to be.

Nagel's prime conceptuality for depicting a "theistic" option is "divine intervention," an intervention which is not itself part of the natural order and therefore leaves the natural order insufficiently explained.[77] Thus, he says,

> theism pushes the quest for intelligibility outside the world. If God exists, he is not part of the natural order but a free agent not governed by natural laws. He may act partly by creating a natural order, but whatever he does directly cannot be part of that order.
>
> A theistic self-understanding, for those who find it compelling to see the world as the expression of divine intention, would leave intact our natural confidence in our cognitive faculties. But it would not be the kind of understanding that explains *how* beings like us fit into the world. The kind of intelligibility that would still be missing is intelligibility of the natural order itself—intelligibility from within. That kind of intelligibility may be compatible with some forms of theism—if God creates a self-contained natural order which he then leaves undisturbed. But it is not compatible with direct theistic explanation of systematic

74. Nagel, "Secular Philosophy and the Religious Temperament," 12, 16, 17.

75. Nagel, *Mind and Cosmos*, 20, 16.

76. Nagel, "Secular Philosophy and the Religious Temperament," 17.

77. Nagel, *Mind and Cosmos*, 8. There may be some internal inconsistency within Nagel's thought in terms of how this interventionism relates to his contention that a religious outlook is "the idea that there is some kind of all-encompassing mind or spiritual principle . . . and that this mind or spirit is the foundation of the existence of the universe." The supposition that God is both the foundation of the natural order and an implicitly arbitrary, interventionist changer of that order is probably incoherent, even though it is an incoherence often found in popular religious discourse. Part of the problem may be the tendency to restrict "creation" to the distant past rather than seeing it as part of God's continuing relation to the world/universe.

> features of the world that would seem otherwise to be brute facts—such as the creation of life from dead matter, or the birth of consciousness, or reason. Such interventionist hypotheses amount to a denial that there is a comprehensive natural order. They are in part motivated by a belief that seems to me correct, namely, that there is little or no possibility that these facts depend on nothing but the laws of physics.[78]

The only apparent alternative to "intervention," which he also depicts as "creationism,"[79] is a form of what historically has been called "deism," though this ends up looking rather like Nagel's own natural teleology.

Towards a Reframing of Gray's and Nagel's Concerns

Issues of such magnitude and complexity obviously require rather fuller treatment than I can give them here.[80] Indeed, I am in full agreement with Nagel's concluding observation about how to proceed: "The best we can do is to develop the rival alternative conceptions in each important domain as fully and carefully as possible, depending on our antecedent sympathies, and see how they measure up. That is a more credible form of progress than decisive proof or refutation."[81]

One possible approach would be in terms of conceptual analysis. Neither Gray nor Nagel offers much analytical reflection on the categories they use. Yet certain questions readily come to mind. For example, is what counts as "meaning" self-evident when speaking of the possible "meaning of life"? What constitutes "intelligibility" in relation to the world, not least in terms of what would count as a point of understanding at which the mind is satisfied? Nagel in particular seems unaware that terms like "divine intervention" or "creationism" are contested in their meaning and appropriate use, and he appears to be unfamiliar with relevant theological literature.[82]

78. Nagel, *Mind and Cosmos*, 26.

79. "A creationist explanation of the existence of life is the biological analogue of dualism in the philosophy of mind. It pushes teleology outside of the natural order, into the intentions of the creator—working with completely directionless materials whose properties nevertheless underlie both the mental and the physical" (Nagel, *Mind and Cosmos*, 94).

80. General discussions of science and religion regularly focus on methodological questions of the value and limits of analytical materialist reductionism and on particular topics like whether the universe is designed, the big bang and the beginning, and the anthropic principle. My present concerns are complementary.

81. Nagel, *Mind and Cosmos*, 127.

82. I presume (on a charitable reading) that Nagel means by "creationism" what most theologians refer to as "creation." But the distinction between these terms in most contexts is

My approach, however, will be to focus on certain implications of the worldview in Scripture in relation to certain implications of the worldview in Gray and Nagel. Such a comparison cannot be made, however, except with a lively awareness of the caveat that when Scripture, with texts in poetic and narrative mode, is set alongside modern philosophy, with texts in abstract and discursive mode, one is not comparing like with like.

There are, of course, accounts by Jewish and Christian scholars which address these general issues. For example, Jonathan Sacks nicely reformulates the tenor of Proverbs 8 in a contemporary idiom, discussing what is necessary for a good human ecology in which life can flourish:

> Families and communities are in turn undergirded by religious faith. In Judaism, at least, the three go hand in hand. Religious faith suggests that our commitments to fidelity and interdependence are not arbitrary, a matter of passing moral fashion. They mirror the deep structure of reality. The bonds between husband and wife, parent and child, and us and our neighbours partake of the covenantal bond between God and humanity. The moral rules and virtues which constrain and enlarge our aspirations are not mere subjective devices and desires. They are "out there" as well as "in here." They represent objective truths about the human situation, refracted through the prisms of revelation and tradition.[83]

This is an interesting example of how one might retain the theological grammar of Proverbs 8 while expressing it in a different idiom in the context of the contemporary world as understood by the natural sciences. However, I would like to take a slightly different tack and suggest that there are easily overlooked aspects of Proverbs and John's Gospel that suggest a particular way of framing the issues, especially in relation to Nagel's account of divine intervention.

The Imaginative Conceptualities of Proverbs 8 and John's Gospel

In Proverbs 8 there is indeed an account of "the beginning" and "creation" in which Wisdom accompanies the LORD and which indicates something of how God creates. Yet the movement in the text suggests modes of understanding rather different from those that Nagel sketches. God is not a "part" of the world that is made. But neither does God create and put a certain potential

important. "Creation" is an integral element of biblical and Christian faith, while "creationism" is a modern corruption of the notion of creation through a well-meaning but misguided attempt to reconcile science and Scripture.

83. Sacks, *Faith in the Future*, 6.

in the world and then "stand back," nor does God periodically "intervene." Rather, wisdom, though not itself God, mediates God. Wisdom is a matter of embracing and attaining *life*, that realization of human existence which Scripture elsewhere consistently associates with response to God.

Moreover, this wisdom which mediates God and which is in some way constitutive of creation is constantly present, active, and response-seeking. Proverbs 8:22–31 reads best, I have suggested, as a movement from before creation (8:22–26), to creation (8:27–29), to the regular order of the familiar world (8:30–31), with no sense that Wisdom "now" is other than "then," before or during creation; she is an enduring and ever-present reality.[84] Wisdom is present in the mundane contexts of life, where she calls to people, challenging them to respond positively to her invitation (8:1–5) as the way of attaining that which is most valuable in life (8:18–21). She is a reality whom some people love and others hate (whether or not people would consciously articulate their desires and priorities in this way) (8:17, 36). One's response to Wisdom mediates life or death. Proverbs presents a picture of a world where the existential reality of life is constituted by the presence and challenge of wisdom, which intrinsically mediates God's presence and challenge.

It is hard to find good terminology to depict this sense of God as being both "beyond" the world yet also, via wisdom, "within" the world. Theology recognizes the need to speak inseparably of both the transcendence and the immanence of God. But it is also clear, at least by implication, that this reality of the world is not self-evident. The book of Proverbs as a whole, and Proverbs 1–9 in particular, is structured around the alternatives of wisdom and folly, both of which appeal to, and are embraced by, humans. Wisdom does not present itself in such a way that people *must* respond positively and embrace it. Rather, life in the world is constituted in such a way that the existential choice between wisdom and folly, as between good and evil, is an inescapable dimension of human reality.

The notion in Proverbs 8 that wisdom is actively present in the world, taking the initiative to engage people and seek a positive response from them, is replicated in the Gospel of John, where the Word, who is the divine agent of creation in the mode of Wisdom, is "the true light [*phōs*] that shines on [*phōtizei*] everyone" and "became flesh and lived among us" (John 1:9, 14 AT). Central to John's portrayal of Jesus is the understanding that Jesus is fully and unreservedly responsive to God the Father, who has sent him, in

84. So too in Prov. 3, the wisdom and understanding by which the LORD creates (3:19) are hardly other than the wisdom and understanding whose attainment constitutes human happiness (3:13).

such a way that Jesus is, as it were, the one in whom God is made visible. This means that, in an important way, an encounter with the human figure of Jesus is also an encounter with God.

A key interpretive passage, in which John articulates how the judgment of God is worked out in Jesus, is John 3:19–21:

> [19]And this is the judgment, that the light [*phōs*] has come into the world, and people loved darkness rather than light because their deeds were evil. [20]For all who do evil hate the light and do not come to the light, so that their deeds may not be exposed. [21]But those who do what is true come to the light, so that it may be clearly seen that their deeds have been done in God.

The imagery here is of a bright torch being thrust into a dark place, like someone carrying a lamp into a dark room full of people—this is what it means when the Word/Wisdom which takes human form in Jesus comes among people. The introduction of the light into the darkness poses an inescapable choice for those in the darkness. Do they welcome and turn to the light (even if it may take a while for their eyes to get used to it), or do they resent the light and shrink back from it, perhaps trying to withdraw to a less affected area that is still dark? Both responses are made. Significantly, the challenge posed by Jesus is intrinsically moral, as is the challenge of wisdom—to embrace good rather than evil—a challenge which some resist. Moreover, it is clearly possible in some sense to "do what is true" *before* coming to the light rather than solely as a consequence of such coming. The intrinsic value of living honestly and truly is affirmed; that is, human dispositions and practices can to some degree be open and attuned to the light of the Creator, even if there is no conscious awareness of this. A positive response of coming to the light—that is, the explicit recognition of Jesus and response in faith to him—will, however, give a more specific context and content and shaping (perhaps reshaping) to that which is affirmed.[85]

At the end of the Gospel of John it becomes clear that the mission of Jesus must become that of his followers too:

> [21]Jesus said to them [his disciples] again, "Peace be with you. As the Father has sent me, so I send you." [22]When he had said this, he breathed on them and said to them, "Receive the Holy Spirit." (John 20:21–22)

85. This coming of the light is reexpressed as active testimony to the truth in Jesus' response to Pilate, in which he redefines his kingship in terms of a mission to the world for all those who belong to the truth and hear his voice (John 18:37). Again, the sovereign God who has made the world is not absent or withdrawn but, through Jesus, is actively confronting people in the world with that moral and existential reality which they need to embrace if they are to live well.

Jesus' followers are enabled to continue to bring God's truth and light into the world. That, in Johannine idiom, is the nature of Christian mission.

The deep similarities between Proverbs 8 and John's Gospel are more at the level of conceptuality than of terminology or imagery. In Proverbs 8, Wisdom *calls out* (*qārāʾ*) to people, while in John's Gospel the Word who becomes flesh in Jesus is a *light* (*phōs*) that *shines on* (*phōtizei*) people. But whether in reference to a calling voice or a shining light, a common understanding is clear: the agent of God's creation, Wisdom or Word, remains active within creation, no less now than then. This dimension of reality engages people and seeks a life-giving response from them.

Interestingly, Proverbs 8 no more tries to explain how folly can be present in a world made by God through wisdom than the Johannine Prologue tries to explain how darkness can be present in a world made by God through the Word who is life and light. The focus in each text is not on the abstract question "Why are there evil and folly in the world?" but rather is on the practically oriented question "How best should the world be understood for the purpose of living well in it?" The inability of monotheistic faith to "resolve" the question of evil and sin at a certain theoretical level is well known (however much partial accounts, primarily in terms of the implications of freedom, may be offered). But the corresponding strength of the biblical witness is its consistent focus on the inescapable reality of the world as known to all humans, with a clear vision of what enhances and diminishes life when confronted by this demanding reality.

Towards a Comparison of Biblical and Secularized Conceptualities

I offer two preliminary observations towards a comparison of ancient biblical and modern secularized conceptualities.

Gray claims that "adopting a world-view is more like selecting a painting to furnish a room than testing a scientific theory. The test is how it fits with your life."[86] In one sense this is clearly right, insofar as the issues here have little in common with testing a scientific theory. Nonetheless, Gray's wording is surely misleading, or else potentially trivializing, since he makes it sound as if it is a matter of consumer choice. The real value in what he says has to do with people existentially encountering a way of seeing the world that enables them to be more authentically and truthfully themselves as they embrace and appropriate it. A key dimension of such a perspective may be less how it fits with *us* (however much that might be an essential

86. Above, p. 38.

element) than how we fit with *it* as a reality to which human beings need to learn to be conformed.

Nagel asks, "Is there a way to live in harmony with the universe, and not just in it?" He takes the religious question more seriously than Gray, even while he reexpresses its core concern in a secular and scientific mode through the notion of a natural teleology. His account, however, focuses on what might be considered formal aspects of life—consciousness, intentionality, meaning, purpose, thought, and value. But these do not prioritize the existential and relational dimensions of life which are so central in the biblical accounts. The biblical portrayals of Wisdom calling out to people and of a light being thrust into darkness so as to elicit a response envisage a dynamic that is elided in Nagel's more abstract conceptualities. The notion that life is constituted by relational realities such as trust, hope, and love is not incompatible with Nagel's formal conceptualities but would reframe them in a particular way. The idea that the human realities of trust, hope, and love are reflections of the divine reality of the Creator, and are our best way of accessing whatever meaning there is in the world, finds no place in Nagel's account.

Conclusion: Towards a Grammar of God's Wisdom and the Created Order

The first facet of what it means to "know that the LORD is God," in the cumulative account in this book, is a recognition that the LORD is the wise Creator of the world. He has created through wisdom, in such a way that wisdom is a constituent element of reality. Right response to the call of wisdom means right response to the LORD God. For the Christian this wisdom, which takes many forms, receives its supreme realization in the Word who becomes flesh in the person of Jesus. This mediation of God through wisdom and Word is not, however, self-evident. Wisdom's call is confronted by folly and rejection, and the light of Christ is confronted by unbelief and rejection. The grammar of God's wisdom is complex. In theological shorthand, fundamental issues of nature and grace cluster here.

In the contemporary world, the challenge of recognizing and responding to God's wisdom is heightened by problems of sheer incomprehension, for particular historical reasons. For example, on Christmas Eve 2019 *The Times* newspaper devoted its prime leading article, "Faith under Fire," to a defense of religious freedom in relation to the "iniquitous" problem of the persecution of Christians, which "is at near-genocide levels in some parts of the world," and also of other religious groups. The writer appealed to Thomas

Jefferson's 1786 Virginia Statute for Religious Freedom as a foundational account of the necessity of liberty for religious belief. Jefferson's document drew a sharp line between private and public in terms of the "inviolable principle of private judgment" and the fact that "there should be no religious test for public office." Yet the article writer's reasonable statement—reflecting a pragmatically constructive, secular outlook—that "the only role of the state in religious matters is to uphold liberty, not to arbitrate between rival claims to truth," is accompanied by the remarkable claim that, "as Jefferson insisted, questions about the origins and purpose of the universe are matters of private conscience alone."

It is one thing to unscramble, and resist the renewal of, certain historic embodiments of institutional religious power in nation-states. It is another to fail to see that understandings of the nature and purpose of the world and of humanity within it can matter profoundly for the ways in which human life is conducted in public as well as in private. In Jefferson's categories, which are apparently shared by *The Times*' writer, the content of Proverbs 8 and John's Gospel becomes opaque and essentially unintelligible.

Much contemporary culture retains a strong intellectual and existential legacy of conceptualities of the seventeenth, eighteenth, and nineteenth centuries. These conceptualities, so fruitful in the development of the natural sciences and nonreligious political arrangements, became oblivious to what lay beyond their scope and thereby increasingly unable to grasp biblical and historic Christian patterns of wisdom. (And the context of Christian-derived belief in the meaningfulness of the world in the natural sciences likewise increasingly disappeared from view.)[87]

Part of the problem lies in the approach one adopts. Questions about possible ultimate meaning—or wisdom, or truth—should surely not be framed in the terms of some concerned thinker who is trying to work out how to go with the grain of the universe and/or discover what might be an appropriate theoretical basis for doing so. Nor should they be essentially framed in terms of trying to specify what primal conditions of the world would be necessary for a sense of meaning to emerge (though that has its place). Instead, going with the grain of the universe should start with how we—in principle, anybody and everybody—find ourselves in the here and now, in response to those dimensions of life which challenge and shape us, and in relationships with others who may also be seeking goodness, wisdom, and truth (or not, as the

87. In addition to Nicholas Lash's *The Beginning and the End of 'Religion'* (see 18n15), groundbreaking work in the history of ideas has been done especially by Peter Harrison, most recently in *The Territories of Science and Religion*, and by Michael Buckley, e.g., *At the Origins of Modern Atheism*.

case may be). Learning to live rightly is an avenue to understanding. Understanding reality through the acquiring of wisdom is relational, responsive, and moral. Such existential dimensions are necessary for reason, over time, to articulate appropriate conceptualities. To use another shorthand of classic theological terminology, we need both love and knowledge.

There comes a point at which rational argument reaches the limits of what it can achieve, something of which both Gray and Nagel are acutely aware. Yet such limits of reason do not mean that intellectual convictions may not be grounded in other ways. There are people whom one recognizes as deserving of trust. These people may embody and represent larger identities within the world—and understandings of it—in which one becomes willing to place trust. In the biblical portrayal, the enduring presence through time and space of a people called by God to live for Him and to bear witness to His priorities is an essential element of the context in which the portrayals of Wisdom and of the incarnate Word are meaningful. Existential responses to the call of wisdom and the shining of the light best find their place within a wider context of people and practices which command respect and earn trust, even while remaining open to discerning wisdom and truth wherever they are found.

The meaningfulness of the biblical portrayals of Wisdom and the Word as constitutive of, and present within, the world cannot be "demonstrated" over against those understandings of the world that are attainable through the natural sciences. It is not, however, just a matter of differing dimensions of reality that require differing approaches, as in the distinction between physics and metaphysics. It is also a matter of which elements within the world one chooses to prioritize in coming to an understanding of what it might mean to be attuned to this world and to be in harmony with it and thereby with its Creator. A fundamental point of Proverbs and John's Gospel—and of "knowing that the LORD is God"—is that the reality of God may be encountered in the mundane human realities of everyday life, even if there is no overtly religious dimension to those mundane realities.

I conclude by drawing out one particular implication of the preceding account. If wisdom is a quality that is inherently intellectual, ethical, and practical, and if it gives access to truth about God's world, then there is something to be said for the notion that what the Bible calls "wisdom," Christian faith calls "theology." I am not in the first instance thinking of "theology" as practiced in the modern university, where it tends to be understood either as a history of ideas or as second-order critical reflection on first-order faith and life. Rather, I am thinking of the ancient, patristic understanding that is classically expressed by Evagrius: "If you are a theologian, you will pray truly.

And if you pray truly, you are a theologian."[88] The point of the saying is that if one is to speak meaningfully of God, one must know that of which one speaks; one can only acquire knowledge *about* God by engaging *with* God. If words about God are not to be mere words, they must arise out of a lived reality of encounter with God that can give substance and meaning to the words (however limited the words may be). Evagrius expresses in his idiom the same fundamental reality that Proverbs expresses in terms of responding rightly to Wisdom's call and that John expresses in terms of having faith in Jesus the incarnate Word. Insofar as people are open and responsive to the reality of God, they become able to speak and live rightly in relation to God and the world; they can grasp something of the grammar of God. This is true for everyone. Professional scholars, qua scholars, have no intrinsic privilege, despite the real value of their knowledge and expertise. The challenge for (would-be) believing scholars is for their technical expertise to become attuned to this overarching and undergirding reality of the God about whom, and to whom, they seek, in one way or another, to speak.

88. Evagrius, *On Prayer*, 62 (text #61).

2

The Mysterious God

The Voice from the Fire in Exodus 3

On the night of November 23, 1654, there was a storm over Paris. In the course of this storm Blaise Pascal had a life-changing experience. He wrote allusively about it on a small piece of parchment, which he then sewed into the hem of his coat so that it would be with him always. Part of what he wrote (which is known as the *Mémorial*) reads thus:

> From about half past ten at night until a half hour after midnight.
>
> FIRE.
>
> God of Abraham, God of Isaac, God of Jacob, not of the philosophers and of the learned. Certitude, certitude, feeling, joy, peace. God of Jesus Christ. . . . Let me never be separated from Him.[1]

Most famous in this is Pascal's sharp distinction between the "God of Abraham, God of Isaac, God of Jacob" and the God "of the philosophers and of the learned." It would of course be worthwhile to linger on what this

A shorter version of this chapter was delivered at the International Organization for the Study of the Old Testament congress in Aberdeen in August 2019 and is published in Maier, Macaskill, and Schaper, *Congress Volume Aberdeen 2019* (VTSup).

1. The translation is taken from Popkin, *Pascal: Selections*, 69–70. Popkin valuably provides a full text. I am grateful to Jan Assmann (*Invention of Religion*, 121) for reminding me of the significance of Pascal's *Mémorial* for thinking about the interpretation of Exod. 3. In the terms of my typology of approaches to the biblical text, Assmann's work, with which I will interact, is a fine example of reading the Bible as a cultural classic (in his own terms, it is a study "from the viewpoint of the cultural sciences" [56]).

meant for Pascal himself. Which particular philosophers and philosophical accounts did he have in mind (Descartes is one obvious candidate), and what exactly did he see as the alternative to them? Despite his speaking of philosophers disparagingly, he himself was a sharp and searching thinker. Although Pascal, as can be seen from his *Pensées*, had a strong sense of the limits of reason, that did not mean for him that reason should be abandoned but rather that intuitive and existential dimensions involving the whole person were needed if faith in the living God were to become a reality.

For present purposes, however, I want to draw attention to two particular facets of the *Mémorial*. On the one hand, Pascal's wording of "FIRE" and "God of Abraham, God of Isaac, and God of Jacob" appears to envisage specifically the account of the burning bush and God's self-introduction to Moses in Exodus 3. On the other hand, Pascal's sharp distinction between God as Scripture portrays Him and God as conceived by philosophers articulates what becomes a recurrent trope in modern biblical interpretation (whether or not use of this trope is always indebted to Pascal). Pascal thus becomes a point of entry into thinking about what is arguably "one of the densest nodal points in the entire Old Testament and one of the most influential texts in world literature."[2]

All this is by way of setting the scene for a reading of what may be the Bible's most famous passage about God, a passage that can hardly not be discussed in a treatment of "the God of the Old Testament" with a view to understanding better what is entailed in "knowing that the LORD is God."

God's Call of Moses

Possible preliminary remarks about reading the book of Exodus could be endless (as is its secondary literature). So I propose to go directly to a reading of the text and to discuss some of the debated issues about the nature of the text as and when they arise.

The first two chapters of Exodus tell of the people of Israel in Egypt, where they have been enslaved. Moses has fled from Egypt after killing a man. He has settled in the land of Midian, where he has married the daughter of a priest. Israel and Egypt are in his past, not his present. Thereby the scene is set.

> [23]After a long time the king of Egypt died. The Israelites groaned under their slavery, and cried out. Out of the slavery their cry for help rose up to God.

2. The wording is that of Thomas Staubli, as cited in Assmann, *Invention of Religion*, 118.

> [24]God heard their groaning, and God remembered his covenant with Abraham, Isaac, and Jacob. [25]God looked upon the Israelites, and God took notice of them. (Exod. 2:23–25)

The style of the passage is slightly repetitive and pleonastic. But Hebrew prose sometimes adopts a style similar to Hebrew poetry: something is said, and then it is said again with an extension or deepening of the original formulation.[3] Here, what is said about both Israel and God is repeated and augmented. Initially, the text's focus is on the human situation and initiative: the enslaved Israelites crying out (v. 23). But then the focus shifts to God (*ʾĕlōhīm*, the generic term), who is the subject of four consecutive verbs which speak of His active awareness of Israel's need (vv. 24–25). If, emphatically, God is thus aware, it raises a basic question: What difference will this make "on the ground"? What follows provides the answer to this question.

> [1]Moses was keeping the flock of his father-in-law Jethro, the priest of Midian; he led his flock to a western area of [*ʾaḥar*][4] the wilderness, and came to Horeb, the mountain of God. (Exod. 3:1)

Moses in Midian has become a shepherd. Although the figure of the shepherd is an image of great resonance elsewhere in the biblical canon, here the depiction of Moses as one seems to be primarily mundane and informational: keeping the flock is what Moses was doing and what brought him to Horeb. Horeb's location in "a western area of" the wilderness—or, better, that Moses went into "the western part of" the wilderness—makes it sound remote. Nonetheless, remoteness does not imply insignificance. On the contrary, Horeb is "the mountain of God [*ʾĕlōhīm*]," a place where, by implication, God is somehow specially present.[5] Interpreters have sometimes supposed that this language indicates that Horeb was already a place of

3. There is a general discussion of this phenomenon in Kugel, *Idea of Biblical Poetry*, 59–95, esp. 59–63.

4. The NRSV's "beyond" misses the most likely idiomatic sense of *ʾaḥar*. The primary meaning of *ʾaḥar* is "behind," which idiomatically in English can become "beyond." By extension, however, since the primary Hebrew geographical orientation is eastward-facing, *ʾaḥar* can mean "west," implying that Moses is to the west of/in the desert, presumably from the perspective of Midian. Although *ʾaḥar* could mean "west of," in the sense of westward beyond the desert, it more likely refers to a western area within the desert; the wider Exodus context makes clear that Horeb, the mountain of God, is indeed within, rather than beyond, the desert.

5. The question of why this mountain is sometimes termed "Horeb" and sometimes "Sinai" lies beyond our present purview. The term for "bush" in Exod. 3:2, *sĕneh*, is widely recognized to be connected to "Sinai" (*sīnay*), though one might have expected the wordplay to take the form "at *sīnay* there was a *sĕneh*."

religious significance for the Midianites, perhaps the location of a shrine. This is possible. Moses, however, is not portrayed as in any way expecting to meet God, and he appears to be surprised and curious when he sees the strange phenomenon of the bush.[6] So it is probably more likely that "mountain of God" reflects the perspective of the writer in his Israelite context, who has a knowledge of all that will happen there. This is the place which Israel has come to know as the location of a foundational encounter with God, first on the part of Moses alone and subsequently on the part of Israel as a whole. In any case, the reader, even if not yet Moses, now expects something to happen.

> [2]There the angel of the LORD appeared to him as a flame of fire out of a bush; he looked, and what he saw was that the bush was blazing, yet it was not consumed. [3]Then Moses said, "I must turn aside and look at this great sight, and see why the bush is not burned up." [4]When the LORD saw that he had turned aside to see, God called to him out of the bush, "Moses, Moses!" And he said, "Yes, I'm here."[7] [5]Then he said, "Come no closer! Remove the sandals from your feet, for the place on which you are standing is holy ground." [6]He said further, "I am the God of your father, the God of Abraham, the God of Isaac, and the God of Jacob." And Moses hid his face, for he was afraid to look at God. (Exod. 3:2–6)

■ The NRSV rendering of v. 2b ("he looked, and the bush was blazing") is mistaken in a way that merits comment. It omits the Hebrew particle *vĕhinnēh*—traditionally rendered "and behold" or "and lo"—apparently on the assumption that this is no more than a quaint archaism that can be omitted without loss. However, *hinnēh* has a range of idiomatic uses, and one important function, in the form *vĕhinnēh* when following *vayyar'* ("and he looked"), is to transfer the perspective within the story from the narrator to the character so that the readers now see what the person in the story sees.[8] It is like the cinematic shift from seeing a scene with the general perspective of the camera to seeing what is happening as though through the eyes of a participant.[9] Thus, Moses sees the angel of the LORD not in human form, as is common elsewhere, but as fire.[10] My rendering, "he

6. The bush is usually reckoned to be some kind of thornbush, because such bushes are found in desert regions.

7. NRSV: "Here I am."

8. For other uses of this idiom to shift perspective within the world of the story, see, e.g., Gen. 18:2; 2 Sam. 18:24.

9. Robert Alter, who recognizes the idiom, seeks to convey its sense with "and look" (*Art of Bible Translation*, 40–41). In English idiom, however, this may sound more like an invitation to readers to see with their own imaginative eye than a transposition into the character's perspective, even though these can of course merge.

10. Often noted is the possibility that the preposition *bĕ* before "flame of fire" might have the sense of identity, "as" (as in Exod. 6:3, "as El Shaddai," *bĕ'ēl shaddāy*), rather than of location, "in"; the traditional but unilluminating grammatical designation for this usage is *beth essentiae* (see *GKC* #119i; JM #133c). When the force of the idiom of what Moses sees

looked, and what he saw was . . . ," is perhaps a little wordy, but it seeks to capture the full sense of the Hebrew idiom.[11] ■

It is perhaps surprising that the LORD speaks to Moses only when Moses turns aside to look more closely at the bush. If the LORD wanted to speak to Moses, why not take the initiative and call to him directly without more ado? We are not told the reason. One supposition is that Moses' turning aside indicates not just curiosity but also a kind of openness or responsiveness, and that such openness creates an appropriate context for hearing the divine address. It is as and when Moses responds to the first divine initiative, the surprising appearance in nondestroying fire, that he receives the further divine initiative of being personally addressed.

The nondestroying fire that Moses sees in the bush has enormous resonance within the Old Testament: fire is a prime symbol of the presence of the LORD (the other prime symbol being a cloud).[12] When Israel as a whole subsequently comes to this same mountain, the LORD descends and the mountain blazes with fire (Exod. 19:18).[13] Indeed, Deuteronomy portrays Israel's experience at Horeb as directly parallel to that of Moses: "Then the LORD spoke to you out of the fire. You heard the sound of words but saw no form; there was only a voice" (Deut. 4:12). Significantly, in no place when the LORD appears as fire is anything said to be consumed, even though this point is made explicitly only here in Exodus 3. The fire that symbolizes the LORD's presence is intrinsically unlike regular fire.[14]

Why fire? Although the Old Testament does not explain the symbols it uses,[15] it is almost always worthwhile to allow the imagination to linger on biblical symbolism to try to probe something of its significance. One of the

---

is taken into account, "as" surely becomes the most likely rendering, so I have emended the NRSV's "in" accordingly.

11. This same issue recurs in Gen. 33:1. See ch. 4, p. 150.

12. The fire and the cloud are both constitutive of the "pillar" that leads Israel in the wilderness (Exod. 13:21–22). Its variable appearance as a cloud by day and fire by night may be a matter of what enables the pillar to be most visible and thus, presumably, most easily followed—as well as being a symbolic assurance of the LORD's presence.

13. Other significant instances of fire as the LORD's presence are 2 Kings 2:1–18—esp. v. 11, where a chariot and horses of fire separate Elijah from Elisha as Elijah is taken up to heaven in a whirlwind—and 2 Kings 6:8–23, esp. vv. 16–17, when the LORD opens the eyes of Elisha's servant to see horses and chariots of fire, which show that the attacking Arameans are not to be feared because "there are more with us than there are with them."

14. The LORD can, however, send regular fire, as in Num. 11:1–3.

15. It is possible that the seven-branch lampstand, the menorah in the tabernacle (Exod. 25:31–40)—which in the course of history becomes a prime symbol of Judaism—should be seen as a symbolic representation of the burning bush. The basic appearance of each—stem, branches, flames—is not dissimilar.

most famous twentieth-century accounts of the nature of religion was Rudolf Otto's *The Idea of the Holy*. Otto argues for the sui generis nature of religious experience, which he characterizes as "numinous"; and he famously depicts God as *mysterium tremendum et fascinans*, a mystery which engenders both fearful shrinking back and a sense of attraction. Otto focuses on the language and experience of "holiness" and does not discuss the symbolism of fire. Nonetheless, it is notable that fire simultaneously attracts, through its warmth and the eye-catching movement of flame, and repels, through the pain it causes if one gets too close. This quality of both drawing close and driving back is surely part of the intrinsic symbolic significance of fire as indicative of the LORD's presence; the LORD invites and is approachable, yet there are necessary limits on the human approach to the divine. Fire is also symbolically suggestive (again, like a cloud) in that by its nature it cannot be grasped or readily controlled by humans.[16] It is thus an appropriate symbol for a God who is beyond human control or manipulation. At any rate, Moses is both attracted to the divine presence in the fiery bush and then is checked in his approach; and although he has a choice in how to respond, he has no control over the voice that addresses him.

■ Readings of the symbolic significance of the burning bush are many and varied in both Jewish and Christian tradition—be it, for example, the people of Israel burned yet not destroyed by their sufferings and persecutions,[17] or the Virgin Mary carrying a divine child in her womb yet remaining unscathed by it. The symbolism of the burning bush lends itself to many a context in the continuing traditions of faith that look to this passage as Scripture.[18] For present purposes I note just one suggestive recent reading by Katherine Sonderegger which complements my concerns in this chapter:

> The Lord God burns in that bush; His Nature as Fire is disclosed in the wilderness near the holy mountain of God. And the bush is not consumed. This is what Augustine means when in the *Confessions* he says that God is "more intimate to me than I to myself" . . . : only God can be compatible with the creature He has made in such a way that two, wholly and utterly otherwise to each other, can be together as one. This is not *explained* in Holy Scripture, and we are not given a *theory* of God's indwelling His creation. Rather, we are *shown* it. And this is "wonder."[19] ■

16. Today, fire is more subject to human control than it was in antiquity, so this dimension may have more limited contemporary resonance—though the experience of fire raging in buildings or in the countryside always gives pause.

17. For a recent argument that this is indeed the intrinsic biblical significance of the imagery, see Janzen, ". . . and the Bush Was Not Consumed."

18. There is a suggestive collection of interpretations in Levine, *Burning Bush*. See also Langston, *Exodus through the Centuries*, 45–61.

19. Sonderegger, *Systematic Theology*, 1:213.

God calls Moses by name. The address is not general but specific, not abstract but personal. Moses' response, "Yes, I'm here," has to do not with geographical location but rather with existential openness.[20]

■ The consistent biblical depiction of God calling people by name may acquire fresh resonance in the modern world, in which people are sometimes dehumanized by replacing their names with bureaucratic numbers. This happened most notoriously to prisoners in Nazi concentration camps. In *Les Misérables*, Victor Hugo gives a memorable literary anticipation in his account of the imprisonment of Jean Valjean, set in the late eighteenth century: "Everything that had been his life was blotted out, even to his name. He was no longer Jean Valjean, but No. 24601." Valjean himself remembers that his former prison companions had "lived without names, were known only by numbers and to some extent turned into numbers themselves."[21] Perhaps the most memorable and moving example of being called by name in the Bible is when the risen Christ calls out to Mary Magdalene and thereby enables her to recognize him (John 20:16). ■

The first divine words speak of the specialness of the ground, which is holy—implicitly because of the divine presence—with the consequence that ordinary practice is suspended: Moses must remove his shoes. This command may imply that the movement appropriate to this place is not regular walking but standing still and/or bowing down; or it is perhaps a symbolic act of purification, removing what is likely to be dirtiest on Moses' body. Moses' obedience is not specified because it does not need to be; he is in responsive mode. When God speaks, Moses hides his face, which might be done by turning his head or by putting his garment or hands over his face (as in the picture on this book's cover).

God introduces Himself with reference to the ancestors of Israel in Genesis: Abraham, Isaac, and Jacob.[22] That is, this God has had specific dealings with

20. Commenting on Abraham's similar response to God in Gen. 22:1, Jon Levenson says that "Here I am" is "a pallid rendering of the Hebrew *hinnēnî*" and suggests that a better rendering (at least in that context) would be "Ready" (*Death and Resurrection of the Beloved Son*, 126). Comparably, Cornelis Houtman opts for "Yes, I'm listening" (*Exodus*, 18, 345).

21. Hugo, *Les Misérables*, 94, 488.

22. Surprisingly, God says, "I am the God of your *father*" rather than "fathers," despite the plural fathers who are then specified and despite the consistent use of the plural "God of your fathers/ancestors" in the dialogue that follows (Exod. 3:13, 15, 16). Scribes and commentators from antiquity onwards have naturally wondered whether this singular ought really to be a plural (see *BHS* ad loc.). When, for example, this passage is cited in the NT in Stephen's speech, the plural form is used (Acts 7:32). To be sure, the singular form "God of your father" is used in Genesis (Gen. 46:3), and it might be in direct imitation of this Genesis usage that the singular is used here; or it might refer to Moses' actual father, Amram (Exod. 6:20), or even conceivably his father-in-law, Reuel/Jethro (2:18; 3:1).

The issue has been complicated by twentieth-century debates about the possible historical form and nature of the religion of the patriarchs, of which this singular usage might be

Moses' forebears and is known in terms of His relationship with particular people. The Israel that had become part of Moses' past is brought back into his present by the God who is God of that past and present.

God speaks further and conveys to Moses what is in effect both good news and something less straightforward.

> [7]Then the LORD said, "I have observed the misery of my people who are in Egypt; I have heard their cry on account of their taskmasters. Indeed, I know their sufferings, [8]and I have come down to deliver them from the Egyptians, and to bring them up out of that land to a good and broad land, a land flowing with milk and honey, to the country of the Canaanites, the Hittites, the Amorites, the Perizzites, the Hivites, and the Jebusites. [9]The cry of the Israelites has now come to me; I have also seen how the Egyptians oppress them. [10]So come, I will send you to Pharaoh to bring my people, the Israelites, out of Egypt." (Exod. 3:7–10)

As in the introductory paragraph 2:23–25, the style of these verses is somewhat pleonastic—so much so that numerous commentators who focus on compositional matters have opined that verses 9–10 essentially duplicate verses 7–8. Nonetheless, there is an important difference. In verses 7–8 Moses hears good news: the God now speaking to Moses knows of Israel's sufferings (as in 2:23–25) and is taking the initiative to remedy the situation: "I have come down to deliver them." But God's awareness of Israel's plight has consequences for Moses too: "I will send you to Pharaoh." In this seemingly simple juxtaposition of the divine "I have come" with "I will send you," we have the heart of the biblical conception of prophecy.[23]

■ To be "sent" by God (Heb. *shālaḥ*; Gk. *apostellō*, with the noun *apostolos*)—to act in response to an initiative from God and not on one's own initiative—is a core conception of Hebrew prophecy. For example, it is specified in the call of both Isaiah and Jeremiah (Isa. 6:8; Jer. 1:7), and those who claim to speak for God without being sent by Him are not prophets at all (Jer. 23:21–22). In the NT, being sent by God is a core conceptuality of Jesus' presence and purpose in John's Gospel (e.g., John 3:17; 6:29; 17:3), one that is extended also to his disciples: "As the Father has sent me, so I send you" (20:21). Thus, the biblical conceptuality of both prophets and apostles is that they are humans whose

---

an indicator. A foundational essay by Albrecht Alt gave rise to extensive traditio-historical discussion of the forms of religion that might underlie the present text of Genesis ("The God of the Fathers"). This debate, however, has now largely faded away. Alt's confidence about the possibilities of traditio-historical investigation of what lies behind the written traditions is no longer widely shared. The fashionable tendency is to lower the date of non-P pentateuchal texts to roughly half a millennium later than Alt assumed and, concurrently, to be doubtful about how much history "behind the text" is recoverable.

23. The pattern of prophecy is notably absent in Genesis, and Exod. 3 is its first appearance in the canonical sequence.

words and deeds in some way mediate God's prior initiative—which is reflected not only in the biblical documents associated with them (which are normative for faith) but also in people who continue to respond faithfully to the divine call. ■

This juxtaposition is also characteristic of the biblical understanding of the divine and the human more generally. God acts, and this action is realized in and through the actions and words of those humans whom He calls to His service. Humans are given the dignity and privilege of implementing the purposes of God on earth, which are best realized insofar as people become consciously open and responsive to God.

■ The biblical conception of the relationship between the divine and the human, not least as focused in OT prophecy, is easily misread in the contemporary world, which is generally not at home in biblical and Christian idiom and thought. There is a recurrent tendency to assume that the divine and the human are somehow in competition with each other and that the presence of the divine in relation to the human constitutes a zero-sum game. That is, the more God is present in a human life, the less space there is for that person to be him/herself. "More" of God means "less" of the person; their humanity is diminished or inhibited because it is in some way "squeezed out" by the divine presence and vocation.[24] But the opposite is in fact the case. God's relationship to His creation is noncompetitive and creative: the more humans are open and receptive to God, the more fully they become their true selves. Christian theology has regularly articulated this understanding, which is consistently presupposed but never as such spelled out in the biblical documents. This is a good example of how classic theology has helpfully drawn out and clarified what stands in the biblical text, and how it is still needed to prevent misreading. The application of classic theology to the OT needs, however, to be done judiciously, as the OT's own categories often do not neatly align with those of classic theology. ■

In one sense, the invitation to implement God's purposes is a privilege and responsibility; it can give meaning and direction to human life. But in another sense, at least in terms of initial reception and realization, it may be less than good news. For it brings with it a demand that Moses should go and do something that will change his life completely. He must not only return to Egypt, from which he fled for his life, but he must also confront its ruler, the pharaoh, who may not think that setting free the people of Israel sounds like a good idea. God's commission might sound to Moses uncomfortably like a death warrant. One can readily imagine Moses thinking that a quiet life of shepherding sheep in Midian, with his wife and children not too far away at home, suddenly seems much more attractive than perhaps it had been recently! At any rate, Moses' immediate response to God's words is not wonder and joy

24. I have discussed this more fully in *Prophecy and Discernment*, ch. 1, esp. 25–38, and ch. 6, esp. 227–29.

but rather apprehension and reluctance. He feels overwhelmed and inadequate for the task that God is giving him. And he says so.

> [11]But Moses said to God, "Who am I that I should go to Pharaoh, and bring the Israelites out of Egypt?" [12]He said, "I will be [*'ehyeh*] with you; and this shall be the sign for you that it is I who sent you: when you have brought the people out of Egypt, you shall worship God on this mountain." (Exod. 3:11–12)

Moses articulates a kind of "How on earth could I do this?" objection to God's commission. God characteristically does not answer the question on its own terms, but rather recasts the issue: "I will be with you." That is, if God is there to enable Moses, then Moses, whatever his sense of inadequacy or unsuitability, will indeed be able to do what God requires of him.

This promise is accompanied by a sign which is puzzling, as it offers reassurance not in the present, when Moses wants it, but in the future. Its tenor is perhaps along the lines of: "When eventually you return to this place, bringing the people of Israel with you, you will understand and know then how I was with you all the way." If Moses acts faithfully in the midst of uncertainties, confirmation of God's presence will come in due course. However, the puzzle of the sign is a detail that we need not linger on.

More important is the fact that this hesitancy, this objection, from Moses initiates a series of further objections, each of which God takes seriously and responds to in ways that address Moses' concern. There is no sense of God's swatting aside Moses' objections ("Don't argue. Just get on with it"); rather, the narrative conveys a sense of space in which genuine interacting with God, a real to-and-fro, is possible. The clear implication is that God does not want to coerce Moses, instead meeting his anxieties with appropriate reassurance. The space and freedom to raise questions are not unlimited—as Moses goes on, what he says begins to sound less like feeling overwhelmed and more like making excuses, and eventually the LORD becomes angry (4:14)—but the space and freedom are real nonetheless.

Thus, after the second question, which is about God's name (3:13–22), Moses' third question envisages the difficulty of people not taking him seriously (despite God's initial assurance otherwise in 3:18a): "But suppose they do not believe me or listen to me, but say, 'The LORD did not appear to you'" (4:1). The LORD responds by enabling Moses to perform signs that should lead the people to believe him (4:2–9). Moses' fourth objection expresses a sense of his own incapacity in relation to the public speaking that his commission will involve: "O my Lord, I have never been eloquent, neither in the past nor even now that you have spoken to your servant; but

I am slow of speech and slow of tongue" (4:10). Again, the LORD gives appropriate reassurance: He will enable Moses to say what he needs to say (4:11–12). Yet after all these reassurances, Moses then tries to get out of the commission altogether: "O my Lord, please send someone else" (4:13). At this point, the LORD becomes angry, which implies that although difficulties with responding to God's call are taken seriously, the attempt to evade and decline God's call altogether is unacceptable. The LORD reminds Moses of his brother, Aaron, who can go with him—but not *instead* of him—and can assist with the speaking; and with that, the dialogue between God and Moses comes to an end (4:17).

The recurrent concern in this lengthy exchange is both Moses' existential sense of not being suitable for the commission he is receiving and God's repeated reassurance. In this way the narrative readily reads as an archetypal account of the difficulties that humans may have with responding to God's call,[25] even if most calls from God involve less than Moses is required to do.[26] Whatever the in-principle dignity for a human to fulfill God's will on earth, the in-practice challenge and cost may be great.

The Giving of the Divine Name

It is to Moses' second objection that we must now turn. Here Moses raises the all-important issue of God's name.

One preliminary point to register is that our passage continues to be dialogue. Whereas much classic Christian theologizing has preferred, and prefers, abstract forms, it is characteristic of the biblical portrayal to prefer dialogue. Dialogue not only has a concreteness and accessibility that abstraction often lacks, but it also roots theological understanding in the relational dynamics of an "I-thou" encounter (which is also in line with the existential openness for responding to Wisdom's call that is envisaged in Prov. 8).

Another preliminary point is that in the Old Testament, names can not only have meaning but also say something about the bearer of the name (though

25. In prophetic call narratives elsewhere in the OT, the prophet characteristically expresses a sense of inadequacy (e.g., Jer. 1:4–10).

26. This is not always the case. Joan of Arc's call to go to the court of the beleaguered Charles VII, resulting in her leading the French against the English to relieve the siege of Orléans—so that, for the only time in history, a teenage woman became the leader of a country's armed forces—arguably is comparable to Moses' confronting the pharaoh. For Joan, the call led also to a cruel death in just over two years, after she was, in effect, abandoned by Charles VII and corruptly tried and burned by the English in Rouen. However, Joan's faithfulness to her call and her integrity in adversity remain a beacon of light in an otherwise bleak period of history.

they do not always do so).[27] When Naomi returns from Moab a disappointed and broken woman, she says to the women of Bethlehem, "Call me no longer Naomi ["Pleasant"], / call me Mara ["Bitter"], / for the Almighty has dealt bitterly with me" (Ruth 1:20). When Abigail is persuading David not to be violent towards her husband Nabal and his men, she says, "My lord, do not take seriously this ill-natured fellow, Nabal; for as his name is, so is he; Nabal ["Foolish"] is his name, and folly is with him" (1 Sam. 25:25).[28] This convention indicates that the name of God may be expected to say something about the nature of God. Our text reads:

> [13]But Moses said to God, "If I come to the Israelites and say to them, 'The God of your ancestors has sent me to you,' and they ask me, 'What is his name?' what shall I say to them?"
>
> [14]God said to Moses, "*'ehyeh 'ăsher 'ehyeh* [I AM WHO I AM]."[29]
>
> He said further, "Thus you shall say to the Israelites, '*'ehyeh* [I AM] has sent me to you.'"
>
> [15]God also said to Moses, "Thus you shall say to the Israelites, '*yhwh* [YHWH / the LORD], the God of your ancestors, the God of Abraham, the God of Isaac, and the God of Jacob, has sent me to you':
>
> This is my name forever,
> and this my title for all generations."
> (Exod. 3:13–15 [NRSV modified])

In terms of appreciating the flow of the text, it is significant to note the repeated speech introductions in 3:14–15 (i.e., 3:14b; 3:15a), even though God is already speaking (3:14a). Modern commentators have often seen this as "clumsy" wording[30] and thus evidence of underlying sources and/or redaction—which is of course possible—but a more literary perspective offers

27. In a modern context, names generally do not have this significance. They are usually chosen because of their resonance with someone who is family or a friend, or who is admired, or simply because a parent likes the name and wants to give it to their child. Nicknames, however, often still say something about the character of the bearer. Moreover, Christians can take a new name at significant moments—such as at confirmation or at the taking of monastic vows—in which the name, almost always that of a saint, is chosen because of the character/story of the saint. So there are still some connections with the convention in the Bible.

28. It is hard to imagine proud parents naming their child "Fool"! Perhaps the name "Nabal" originally had a different meaning, or it may be that the tradition has given this name to Abigail's first husband on account of his behavior. Comparably, Abel (Heb. *hevel*, "vapor," "breath," something that disappears quickly) may have been given this name by tradition in light of the brevity of his presence in the story before he is killed (Gen. 4:1–8).

29. The translation of the divine name will be discussed below. For the present, I want to keep the Hebrew with its wordplay to the fore, while still indicating my preferred translation.

30. "Clumsy" is the term of Magne Saebø ("God's Name in Exodus 3.13–15," 82).

a different angle of vision. In Hebrew literary convention, speech introductions in the course of a speech can serve a function akin to paragraph divisions in modern writing, whereby one point is distinguished from another.[31] The idiom might also invite a pause for reflection or imply a silence on the part of the one addressed.[32] I have thus laid out the text accordingly (departing from the NRSV's format).

What is the sense of the question and the answer in 3:13–15? In verse 13 Moses imagines himself saying to the Israelites, "The God of your ancestors has sent me to you." In terms of the flow of the story, Moses seems to take up the title with which God initially spoke to him (3:6)[33] as his own way of speaking of the God who has sent him. But this could invite a question from the Israelites about the actual name of this God of the ancestors: "What is his name?" In verse 15a, God's response combines the initial title "God of your ancestors" with the Tetragrammaton, *yhwh*—the specific name "YHWH" / "the LORD"—to name the one who has sent Moses. This addition of name to title answers the imagined question about the name of the "God of your ancestors" who has sent Moses. There is then a note in verse 15b, apparently in poetry (which is often used in speech of heightened significance),[34] about the definitive and enduring nature of this name as God's name.

If verse 15 gives the answer to the question of verse 13, what is the role of verse 14? It appears to be saying something about the meaning and significance of God's name, and doing so through an association of the divine name, *yhwh*, with the Hebrew verb "to be," *hāyāh*—a weighty play on words. Although one might expect the name to be given first and then have its meaning brought out, it still makes good sense for the meaning to be given before the name, so that the name is inseparable from its meaning.

31. A good example is God's address to Noah after the flood (Gen. 9:8–17). Initially, God promises a covenant which entails that there will not be another flood ("God said to Noah and to his sons," 9:8–11); then He specifies the rainbow as a sign of the covenant ("God said," 9:12–16); then He summarizes and concludes ("God said to Noah," 9:17). As another example, when David is persuading Saul to let him fight Goliath (1 Sam. 17:34–37), David initially makes his case in terms of the usually deadly wild animals he has already overcome ("David said to Saul," 17:34–36); he then concludes on a different note by ascribing his victories, both achieved and anticipated, to the LORD ("David said," 17:37).

32. Jean-Pierre Sonnet imagines Moses as being temporarily at a loss about how to respond to God ("*Ehyeh asher Ehyeh*," esp. 341).

33. The problem here is that Moses uses the plural "fathers/ancestors," whereas God's initial address used the singular "father." As already noted, this is presumably a factor in a plural form finding its way into some ancient versions of Exod. 3:6. Nonetheless, Moses' intention to speak of God in terms of His being the ancestral deity of Israel is clear on any reckoning.

34. For example, one might compare the poetic form of the man's delighted exclamation about the woman (Gen. 2:23) or of Lamech's boastful claim to his unfortunate wives (Gen. 4:23–24).

Initially (v. 14a), God says something about Himself, *ʾehyeh ʾăsher ʾehyeh* ("I AM WHO I AM" or "I WILL BE WHO/WHAT/AS I WILL BE"). Immediately, however, two developments of this are given (v. 14b). On the one hand, *ʾehyeh ʾăsher ʾehyeh* ("I AM WHO I AM") is reduced to a single *ʾehyeh* ("I AM"), with the implication that the shorter form represents the fuller form. On the other hand, this shorter form is treated as if it is the name of God which can answer the question of the identity of the one who has sent Moses, so that he can say, "*ʾehyeh* ["I AM"] has sent me to you." However, in what immediately follows (v. 15a), *ʾehyeh* is replaced by *yhwh*, the Tetragrammaton, the familiar Old Testament form of the name of God. So *ʾehyeh ʾăsher ʾehyeh* (v. 14a) gives the meaning of the name of Israel's God, who is YHWH / the LORD (v. 15), with the single *ʾehyeh* (v. 14b) serving to enable the transition.

In the central wordplay between *ʾehyeh* and *yhwh*, an important distinction is that, as God Himself is speaking, He uses the first-person "I" (an initial *aleph*), whereas the form of the familiar name is the third-person "he" (an initial *yod*), as would be appropriate for people speaking about God. This suggests that the name "YHWH / the LORD" is to be understood as having the sense both of "I AM," on His lips, and of "HE IS," on the lips of everyone else.

■ Another difference in form between *ʾehyeh* and *yhwh* is that the linkage utilizes a rare form of the verb "to be," which is usually *hāyāh* but is here *hāwāh* (as in Gen. 27:29a and Isa. 16:4a in imperative form, and Neh. 6:6b and Eccl. 2:22a in participial form). Although modern scholars have often conjectured that, in etymological terms, the root of *yhwh* might have been the verb *hāwāh* with a meaning other than "to be," such a conjecture does little to illuminate Exod. 3:14, where, as is customary with wordplay in the OT, the association between *ʾehyeh* and *yhwh* is not etymological but rather one of sound and meaning.

There is a further question about the vocalization and pronunciation of *yhwh*, which is unknown because of the ancient and continuing Jewish reverential practice of not pronouncing or spelling out the divine name (a practice still followed in most modern English translations, though not in most modern scholarly discourse). In terms of *hāwāh*, the grammatical form of *yhwh* is imperfect/*yiqtol*, third masculine singular—but of which conjugation/*binyan*? As *ʾehyeh* is first-person imperfect *qal*, the counterpart third-person imperfect *qal* would be *yihweh* ("he will be / is"). The problem is that when names are compounded with what appears to be a form of the divine name, they consistently have the vowel "a"—*yah*—hence (to simplify) the scholarly consensus that the intrinsic pronunciation of the divine name is "yahweh." In grammatical terms, an initial "ya-" is indicative of the *hiphil*, the (commonly but not always) causative form of the verb. Thus, the third masculine singular *hiphil* of *hāwāh* ("to be")—i.e., *yahweh*—would mean "he causes to be." This has led to much discussion about the divine name as perhaps indicating a creator deity, "he who causes things to be." Again, however, this is not greatly illuminating for Exod. 3:14, which makes the association with the intransitive "I am," and by implication "he is," rather than the transitive "he causes to be." The issues here are perhaps indicative of the difference between (a) a modern reconstruction of possible original forms of terms and/or practices in Israelite religion and (b) a focus on the meanings that the tradents of Israel's religious traditions in their mature understanding sought to convey to future generations. ■

Beyond this outline of the flow of the interaction between God and Moses, one further particularity of the text should be noted. The content of 3:14a is not presented as something that Moses is to convey to the people of Israel. The understanding of the divine name in the story is given to Moses alone; but it is also given to the reader who is privileged by the omniscient narrator to hear what Moses hears from the lips of God and to know what Moses knows. Moreover, in the narrative that follows, although reference is often made to both Israel and Egypt coming to "know that I am YHWH" (e.g., 7:17; 10:2), the particular content expressed by 3:14a is never repeated or alluded to. This is not to say that knowledge of the meaning of the name is in any way "occult" or restricted, something to be kept from Israel. But the lack of an explicit command to convey this content to Israel may mean that the reader of the text is meant to know and ponder something about the name of God that is not necessarily envisaged on the part of the characters in the narrative also.

Excursus: Four Technical Issues concerning Israel's Question and the Divine Name

My primary purpose in this chapter is to probe the theological question of the meaning of the divine name—what it means that God is YHWH / the LORD. There are, however, numerous other issues that attend the interpretation of Exodus 3 and that feature prominently in the literature of commentary (few other passages in the Old Testament have greater complexities surrounding them). In this excursus I look briefly at four issues which I find interesting and instructive in terms of how historical-critical questioning can open suggestive avenues of thought about the biblical text. However, their bearing on the meaning of the divine name as such is oblique. Some readers may prefer to regard this excursus as optional, according to their interests. Discussion of the meaning of the divine name resumes on the second half of page 69.

The Distinctiveness of Exodus 3:13–15 in Context

One peculiarity of both the question that Moses envisages the Israelites raising, and his question about that question, is that they are different in kind from those that Moses otherwise raises. Moses' question about the imagined question reflects no sense of his existential difficulty or inadequacy—only his apparent ignorance of God's name in the event of the Israelites asking about it. Strikingly, the immediately following narrative in 3:16–22 does not develop the issue of God's name (though it uses the name), instead dealing with the practical question of what Moses is to say to the people of Israel and the king of Egypt (3:16–18). There is also reassurance that the LORD is well aware that the king will not want to let Israel go. However, He will override this refusal, such that not only will Israel be able to leave Egypt but also they will not leave empty-handed (3:19–22). This sequence in 3:16–22 could well be read as an answer to a question from Moses to the LORD along the lines of "But how am I to do such a great task?" (perhaps *ʾēkāh ʾaʿăseh ʾet haddāvār haggādōl hazzeh*)—a question with an existential edge—rather than the question about the name of God that actually stands in the text.

Moreover, the imagined question of 3:13 has no resonance with the surrounding narrative. The narrative that precedes does not prepare the ground for such a question (other than by God's self-introduction as "God of your father" in 3:6), nor does the narrative that follows depict the Israelites actually asking it, or anything like it, when Moses encounters them.

I will be arguing that, contextually, the burning bush provides a fully appropriate symbolic resonance for the divine name "I AM WHO I AM." Thus, although Exodus 3:13–15 does not resemble Moses' other questions/objections, it does fit well with the opening narrative of 3:1–10.

We may note also the common observation that the dialogue in 4:18–20—where Moses asks Jethro to let him return to Egypt to see whether his family is still alive, and the LORD tells him to return, "for all those who were seeking your life are dead"—would work well as a sequel to the narrative in 2:11–23a, resulting in a narrative about Moses fleeing Egypt, settling in Midian, and then returning to Egypt, without reference to the burning bush and his commission. There is some reason to think, therefore, that the present text of Exodus 3–4 may perhaps have been formed from once-distinct accounts of Moses that have in some way been combined and reworked. A concern to read the received text with full imaginative seriousness does not preclude the recognition of unevennesses in the text which may be indicative of aspects of its compositional history.

Does Exodus 3 Depict Israel's First Knowledge of God as YHWH?

There is an implicit difficulty with the imagined question of 3:13: *Why* would Moses envisage the Israelites as asking about the name of God? As was just noted, nothing in the preceding narrative prepares the reader for the question, and in what follows the question is never asked. So interpreters must offer intelligent conjecture. There appear to be two main alternatives.

On the one hand, it could be that, as yet, neither Israel nor Moses knows the personal name of the "God of [their] ancestors"; although the Exodus narrator has used "the LORD" in telling the story so far, the name has not been used in divine words to Moses. The Israelites might wonder whether He has a personal name at all. If their God is doing something major through Moses, then it would help to have further knowledge about this God as expressed by a name—hence their request for such knowledge. In such a case, Exodus 3 depicts the momentous occasion of the first giving to Israel, via Moses, of the name of God, YHWH / the LORD. Israel's knowledge of God as YHWH is something both given by God Himself and inseparable from the foundational role of Moses in Israel's faith. In support of this is the related passage in Exodus 6:2–3, where God says to Moses, "I am the LORD. I appeared to Abraham, Isaac, and Jacob as God Almighty [Heb. *El Shaddai*], but by my name 'The LORD' I did not make myself known to them." The prima facie sense of this is that the name of God given to Moses in 3:14–15 is a name only now given to Israel. This name was unknown to Israel's ancestors, who instead knew their God as El Shaddai.

On the other hand, it could be that Israel is supposed to know the name but that Moses as yet does not. In that case the question would be some kind of test of Moses, perhaps to establish whether he truly shares Israel's special knowledge of God and/or to establish his credentials as a prophet. The divine answer would then presumably be telling Moses for the first time what Israel already knows. This reading of the question is predominant among interpreters down the ages.[35] In support of it is the extensive use of the name YHWH already in the book of Genesis, not only on the part of the narrator but also on the part of various characters, including occasionally God Himself.

I still hold to the basic thesis of my *The Old Testament of the Old Testament*, in which I argue that the divine name is indeed to be understood as newly given to Moses and that all the uses in Genesis are readily explicable as a straightforward storytelling phenomenon: they are retrojections of Israel's familiar name for God into the world of the ancestors—technically

35. Thus Maimonides in the twelfth century: "Everyone who lays claim to prophecy should be spoken to in this way until he brings proof" (*Guide of the Perplexed*, 153); or Martin Noth in the twentieth century: "Moses . . . requires some proof to give to the Israelites" (*Exodus*, 42); or Jeffrey Tigay in the twenty-first century: "Not having been raised among his own people, Moses . . . is ignorant of their God's name and fears he will therefore lack credibility with them" ("Exodus," 103).

anachronistic, but a natural storytelling device. The biblical writers could have shared a common understanding that the name YHWH was first given to Israel in the context of the story of Moses, yet they nonetheless felt free to use it when telling of the ancestors (mainly Abraham), on the understanding that the God of the ancestors is none other than YHWH, the God of Israel. In the light of the transformation of pentateuchal criticism in recent years, this thesis needs restating with revision and qualification, which I believe can be done; but this is not the place for that task.

Does Israel's Imagined Question Envisage a Polytheistic Background?

There is also an interesting methodological question about which context one considers the most appropriate for interpreting Israel's imagined question: How far should one appeal to the possible cultural background of the ancient Near East?[36] For example, if one thinks in terms of a wider "polytheistic" culture, one can imagine a possible problem for Moses or the Israelites in knowing that the deity who spoke really was their deity rather than some other deity.[37] There is no evidence within the Old Testament itself, however, that this would ever have been conceived of as a difficulty for Moses or Israel; no biblical writer entertains the possibility that a deity other than YHWH might speak to or within Israel.

Alternatively, it appears that, in Egypt, not only did divine names convey power, but also knowledge of the name of a deity gave its possessor some kind of power over that deity, perhaps via magical incantations.[38] The issue at stake in Exodus 3:13 can then be viewed in this light. Thus, Gerhard von Rad sees the question about the name as expressing the people's desire "to get God permanently into their own power," such that the question "is the expression at the same time of the human need for God and of human impudence in relation to God." This means that, in God's answer in 3:14a, YHWH reserves His freedom to Himself and "censures" Moses' question insofar as God "does not allow anyone to lay claim to him, as humans would so gladly do."[39] But although this is a conceivable scenario, it introduces the notion of the question as a problematic desire for power into a passage that in itself gives no hint that such is at stake.

36. Such questions are best handled on a case-by-case basis. A memorable account of some of the in-principle issues is Sandmel, "Parallelomania."

37. Thus, e.g., Fischer, *Jahwe unser Gott*, 146.

38. See, e.g., the Egyptian text presented under the heading "The God and His Unknown Name of Power," in *ANET*, 12–14.

39. Von Rad, *Moses*, 17–18; von Rad, *Old Testament Theology*, 1:182.

The Kenite Hypothesis

Finally, I should briefly take note of older, twentieth-century accounts of "what really happened" in terms of how Moses came to know the name YHWH. Best known and most prevalent has been the Kenite Hypothesis. Put simply, this is the hypothesis that (a) possible earliest uses of the divine name are associated with regions that might be designated "Midianite" or "Kenite," and that (b) Moses acquired knowledge of the Midianite/Kenite deity *yhwh* after marrying into the family of a Midianite priest. This theory has largely faded away amid the increasing scholarly agnosticism about Israel's early history, though it still has some advocates.[40] It is also not uncommon in recent literature to find nonspecific claims, such as: "For sure, neither Exodus 3 or Exodus 6 are historical texts. But they may preserve a 'longue durée,' a long-term memory of the 'adoption' of the deity Yhwh in relation to Egyptian or southern traditions. . . . The biblical texts of the divine revelation of Yhwh's name . . . retain 'traces of memories' . . . of a non-autochthonous origin of Yhwh."[41]

Such proposals make sense on their own terms. Nonetheless, they do not address the specifically theological issue that has made Exodus 3 most interesting and significant to interpreters down the ages: that knowledge of God as YHWH (understood as "I AM WHO I AM") is in some way given by God Himself (whoever/whatever the human channel) and truly depicts the One God.

On Translating *ʾehyeh ʾăsher ʾehyeh*

Thus far I have sidestepped the question of how best to translate God's initial statement about Himself in 3:14a, *ʾehyeh ʾăsher ʾehyeh*. The problem of translation, which is simultaneously an issue of interpretation, requires engagement with Hebrew. The section that follows is the one discussion of Hebrew that is not in a smaller font because of its intrinsic importance to the overall discussion. Still, I hope it will be understandable by the non-Hebraist; and the final paragraph provides a summary of what is necessary for subsequent interpretive discussion.[42]

The problem of translation revolves around two issues. One is a matter of syntax; the other is a problem of tense. The matter of syntax is straightforward, as the particular Hebrew idiom is well represented in the Old Testament.

40. A classic exposition is Rowley, *From Joseph to Joshua*, 148ff. For a recent account, see Blenkinsopp, "Midianite-Kenite Hypothesis Revisited."

41. Römer, "Revelation of the Divine Name to Moses," 312, 314.

42. See the final paragraph on p. 71 below.

In terms of syntax, the repetition of a verb with an intervening particle of relation, *ʾăsher*, is a well-attested Hebrew formulation, known in scholarly parlance as *idem per idem*. The particle of relation has no particular sense of its own but serves to connect that which precedes with that which follows. In translational terms, one should translate *ʾăsher* with a word that meaningfully holds the two instances of *ʾehyeh* together: "who," "as," "where," "that," and "how" are all legitimate renderings of *ʾăsher*. The idiomatic sense of the *idem per idem* formulation is well captured by a much-cited definition by S. R. Driver: "a Semitic idiom . . . employed where either the means, or the desire, to be more explicit does not exist."[43]

The problem of tense, however, is genuinely difficult, a result of biblical Hebrew not having tenses, as we usually understand that term. Rather, Hebrew has two aspects for verbs, one for complete action (perfect/*qatal* form, which tends to be used for present or past tense) and one for incomplete action (imperfect/*yiqtol* form, which tends to be used for present or future tense and is regularly used for habitual action). The form of *ʾehyeh* is *yiqtol* and thus present and/or future tense. Precise temporal sense, insofar as precision is possible, is usually indicated by context or perhaps sentence structure. But in the case of *ʾehyeh ʾăsher ʾehyeh*, neither of these really help.

One weighty consideration is that the verb *hāyāh* ("to be"), of which *ʾehyeh* is an imperfect form, is not, as a matter of regular Hebrew idiom, used in the present tense in the way that the verb "to be" is used in English. If Hebrew expresses "I am," as in "I am the LORD," such a subject-predicate clause does not use the verb "to be" at all, but simply juxtaposes subject and predicate in a verbless clause (e.g., *ʾănī*/*ʾānōkhī yhwh*, Gen. 15:7; Exod. 20:2). Or when the psalmist says, "The LORD is with/for me" (*yhwh lī*, Ps. 118:6 AT), again no verb is used. In such subject-predicate clauses the subject is always specified with either a noun or a pronoun; and there is neither a noun nor a pronoun in *ʾehyeh ʾăsher ʾehyeh*. So the three words cannot be a subject-predicate "I am X" clause.[44] If the meaning is not subject-predicate but verbal-first-person-as-

43. Driver, *Notes on the Hebrew Text and the Topography of the Books of Samuel*, 185–86.

44. There are, however, two possible exceptions in which *ʾehyeh* may be used in the present tense in a context of subject and/or predicate. First is Hosea 1:9, where "You are not my people" (*ʾattem lōʾ ʿammī*) is paired with "and I am not yours" (*vĕʾānōkhī lōʾ ʾehyeh lākem*); both clauses appear to be present tense, and so *ʾehyeh* has the sense "I am." However, this example is not straightforward. This is partly because Hosea 1:9 may be a citation of Exod. 3:14b (i.e., "I am not *ʾehyeh* for you")—in which case the verb *ʾehyeh* would be functioning like a nominal predicate—and partly because it can be not implausibly suggested that *ʾehyeh lākem* could be a textual corruption of *ʾĕlōhēkem* (so *BHS* ad loc., though no ancient versions are cited in support). Second is Ps. 50:21, where God is speaking to the wicked: "These things you have done and I have been silent; / you thought that I was one just like yourself [*hĕyōt-ʾehyeh kāmōkā*]." Here,

verbal-first-person, it is unclear what tense or sense in English best expresses such an idiom.

The nonuse of the verb "to be" in present-tense statements of identity, together with the straightforward use of *ʾehyeh* as "I will be" in Exodus 3:12, leads many to conclude that the sense of the repeated *ʾehyeh* in 3:14a should be in the future tense. However, partly for the very reason that Hebrew does not have tenses as English does, it is a mistake to infer that a present-tense sense of *ʾehyeh* is in any way precluded. Periodic claims that it is impossible or mistaken to understand 3:14a as other than the future-tense "I will be" are rhetorically overstated.[45] In particular, it would be inappropriate to render *ʾehyeh* with a future "I will be" if that were taken in any way to imply something other than what is already the case in the present (i.e., to imply "though I am not now/yet").[46] This would neglect the regular use of the imperfect for habitual action in a continuous present (e.g., Gen. 2:24, *yaʿăzov ʾīsh*, "a man leaves"; Prov. 8:1, *ḥokmāh tiqrāʾ*, "wisdom cries out"; Ps. 145:2, *bĕkol yōm ʾăvārăkekā*, "every day I bless you").

Exodus 33:19b is the most important intertext for Exodus 3:14a; the repeated verbal form displays the same idiom as in 3:14, and it is again a passage in which the LORD is speaking about His name. A conventional translation of God's words uses the future tense: "I will be gracious to whom I will be gracious, and will show mercy on whom I will show mercy." God is speaking of what He is about to do for Moses in response to the request to see His glory. It is clear, however, that God is saying not that He will be different in the future from how He is at the moment of speaking, but rather that how He is at present is how He will act and show Himself to be. It would therefore not be wrong to translate Exodus 33:19b as "I am gracious to whom I am gracious, and I show mercy on whom I show mercy."[47]

In summary, translating *ʾehyeh ʾăsher ʾehyeh* either with the future-tense "I WILL BE WHO/WHAT/AS I WILL BE" or with the present-tense "I AM WHO/WHAT/AS I AM" seems possible, as the philology is open-ended. I am inclined to give particular weight to the continuous present of verbs as significant

whatever the best modal form for rendering *ʾehyeh* in English—"was," "would be," "am"—this clearly seems to be a perception on the part of the wicked about God's character at the time of their thinking—i.e., as a present reality.

45. Thus Bartelmus, *HYH*, 228; Sacks, *Future Tense*, 232.

46. Robert Carroll once proposed restricting the sense of *ʾehyeh* to the future, in an ever-receding sense: "It is in the future that YHWH will be. And like *mañana* that future never comes because it is always future to now. It is a self-fulfilling prophecy that can never be falsified" ("Strange Fire," 55).

47. Compare NJPS: "I will proclaim before you the name LORD, and the grace that I grant and the compassion that I show."

for *ʾehyeh ʾăsher ʾehyeh*. Because I also want to keep the history of interpretation in play without diminishing it as a category mistake based on a philological error, I will opt for the time-honored "I AM WHO/AS I AM" as my preferred translation, which is to be understood in the light of the qualifications just noted.

The Interpretation of the Divine Name

Towards Framing Assumptions for Interpretation

If "I AM WHO I AM" gives the meaning of the divine name, YHWH, what is that meaning?

The form and content of the divine words in 3:14a is striking and unusual, since "I AM WHO I AM" is a tautology. Although the tautological character of 3:14a is usually discussed in terms of the specific Semitic *idem per idem* idiom (as in S. R. Driver's construal),[48] it may be fruitful to reflect more generally on the nature and use of tautology—and to do so in the context of the relation between form and content, an issue that is more important in the Bible than in much contemporary writing. As translation specialist Sarah Ruden puts it,

> These [ancient biblical] languages were not like modern globalized ones, serving mainly to convey information in explicit and interchangeable forms—but with a dimension called "style" for artistic uses on the side. Instead, the original Bible was, like all of ancient rhetoric and poetry, primarily a set of live performances, and *what* they meant was tightly bound up in *the way* they meant it.[49]

Comparably, Robert Alter says,

> The literary style of the Bible in both the prose narratives and the poetry is not some sort of aesthetic embellishment of the "message" of Scripture but the vital medium through which the biblical vision of God, human nature, history, politics, society, and moral value is conveyed.[50]

How might the verbal form of tautology best be understood in this context? John Wevers once commented on the future-tense rendering "I will be who I will be" (as found in the Greek of Theodotion) that "a Greek reader would

48. Above, p. 70.
49. Ruden, *Face of Water*, xxi.
50. Alter, *Art of Bible Translation*, xiii.

find this an absurd tautology."[51] But what makes a tautology absurd? For an ancient reader, as for a modern, a decision as to whether a tautology is absurd would surely depend upon judgments about the register and inflection of such wording in its overall literary context.

Tautology entails logical redundance, but rhetorically and contextually it may be significant in more than one way. A tautology can commonly convey a sense of trying to close down discussion: "That's that" or "What I have written I have written."[52] But that is not its only force. "You've gotta do what you've gotta do" and "It ain't over till it's over" express the determination to persevere in a difficult situation. The popular idiom "It is what it is" can convey a wide range of nuances, from reticence to admiration to exasperation. The precise force of the tautology in Exodus 3:14a is not self-evident, and such wording on the lips of God gives one pause.

The question of how best to gauge the tone of the text and be attuned to it can be approached via an occasional modern reaction to its long history of weighty theological and philosophical interpretations. Some commentators have suggested that such interpretations may, in reality, be missing the point. Samuel Sandmel, for example, in the course of arguing for a high level of haggada (creative retelling of stories, as distinct from the combining of sources) within the biblical text, says,

> The passage Exod 3 13–15 can be ascribed to some ancient document only by ignoring the high good humor of the haggadic passage. The "I am who I am" is simply a good-natured pun, the humor of which has escaped the long-faced grammarians. . . . A wag could write *I am has sent me*; an ancient source scarcely. The wag was indulging in his very early times in the by now age-old pursuit of giving a supposed etymology of Yahve, and has done so almost as well as modern scholars.[53]

Alternatively, Robert Carroll laments the working assumptions of philosophers at a Cambridge conference he attended: "What disappointed me about the Cambridge conference was the way all the philosophers took up the complex philosophical implicatures of various translations of 3.14, without ever stopping to allow some thought or time for the simplicities of the original text." While he acknowledges the difficulty of determining the tone of the

51. Wevers, *Notes on the Greek Text of Exodus*, 32.

52. For a British writer in 2019, it is hard not to think also of Theresa May's "Brexit is Brexit."

53. Sandmel, "Haggada within Scripture," 113. In certain respects, Sandmel's essay is a forerunner of recent moves both towards inner-biblical interpretation and towards a strongly redactional emphasis in pentateuchal criticism.

text, Carroll offers his own forthright construal of what is going on in those textual "simplicities":

> I read the simple punning tautology of 3.14 as a dismissive rejection of Moses' kvetching questions. . . . I take the response to be somewhat short-tempered and dismissive. It says nothing and then twits Moses by inviting him to speak nonsense to the people of Israel. . . . It is playful rather than serious linguistics.[54]

Sandmel has YHWH as comic, while Carroll sees Him as grumpy.

Such readings raise a difficult point of method. In effect they privilege a conjecture about the motives of the person responsible for the wording of the text, in such a way that those words become harder to take at face value. Not the nature of God but the putative playfulness of an ancient scribe becomes the real focus of attention. Given our extensive lack of evidence and ignorance, we will never know what went on in the formation of the text. Judgments about likely scenarios will relate to one's wider judgments about the nature of the text as a whole. Those who read the text as Jewish or Christian Scripture are likely to be predisposed to give prime attention to the subject matter of the text in its received form. In terms of possible compositional processes, one option is to think in terms of tradents who, like many great storytellers, subordinated themselves to the content of the text.[55] It is possible that they effaced themselves precisely so that attention could be focused on the subject matter of their material.[56] An approach along these lines underlies the classic theological and philosophical discussions of Exodus 3:14. But other approaches and working assumptions that speculate about what may lie behind the text cannot be ruled out, even if one chooses not to adopt them.

Towards Understanding ʾehyeh ʾăsher ʾehyeh

How, then, should we understand the tautologous "I AM WHO I AM"? Frank Polak makes a nice observation about *ʾehyeh ʾăsher ʾehyeh* that takes seriously the form of the wording and is similar to the well-known point about the non-explicit nature of the Hebrew idiom: it is "unlimited in its implications but without going beyond implication."[57]

54. Carroll, "Strange Fire," 47. Unsurprisingly, in the light of such a reading, Carroll was strongly not in favor of using the Bible for constructive theology. See his *Wolf in the Sheepfold*.

55. For an interesting discussion of the "self-subsumption" of the tradents of canonical texts, see Chapman, *The Law and the Prophets*, 99–104.

56. The self-effacing anonymity of most of the great sculptors and glaziers in medieval European cathedrals would be analogous.

57. Polak, "Storytelling and Redaction," 464.

However, my impression is that many interpreters prefer not to linger long on possible unlimited implications but rather seek to provide some specific takeaway meaning for their readers (a natural instinct for a commentator!). Thus, for example, Jeffrey Tigay comments that *ʾehyeh ʾăsher ʾehyeh* means "My nature will become evident from my actions."[58] Relatedly, one common interpretive move is to focus on the single *ʾehyeh* of 3:14b in conjunction with the single *ʾehyeh* of 3:12a and to take this more straightforward formulation (despite its transitional role in context) as that which gives the meaning of the divine name. Jan Assmann, representing significant scholarly consensus, observes, "This 'to be' denotes a supportive being-there or being-with. That the name *ʾehyeh* is meant to be read in this way emerges clearly enough from the context, since from this point on God is constantly making his presence felt in both word and deed as he watches over the fluctuating fortunes of his people."[59] These interpretations make good sense.

Nonetheless, the question of how well they do justice to *ʾehyeh ʾăsher ʾehyeh* is worth pressing a little.[60] For example, with regard to the options expressed by Assmann, Hebrew has regular words for "there" (*shām*) and "with" (*ʿīm* or *ʾet*) which it can combine with *ʾehyeh*, as in Exodus 3:12. Yet these words are absent from 3:14a, although they could have been included. Perhaps this should give the reader pause to ask whether something other than what we find in 3:12 might do more justice to the wording of 3:14a.

Put differently, a recurrent note that is sounded in modern biblical commentary on the meaning of *ʾehyeh ʾăsher ʾehyeh* is that it is important to eschew metaphysics and/or certain modes of classic philosophical thought in favor of keeping to the thought-world of the Hebrew text. We regularly read statements such as these: "The early Hebrew mind was essentially practical, not metaphysical."[61] "All interpretations which speak of Being in an abstract metaphysical sense are inappropriate. . . . Our verse did not seek to understand God metaphysically, but historically."[62] "Not conceptual being, being in the abstract, but active being, is the intent of this reply."[63] On one level, this is clearly right. There is unarguable value in recognizing that the philosophical thought expressed in the Greek language of late antiquity and

58. Tigay, "Exodus," 103.

59. Assmann, *Invention of Religion*, 131–32.

60. So also G. I. Davies: "The . . . undefinedness and generality of v. 14 is the distinctive characteristic of this particular 'exegesis of the divine name' and is not to be lost sight of" (*Exodus 1–18*, 275).

61. McNeile, *Book of Exodus*, 22.

62. Jacob, *Second Book of the Bible*, 72, 77.

63. Durham, *Exodus*, 39.

thereafter differs in many ways from the Hebrew thought-world within which Exodus 3 was written and initially preserved. It can be asked, however, whether assertions such as these are an unintended consequence of Pascal's distinction between the biblical God and the deity of the philosophers, one which may not be what Pascal himself envisaged but which has nonetheless entered the bloodstream, as it were, of modern biblical scholarship. It is one thing to recognize appropriate differences in the history of thought. It is another to set aside and ignore questions about the semantic and conceptual potential of wording such as *ʾehyeh ʾăsher ʾehyeh* if it is indeed "unlimited in its implications."

Some of the central linguistic and conceptual issues posed by Exodus 3:14—and the biblical text's intrinsic relation to the theological task of speaking appropriately of God—are nicely articulated by Paul Ricoeur. He notes, for example, Aristotle's observation that, in classical Greek, "the simple term 'being' has various meanings."[64] Ricoeur further observes,

> If it is true that the Greek *einai* and the Latin *esse* have always signified more than one thing, . . . who can say whether in the ears of the ancient Hebrews the declaration *ʾehyeh ʾašer ʾehyeh* did not already have an enigmatic resonance? And if so, this resonance would already have at least a double sense: the enigma of a positive revelation giving rise to thought (about existence, efficacity, faithfulness, accompanying through history), and of a negative revelation dissociating the Name from those utilitarian and magical values concerning power that were ordinarily associated with it. . . . If we admit with Hans-Georg Gadamer that there are no specifically philosophical words, but only a philosophical use of words in particular contexts, why not assume that the biblical writer proceeded like the Greek philosophers and raised to a hitherto unheard-of level a verb that was as common in his language as the verb for being in Greek or Latin or contemporary languages?[65]

This proposal merits serious consideration. It may be that the avoidance of a subject-predicate formulation, "I am X," in favor of a repeated use of the verb "to be" should serve in this context to direct the reader away from any particular predicate for God (appropriate though many predicates indeed are, as in, e.g., Exod. 34:6 or Deut. 32:4 or Isa. 6:3) towards thinking of the nature of divine being in itself as an active reality that is inexhaustible and beyond all regular conceptuality—yet who sends Moses to Israel.

64. Aristotle's Greek is *to on to haplōs legomenon legetai pollachōs* (*Metaphysics* E2/1026a33); see Ross, *Aristotle's "Metaphysics"* (no pagination for the Greek text).

65. LaCocque and Ricoeur, *Thinking Biblically*, 340–41. For a fuller account of Ricoeur's thought on this issue, see Meessen, "Penser le verbe 'être' autrement."

The Meaning of the Name: Explanation and Mystery

Further progress can be made by turning again to the work of Jan Assmann. Assmann, beyond offering the common interpretations of "being there" and "being with" (as already noted), also ventures a further, less common interpretive proposal:

> The formula "I am that I am" (or "I will be what I will be") is tautological. . . . It explains nothing. . . . From this perspective, a name is being withheld here rather than shared. By declaring "I am that I am," God leaves the question of his name unresolved. "I AM hath sent me to you" sounds a little like the positively worded counterpart to the "no-one" with which Odysseus introduces himself to Polyphemus, leading the blinded cyclops to lament, "No-one has wounded me"—a cry that ensures no-one comes to his aid.[66]

This seems to me to be on the wrong track, but illuminatingly so. First, even though a construal of God's words as an evasion or refusal of Moses' request is common in the scholarly literature, the contention that God's words indicate that "a name is being withheld" is surely wrong. The answer to the question of 3:13 comes in 3:15. A name is asked for, and a name is given. The Tetragrammaton, YHWH / the LORD, is the name of the God of Israel's ancestors. Assmann's reading depends on discounting 3:15a.[67]

Second, Assmann's linkage with the famous story of Odysseus and Polyphemus surely sets his interpretation in the wrong register.[68] Odysseus's wily giving of his name as "No-one" was designed to outsmart and trick the hostile Cyclops. Odysseus intended no good for Polyphemus. To suggest that God's answer to Moses is in any way analogous creates the impression that the divine words are in some way an outmaneuvering of Moses, leaving him uncomprehending of what is going on (as Carroll clearly proposes). But such words would not be ones that envisaged the good of Moses or Israel.

Third, Assmann's observation that the divine wording "explains nothing" makes the assumption that it ought to be explaining something. But maybe

66. Assmann, *Invention of Religion*, 132.

67. Assmann ignores the logic of the text in its received form—although generally he seeks to work with the received form—because he takes 3:15a (the whole verse up to "This is my name") to be "an addition of the Priestly Source to create a link to Genesis 15 and 17" (*Invention of Religion*, 131, 350); for that reason he excludes it from interpretation. It is a pity when redactional theories about textual formation are permitted, in effect, to disable a reading of the sequential logic of the text as it stands.

68. Assmann's proposal here has analogies to the proposals of Sandmel and Carroll (see above, pp. 73–74).

the meaning given to the name YHWH is not meant to explain anything. If one looks for an interpretive clue in the wider narrative, there is one clue that has not been discussed so far, yet which is a prime candidate as it sets the scene for the dialogue between God and Moses: the burning bush.[69] The bush attracts Moses because the fire that burns without destroying it is like nothing that he has ever encountered, and it is the context for God's speaking to him. Rather than being an arbitrary but convenient sign to attract Moses' attention, the bush is most likely integral—indeed, foundational—to the narrative as a whole. It is easy to forget that, in terms of the narrative scenario, the voice that says "I AM WHO I AM" is still the voice that is speaking from the fiery bush. If we read "I AM WHO I AM" as analogous to the bush which burns without being destroyed, then the bush is the visual symbol that illustrates something of the meaning of the words. The purpose of the "I AM WHO I AM" would be not to explain anything but to engage Moses in such a way that he is drawn into a deeper level of the encounter with God that is already taking place.

In other words, the appearance and speech of God are the archetypal expressions of mystery. There are, however, two important and different meanings of the word "mystery." One meaning is that of a puzzle or problem, where the problem is a lack of information. In a detective story, the story is a mystery because its readers/viewers do not know, and are struggling to work out, what is going on (i.e., "whodunit"); but by the end of the story, when the necessary information has been disclosed, there is no more mystery—everything, or at least everything necessary, has been explained.

The other meaning of "mystery," characteristic of theology, is that of a reality which is understood to be ever greater the more one enters into it. Genuine love is a mystery in this sense, as is human nature. And, supremely, God is a mystery in this sense. It is sometimes supposed that when theologians appeal to "mystery" ("We cannot inquire further, for it is a mystery"), they are prematurely foreclosing a puzzling issue that might in fact be clarified and explained if only one worked harder at it, perhaps by approaching the problem from a different angle. Sometimes this may indeed be the case.

69. This construal is not, of course, novel. Nahum Sarna, for example, observes, "God's pronouncement of His own Name . . . is the articulated counterpart of the spectacle of fire at the Burning Bush, fire that is self-generating and self-sustaining" (*Exploring Exodus*, 52). Or as Christoph Dohmen says, "The thornbush, burning yet not burning up, appears to be removed from transitoriness or mutability [Vergänglichkeit bzw. Veränderung], for which time is constitutive; and thereby it [the thornbush] grasps hold—even if hiddenly—of what God later proclaims about himself in 3:14: 'I will be who I will be'" (*Exodus 1–18*, 149 [my translation]). Nonetheless, the connection between the fiery bush and the divine words is much less well represented in modern commentary than it might be.

Nonetheless, that is a debasement of theology rather than its true exercise. With regard to the meaning of the divine words in 3:14a, the key point is nicely expressed by Terence Fretheim:

> Both God and Moses recognize that God is not demystified through further understanding. In fact, the more one understands God, the more mysterious God becomes. God is the supreme exemplification of the old adage: The more you know, the more you know you don't know.[70]

The recognition of God as a mystery in this second sense aligns well with the bush that burns without being destroyed, the bush whose unconsuming fire is alive and not on a trajectory towards death. The symbolic resonances of this bush are as open and unlimited and resistant to being pinned down as are the implications of God as "I AM WHO I AM" in the privileged disclosure to Moses and to the reader.

Interpretive Clues in the Following Narrative

Another approach to understanding the divine name is to look to the wider context of Exodus for interpretive clues. For example, the first narrative that follows Moses' commissioning—his initial encounter with the pharaoh (Exod. 5:1–6:13)—is framed by uses of the divine name.

Initially, Moses speaks confidently and authoritatively, in classic prophetic mode:

> [1]Afterward Moses and Aaron went to Pharaoh and said, "Thus says the LORD, the God of Israel, 'Let my people go, so that they may celebrate a festival to me in the wilderness.'" (Exod. 5:1)

The pharaoh, however, is unimpressed.

> [2]But Pharaoh said, "Who is the LORD, that I should heed him and let Israel go? I do not know the LORD, and I will not let Israel go." (Exod. 5:2)

The pharaoh does not recognize the authority of the deity in whose name Moses speaks in such a peremptory manner.[71]

70. Fretheim, *Exodus*, 62–63.

71. The pharaoh's dismissiveness thus does not bear on the question of whether the divine name that was given to Moses had hitherto been unknown. The pharaoh is never named. Although one can readily imagine traditio-historical reasons for this, the literary effect is that the pharaoh is seen as an archetypal figure of human resistance towards the LORD.

How does Moses respond? Does he know what to do with this refusal? The narrative suggests that he does not.

> [3]Then they said, "The God of the Hebrews has revealed himself to us; please, may we go a three days' journey into the wilderness to sacrifice to the LORD our God, or he will fall upon us with pestilence or sword." (Exod. 5:3)

Moses and Aaron instantly back down and speak quite differently. There is no confident "Thus says the LORD." The new and definitive name of God is instantly relegated to a secondary mention as recipient of sacrifice, in favor of a descriptive title, "God of the Hebrews," which probably signifies no more than "our national (tribal) deity." In addition, the NRSV, like many recent translations, omits the Hebrew particle *nāʾ* (which comes directly after "let us go") as though it were no more significant than an "er" or "um" in English. Yet *nāʾ* is a particle which idiomatically can have something of the force of "please,"[72] and turns the previous command ("Let my people go") into a polite and deferential request ("We're now asking, and asking nicely"). Finally, Moses and Aaron speak of their deity in terms of immediate and unpleasant retribution, something that should register with the pharaoh's outlook ("If we don't go, he'll kill us all—you understand that sort of thing, don't you?"). The new understanding and hope represented by knowing God as the LORD falls down at the first hurdle.[73]

Yet the pharaoh is no more moved this time than he was previously.

> [4]But the king of Egypt said to them, "Moses and Aaron, why are you taking the people away from their work? Get to your labors!" (Exod. 5:4)

The story then continues with the pharaoh maliciously increasing the difficulty of Israel's labors. When the Israelite supervisors complain, the pharaoh cynically dismisses their complaint as merely showing laziness. After this brusque dismissal, the Israelite supervisors then turn on Moses and Aaron, accusing them of making the Israelites' labors under the pharaoh even worse than they were previously. Moses calls out to the LORD in anguished puzzlement and dismay; this was not at all what he had expected.

72. Compare NJPS: "we pray." See also Gehazi's words to Naaman in 2 Kings 5:22 (below, p. 177). The idiomatic use of *nāʾ* is valuably discussed by Ahouva Shulman ("The Particle *nāʾ* in Biblical Hebrew Prose"), who compares contexts where *nāʾ* is used and is not used, and shows how regularly it functions to express polite request.

73. There is some irony when Moses' wording in 5:3 is compared with that initially prescribed by the LORD in 3:18, as Moses now drops the LORD's name from qualifying "God of the Hebrews" and adds a sense of threat.

> [22]Then Moses turned again to the LORD and said, "O LORD, why have you mistreated this people? Why did you ever send me? [23]Since I first came to Pharaoh to speak in your name, he has mistreated this people, and you have done nothing at all to deliver your people." (Exod. 5:22–23)

It is at this point, when Moses' initial expectations have been completely disappointed, that God speaks again, not only with general reassurance but also with the specific reaffirmation that it is indeed as the LORD that Israel is to know Him, and that in this capacity He will bring them freedom.

> [1]Then the LORD said to Moses, "Now you shall see what I will do to Pharaoh: Indeed, by a mighty hand he will let them go; by a mighty hand he will drive them out of his land." [2]God also spoke to Moses and said to him: "I am the LORD. [3]I appeared to Abraham, Isaac, and Jacob as God Almighty [*El Shaddai*], but by my name 'The LORD' I did not make myself known to them. . . . [6]Say therefore to the Israelites, 'I am the LORD, and I will free you from the burdens of the Egyptians." (Exod. 6:1–3, 6)

The ways of the LORD are not self-evident and do not conform to any natural expectation of what God "ought to do." They require a reordering of thought and practice, which even Moses has to learn. Insofar as Moses' complaint in 5:22–23 is a narrative paradigm of what is regularly depicted in the psalms of lament as part of a recurrent pattern of prayer, then it follows that, however much believers may learn of the ways of the LORD, those ways never cease to puzzle and humble human expectations. Something of this should probably be seen as contained within the "I AM WHO I AM."

Summary of Interpretation of "I AM WHO I AM"

The meaning of God's name, of which the reader, like Moses, is to be aware—the "I AM WHO I AM" which gives content to the familiar form of the divine name, YHWH / the LORD—is best arrived at by utilizing the interpretive clues in the wider narrative context: supremely, the account of the burning bush, but also the confrontation with the pharaoh and the similar wording on the divine lips in Exodus 33:19. The fire that burns without destroying is like the suggestive tautology on the lips of God—a pointer to the mystery which is intrinsic to the nature of God, a mystery of reality which needs to be engaged in order to be in any way understood, and in which the understanding transcends rational categories, but which is active in the life of Israel through the sending of Moses and the continuing association with Israel's ancestors.

In light of this I turn briefly to a little of the history of interpretation of these momentous words.

Exodus 3:14 in the Greek of the Septuagint, the New Testament, and the Early Church

The Greek Translation of Exodus 3:13–15

The most famous and influential translation of the Hebrew *ʾehyeh ʾăsher ʾehyeh* ("I AM WHO I AM") is in the Greek of the Septuagint, where God's words to Moses become "I am The One Who Is."

The Greek of Exodus 3:13–15 for the most part follows the Hebrew closely,[74] with the sole exception being its rendering of *ʾehyeh* and *yhwh*. Its rendering of 3:14a, *egō eimi ho ōn*, which means "I am The One Who Is," is, unlike the Hebrew, a subject-predicate formulation. Exodus 3:14b uses the predicate "the one who is" (*ho ōn*) as the subject of the verb in what Moses is to say: "The one who is [*ho ōn*] has sent me to you." Then 3:15a uses the reverential formulation "Lord" (*kurios*) as the name that is added to the title "God of your fathers."[75] A consequence of this is that the wordplay between the divine name and the verb "to be" is lost. A reader of the text in Greek still sees the parallel between "The one who is has sent me to you" (3:14b) and "The Lord, the God of your fathers, . . . has sent me to you" (3:15a). But the lack of any intrinsic verbal linkage between *ho ōn* and *kurios* makes the relationship between them puzzling. This may have had the effect of encouraging reflection on the meaning of 3:14 in relative isolation from 3:15.

The septuagintal rendering of 3:14a appears to be less a translation than an interpretation.[76] A translation in Greek that preserved the form and syntax of the Hebrew would use either the relative pronoun *hos*,[77] giving *eimi hos*

74. See the full translation in *NETS*, 53.

75. When *kurios* is used in the Septuagint as the name of God, it is anarthrous (i.e., used without the definite article)—*kurios*, not *ho kurios*—and so readily functions as a name. In this it differs from the familiar English rendering "the LORD," even though an anarthrous "LORD/Lord" on its own is used as a form of address in prayer.

76. John Wevers, however, contends that *ho ōn* is probably a "straightforward attempt to make an acceptable Greek version of the Hebrew" (*Notes on the Greek Text of Exodus*, 34). Comparably, Daniel Gurtner renders *egō eimi ho ōn* with "I am who I am" and comments, "Since a first-person subject would not work for the necessary *apestalken* (a third singular form), Exod is forced to resort to the participial *ho ōn*, 'the one who is'" (*Exodus*, 36–37, 206). However, I cannot see that a first-person subject before "has sent me" would be any more puzzling or unable to "work" in Greek than in Hebrew.

77. The Latin relative pronoun *qui* was chosen for the Vulgate rendering: *ego sum qui sum* (3:14a) and *qui est misit me ad vos* (3:14b).

eimi ("I am who I am"), or, perhaps better, the flexible particle of conjunction *hōs*, giving *eimi hōs eimi* ("I am as I am"). The retroversion of *egō eimi ho ōn* into Hebrew would give *ʾănī hahōyeh*, the first-person pronoun followed by the participial form of *hāyāh* ("to be") with the definite article.

The septuagintal wording links God with the concept of being. All-importantly, being is conceived in a personal mode (*ho ōn*, masculine) rather than an impersonal one (*to on*, neuter).[78] Precisely what this means in its ancient context is a moot point. The likelihood is that, in line with Aristotle's observation about the different senses of the verb "to be," "I am The One Who Is" is intrinsically polysemous, suggestive rather than narrowly determinate in meaning. Hence the rich interpretive history.

Exodus 3:14 LXX in the New Testament

The Greek rendering of Exodus 3:14a is utilized and appropriated in the New Testament in the Johannine corpus.

In Revelation, God is spoken of as "he who is [*ho ōn*] and who was and who is to come" (Rev. 1:4, 8),[79] which appears not only to utilize the specific wording of Exodus 3:14 LXX but also to exploit an openness of tense within the verb "to be" such that past and future are also included.[80] The implication seems to be that the God who is eternal is working out His purposes in the temporal order, and that all times, past and future, are present to Him.

The form of God's declaration "I am The One Who Is" in Exodus 3:14 LXX makes it analogous to Jesus' famous "I am" sayings in John's Gospel, such as "I am the bread of life" (John 6:35). This analogy of form is both straightforward and interpretively suggestive. The reader is to ponder the nature and meaning both of Jesus and of God.

There is also the question of how the divine "I am" of Exodus 3:14 relates to Jesus' "I am," without a predicate. Sometimes in John's Gospel, Jesus' saying "I am" (*egō eimi*) without a predicate is essentially an idiom of self-identification: "Yes, I am the one (whom you are expecting / looking for)" (4:26). In itself this raises no particular theological issues, though deeper issues sometimes may be implied, as in the stepping back and falling down of those arresting Jesus when he identifies himself as the one for whom they are searching with *egō eimi* (18:5–6).

78. Although generalizations are perilous, ancient Greek thought would characteristically tend to favor *to on*, to indicate a sense of too-transcendent-to-be-personal-as-we-messy-and-mortal-beings-are.

79. See also Rev. 4:8; 11:17; 16:5.

80. Instead of the future participle of *eimi*—i.e., *esomenos*—John uses the participial form of *erchomai*, "come," perhaps to emphasize existential eschatological challenge.

Of particular interest are two sayings which are difficult to understand as utterances in the Greek language: "You will die in your sins unless you believe that *egō eimi*" (John 8:24) and "Very truly I tell you, before Abraham was, *egō eimi*" (8:58). One needs to be cautious about interpreting the language of 8:24, 58, as a direct appropriation of Exodus 3:14 LXX. Why? In a subject-predicate formulation, the substantive point is carried by the predicate. When Jesus says, "I am the bread of life," we are meant to think of how he, as bread, nourishes true life and to respond accordingly; in other words, we ponder the words "bread of life" more than the words "I am." If John's Greek in 8:24, 58, were appropriating the Greek of Exodus 3:14, whose form is that of subject and predicate, then the predicate "the one who is" (*ho ōn*) would be the substantive focus rather than the subject "I am" (*egō eimi*).

It is thus likely that the sense of John 8:24, 58, lies in the words being an allusion or citation. The words *egō eimi* without predicate occur in the Septuagint, especially in Isaiah 40–48, as a rendering of the Hebrew "I am he" (*ʾănī hūʾ*) on the lips of God. For example, the Lord speaks of His choosing Israel "so that you may know and believe me / and understand that I am he [Heb. *ʾănī hūʾ*; Gk. *egō eimi*]. / Before me no god was formed, / nor shall there be any after me" (Isa. 43:10). The point is that Israel should recognize their deity as the one and only true God; the idiom indicates that the God of Israel is unique, sovereign, incomparable. It is widely recognized that these Isaianic passages and the similar Deuteronomy 32:39 are the primary intertexts for Jesus' words.[81] The divine implication of Jesus' words is clear, even if Exodus 3:14 is not being cited.

However, a synthetic theological construal within the wider canon as the context for interpretation can readily recognize further resonances and links. The Isaianic "I am" sits alongside regular use of the Tetragrammaton,[82] so there is a ready association between "I am" and the divine name. There is also some evidence for ancient Christian reflection on God and Jesus as "the first and the last" / "Alpha and Omega"; and the vowels *a* and *ō* are the vowels used in *Adōnai*, a common reverential substitute for the divine name in the Jewish reading of Scripture. So there may be an ancient inner-biblical linkage of the divine name with *ʾănī hūʾ* / *egō eimi*.[83] The "I am" sayings of Isaiah 43:10 and comparable passages express the identity and uniqueness of the God whose name is "the Lord." When these same words are heard on the lips of Jesus, it means that Jesus, in whom the divine Word becomes

81. See esp. C. Williams, *I Am He*.

82. The "I am" of Isa. 43:10 is directly followed by "I, I am the Lord" in 43:11 in the Hebrew, though the Greek at this point has "I am God" (*egō ho theos*).

83. See Macaskill, "Name Christology," esp. 226–28.

flesh, is the appearance in space and time of the God who is beyond space and time.

The potential significance of the Greek rendering of Exodus 3:14 is nicely brought out by Rowan Williams, in what is almost a passing remark:

> Greek-speaking Christians (and Jews) translated the "I am who I am" of Exodus as "I am the One who is"—as an affirmation of God's transcendent, independent existence. Some moderns have complained that this reduces the "dynamic" language of the Hebrew Bible to a philosophical concept, but this is too crude a criticism. The Greek vision is precisely of a divine life that needs no "maintenance" from outside itself, that is free from the conditioning of any particular reality. What is distinctive about the Jewish and Christian reading of this is simply that the freedom of God is grasped as fully shown in certain events and transactions in our world: in the liberation of the Hebrew slaves; in the human life and death of Jesus.[84]

This adroitly recognizes and reframes familiar problems.

Hilary of Poitiers on Exodus 3:14 LXX

That an ontological reading of Exodus 3:14 may, despite its nonidentity with the Hebrew original, retain intrinsic dynamic and existential resonance can be seen in the personal testimony of Hilary of Poitiers in the fourth century. Hilary begins his treatise *The Trinity* (*De Trinitate*) with an account of how, as a young man, he sought to know what would make for the good and true life. In the course of this search he read widely and significantly:

> I began the search for the meaning of life. . . . At first I was attracted by riches and leisure. . . . But most people discover that human nature wants something better to do than just gormandize and kill time. . . .
>
> Then I sought to know God better. . . . Some religions . . . imagine male gods and female ones and can trace the lineage of these gods born from one another. . . . Most, however, admit that God exists, but hold him to be indifferent to human beings. . . .
>
> I was reflecting on these problems when I discovered the books which the Jewish religion says were composed by Moses and the prophets. There I discovered that God bears witness to himself in these terms: "I am who I am," and, "Say this to the people of Israel, 'I AM has sent me to you.'" I was filled with wonder at this perfect definition which translates into intelligible words

84. R. Williams, *Christ on Trial*, 21–22.

> the incomprehensible knowledge of God. *Nothing better suggests God than Being*. "He who is" can have neither end nor beginning.

The account continues with Hilary reflecting further on the Law and the Prophets until he "made the acquaintance of the teaching of the Gospel and of the apostles." Specifically, he encounters the Prologue to John's Gospel and is struck by the significance of the Word made flesh:

> My intellect overstepped its limits at that point and I learnt more about God than I had expected. I understood that my Creator was God born of God. . . . Without surrendering his divinity God was made of our flesh. . . . My soul joyfully received the revelation of this mystery. By means of my flesh I was drawing near to God, by means of my faith I was called to a new birth. I was able to receive this new birth from on high. . . . *I was assured that I could not be reduced to non-being*.[85]

Hilary's combined reading of Exodus 3 and John's Prologue enables him to see that his perishable, mortal flesh is not an ultimate problem. Because the Word became flesh, it follows that perishable flesh, instead of being reduced to nonbeing, can attain that reality of being which is God Himself. Hilary, like Pascal, encountered a mystery in the full sense of the word—not a puzzle for the mind to solve but a reality by which the whole human being is to be transformed.

Hilary's reading of Scripture is not a good guide to the meaning that Exodus 3:14 may have had for its Hebrew author in its context of origin or for the Greek translators of the Septuagint. But when Israel's scriptures are recontextualized as part of the Christian Bible, and are read not only in conjunction with the writings of the New Testament but also in relation to the developing conceptualities of early Christian thought, Hilary's reading can appropriately evoke an affirmative response to the following question: Has he not seen some genuinely possible implications of Exodus 3 in its depiction of God's self-revelation to Moses as the God who can be known yet is beyond knowledge, as the living God who can cause Hilary to be alive and stay alive—like a fiery bush which neither consumes nor is consumed—and whose self-revelation is for the enduring good of His people? This does not mean that contemporary reading and appropriation of this biblical passage should straightforwardly emulate Hilary's reading. Yet Hilary's combination of conceptual discipline

85. Hilary of Poitiers, *The Trinity* 1.1–13. The Latin text is conveniently available in Hilaire de Poitiers, *La Trinité I*. I have utilized the fluent interpretive rendering in Olivier Clément's great work, *The Roots of Christian Mysticism*, 18–21. The italics are mine.

and existential openness and engagement offers a suggestive model of theological inquiry from which (would-be) believers today can still learn.

What Term Should Be Used to Speak of Israel's God?

I would like briefly to touch on one further issue, though only in an indicative way which cannot do justice to the complexities of the issue (and its literature).

In rendering the Tetragrammaton, there is a divergence between the predominant practice of mainstream, modern biblical translations, which use the reverential form "the LORD"—following the precedent set by the Septuagint, which uses *Kurios*—and the predominant practice of mainstream biblical scholars, who use the divine name with its likely original pronunciation "Yahweh." The appropriateness of one usage or the other has been extensively argued both ways.

This issue illustrates significant in-principle questions which, in my judgment, revolve around the difference between reading Israel's scriptures as ancient history in relation to their context of origin, and reading them not only as ancient history but also as Christian or Jewish Scripture in relation to faith in the contemporary world. Insofar as the interpreter's concern is to read Israel's religious writings as analogous to other religious writings of the ancient Mediterranean / Near Eastern world ("interpret the Bible like any other book," in shorthand), a good rationale exists for using the divine name in the most likely form that it had in that world.[86] As a point of history, in a world where different peoples had different deities, Israel's deity is thus identified and distinguished from other deities by a proper name. But insofar as Israel's scriptures are being read as Christian Scripture ("interpret the Bible unlike any other book," in shorthand), they are recontextualized in a frame of reference in which Israel's deity is believed to be the one true God in a way that is continuous with, but not identical to, the conceptualities within their context of origin. Moreover, since Marduk and Zeus are generally no longer considered to be live options for belief, there is no longer the same need or propriety for distinguishing the deity of Israel's scriptures from them, as once might have been the case. There is thus good reason to use not the proper name of God but rather a reverential and honorific alternative, of which "the LORD" is the most commonly accepted Christian form.

86. There is the added complication that the divine name is a Qere-Ketiv in the Hebrew Bible (i.e., what is read aloud is other than what is written in the text), though it is unclear how far back this tradition of alternative pronunciation goes.

■ I realize that "the LORD" introduces gender into the divine name in a way that grates for some in a contemporary context. A not-uncommon Jewish alternative, "the Eternal," has advantages in this regard. The common Jewish rendering *HaShem* ("The Name") is also non-gender-specific. However, for many Christians the resonances with Paul's succinct summary of Christian faith, "Jesus is Lord" (*kurios Iēsous*, 1 Cor. 12:3; cf. Rom. 10:9; Phil. 2:11), are theologically and existentially important. Common uses of "Lord" in liturgy and practice focus primarily on God as the appropriate recipient of fundamental trust, allegiance, and obedience. It is possible for the gender implications to recede into background invisibility. This background invisibility is akin to, say, the Christian implications of the names of certain Oxford and Cambridge colleges—Jesus, Corpus Christi, Trinity—for most of those who live and work there, or to the various connotations of "Amazon," which hardly brings to mind a female warrior with a breast removed or a river in the South American continent for most of those who shop there. ■

Conclusion: Towards a Grammar of God as Self-Revealing Mystery

A second facet of what it means to "know that the LORD is God," in the context of this book, is a recognition that God's nature is expressed in His name, YHWH / the LORD, which is itself to be understood as "I AM WHO I AM" or, from the human perspective, "HE IS WHO HE IS." I have argued that the burning bush and the "I AM WHO I AM" should be taken together as mutually interpretive of each other. They are mutually expressive of the mystery of active being that is intrinsic to the name and nature of Israel's deity. As such they should evoke an existential openness and a practical responsiveness towards that mystery, a responsiveness akin to that envisaged in Proverbs 8.[87] The meaning of Exodus 3 may also be extended in more than one way, as can be seen in its appropriation both in the Septuagint and in the New Testament, where its resonances help frame John's portrayal of Jesus. There is also, I think, a pleasing paradox in my contention that a passage in which God gives His name is well appropriated via nonuse of that name on the part of those who inhabit the continuing traditions of faith that are rooted in the biblical text.

The study of Exodus 3 brings readers to the issue of revelation and the core understanding of Jews and Christians and Muslims that human knowledge of the one God is possible because this one God has given Himself to be known. Questions about divine self-revelation and questions about the nature of the scriptural text that mediates and witnesses to that revelation become inseparable.

One facet of a belief in revelation is the time-honored notion of *divine accommodation*, the understanding that any revelation from God, if it is

87. See ch. 1 of this book.

to be comprehensible, must use recognizable categories of human thought and language, which may have their limitations but which are meaningful and appropriate nonetheless. Much modern thought, however, has followed the lead of Feuerbach and reversed the direction, as it were, by preferring to speak of biblical content in terms of *human projection* rather than divine accommodation: the divine becomes increasingly—and, for many, exclusively—a coded form of the human. But if one is disinclined to follow the dogmatic contention that projection in relation to God is always and only *mere* projection, there should be no intrinsic difficulty with seeing that, as Marilynne Robinson puts it, "projection is our method of inquiry, the grounds of speculation and hypothesis."[88] In theological terms, the question is whether human inquiry may be in some way responsive to an antecedent divine initiative; human projection may be essentially a counterpart to divine accommodation.

Nonetheless, the appreciation of the likely complex human processes involved in the formation and composition of the books of the Bible has tended to strengthen a sense of its human construction in a reductive mode. For many people, the impact of modern biblical criticism has had a debunking effect on the Bible's status as a sacred text. What the Bible says about God and humanity is thus illuminating primarily in terms of the ideologies and conflicts of the ancient world in which it arose. It is no longer trusted as an authoritative witness to enduring truth about ultimate reality, in a reversal of the historic affirmation of Jews and Christians who regard it as Scripture.

With regard to Exodus 3, let me offer a succinct formulation of the key issue: If Exodus 3 is not a transcript by Moses of what God said to him on a particular momentous day in the desert (as was in general implicitly held by premodern interpreters), but a text whose author, date, tradition history, and relation to Israel's origins cannot be determined with any precision (in line with insights from modern historical-critical work) and a story in which an omniscient narrator gives access to the intentions and words of God and Moses (in line with postmodern literary insights), then what follows? Certainly, one will regard the nature and genre of the text otherwise than premodern readers did. Does that mean that a reader cannot seriously engage the narrative world and the subject matter that the text presents? Clearly not, as I have tried to show in the preceding pages. Does it mean that the text does not *really* speak of the one God? For many and various theological and philosophical reasons, the short answer is *no*. Such a conclusion would simply

88. M. Robinson, *What Are We Doing Here?*, 228.

be a non sequitur. As Jon Levenson succinctly puts the point in relation to modern biblical scholarship,

> The relationship of compositional history to religious faith is not a simple one. If Moses is the human author of Genesis [or Exodus], nothing ensures that God is its ultimate Author. If J, E, P, and various equally anonymous sources and redactors are its human authors, nothing ensures that God is not its ultimate Author.[89]

I conclude with three brief reflections on offering a renewed account of divine revelation in the context of Scripture. First, from the perspective of both the Jewish and the Christian faiths, it is important to maintain that the human processes involved in articulating the content of the biblical text could have been open and responsive to the initiative of God, unless there is good reason to suppose otherwise. Moreover, a core theological principle is that the human and the divine are not in competition with each other. Thus, the ability to offer a comprehensive account of the biblical text's formation in human terms—which is a point of principle rather than a reality in practice, given how little we actually know—does not resolve the question of whether its content should be understood to be also mediating a transcendent reality from beyond itself within the conventions and constraints of human language.

Second, the in-principle possibility that the biblical text mediates divine reality should not be considered in isolation from the question of how and why it may be possible today to handle responsibly the content of the biblical portrayal of YHWH differently from how one handles the portrayal of other ancient deities and religions (e.g., Marduk in Babylonian religion, Zeus in Greek religion). That is, on what basis might we today responsibly privilege the one and believe it to be in some way from God, and thus find in it enduring truth and wisdom that is not found in the others? How such judgments and discernments might appropriately be made is not an easy question, and it goes well beyond the familiar parameters of modern biblical scholarship, which generally prefers not to address such questions.[90] It requires engagement with the expectations and understandings that have arisen through the

89. Levenson, "Genesis," 10.

90. For example, a significant recent collection of essays—J. van Oorschot and M. Witte, *The Origins of Yahwism*—has thirteen contributions, all focused on questions of religio-historical origins in antiquity, but not discussing possible origin in God, or even asking what would be necessary for that issue to be raised meaningfully. Even the most hermeneutically focused essay, F. Hartenstein, "Beginnings of YHWH and 'Longing for the Origin,'" fascinatingly ponders questions about the distinctiveness and particularity of Israel's religion, together with historiographical puzzles about its origins, but does not address the theological issue which I am trying to articulate here.

continuing life-giving generativity of the biblical writings in those ongoing Jewish and Christian communities that have received them as Scripture and still use them in worship and in daily life.[91]

Finally, an appropriate note on which to end has to do with the intrinsic quality of the biblical content itself. Erich Auerbach once famously said, "The Bible's claim to truth . . . is tyrannical—it excludes other claims."[92] Put more modestly, there is much in the inherent nature of the biblical portrayal of God and Moses in Exodus 3 that has persuaded people down the ages that here is something beyond familiar ideologies and philosophies and conflicts, something self-authenticating, something that mediates a transcendent and life-giving reality—as memorably happened one night for Pascal.

91. I have discussed this more extensively in my *The Bible in a Disenchanted Age*.

92. Auerbach, *Mimesis*, 14. Auerbach made the point with reference to Gen. 22, and it is a strong generalizing claim that does not apply everywhere: the characteristics of Gen. 22 are not equally present in Gen. 23! Nonetheless, Exod. 3 does share some of the key characteristics that Auerbach identified in Gen. 22.

3

The Just God

The Nature of Deity in Psalm 82

In an episode of the American TV spy thriller *Homeland*, senior CIA operative Saul Berenson visits his sister Dorit, who lives in the West Bank in a Jewish settlement built directly opposite a Palestinian village.[1] There are some preliminary exchanges about their families: Dorit has children and grandchildren; Saul had a childless marriage that has failed. The conversation turns to how Saul and Dorit have drifted apart despite their childhood closeness. Both recognize that the drift began when Dorit married Moshe, who was an ardent Zionist. Saul laments that Moshe was an unbending fanatic, while Dorit says that Moshe "opened my eyes . . . made me proud to be a Jew." The conversation continues:

Saul: "He turned you against your family. . . . He brought you to live in a place that's not yours, where *you* don't belong. . . . Haven't you driven enough people from their homes already, bulldozed their villages, seized their property under laws they had no part in making?"

Dorit: "This land was promised to Avraham."

An earlier version of this chapter was published as "Justice and the Recognition of the True God: A Reading of Psalm 82," *RB* 127 (2020): 215–36.

1. The scene comes in the third episode of the sixth season.

Saul: "Ah yes. (*pause*) Promise. (*pause*) Covenant with God made thousands of years ago. (*pause*) Doesn't that strike you as a form of *insanity*?"

Dorit: "You don't understand, Saul. . . . I love the life that God has given me."

Saul: "How can you love making enemies? How can you love knowing that your very presence here makes peace less possible?"

Dorit: "I have a family, a community, a life filled with faith and purpose. Saul—what do *you* have?"

Dorit turns and walks away, while the camera lingers on Saul sitting in silence.

My interest here is not in the rights and wrongs of Zionism, which is an extremely complex phenomenon. Rather, I'm interested in the differing outlooks that characterize Saul and Dorit. Dorit appeals to the Bible, talks about what God has promised in the past and is doing today, and speaks of the difference that faith makes to her life—concerns to which Saul seems impervious. Saul, however, is concerned with justice and peace for the Palestinians—something to which Dorit seems impervious. Saul also directs his strongest language against the idea that something long ago attributed to God in the Bible could still be valid for sociopolitical realities today. Their views are not only starkly polarized, but communication between them in this area seems impossible; they talk past each other in a way that seems all too characteristic of our contemporary world. However, I would like to let this antithesis between God and the Bible, on the one hand, and the priorities of justice, on the other, linger in the background of the discussion that follows.

Quite apart from the problematic dynamics of this exchange between Saul and Dorit, many ordinary believers, both Jewish and Christian, struggle to understand and express the content of the Bible not just through time-honored wording and familiar liturgical formulations but in ways that genuinely engage the realities of life in the contemporary world. One prime challenge for anyone interested in the Bible as Scripture is to find fresh conceptualities and interpretative practices that do justice to the content of the Bible in relation to the needs and hopes of today.

The next step in our exploration of what it means to "know that the Lord is God" will be to consider the moral nature of God, with particular reference to the question of justice. This is a well-known issue in the Old Testament, and an "obvious" place to go would be the prophets,[2] and also perhaps some selected passages in the legal material of the Pentateuch. I propose, however,

2. I do make this move in ch. 6, pp. 214–16.

to look at a psalm that is not usually considered in this context and which, prima facie, may appear unpromising. Yet I will argue that it is a core expression of the Old Testament understanding of God.

Introduction to Psalm 82

Psalm 82 is one of the most intriguing and challenging of the Psalms.

A Psalm of Asaph.

> [1] God [*ʾĕlōhîm*] has taken his place in the divine council;
> in the midst of the gods [*ʾĕlōhîm*] he holds judgment:
> [2] "How long will you judge unjustly
> and show partiality to the wicked?
> [3] Give justice to the weak and the orphan;
> maintain the right of the lowly and the destitute.
> [4] Rescue the weak and the needy;
> deliver them from the hand of the wicked."
>
> [5] They have neither knowledge nor understanding,
> they walk around in darkness;
> all the foundations of the earth are shaken.
>
> [6] I say, "You are gods [*ʾĕlōhîm*],
> children of the Most High, all of you;
> [7] nevertheless, you shall die like mortals,
> and fall like any prince."
>
> [8] Rise up, O God [*ʾĕlōhîm*], judge the earth;
> for all the nations belong to you![3]

The psalm's date and context of origin are elusive. Scholars usually date the psalm by locating its content at a seemingly appropriate stage within their overall conception of the nature and development of Israelite religion. Responsible scholars have, however, ascribed the psalm variously to almost every period, from the premonarchic period to the Maccabean period.[4] Since dates ranging over a full millennium have been seriously proposed, the only safe inference is that we simply do not know when the psalm was written, other

3. Here I straightforwardly use the NRSV. Later, when I comment on the psalm, I will suggest some modifications of the NRSV.

4. For an overview of the options, see, e.g., Anderson, *Psalms*, 2:591–93; Tate, *Psalms 51–100*, 332–34.

than that it originates at some point within the life of ancient Israel. Such ignorance may or may not matter, however—it all depends on the purposes for which one is reading the psalm.

Psalm 82's genre is distinctive. Strikingly, apart from the first and last verses, God is not the addressee but (apparently) the speaker. The psalm has been variously described as a didactic psalm, a prophetic oracle, a scribal prophecy, or a part of a temple liturgy—even, specifically, a New Year liturgy.[5] But such attempts to articulate the psalm's genre via a historically imaginative construal of the possible nature and purpose of its content show that this psalm fits none of the recognized categories of psalms. It is sui generis. Most of Psalm 82 is a poem about God and the gods in a divine council, a poem whose genre is not that of prayer, apart from its final verse. It might even be possible to imagine it as originally a piece of freestanding theological poetry which has been transformed into a psalm.

■ What makes this distinctive material a psalm in the first place? There are three indicators of its nature as a psalm. First is its inclusion in the psalter. Second is its heading, *mizmōr lĕʾāsāph*.[6] In light of the LXX rendering of *mizmōr* with *psalmos*, from which we derive our English term "psalm," there is a sense in which a poem headed with *mizmōr* is unarguably a psalm. Relatedly, the linkage with Asaph clearly ties this poem into the liturgical tradition of Israel.[7] The third indicator is Ps. 82's last nine words, its final verse (v. 8), which is explicitly a prayer to God ("Rise up, O God, judge the earth"). The heading and the prayer frame the material as a whole and thereby enable its content to be part of the worship of Israel.

In the remainder of the psalm—i.e., everything in between its heading and conclusion—there is little that is intrinsically psalmic, other than the question "How long . . . ?" in relation to injustice, which is common in psalms of lament. That is, there is no prayer or the recounting of a situation of distress or deliverance that might typically give rise to prayer in the form of lament or praise or thanksgiving. To be sure, the depiction of the divine council, with its account of injustice, does indeed lead to the prayer that concludes the psalm. But this portrayal of the divine council, a council intrinsically inaccessible to any ordinary human being, is unlike any of the recognizable (albeit poetically depicted) situations of life on earth that give rise to prayer elsewhere in the Psalter.

Whether or not one would find persuasive a conjecture about a possibly independent poem being transformed into a psalm is not greatly important, not least because it is impossible either to prove or disprove. For present purposes, the potential value of such a traditio-historical and redactional conjecture lies not in "recovering" some original pre-Psalter *Sitz im Leben* for this account of a divine assembly without its first two and last nine words.

5. For the options, see Anderson, *Psalms*, and Tate, *Psalms 51–100*.

6. *Mizmōr* is a nominal form of the verb *zammēr*, "to sing / make music," and it only appears in the OT in psalm titles as a term for a particular kind of composition.

7. Elsewhere in the OT, Asaph is a Levitical ancestor of singers (Ezra 2:41) and a significant musician appointed by David (1 Chron. 16:5; 2 Chron. 5:12). There is also a collection of psalms associated with Asaph, of which this psalm is a part (Pss. 73–83).

Rather, the point is to gain a greater analytical sharpness for thinking about the psalm as a whole if we recognize the distinctiveness of its introduction and conclusion in relation to its main body, even as they now shape that main body to serve as a basis for prayer. ■

How should this psalm about an assembly of deities, in which all but one of its members are condemned to die, best be understood?

Traditional Christian and Jewish Understandings of Psalm 82

Classic Readings

Interestingly, the classic reading of this psalm among both Jews and Christians for most of their histories is that the psalm is not about an assembly of ancient deities at all. Rather, it is a reminder to all *human* judges of their responsibilities, an admonition to them genuinely to practice justice, and a warning of their accountability to God for faithless failure. For example, John Calvin introduces his commentary on the psalm thus:

> As kings, and such as are invested with authority, through the blindness which is produced by pride, generally take to themselves a boundless liberty of action, the Psalmist warns them that they must render an account at the bar of the Supreme Judge, who is exalted above the highest of this world.[8]

Martin Luther is characteristically expansive:

> These next three verses [i.e., vv. 2–4], indeed the whole psalm, every prince should have painted on the wall of his chamber, on his bed, over his table, and on his garments. For here they find what lofty, princely, noble virtues their estate can practice. . . . For how could one praise this rank more highly than by saying that they are called, and are, gods?[9]

Charles Spurgeon is also eloquent. He introduces his commentary on the psalm with "This poet of the temple [i.e., Asaph] here acts as a preacher to the court and to the magistracy," and his "sermon before the judges is now before us." Judges are called "gods" because God "lends them his name, and this is their authority for acting as judges, but they must take care that they do not misuse the power entrusted to them, for the Judge of judges is in session among them." Thus,

8. Calvin, *Commentary on the Book of Psalms*, 327–28.
9. Luther, *Selected Psalms II*, 51–52.

> judges shall be judged, and to justices justice shall be meted out. Our village squires and country magistrates would do well to remember this. Some of them had need go to school to Asaph till they have mastered this psalm. Their harsh decisions and strange judgments are made in the presence of him who will surely visit them for every unseemly act, for he has no respect unto the person of any, and is the champion of the poor and needy.[10]

On this reading, the demise announced in verses 6–7 refers to human judges being reminded of their mortality and being called to account by God: "The dignity, therefore, with which they are clothed is only temporary, and will pass away with the fashion of the world" (Calvin).[11] "To every judge this verse [v. 7] is a *memento mori*! He must leave the bench to stand at the bar, and on the way must put off the ermine to put on the shroud" (Spurgeon).[12]

Although Calvin, Luther, and Spurgeon are quintessential Protestants, Roman Catholic interpreters do not differ. The famous Old Testament commentary of the seventeenth-century Jesuit Cornelius à Lapide does not extend to the Psalms, but one standard edition of his commentaries includes the Psalms commentary of his fellow Jesuit and contemporary Robert Bellarmine, who summarizes the psalm thus: "The subject of this psalm is an exhortation to judges, that they should judge justly. But to strengthen the exhortation, God is represented as the supreme Judge who reproves lesser judges."[13]

It can come as something of a shock to those who are familiar only with modern biblical commentaries to realize that premodern interpreters generally agreed that human judges were the addressees of Psalm 82[14] and that, as such, neither the sense nor the enduring and vital significance of the psalm was in doubt.

Such a reading is not an evasive or strained construal of the "plain sense" of the Hebrew text. It has two bases which dovetail so as to enable the reading. On the one hand is the characteristic Old Testament understanding that the role of a judge is to be representative of, and accountable to, God. In the epigrammatic formulation of Moses in Deuteronomy, "justice/judgment is God's" (*hammishpāt lēʾlōhīm hūʾ*, Deut. 1:17). However, this divine justice/

10. Spurgeon, *Treasury of David*, 39–40.

11. Calvin, *Commentary on the Book of Psalms*, 335.

12. Spurgeon, *Treasury of David*, 41.

13. "Argumentum huius Psalmi est exhortatio ad Judices, ut juste judicent. Sed ut maiorem efficaciam habeat exhortatio, inducitur Deus summus Judex increpans Judices minores" (Bellarmine, *Commentarii in Scripturam Sacram*, 322 [my translation]).

14. This can be qualified to some extent by ancient Christian interpretation, in which godly humans in general could be called "gods," divine by grace. Material is conveniently collected in Wesselschmidt, *Psalms 51–150*, 145–48.

judgment is mediated by humans. As the Moses of Exodus puts it with regard to his role as judge, "The people come to me to inquire of God . . . and I decide [*vĕshāphattī*] between one person and another, and I make known to them the statutes and instructions of God" (Exod. 18:15–16). Human judges should mediate the justice of God.

On the other hand is a traditional understanding, which originated among Jewish interpreters and was adopted early by Christians, that the Hebrew term for "God/gods," *ʾĕlōhīm*, could sometimes refer to certain exalted humans—namely, judges and kings. (Judges and kings would often be one and the same person, insofar as one of the major responsibilities of an ancient king was the exercise of justice.)[15] This understanding was based on a few specific texts, primarily Exodus 21:6 and 22:8 (Heb. 7), where it was reckoned that *ʾĕlōhīm* actually meant "judges."

Exodus 21:6 specifies that if a slave declines freedom because he loves his master, his wife, and his children, then "his master shall bring him before God [*ʾel hāʾĕlōhīm*]. He shall be brought to the door or the doorpost; and his master shall pierce his ear with an awl; and he shall serve him for life." Similarly, in Exodus 22:8 (Heb. 7) we read, "If the thief is not caught, the owner of the house shall be brought before God [*ʾel hāʾĕlōhīm*], to determine whether or not the owner had laid hands on the neighbor's goods." Bringing a legal issue "before God" was not unreasonably supposed, at least from Targum Onqelos onwards,[16] to envisage bringing the matter before human judges as those who mediate God.[17]

This classic Jewish construal was still well established in the early twentieth century. It is found in Brown, Driver, and Briggs's *Hebrew and English Lexicon of the Old Testament* (BDB), where the first meaning offered for *ʾĕlōhīm* is "*rulers, judges*, either as divine representatives at sacred places or as reflecting divine majesty and power."[18] It is also found in standard commentaries.[19]

15. See, e.g., the archetypal portrayal of Solomon and his prayer for wisdom to judge rightly in 1 Kings 3, where Solomon's elevation to the throne as king (3:6–7) requires most of all that he have wisdom in judging (*shāphat*) Israel (3:9, 11). Equally paradigmatic is Jeremiah's account of Josiah. Unlike his son Jehoiakim, whose priority was a prestige building project enabled by forced labor, Josiah demonstrates the true meaning of kingship through his doing justice and righteousness (Jer. 22:13–16). Alongside the administration of justice, the conduct of warfare was the other prime responsibility of ancient rulers.

16. Onqelos's text reads *dynyy*ʾ, "judges" (Sperber, *Bible in Aramaic*, 123).

17. This is the consensus understanding among the great medieval Jewish commentators. See Carasik, *Commentators' Bible: Exodus*, 170.

18. BDB, 43. There is almost identical wording in Burney, *Outlines of Old Testament Theology*, 15.

19. E.g., Charles Briggs (of BDB fame), in his 1907 International Critical Commentary, says of the *ʾĕlōhīm* in v. 1, "They are the wicked governors of the nations holding Israel in subjection,

And the NRSV still maintains this understanding with its marginal notes to Exodus 21:6 and 22:8 (Heb. 7), "Or *to/before the judges*." Some conservatively and traditionally minded interpreters also offer this interpretation straightforwardly.[20]

The Emergence of an Alternative Modern Reading

Over the course of the twentieth century, however, comparative religio-historical considerations increasingly changed the interpretive frame of reference. It became doubtful that *ʾĕlōhîm* did in fact mean "judge."[21] Although it remains unclear exactly what is envisaged in coming "before God" (*ʾel hāʾĕlōhîm*) in Exodus 21:6 and 22:8 (Heb. 7), the context of these verses sounds more like the home than the city gate, where issues of law and justice would usually be handled.[22] In this light, the *ʾĕlōhîm* are likely sacred objects of some sort, either within the home or perhaps in a sanctuary.[23] They are unlikely to be human judges.[24]

Moreover, as the wider ancient Near Eastern context of origin of the biblical documents has come more clearly into view, scholars have begun to take Psalm 82's depiction of a council of deities at face value. Portrayals of ancient deities in a pantheon have always been known from Homer. But whereas biblical scholars generally used to emphasize the differences and distinctiveness of the biblical material in relation to its wider world of origin, they now tend to emphasize similarities and continuity.[25] The scenario of numerous gods gathered

---

cf. Ez. 28[11–19]. All of these are called gods, because as rulers and judges they reflect the divine majesty of Law and order in government" (*Book of Psalms*, 2:215). Comparable is the construal of *ʾĕlōhîm* as "judges" by that acute (and unpredictable) interpreter, Arnold B. Ehrlich, in *Die Psalmen*, 199–200.

20. So, e.g., Konrad Schaefer comments, "The 'divine council' or 'gods' (v. 1b) are judges or governors who share God's responsibility to administer justice and protect the rights of the downtrodden and defenseless (cf. Exod 21:6; 22:8; 2 Chr 19:5–6)" (*Psalms*, 201).

21. See, e.g., Cyrus H. Gordon, "*ʾlhym* in Its Reputed Meaning of *Rulers, Judges*."

22. See, e.g., Boaz meeting with the elders in the gate (Ruth 4) or Job remembering how he used to go to the city gate, where he sought justice for those in need (Job 29).

23. In a number of ancient cultures, a shrine could be the context for manumission. See Falk, "Exodus XXI:6."

24. In the late twentieth-century *Dictionary of Classical Hebrew* (ed. David J. A. Clines), "judge" is not offered as a possible meaning for *ʾĕlōhîm*. Exodus 21:6 and 22:7 (Eng. 8) are simply listed as examples of *ʾĕlōhîm* following the preposition *ʾel*, with no meaning other than "God" suggested (1:284).

25. Scholarship does not develop in straight lines, and the mid-twentieth-century biblical theology movement laid great emphasis on the distinctiveness of the biblical material. Nonetheless, the tenor of much biblical scholarship in recent years has been in many ways comparable to that of the early twentieth-century *Religionsgeschichtliche Schule*. The dominant emphasis has been on continuities between Israel and its neighbors, and those distinctives that the biblical

in council in Psalm 82 can thus be seen as comparable to the divine assemblies depicted in material from Mesopotamia and Ugarit, Israel's near neighbors.

In light of these developments, it is now generally taken for granted that if Psalm 82 appears to depict a council of deities, then that is what it actually depicts. The judges are divine, not human. Thus, Psalm 82 stands as a parade example of how traditional theological and ecclesial understandings of the biblical text may need to be modified in the light of modern philology and the rediscovery of the world of the ancient Near East from which the Old Testament arose.

■ In terms of philology and history, I share this new consensus understanding that Ps. 82 envisages a gathering of deities. However, it is doubtful whether one should consider the issue entirely settled. There are still occasional voices which argue in favor of seeing the *ʾĕlōhīm* as earthly rulers, and not for the reason that such a construal is traditional and/or theologically fitting. There is at least one passage in the OT in which *ʾĕlōhīm* does seem clearly to envisage a human referent, a king, in a context of poetic panegyric.[26] If one such usage exists, some scholars not unreasonably ask whether there may not be others also. They do so partly because the OT understanding that human judges should mediate the justice of God remains clear, and partly because a reading of *ʾĕlōhīm* as envisaging human kings can make sense in an ancient context. Moses Buttenweiser, for example, sees the Hellenistic period as the original context for Psalm 82, in which a prophet-like psalmist unmasks the pretensions of contemporary rulers: "The author assails the deification of kings in vogue in his day and confesses [in 82:6] that for a time he himself believed in their divine descent. . . . The Jews of Alexander's age shared with the rest of the world the belief in his divine descent."[27] Recently, James Trotter has also made a thorough argument that the *ʾĕlōhīm* who are addressed and doomed to die are human kings who were regarded as divine.[28] ■

Characteristic Contemporary Readings of Psalm 82

If the deities in assembly in Psalm 82 are indeed deities in assembly, how should the psalm be understood? It is now regularly cited as a rare example

documents highlight in their canonical form tend to be seen as late developments that are in significant ways uncharacteristic of ancient Israel's religion for much of its history. Debates and disagreements here are of course not unrelated to differences concerning the purpose for which the biblical text is studied, and differences between focusing on context of origin and on canonical context.

26. This is the use of *ʾĕlōhīm* in Ps. 45:6: "Your throne, *ʾĕlōhīm*, endures forever and ever." In the verses that both precede and follow, a human king is the addressee. Comparable is the use of *ʾēl* ("God") in Isa. 9:6 (Heb. 5), where the referent is a royal figure who will sit on the throne of David.

27. Buttenweiser, *Psalms*, 770.

28. Trotter, "Death of the *ʾlhym* in Psalm 82."

of full-blown myth in the Old Testament and as significant evidence for the indebtedness of Israel's religion to Canaanite influence—that is, that Israel's religion was rooted in polytheism. Plural terms for deity are used in Psalm 82, and a plurality of deities is envisaged. As Jon Levenson succinctly puts it,

> It is by no means certain that the "God" (*'ĕlōhîm*) who takes his stand is the same as the "God" (*'Ēl*) in whose assembly he speaks (v 1), nor is it at all clear that these two are identical to the "Most High" (*'elyôn*) whom v 6 identifies as the father of the gods. In fact, the context is redolent of the polytheism that we see in a scene from a Canaanite poem from not later than about 1400 B.C.E., when mighty Baal takes his stand in the divine assembly and spits in defiance.[29]

The psalm is also generally seen as marking a significant step in the development of Israel's religious thought, though this can be envisaged in more than one way.

There are, I think, two main, and closely related, options in the scholarly literature. First, one can see in Psalm 82 an early Israelite version of the common ancient understanding that different peoples had their own distinct tutelary deities. Scholars regularly associate Psalm 82 with Deuteronomy 32:8–9:

> [8] When the Most High [*'elyōn*] apportioned the nations,
> when he divided humankind,
> he fixed the boundaries of the peoples
> according to the number of the gods;[30]
> [9] the LORD's [*yhwh*] own portion was his people,
> Jacob his allotted share.

This text apparently envisages YHWH as being responsible solely for Jacob/Israel in the way that other deities were apparently responsible for other nations.[31] Thus, scholars commonly find in Psalm 82 a modification or abrogation of Deuteronomy's scenario, in which YHWH now takes to Himself those peoples who hitherto had been allocated to other deities.[32] Such a construal

29. Levenson, *Sinai and Zion*, 61.

30. The NRSV goes with the general scholarly preference for "the gods" (LXX and 4QDeuteronomy) rather than "the Israelites" (MT). It supposes a *Vorlage* of *bĕnē 'ēl* (or *bĕnē 'ēlīm*) instead of *bĕnē yisrā'ēl*; see *BHS* ad loc. Nonetheless, the implication of tutelary deities remains present, whichever reading is adopted.

31. The textual and interpretative problem is helpfully set out in Tigay, *Deuteronomy*, 302–4, 513–18, though Tigay passes over the issue of whether *'elyōn* in Deut. 32:8 might originally have had a referent other than the deity of Israel.

32. See, e.g., Smith, *Origins of Biblical Monotheism*, 156.

has a certain conceptual similarity to the rise of Marduk to supremacy over his fellow deities in *Enuma Elish*. A struggle among the gods is envisaged, albeit in a highly distinctive mode, in Psalm 82: a martial struggle is recast in juridical terms.

The second option is to see a religious development which takes the form of a transition, in some way, from many gods to one. If there was a rejection of the notion of tutelary deities, such a move would have been its natural corollary. But a rejection of many gods in favor of one can make sense on its own terms. As Robert Alter puts it, "One could describe [Ps. 82] as a poem about the transition from mythology to a monotheistic frame of reference because in the end the gods are rudely demoted from their divine status."[33] Or, in Jon Levenson's formulation,

> The psalm that begins with a scene familiar to any student of (polytheistic) Canaanite religion ends with the death of the other gods and the assertion that "God" will take possession of all the nations, whomever it is they worship. Psalm 82 thus opens in polytheism and closes in monotheism.[34]

One might perhaps summarize the difference between these construals as *one over many* or *one instead of many*; or, in convenient but questionable modern categories, it is a matter of either henotheism or monotheism. Either way, perhaps the most interesting point for the historian of religion is that the biblical text preserves the outlines of the older religious outlook that it is rejecting and seeking to replace. The older outlook was preserved because it was amenable to reinterpretation: El and Elyon, which in religio-historical terms can be taken as terms for a supreme Canaanite deity, became terms for YHWH (as is common elsewhere in the OT),[35] while other deities can be reconceived as angelic or human beings. But, in contemporary readings of Psalm 82, the historian of religion penetrates behind such reinterpretation to the putative antecedent and likely original form of thought, which was polytheistic, thereby achieving a richer and more differentiated understanding

33. Alter, *Book of Psalms*, 291.

34. Levenson, *Sinai and Zion*, 62. Elsewhere Levenson fills out the picture in Ps. 82 in a way more akin to Smith, if one allows that "God" and "El" in v. 1 are not necessarily to be identified. Then there is a "striking resemblance" to Marduk's rise to power in the *Enuma Elish* (*Creation and the Persistence of Evil*, 6–7).

35. In Ps. 83, which immediately follows and which is addressed to the *ʾĕlōhîm* who is *yhwh* (83:16, 18 [Heb. 17, 19]), the terms *ʾēl* and *ʿelyôn* are both used as appellations (83:1b, 18b [Heb. 2b, 19b]). Elsewhere, e.g., Josh. 22:22, the people twice exclaim *ʾēl ʾĕlōhîm yhwh*, and the referent is clearly the same for each appellation; also, in Ps. 91:1–2, 9, *ʿelyôn* is an alternative appellation for *yhwh*.

of the development of Israelite religion and its relationship with neighboring cultures in its world of origin.[36]

Towards a Fresh Reading of Psalm 82

So how best might someone who wants to read Israel's scriptures as Christian Scripture read the psalm?

■ I do not propose to discuss NT and patristic interpretations of Ps. 82 in which the "I say, 'You are gods'" of v. 6 plays an important role because of its citation in John 10:33–36. The issues raised by the citation lead into fascinating areas that are nonetheless distinct from the psalm's own concerns. The psalm's content is open to a different use and construal when thus recontextualized; but that is not my present concern.

A good entrée to the scholarly literature is Carl Mosser, "The Earliest Patristic Interpretations of Psalm 82, Jewish Antecedents, and the Origins of Christian Deification." Mosser shows, for example, how Irenaeus read Ps. 82:6 "as a prophecy of the Pauline soteriology of adoption to divine sonship"; Mosser also argues that "the patristic notion of deification represents a remarkable instance of fidelity to the early Jewish roots of Christian belief."[37] See also the comprehensive and illuminating discussion in Christian Gers-Uphaus, *Sterbliche Götter—göttliche Menschen.* ■

Some General Considerations

The main difficulty is self-evident: If human judges recede and an assembly of ancient Near Eastern deities takes their place, how is this scenario meaningful for contemporary Christian thought and practice? A better understanding of the possible development of Israelite monotheism in the ancient world has value in terms of the history of ideas but seems to have little to do with the priorities of constructive thinking and faithful living in the twenty-first century. Patrick Miller, with an eye on the practicalities of Christian preaching, nicely articulates the challenge:

> Psalm 82 is so thoroughly a mythopoeic text, assuming the world of the gods as an operative image, that it is very difficult to translate the claims of the psalm into the language of proclamation. The setting is intimately what it is about. It resists demythologization. A sermon about . . . the assembly of the

36. Uncertainties over the dating of OT texts make religio-historical accounts somewhat provisional. Some of the methodological complexities with reference to Ps. 82 are interestingly set out by Konrad Schmid in his "Gibt es 'Reste hebräischen Heidentums' im Alten Testament?"

37. Mosser, "Earliest Patristic Interpretations," 73.

gods may be possible, but there are inherent obstacles to [it] as the subject of preaching.[38]

There is also a further difficulty, lesser but not insignificant: Is it possible to retain the significance of the poem as a poem? The psalm's possibly substantive point about divine justice—the direction which most Christian commentators take—may easily be considered more or less independently from the specific imagery of the psalm and the dramatic movement within it. So there is a further question about holding together, in one way or another (if at all), form and content, the medium and the message.

In general terms, there are issues related to one's interests and concerns in the biblical text, as in my typology of reading the text as ancient history, as cultural classic, or as holy Scripture. *How* we read the text relates to *why* we read it. A Christian theologian is likely to make conceptual moves different from those of the historian of religion. A theologian who inhabits a living Christian or Jewish tradition may reasonably have a predisposition to work with those voices and understandings that have been preserved and privileged by the tradition. That is, a theologian may be inclined to go *with* the flow of the text—and see what existential and conceptual possibilities are opened up by the mature understandings represented in the received form of Israel's canonical texts—rather than go *against* the flow so as to recover possible earlier understandings that may have been deliberately displaced and obscured. So, for example, even if the original scenario of Psalm 82 envisaged YHWH as one deity among others in the council of the distinct and supreme Canaanite deity El—the material is certainly open to being read thus—the poem as recontextualized in the Psalter in the wider context of Israel's scriptures reads differently. "El" and "Elyon" become epithets for YHWH, who is the sovereign deity in whose council the other deities gather. Of course, theologians can still learn from historians of religion and approach the biblical text with greater historical and conceptual nuance as a result, discerning better what are appropriate and inappropriate inferences to make.

■ Reasons for reading against the grain of the canonical text can be varied. As already outlined, a characteristic modern concern has been to recover a sharper understanding

38. Miller, "Old Testament and Christian Faith," 656. Characteristically, Miller does not leave the issue there but goes on to tackle the problem in terms that resonate with my own proposal here: "What *Psalm 82* makes radically clear and unequivocal is that [divine] power is in behalf of *just* rule, that the divine world, indeed the whole cosmos, stands or falls over the maintenance of justice for the weak and poor of the earth. The claim to deity is in effect a claim that the universe has a moral character to it, that God is the righteous ground of history and its end" (657).

of the development of Israelite religion. Further, in recent years there has been a growth in ideological critiques of the biblical text. Here the primary concern is often to combat what are perceived to be problematic and oppressive effects of the biblical text when its content is treated as religiously authoritative in the contemporary world. Debates over violence, gender, and sexuality have become extensive. There is also sometimes a more general moral concern to read against the grain so as to recover the voices of the marginalized—to attend to the "losers" as well as the "winners" in past controversies. These are all concerns that need to be heeded and taken seriously by those who inhabit the continuing traditions of faith.

Nonetheless, sometimes it is perhaps too easily forgotten that at least some of the biblical writers themselves, and those about whom they write, may have been the minority voices in their original context. Jeremiah is self-confessedly a minority voice during his lifetime. Yet the fact that such minority voices, and not other voices from their time, have been preserved and privileged attests to a substantive, and probably long-term, process of moral and spiritual discernment on the part of those responsible for the canonical collection. This process of discernment seeks a deeper understanding of God's priorities than would be reached by attending primarily to majority views, the wielding of power, or successful outcomes; and such discernments have been found truthful and life-giving in the continuing religious traditions. ■

Textual Clues Towards a Fresh Reading

The springboard for my reading of Psalm 82 is the observation of two silences or absences in the text. The first is the lack of any language for, or apparent interest in, the one or the many in relation to the divine realm. There is no use of *ʾeḥād* ("one") or *rabbîm* ("many"). To be sure, the Old Testament's regular idiomatic epithet for deities other than YHWH is not *rabbîm* ("many") but *ʾăḥērîm* ("other"). It is not their plurality on which emphasis is laid, but the fact that they are not-YHWH: they are *other*. But *ʾăḥērîm* is not used in the psalm either. Rather, its consistent interest throughout is in the matter of justice in relation to the divine realm.[39] Not the number of the gods but the moral content of their practice is the psalm's concern.

The second absence is the name of Israel's deity, YHWH. For both of the history-of-religious-thought accounts outlined above—YHWH becoming either supreme deity or sole deity—this is prima facie a puzzling problem. The divine name *ought* to be the psalm's first word (after the heading), as the logic of the psalm, when read in these terms, requires it: "*YHWH* takes a stand," rather than the actual wording of the text, "*God* takes a stand."[40]

39. Neither noun of the common pairing *mishpāt* ("justice") and *tsĕdāqāh* ("righteousness") is used. But this is incidental rather than significant; verbal forms of each root are used, as are other terms in the same semantic domain.

40. It would also seem appropriate to appeal to YHWH by name in the concluding prayer in v. 8.

However, the puzzle has a ready solution—namely, the argument that the original proper name in the Hebrew text, *yhwh*, has been changed into the generic term for deity, *ʾĕlōhīm*, by an editor.[41] This supposition is not simply a matter of appealing to the internal logic of the psalm in its supposed religio-historical context, but is based also on the location of Psalm 82 within the "Elohistic Psalter" (Pss. 42–83).[42] Here, contrary to the predominant usage elsewhere in the Psalter, *ʾĕlōhīm* is preferred to *yhwh*, and there is reason to suppose that at least sometimes *ʾĕlōhīm* may have displaced an original *yhwh*.[43] The critical judgment that an original *yhwh* has been replaced by *ʾĕlōhīm* in Psalm 82:1a is, as far as I can see, considered secure and uncontroversial—so much so that Hans-Joachim Kraus in his major commentary actually inserts the divine name into his translation of the text in both verse 1 and verse 8.[44] The displacement of an original *yhwh* in favor of *ʾĕlōhīm* is certainly a possibility.

Nonetheless, I wish to take seriously the fact that the generic term for deity stands in the text rather than the proper name of Israel's deity.[45] No doubt this is in part because of my general predisposition to work with the received text that we actually have rather than a putative original that has no known reading or reception.[46] But there is warrant also in the fact that the Old Testament often prefers the generic *ʾĕlōhīm* over the Israel-specific *yhwh* for conceptual reasons.[47] In Genesis 1 the use of the generic *ʾĕlōhīm* seems to be related to the chapter's depiction of the entire world as the creation of the one God, from whom all receive and to whom all are in some way accountable. In this depiction the focus is consistently on the world as a whole, and the

41. Thus, typically, Anderson: "We should probably read 'Yahweh' (*yhwh*), which must have been changed into 'God' (*ʾelohim*) by the Elohistic editor" (*Psalms*, 2:593).

42. Standard introductions to the Psalter set out the evidence; see, e.g., Anderson, *Psalms*, 1:25. There is a fresh discussion in Zevit, *Religions of Ancient Israel*, 675–79.

43. The parade example is a comparison of Pss. 14 and 53, which are effectively doublets. In three clear instances Ps. 53 reads *ʾĕlōhīm* where Ps. 14 reads *yhwh*. Of course, it is not inconceivable that an original *ʾĕlōhīm* has been replaced by *yhwh* rather than vice versa. Comparisons elsewhere, however, show that *yhwh* in an old text (Num. 10:35; Judg. 5:4–5) has become *ʾĕlōhīm* in Ps. 68:1, 8 (Heb. 2, 9).

44. Kraus, *Psalms 60–150*, 153–54.

45. To the best of my knowledge, the most significant recent dissenter from the scholarly consensus about an original *yhwh* is Peter Machinist, who argues that "*ʾelohim* is the key term of Psalm 82," in that the recurrent double usage, referring both to the God of Israel / *ʾĕlōhīm* and to the other gods/*ʾĕlōhīm* in the divine council, together with the play on this duality, "tie[s] the text together" ("How Gods Die," 194). There are significant affinities between my reading of the psalm and Machinist's.

46. I think that judgments about textual emendation in relation to reading the text as Scripture should be made on a case-by-case basis.

47. It is arguably the case that sometimes *ʾĕlōhīm* may in effect function as a proper name.

people of Israel and their location in the world are not even mentioned, let alone privileged.[48] This portrayal differs from Genesis 2's creation account, in which *ʾĕlōhīm* is now qualified by *yhwh*; in this account there are numerous subtle resonances with the particularities of Israel.[49] Relatedly, biblical writers often use *ʾĕlōhīm* instead of *yhwh* when they depict non-Israelites as those who can have, or at least ought to have, some genuine knowledge of the one God. For Israel, the one God is known as YHWH, as is foundationally depicted in Exodus 3.[50] When the biblical writers recognize that other peoples' knowledge of God is not conceived in terms of God as *yhwh*, the generic *ʾĕlōhīm* becomes the appropriate term.

This conceptual difference between *ʾĕlōhīm* and *yhwh* is most commonly observed in the distinction between "fear of God" (*yirʾat ʾĕlōhīm*) and "fear of the LORD" (*yirʾat yhwh*). The former is consistently used when speaking of appropriate response to God on the part of non-Israelites.[51] On the one hand, this distinction means that Israel's knowledge of God has a particular content, which is fuller and more demanding than that of other nations. On the other hand, because "fear of God" lacks the specific content of Israel's knowledge of God, it may be helpful in many contexts not to construe it narrowly or too religiously, but rather to read it as a term for what we today would call following one's conscience.[52] "Fear of God" generally envisages a moral awareness that constrains human behavior in the absence of human sanction or redress. It is expected of all humans, both non-Israelites and Israelites, and is part of their humanity in a world created by, and accountable to, God. Having a conscience is constitutive of being human.

■ Some examples of OT usage of "fear of God" include Abraham, who supposed that he might be killed by Abimelech's people because of their lack of fear of God (Gen.

48. The difference from *Enuma Elish*, which culminates in the primacy of Babylon under Marduk, is striking. The wider pentateuchal context, however, sets things in a different light, since the construction of the tabernacle at the end of Exodus has verbal resonances with Gen. 1's creation account. This may suggest that Israel's worship in the tabernacle is in some sense a goal of creation (see Levenson, *Creation and the Persistence of Evil*, esp. part 2).

49. Influential has been Wenham, "Sanctuary Symbolism in the Garden of Eden Story." The notion that Eden has strong resonances with Israel's tabernacle/temple has become widely accepted. See, e.g., Held, *Heart of Torah*, 191–92.

50. See ch. 2 of the present book.

51. The distinction is not entirely consistent in that sometimes within the context of Israel the terminology is also "fear of God" (*yirʾat ʾĕlōhīm*), as in Moses' interpretation of the Ten Commandments to Israel (Exod. 20:20).

52. For suggestive recognitions that "fear of God" in some way corresponds to a notion of conscience, see, e.g., Weinfeld, *Deuteronomy and the Deuteronomistic School*, 274–81; Cox, "Fear or Conscience?"; Fox, *Proverbs 1–9*, 70–71.

20:11). Since Abraham was a *gēr* ("immigrant," 20:1)[53] in Abimelech's territory, he lacked the supportive network of kin to protect or avenge him, and so he could easily be victimized and disposed of. But the story highlights Abimelech's moral responsiveness when God speaks to him; thus, Abraham's supposition that there was no fear of God in Gerar was mistaken. Joseph, speaking to his unrecognizing brothers as a supposed Egyptian, appeals to his fear of God as a reason why his brothers need not be afraid that he will maltreat them (Gen. 42:18). In Israel's legislation, to mock the deaf or trip the blind, both of which could be done with seeming impunity, are prohibited since they would constitute an absence of fear of God—i.e., a lack of appropriate moral restraint that comes from a sense of accountability to God (Lev. 19:14). Even the Amalekites (who are the most problematic people in the OT)[54] were seen as capable of displaying the fear of God and are reprobated precisely because they picked off the weak and vulnerable among Israel in the wilderness and thereby did not display such fear (Deut. 25:18).

Another good narrative example is the exemplary repentance of the Ninevites in the book of Jonah, in which they turn to *ʾĕlōhîm*, not *yhwh* (Jon. 3:5–10). The writer conveys that they are truly turning to God because they are repenting, even while they still do not know God as Israel knows God. So they are not "converting," and they remain within their own religious frame of reference. By contrast, the sailors earlier in the story are indeed portrayed as embracing Israel's knowledge of God. Although initially each cries to his god (1:5), they subsequently pray, make a sacrifice, and offer vows specifically to the LORD (1:14, 16). They do "convert," presumably because of the combination of Jonah's words (1:9–10) and the following sequence of events. ■

My proposal, therefore, is that the *ʾĕlōhîm* of Psalm 82:1a is intrinsically meaningful and that the psalm is an exercise in defining the meaning of this term.[55] Or in other words, to put it in unashamedly contemporary categories, I suggest that the psalm can well be read as a conceptual analysis of what is, and is not, meant by the term *ʾĕlōhîm*.[56] This analysis, however, is conveyed in imaginatively concrete form rather than in a theoretical or abstract mode, for this is the biblical writers' preferred way of doing theology.

53. For a discussion of the best translation of *gēr*, see ch. 6, 214n36.

54. See Jon Levenson's searching essay "Is There a Counterpart in the Hebrew Bible to New Testament Anti-Semitism?"

55. Definitions of "god" as offered by ancient historians tend to be phenomenologically descriptive with limited theological content. M. West, for example, interestingly says, "I will define a god (and gods, of course, embrace goddesses) as an entity identified or postulated, by one or more members of the species *homo sapiens*, as a wilful agent possessing or exercising power over events that appear to be beyond human control or not governed by other intelligible agencies" ("Towards Monotheism," 21).

56. Peter Machinist also argues that "Psalm 82 is ultimately about the meaning of the term *ʾelohim*." He further contends that Ps. 82 shows "religion in the making: the making of monotheism, which involves nothing less than a restructuring of the cosmic order" ("How Gods Die," 232, 235). His account is more oriented to the developmental history of religious thought than is mine.

A Fresh Reading of Psalm 82

The poem's imaginative scenario unfolds in four parts.

A Psalm of Asaph.[57]

> [1] God [*ʾĕlōhīm*] has taken his stand [*nitstsāv*] in the divine council;
> in the midst of the gods [*ʾĕlōhīm*] he pronounces judgment.[58] (Ps. 82:1)

The poem envisages a divine assembly (*ʿădat ʾēl*)[59] in which one particular deity (*ʾĕlōhīm*) takes a stand among other deities (*ʾĕlōhīm*). Insofar as it is appropriate to infer the purpose of the assembly from the verb used to depict the action of the deity taking a stand, "pronounces judgment" (*yishpōt*), then this assembly of rulers is gathered with reference to that prime activity of ancient rulers, the judicial exercise of judgment for the purpose of enacting justice. The assembly is imagined by analogy with typical human assemblies in which people gather and someone stands up and speaks. In this case, however, the rulers are divine rather than human.

■ There is a question about the symbolic significance of "standing." In particular, does it imply either precedence (standing over others) or subordination (since a figure of authority might sit and preside over proceedings, as kings and judges from general antiquity, and bishops from late antiquity, have done)?[60] Certainly, it is the normal posture of a judge to sit while others stand, just as "Moses sat as judge for the people, while the people stood around him" (Exod. 18:13). James Trotter, for example, makes much of this and argues that "Psalm 82 depicts the council of El with Yahweh standing among the other gods in the presence of the seated El."[61] However, there is no reference to El or anyone else being seated (*yāshav*); and, for reasons already given, I am disinclined to read *ʾēl* as the distinct deity El. I find persuasive the scenario imagined by Matitiahu Tsevat: "What might normally be a routine assembly, where the gods report or participate in deliberations, has

57. The possible interpretive significance of the Asaph collection of psalms (Pss. 73–83) will not be discussed here. A suggestive reading of Ps. 82 in canonical context as part of the psalms of Asaph, with many resonances with the reading I offer here, is Gers-Uphaus, "Gott als wahrer *elohim* und Retter der Armen." He observes that the Tetragrammaton is used in every other Asaph psalm, from Ps. 50:1 to Ps. 83:19, with Ps. 82 as the sole Asaph psalm lacking it. He sees this as most likely indicative of a strategy of depicting YHWH as the only true deity (see esp. p. 43).

58. I make various emendations to the NRSV. "Take his stand" is better than "take his place" because the difference between standing and sitting can be interpretively significant.

59. A natural construal of *ʾēl* within the literary/canonical context of the OT is as a generic term for deity, akin to *ʾĕlōhīm*. This is also the LXX rendering—*en sunagōgē theōn*—though conceivably the Greek translators had a different *Vorlage* (e.g., *ʾēlīm*).

60. One might perhaps see university professors and their chairs as a more recent addition to the list.

61. Trotter, "Death of the *ʾlhym* in Psalm 82," 228.

unexpectedly turned into a tribunal; God has stood up to judge the assembled."[62] Trotter resists this reading on the grounds that Tsevat can cite no precise parallel in extant biblical texts (though Isa. 3:13 comes closer than Trotter wants to allow).[63] Yet the scenario is so common an occurrence in human assemblies that its plausibility does not require precise extant parallels. Thus I am inclined to think that the deity standing to speak has no special symbolic significance. Either way, I do not think that the issue makes any substantive difference to my reading. ■

The relationship between the *ʾĕlōhīm* who takes a stand and the other *ʾĕlōhīm* is not specified. However, the *ʾĕlōhīm* in the second part of the verse are plural, as one can stand "in their midst,"[64] while the deity who takes a stand is singular, as indicated by the form of the verb "take a stand" (*nitstsāv*). The deity taking a stand is thus implicitly the deity of Israel, YHWH, in line with the regular (though not invariable) idiom of the Hebrew scriptures in which YHWH is depicted by singular verbs and adjectives while "other" deities are depicted with plural verbs and adjectives.[65] This idiomatic distinction justifies the English rendering of the first *ʾĕlōhīm* with a capital letter (God) and of the further *ʾĕlōhīm* in lowercase (gods/divine beings).

Who are these other members of the divine assembly? Interestingly, we are not told. One could easily imagine the poet lining up deities from Israel's neighbors—say, Dagon, Chemosh, and Baal—to make a polemical point about their demotion or demise.[66] But the presentation of the assembly is generalized and anonymous (as is often the case with "other gods"). The silence about their identities suggests that the poem's concern is generic: it is about "other gods" as such rather than specific deities.

If the poet is able to depict what happens in this divine assembly, then he himself is implicitly in some way present and thus able to describe what he sees and hears.[67] In other words, the poet is imagining himself to be Moses or one of the prophets. In Deuteronomy's memorable portrayal, Moses is given the weighty responsibility to draw so near to the LORD that he can

62. Tsevat, "God and the Gods in Assembly," 127.

63. Trotter, "Death of the *ʾlhym* in Psalm 82," 226.

64. Interestingly, the LXX reads *ʾĕlōhīm* as the object of the verb "judge": *en mesō de theous diakrinei* (not *en mesō theōn*). The overall scenario does not differ.

65. Good examples are the plural adjective and verb on the lips of the Philistines (1 Sam. 4:8) and the plural verb on the lips of Jezebel (1 Kings 19:2). Two exceptions are the idiom for YHWH as "living God" (*ʾĕlōhīm hayyīm*, not *hay*; so Deut. 5:26; 1 Sam. 17:26) and the plural *shōphĕtīm* with *ʾĕlōhīm*, with apparent reference to YHWH, in Ps. 58:12 (Eng. 11).

66. E.g., Astarte, Milcom, Chemosh, and Molech are all enumerated as recipients of Solomon's misguided worship (1 Kings 11:5–8).

67. A prime analogy elsewhere in the OT is the presence of Daniel at the divine court of justice in Dan. 7, which is presented as the content of a dream.

hear the LORD's words and thereby instruct Israel (Deut. 5:22–31, esp. 27–28, 31). This paradigmatic portrayal of the role of a prophet is reflected in the prophetic books in references to the prophet standing in the "council" of the LORD.[68] The point is that proximity to the LORD enables a knowledge of the LORD's will, imaginatively depicted in Psalm 82 in terms of overhearing the pronouncements of a divine king to his courtiers gathered in council. When the poet writes what he sees and hears and it is preserved and made available to others, then we too, as subsequent readers, are given access to this scenario.

Put differently, the implications of the psalm's literary genre are crucial for its right reading. Why does the poet portray a heavenly scenario? If one thinks of contemporary analogies—say, accounts of conversations with St. Peter at the Pearly Gates, or wry accounts of the surprising discoveries that certain people make when they get to heaven—the point is clear. Heavenly scenarios refract and impact mundane realities; the situation "up there" is described to make a difference to what people think and do "down here." What God says about the gods in the heavenly setting is spoken aloud for the benefit of those whom the poet enables to hear what is said. That is, everything is for the benefit of the ordinary person who is located in the context of everyday life.

■ I am proposing that there is no need to see the psalm as rooted in an actual vision. An actual vision is, of course, possible. As John Goldingay puts it, "The psalm does not tell us what occasion it refers to. My working assumption is that it relates a visionary experience that the psalmist had."[69] This makes sense. Nonetheless, the psalm is fully meaningful as a dramatic scenario in which the poet is taking the well-known notion of an assembly of the gods and using it imaginatively to make a point.

I am persuaded that the other two OT portrayals of a divine assembly also function in precisely this way. This function is widely recognized with regard to the divine assembly depicted in Job 1:6–12 and 2:1–6, which give the reason and meaning of what happens to Job on earth.[70] The genre and purpose of Micaiah ben Imlah's famous vision in 1 Kings 22:19–23, in which a lying spirit is commissioned to deceive Ahab, is more controverted. Micaiah indeed had a vision whose warning content, in relation to the king's desire to go to war over Ramoth-gilead, he had already conveyed to the king (1 Kings 22:17). But the king did not want to listen, even though this was a matter of life and death. So there is a good case for seeing Micaiah's second "vision" in vv. 19–23 as a persuasive, imaginative rhetorical construct, an attempt to break through the king's hardness of heart, akin to Nathan's parable to David in 2 Sam. 12:1–7. The fact that Micaiah failed to dissuade Ahab from going to battle should not obscure the skill and seriousness of his attempt.[71] ■

68. See further Moberly, *Prophecy and Discernment*, 5–10, 73–75.

69. Goldingay, *Old Testament Theology*, 2:57.

70. See my *Old Testament Theology*, 244–61.

71. See my "Does God Lie to His Prophets?," esp. 8–12; or my *Prophecy and Discernment*, 109–29, esp. 116–20.

Now that the scene is set, weighty words are spoken.

> [2] "How long will you judge unjustly
> and show partiality to the wicked?
> [3] Give justice to the weak and the orphan;
> maintain the right of the lowly and the destitute.
> [4] Rescue the weak and the needy;
> deliver them from the hand of the wicked." (Ps. 82:2–4)

Here and subsequently, there is a question about who is speaking, as there is no formal speech introduction (*wayyōmer*). Some interpreters find a human voice here, speaking in prophetic mode. This makes sense.[72] However, I am inclined to go with the natural contextual inference that these are the words of the God who has taken a stand to pronounce judgment on the other deities present. Little, however, hangs on the issue.

Verses 2–4 begin with a rhetorical question making clear that the subject matter of the gathering is injustice and corruption. The deities addressed are implicitly seen as entangled in, or representative of, corrupt human power dynamics. This opening question is followed by four imperatives which prescribe behavior that is the opposite of injustice and corruption. These imperatives come in two pairs.[73] The first pair relate specifically to what those in positions of power in a court of law should do: judge (*shiphtū*) and vindicate (*hatsdīqū*). The second pair of imperatives, while still applicable to practices in a law court, could readily refer also to actions in situations of oppression or danger in life generally: rescue (*pallĕtū*) and deliver (*hatstsīlū*). The recipients of these actions are those who are poor and vulnerable, those whose life situation is diminished and under threat, as expressed by the repeated key word "wretched" (*dal*).[74]

Psalm 82:2–4 is thus a prime expression of the characteristic Old Testament understanding of justice. The critical test of justice is its practice in contexts not only where there is great human need but also where there is little or no social or financial benefit for the judge. If justice is practiced here, it will also be readily practiced elsewhere. In a different idiom, this can be seen as an Old Testament formulation of a preferential option for the poor.

72. John Goldingay, for example, offers a meaningful reading in which a prophetic voice speaks throughout the psalm (*Psalms 42–89*, 559, 563, 568).

73. In the MT the imperatives neatly balance each other as the first and last words of each pair of clauses.

74. Some have proposed emending the first occurrence of *dal* with *dak* ("crushed")—so *BHS* ad loc.—probably because the repetition of *dal* is less poetic than the use of different terms, and so the repetition indicates possible textual corruption. I note, however, that the *BHS* editor offers no ancient textual variant to support this proposal. The overall sense is unaffected either way.

Suddenly, the focus changes. In place of strong words, a pitiable scene is sketched.

> [5] They have neither knowledge nor understanding,
> they walk around in darkness;
> all the foundations of the earth are shaken. (Ps. 82:5)

This third part of the poem is initially difficult, as it is again unclear who is speaking. The identity of the "they" is also unclear. Although God could still be the speaker,[75] I propose that we should hear the voice of the poet interjecting a comment in response to the scene just described, momentarily shifting away from the divine assembly—implicitly located in the celestial realm—to a brief glimpse of life on earth. The referent of "they" is usually taken to be the gods of the previous verses. If so, this brief moment of vision would be a redescription of the deities who are gathered in assembly, to show that their reality is that they ignorantly blunder in darkness.[76] Yet the point of the two verses that follow is precisely to offer a redescription of the deities and their reality, so a redescription here in verse 5 would surely be premature. Rather, "they" can well be read as the poor, the victims of these deities' malpractice.[77] The picture of incomprehension, bleakness, and life on earth being utterly unstable well portrays the existential situation of the needy and vulnerable when justice is denied them.[78] But whatever one's decision about the precise referent of the verse, on any reading we briefly see something of the dire consequences when corruption displaces justice. As Robert Alter puts it, "The perversion of justice is the first step toward the apocalypse."[79]

We now come to the poem's dramatic climax.

75. If God is still speaking to the other deities, the use of the third person rather than the second is awkward. Curiously, the NEB resolves this awkwardness by silently (i.e., with no marginal note) emending the text to second person.

76. For example, the exact Hebrew wording for "they have neither knowledge nor understanding" is used of idols in Isa. 44:18, which could support a reading of the deities as the referent here. Along similar lines, in personal correspondence Jon Levenson has suggested a possible linkage with Ps. 115:2–8. He notes that in each case there is language of invective against the falseness of other gods—in Ps. 115 their lack of understanding and vision, in Ps. 82 their indifference to justice and the fate of the vulnerable. The tottering of the earth in 82:5 would then introduce the following divine speech and would have to do with the momentousness of God's pronouncing judgment on the would-be gods. The imagery is open to this reading, even if I am inclined to read otherwise.

77. The antecedent of "they" could also be the immediately preceding "wicked" of v. 4, which also yields a meaningful reading; thus Goldingay, *Psalms 42–89*, 565–66.

78. Brent Strawn compellingly makes the case that the primary referent of v. 5 is most likely the oppressed ("Poetics of Psalm 82").

79. Alter, *Book of Psalms*, 292.

[6] "I had taken you for [*ʾănī ʾāmartī*] gods [*ʾĕlōhīm*],
children of the Most High, all of you;
[7] but [*ʾākēn*] you shall die like mortals,
and fall like any prince." (Ps. 82:6–7)[80]

Remarkably, here we have a kind of *Götterdämmerung*, a twilight of the gods. Yet it is an unusual vision. Although the notion of one god being superior to, defeating, or even killing other gods is common in ancient Mediterranean religions, the notion that one deity should deny divine status to other supposed deities appears to be unprecedented.[81] This reshaping of heavenly conflict is peculiar to the Old Testament.

The precise tenor of these remarkable words is easily missed. Some translators, perhaps unduly swayed by the judicial scenario in the psalm as a whole, find here that God is pronouncing a judicial verdict on the other gods:

- "This is my sentence: Gods you may be . . . yet you shall die." (NEB)
- "I hereby declare, 'You are gods. . . . But you will die.'" (CEB)
- "Now I declare: Indeed you are gods. . . . Nevertheless, you will die."[82]
- "I even declare it, You are gods. . . . Nevertheless, you will die."[83]

Although this reading makes sense, this is not the precise meaning of these words. Rather, the poem utilizes a specific and not-uncommon Hebrew idiom: the use of *ʾănī ʾāmartī* ("I said / thought / had taken you for") followed by *ʾākēn* ("but in fact"). This idiom expresses an initial faulty understanding of something that appeared to the speaker to be the case that is subsequently corrected by a better and more accurate realization. The sense of the idiom is not a judicial verdict but the correction of a mistaken supposition about something initially plausible.[84]

■ Examples of the idiom are clear. The Isaianic servant at one point supposed (*vaʾănī ʾāmartī*) that he had labored in vain but then realizes that in fact (*ʾākēn*) his rightness and the value of his cause are secure in God's hands (Isa. 49:4). The psalmist's initial supposition (*vaʾănī ʾāmartī*) that he had been removed from God's sight is corrected by

80. The NRSV lacks quotation marks at the beginning of v. 6 and presumably takes the speaking voice to be that of the psalmist. I take the speaking voice to be God, as in vv. 2–4, and so have added quotation marks at the outset.

81. So also Miller, "God and the Gods," 365–96, esp. 387–88.

82. Thus Hossfeld and Zenger, *Commentary on Psalms 51–100*, 328–29.

83. Terrien, *Psalms*, 588.

84. My preferred translation, "I had taken you for," follows the NJPS in its recognition of the idiom.

the realization that in fact (*ʾākēn*) the LORD has heard his prayer (Ps. 31:23 [Eng. 22]). The LORD's initial supposition (*vĕʾānōkī ʾāmartī*) that His relationship with His people would be good and strong is corrected by the realization that in fact (*ʾākēn*) Israel is faithless (Jer. 3:19–20). Elihu initially supposed (*ʾāmartī*) that age would bring wisdom, but in fact (*ʾākēn*) understanding is a gift of God (Job 32:7–8). The LORD's initial supposition (*ʾāmartī*) that a chastised Jerusalem would renew its fear of Him is corrected by the realization that (*ʾākēn*) the people's eagerness for corrupt practice is undiminished (Zeph. 3:7).

The idiom is clearly set out in BDB, s.v. *ʾākēn*, and was lucidly analyzed a century ago in a well-known article by K. Budde.[85] Despite the clear usage of the idiom, it is dismaying that some translators and interpreters do not recognize its presence and significance in Ps. 82. Marvin Tate, for example, observes that the number of occurrences is "limited" and finds its precise meaning "debatable" because he focuses on the secondary (indeed, irrelevant) issue of whether *ʾāmartī* means "said" or "thought."[86] Remarkably, Frank Hossfeld and Erich Zenger, with no philological discussion (though the Budde article is in their bibliography), dismiss the possibility of a specific idiom here as "most improbable" (*am unwahrscheinlichsten*) and prefer "reading the formula as a solemn introduction to the discourse," the making of a formal pronouncement of the termination of the arrangement envisaged in Deut. 32:8–9.[87] Of course, semantic decisions and interpretive judgments mutually interact. Nonetheless, I find it hard to resist the impression that a decision about what is appropriate to this judicial scenario, what the text "must" mean, has been allowed to overrule attentiveness to what the Hebrew idiom in fact means. ■

Let me offer an analogy. In the UK, Jimmy Savile was once thought to be not only a great entertainer but also a fine, albeit eccentric, philanthropist. He had prime-time television shows for many years, raised money for charities, and "fixed it" for people, especially children, in need.[88] For his contributions to society he received formal recognition and honor through a knighthood and also a papal medal. But the posthumous discovery of his extensive and degraded sexual exploitation of others has led to his disgrace and his becoming a byword for corrupt sexual predation. I, as a member of the general public, once supposed (*ʾănī ʾāmartī*) that Jimmy Savile was one of the great and good; but in fact (*ʾākēn*) he was a cunning pervert.

The faulty supposition in Psalm 82 is that those gathered in the assembly really are *ʾĕlōhīm* (deities). But, in fact, they are not, because of the injustice they do. This does not mean that instead of being *ʾĕlōhīm* they are *ʾādām* (humans). Rather, they are no different from, no better than, *ʾādām*—either humanity generically or the particular figure Adam—in that they will suffer

85. Budde, "Ps. 82 6f."
86. Tate, *Psalms 51–100*, 330.
87. Hossfeld and Zenger, *Commentary on Psalms 51–100*, 329, 334–35.
88. There was a long-running TV show, "Jim'll Fix It."

that defining human fate, death, which comes even to the noblest of humans, such as princes. The poet is not really interested in whether this death will come soon (perhaps as a sentence of death to be carried out directly) or at some unspecified time in the future (possibly as a consequence of immortality being replaced by mortality). Rather, the fact that they will die demonstrates their true nature—that they are not *ʾĕlōhîm*, as initially supposed—for immortality is clearly integral to the conceptuality of *ʾĕlōhîm*.

Why should it have been supposed that these other members of the divine assembly were *ʾĕlōhîm* in the first place? It is not easy to find good conceptual categories here, not least because of a modern tendency to see issues of metaphysics and ontology as integral to discussions about the possible reality of God and gods. I suggest that the reason is essentially phenomenological and pragmatic. In other words, there simply *were* many *ʾĕlōhîm* in Israel's world, deities to whom people looked in prayer and hope, deities whose cult was observed in a way that gave identity and order to their worshipers, deities who were expected to give people victory over their enemies. (To avoid misunderstanding: this is not a claim about metaphysical ontology, but about the way life was lived and experienced.) If this was Israel's world, and Israel with its God existed in its midst, then it would have been meaningful for an Israelite poet to project this world imaginatively into the heavenly realm and envisage these deities as constituting a divine assembly among whom Israel's God was also present.

What, then, follows from God being the determinative figure in this assembly and recognizing that these others who were supposed to be deities are not really so? On the one hand, in relation to literary genre, it surely displays a distinctly wooden handling of the text to worry about implicit limitations within God and ask a question such as, "Is it likely that Yahweh would have been fooled in his judgment about the true nature of the gods?"[89] All sorts of things are dramatically possible in an enacted scenario that is making a point. In dramatic terms, what matters is what the onlookers/listeners need to know—in this instance, what they need to know about those they have taken to be gods.

89. Thus Tate, *Psalms 51–100*, 338; cf. 330. Even more forceful is Alastair Hunter (admittedly in a section of his discussion of the psalm entitled "Deconstructive Readings"): "What do we find there but the omnipotent God who used to think these ignoramuses were gods! What kind of 'God' is this who cannot tell the difference between fools and deities? Is this a God who learns from his/her mistakes? But can we tolerate belief in a God about whom we cannot even be sure that he/she has reached full maturity?" (*Psalms*, 170). It is notable that, besides Ps. 82:6–7, two other uses of the idiom for correction of the speaker's initial faulty supposition have the LORD as their speaker (Jer. 3:19–20; Zeph. 3:7). The biblical writers appear to have been more relaxed about religious language and imaginative scenarios than some moderns.

On the other hand, in conceptual terms, the presence of the other deities in the divine assembly would lead one to assume that they would be responsible rulers, concerned with the practice of justice. The appropriate inference from their corruption and failure to practice justice is that they were not really deities at all. They may have *appeared* to be so, for many possible reasons; but the critical test showing that their divinity is only apparent and not real is their lack of moral integrity, as evidenced by their unconcern for justice. The correlative logic of the scene is that the *ʾĕlōhīm* who pronounces this judgment about the others is thereby appropriately understood to be a God of justice and integrity, not incidentally but constitutively: this *ʾĕlōhīm* would not be God unless justice and integrity were essential to His nature. The poem is thus, in its own way, a conceptual analysis of the nature of deity.

One good intertext for this psalm (besides Deut. 32:8–9) might be Deuteronomy 10:17–19, which initially presents YHWH as the sovereign deity in a way that does not deny but rather relativizes all other deities: "For the LORD your God is God supreme and Lord supreme [lit., "the God of gods and the Lord of lords"], the great, the mighty, and the awesome God." How is God's sovereign power made known? "The awesome God . . . shows no favor and takes no bribe, but upholds the cause of the fatherless and the widow, and befriends the immigrant, providing him with food and clothing." YHWH's nature as the sovereign God of supreme power is clearly expressed in the exercise of justice for the poor and marginalized. And there are implications also for Israel's practice: "So you should love the immigrant."[90]

How might such a poem appropriately be used? An initial answer is present within the psalm itself, in the words that conclude it:

> [8] Rise up, O God [*ʾĕlōhīm*], judge the earth;
> for all the nations are your possession [*tinḥal bĕ*]! (Ps. 82:8)

The realization that justice is constitutive of true deity is in the first instance an insight neither for intellectual satisfaction ("It is good to understand the nature of reality") nor for intellectual puzzlement ("If the true God is just, why does the world have so much injustice?"), even if such responses have their place and time. Rather, it is an understanding that requires active engagement with this deity in the form of prayer. In a way that is characteristic of the biblical literature more generally (as seen in the discussions of Prov. 8 and Exod. 3 in the previous chapters), theological understanding, as articulated here in Psalm 82, is not only intellectual but also existential and participatory,

90. My translation of Deut. 10:17–19a.

and the reality of which it speaks is not just a given but also a goal, something to be entered into and appropriated.[91]

The precise meaning of the prayer is not entirely clear. Is it a prayer for ultimate judgment on a day of the LORD, or is it a prayer for the immediate display of justice in the here and now? And in what sense are all the nations the possession of the LORD, when nations other than Israel do not recognize or acknowledge the LORD? The universal scope of the wording of the prayer may lead one to think of an eschatological scenario, but the psalm's earlier depiction of oppression and consequent dark bewilderment may also lead one to think of change for the better in the here and now. If the wording is open to both readings, it may be unwise to see them as alternatives and preferable to see them as complementary dimensions of meaning.

■ There is a difficult question about the precise sense of *tinḥal bĕ*. It is often proposed that the MT's *qal*, "inherit"/"possess," should be repointed as a *hiphil*, "apportion" / "take in possession." The key issue, in my judgment, is less philological than contextual: How does this concluding prayer follow on from the scenario of vv. 1–7? Is God demoting the other deities and taking on their previous role in a new arrangement? This could indicate the *hiphil* sense. Or is the point of the scenario to demonstrate the nature of the true God, with a final affirmation of what this means? This would make the *qal* sense preferable. I incline to the latter, although imaginatively there is a gray area in which both options are meaningful.[92] ■

As noted at the outset, the classic Christian and Jewish reading of Psalm 82 has to do with the need for justice to be practiced on earth by human judges. On one level, in terms of the semantics of *ʾĕlōhîm*, this is most likely a misreading. Human judges are not being addressed and admonished. Nonetheless, the implications not only of the psalm's literary genre but also of a basic theological principle still give warrant for the classic judgment about the implications of the psalm. In terms of literary genre, the imagined scenario in the poem is indeed about God and supposed gods, but the existential freight of the genre applies to humans who live under God. In theological terms, one widespread ethical principle in the Old Testament is *imitatio Dei*: in significant ways, humans are to become like God in how they live and conduct themselves.[93] The prayer that concludes Psalm 82—that God should

91. As Brent Strawn nicely puts it, "God's rule is in process, not yet fully accomplished. But the psalmist prays for it with the equivalent of 'Your kingdom come'" ("Psalm 82," 219). A number of other psalm commentators also draw this link with the Lord's Prayer.

92. Peter Machinist discusses the issue at length and concludes that "we are still . . . in a quandary about how to understand *nāḥal bĕ* in our v. 8b" ("How Gods Die," 225).

93. John Barton gives a helpful account of the imitation of God as "part of what may be called the moral atmosphere of the Old Testament" (*Ethics in Ancient Israel*, 266).

judge the earth—has self-involving implications for any who pray it. They themselves should seek to realize the justice of God on earth—even though, of course, the implications are strongest for those with formal responsibilities to administer justice.

On Going with the Flow of Psalm 82

To conclude this reading of the psalm, I return to a couple of issues noted earlier. Is the picture of an assembly of ancient deities imaginatively too remote from the world of the twenty-first century to be usable in Christian preaching and worship? And how can one hold together the medium of the poem with the message that one may want to take from it?

The problem of remoteness is real but can easily be overstated. We live in a culture where many have no difficulty whatsoever in taking with full imaginative seriousness scenarios that are far removed from our everyday world. These may be set "a long time ago in a galaxy far, far away"; or else they may envisage superhuman heroes both ancient and modern, from Thor to Captain America, who save the world. The issue is not, I think, that people in general lack imaginative flexibility, but rather that they often struggle to exercise it in the context of biblical interpretation, where a certain kind of woodenness all too readily sets in. Prepossession with questions such as "Is it literally true?" or "But did it actually happen like that?" or "How could God have been ignorant and then come to realize something?" too easily displaces robust literary awareness. The ability to read diverse literary genres with full imaginative seriousness, and to see a variety of metaphorical and analogical ways of engaging with the subject matter of the text, is a necessary dimension of biblical literacy. Poetry should stimulate the imagination.

The question of whether an imaginative construction should be recognized as in some way responsive to antecedent divine initiative, thus mediating the reality of which it speaks, is independent of decisions about literary conventions. The key issue has to do with the rich cluster of judgments embodied in approaching the biblical documents as Scripture.[94]

I also suggested above that the psalm's approach to other deities is essentially phenomenological and pragmatic: there simply *were* many gods, *ʾĕlōhīm ʾăḥērīm*, in Israel's world. I suggest that the same is true of the world of the twenty-first century. By this I do not mean that people today generally hold religious outlooks characteristic of the ancient world. This is clearly not the case. Rather, I have in mind the long-standing Christian tradition, which has

94. See also my remarks at the end of ch. 2 (above, pp. 89–91).

strong biblical roots, that a primary meaning of the term "god" is that upon which people fundamentally set their hearts and towards which they orient their priorities.[95] In this sense, although many people today may have no use for the little three-letter word *g-o-d* other than in exclamations, this does not preclude, in a biblically informed frame of reference, their treating people, things, and ideas as gods. The question of whether the realities which people treat as gods *should* be appropriately treated as gods is an enduring issue of life that does not go away. One of the most characteristic affirmations of those who come to faith in God, in the context of a continuing tradition of thought and life rooted in the Bible, is that certain things they had previously reckoned to matter most do not in reality have that importance: "I had taken you for gods, . . . but in fact you die like mortals."

Conclusion: Towards a Grammar of God as Just

This chapter's facet of what it means to "know that the Lord is God" is a consideration of the term "God." I argue that Psalm 82 offers a conceptual analysis of deity in terms of the practice of justice. If the Lord is God, then justice is intrinsic to His nature. The gods who are dismissed as not really gods and who are doomed to die are those whose intrinsic lack of justice shows that they are not really divine in the way that they were initially supposed to be. This is not to deny that ancient peoples other than Israel also associated their deities with the practice of justice.[96] The key issue that Psalm 82 poses is whether justice is constitutive of true deity.

■ My reading of Ps. 82 is not unprecedented or unparalleled. In the literature on Ps. 82 of which I am aware, the discussion that perhaps has the most affinities with my thesis, other than the essays of Machinist and Gers-Uphaus,[97] is J. Clinton McCann's "The Single Most Important Text in the Entire Bible." McCann's title and discussion commend an enthusiastic account of the content of Ps. 82 by John Dominic Crossan in *The Birth of Christianity* (575–76). For both Crossan and McCann, the issue of justice is part of

95. See further Moberly, *Old Testament Theology*, 35–40.

96. See, e.g., Weinfeld, *Social Justice in Ancient Israel and in the Ancient Near East*; Lloyd-Jones, *Justice of Zeus*. There is a recurrent temptation for those who inhabit the Jewish and Christian faiths as living traditions to indulge in some degree of misrepresentation and/or caricature of other ancient religions which have not similarly endured. For example: "The pagan gods had always been believed to have no restraints whatever in their dealings with man" (H. Cohn, "Justice," 515). The reality was usually more of a middle ground between justice as constitutive and "no restraints whatever."

97. See above, 107n45 and 110n57.

"the essential character of the biblical God."[98] Walter Brueggemann strikingly sees that Ps. 82 "engages in a question about what constitutes 'godness,'" to which the answer is that "godness is constituted by solidarity with the weak and needy" (although when he expounds "justice as the core focus of Yahweh's life in the world and Israel's life with Yahweh," Ps. 82 is absent from his account).[99] ■

This approach brings with it the corollary issue of how humans might be expected to recognize true deity when they encounter it. On this reading, the psalm offers a criterion for critical discernment. Insofar as the goal on which people set their hearts is intrinsically related to the realization of justice on earth, then that goal can be affirmed as responsive to the initiative of the true God, whether or not people in general conceive it in those terms. It becomes possible to affirm that wherever on earth there is justice, there, in some way, God is present: *Ubi iustitia, Deus ibi est.*[100] God's justice represents a reality into which all humans need to enter.

This understanding of God, however, must not be taken in isolation. That is, the biblical witness associates numerous intrinsic qualities other than being just with the deity who is God. Psalm 82 is one voice among many others. A faith rooted in the canonical collection as a whole is committed to a synthetic construal of many biblical voices as witnesses to the mysterious reality of God. Simply holding together the two qualities of justice and mercy (never mind the wisdom of Prov. 8) in relation to God and among humans is endlessly demanding in both thought and practice.[101]

Moreover, the question of what counts as justice is often difficult to discern in practice, and changes over time. For example, what constitutes justice in cultures that have experienced the emancipation of women in their laws and social reality will differ from what counts as justice in cultures where social roles and responsibilities are differently understood. A second set of challenges

98. McCann, "Single Most Important Text," 65.

99. Brueggemann, *Theology of the Old Testament*, 143–44, 735–42.

100. I am here playing on the historic Christian hymn/antiphon *Ubi caritas, Deus ibi est*—"Where love is, God is"—which has a renewed role in contemporary worship, not least through its memorable rendering as a Taizé chant.

101. Rabbinic tradition developed the distinction between divine justice and divine mercy in terms of the distinction between *ʾĕlōhîm* and *yhwh*. This was not exegetical in a modern sense, but rather an attempt to probe a fundamental issue of theology and life in a context of reading and reflecting on the implications of the biblical text. A fine account is offered by Kadushin, *The Rabbinic Mind*, 215–17. Among other things, Kadushin gives a footnote reference to Genesis Rabbah 12:15, the text of which merits citation: "Said the Holy One, blessed be He: 'If I create the world on the basis of mercy alone, its sins will be great; on the basis of judgment alone, the world cannot exist. Hence I will create it on the basis of judgment and mercy, and may it then stand!' Hence the expression, The Lord God [in Gen. 2:4]" (Freedman, *Midrash Rabbah: Genesis I*, 99).

is in a sense methodological. What constitutes justice in a culture that prioritizes procedural correctness over principled rightness will differ from what counts as justice in a culture that prioritizes principle over procedure. This can regularly be challenging for many people in relation to the bureaucratic and litigious priorities of much contemporary culture. It is worth remembering, however, that whatever the difficult structural and political questions about justice, everyday issues in the family, the local community, and the workplace will always provide opportunities for people to attend to those in need, to resist corruption, and to display priorities that are attuned to God's priorities.

Finally, if we revisit the standoff between Saul and Dorit with which this chapter opened, we can see that neither character associates God with issues of public justice or the common good. This surely reflects the de-moralizing of God and the marginalization of God away from the public sphere and the common good of human life that has been so characteristic of post-Enlightenment Western modernity. Numerous theologians, not least those associated with liberation theology, have protested this move, as have some justice-oriented groups, such as the Mennonites and certain neomonastic communities. Nonetheless, much contemporary understanding of God remains unduly individualistic and privatized, not to mention self-serving. To say this does not resolve the challenges posed by the legitimate concerns of the modern state of Israel in relation to the legitimate concerns of the Palestinians. But perhaps that essentially means that the challenges of living justly and well under God must always—time, time, and time again—be confronted afresh as life goes on. The prayer of Psalm 82:8 still needs to be prayed and appropriated.

4

The Inscrutable God

Divine Differentials and Human Choosing in Genesis 4

In November 1499, John Colet, who at that time was lecturing in Oxford on the Letters of St. Paul, hosted a dinner party. Among his guests was the itinerant scholar Erasmus, who, in a letter to a friend, tells of a delightful evening of good company, good food, and good drink.[1] A particular topic of amicable disagreement was the question of how Cain had displeased God. Colet advanced the thesis that Cain's fault was that he doubted the Creator's goodness in that he relied too much on his own efforts and so became the first to plow the earth. Abel, by contrast, tended sheep, being content with what grew of itself. Erasmus apparently responded to Colet with arguments that he called "rhetoric," while another theologian present responded with syllogisms. Yet Erasmus credits Colet with "having the better of us all"; Colet went into "a sort of holy frenzy" whereby "his voice was altered" and "his eyes had a different look"—which is no doubt a tribute to Colet's passion for his subject (though one suspects that the wine may perhaps have made some contribution also). Erasmus then lightened the tone with an amusing retelling of Cain's sin in a different mode, in which Cain becomes a Prometheus-like figure who

In this chapter I draw on and develop my previous discussions of Gen. 4:1–17: "Is Monotheism Bad for You?"; *Theology of the Book of Genesis*, 22–28, 88–101; "Exemplars of Faith in Hebrews 11: Abel"; and "Theological Interpretation," esp. 667–70.

1. See Erasmus, "Letter 116: 'To Johannes Sixtinus.'" The episode is contextualized in Huizinga, *Erasmus and the Age of Reformation*, 29–33.

deviously persuades the angel guarding Eden to give him some seeds from the garden, which he plants outside Eden and whose flourishing growth outside Eden then provokes God's anger and leads Him to reject Cain's sacrifice.

The issue of what Cain did wrong has been a time-honored interpretive crux—and, in this case, a suitable topic for a friendly dinner discussion between Renaissance Christian humanists. Colet's proposal would hardly feature in a short list of the most common resolutions of the problem, while Erasmus's jocular story is off the scale. Nonetheless, Colet's thesis represents an interesting attempt to offer a fresh resolution on the basis of a return to certain theological and moral first principles such as he and Erasmus tried to promote. What's notable, however, is that both Colet and Erasmus share the assumption that Cain must have done something wrong, and that the real puzzle in the story is what that was, since the text does not say. But maybe the seemingly obvious assumption that Cain was at fault was really what should have received their attention.

The question of what, if anything, Cain did wrong is our way into the next facet of "knowing that the LORD is God." I will argue that the story of Cain and Abel sounds a very different note to that sounded in Psalm 82, where justice is constitutive of God. Here a key question will be "Is God unfair?"

Introduction to the Story of Cain and Abel (Gen. 4:1–17)

Some preliminary words about the genre of the story of Cain and Abel are appropriate, as there are certain obvious difficulties that have confronted readers down the ages. The essential problem is that certain internal details of the story are at odds with its narrative context. The narrative context is the beginnings of human life on earth, in which there appears to be only a handful of people. Yet the internal features of the story presuppose the regular conditions of life in a populated earth. The perennially popular form of posing the issue has been to refer to the immediate sequel to the main story in Genesis 4:17, "Cain knew his wife," and ask the question "Whence Cain's wife?" On one level, this can be answered by appealing to the reference to Adam and Eve having other children (Gen. 5:4): Cain must have married a sister.[2] Yet the popular question is not the sharpest question, as arguably it would be more to the point to appeal to the latter part of Genesis 4:17, "and he built a city," and ask, "Whence sufficient people for a city?" (even if the

2. This was the approach of St. Augustine in late antiquity (and of many others down the ages). See his *Questions on the Heptateuch* 1.1. He also discusses the necessary marriage of brothers and sisters in earliest times in *City of God* 15.16.

term traditionally rendered "city" envisages a settlement far smaller than what is implied by "city" in contemporary English).[3] But appealing to any particular reference in isolation misses the point that the Cain and Abel story as a whole presupposes the regular conditions of life in a populated earth:

- the differentiation of labor, where Abel is a shepherd while Cain is a farmer (4:2);
- the assumption that the offering of sacrifice is a regular, established practice that needs no explanation (4:3–4);
- Cain's proposal to Abel that they go out "to the field"—that is, away from where people are likely to be present (4:8);[4] and
- Cain's anxiety that if he becomes a restless wanderer, anyone who finds him may kill him (4:14), which envisages the vulnerable role of the nomad/vagrant on the fringes of settled communities.[5]

The most likely explanation for this internal tension between story and narrative context is that the story has a history. That is, the story originated in a context in which the familiar conditions of life on earth were as natural to this story as to most of the other stories in the Old Testament. But the story was moved to its present location in a narrative that describes how things were *before* regular life on earth. It was adapted sufficiently to follow the story of Adam and Eve, which precedes it, but its details were not otherwise changed—hence the mismatch. If the story was in fact recontextualized into a narrative that describes the beginning of human life on earth, one reason why may be that it sounds a keynote and/or offers a lens whereby much that follows may be understood. Such recontextualization also makes the story a story of humanity in general involving "Everyman" characters, however much it may also sound notes that anticipate the particular story of Israel.

3. There is a problem of translation, coupled with a problem of what to envisage. The Hebrew term *ʿîr* (conventionally rendered "city," "town") is essentially a counterpart to *śādeh* (conventionally rendered "field," "countryside"). The former envisages a human settlement of any size where people live and have domesticated animals, while the latter envisages open territory where people generally do not live and where animals are wild, though it is also where flocks are pastured. When *ʿîr* and *śādeh* are used together, they specify the whole of a region or territory (Gen. 34:28; Deut. 28:3, 16; 1 Kings 14:11; Jer. 14:18).

4. There is a text-critical problem, in that the MT of Gen. 4:8 lacks Cain's words to Abel. However, the wording in the ancient versions, "Let us go to the field [*śādeh*; i.e., away from any *ʿîr*]," gives the best text, even though the MT's silence can perhaps intrigue the imagination.

5. If the world were populated only by a few offspring of Adam and Eve, then the more Cain (and his descendants) wandered, the further away he (they) would be from these few other people.

If the story has such a history, leading to certain incongruities in the text, it does not follow that one should not still read it with full imaginative seriousness as a story setting out something fundamental about life in God's world. But it does mean that one needs to recognize that the conventions embedded in the story have more in common with traditional storytelling than with modern historiography.

■ Another preliminary question concerns how best to read the story in light of some of its wider resonances. For example, the murderous rivalry between Cain and Abel resonates strikingly with the story of Romulus and Remus, a story of paradigmatic significance for ancient Rome. Although it is impossible to trace any direct linkage between these two stories of sibling murder, the imagination readily connects them in terms of the similar subject matter. At the very least, their similarity reminds us of the deep, even deadly, divisions that can arise between those who, through their birth and familial context, should be closest to each other, or of the serious failings in those whose influence for later generations is considered great. Yet it is important to establish how—if at all—such resonances contribute to the particular point or purpose that the biblical story may have.

Alternatively, biblical scholars have often wanted to find in the story evidence for certain patterns of life in ancient Israel. Scholars have wondered whether the tensions between Cain and Abel might in some way embody ancient tensions between, for example, shepherds and farmers in Israel, or between particular tribal groupings (Israelite and Kenite), or between the inhabitants of arable land (say, the central hill country of Canaan) and inhabitants of the desert (say, the Negev). But such suggestions at best indicate possible background resonances which may give a certain local color to the biblical story in its putative context of origin, but which most likely do not address the role that the story now has in its strategic location at the outset of human life on earth.

Possible readings of the story in a Christian context are also many and varied. Samuel Wells, for example, proposes that this story can be read as (1) everybody's story, in which the issue is the often-complex dynamics of family life; (2) Israel's story, in which Cain and Abel are coded representations of the Northern and Southern Kingdoms and of exile; or (3) your personal story, in which people have to face the existential issues of personal accountability and responsibility for others.[6] These are all meaningful readings, even if they are less exegetically rooted than they might be. ■

A Reading of Genesis 4:1–17

The story of Cain and Abel directly follows that of Adam and Eve in Eden.[7] Although the story is told with seeming simplicity, the reader nevertheless needs to be alert.

6. Wells, *Learning to Dream Again*, 130–35.

7. Ancient traditions of interpretation of the story are helpfully introduced in Kugel, *The Bible as It Was*, 83–96.

> [1]Now the man knew his wife Eve, and she conceived and bore Cain, saying, "I have produced a man with the help of the LORD." [2]Next she bore his brother Abel. (Gen. 4:1–2)

Apart from some minor interpretive issues,[8] there is a significant silence in the wording. The text twice says that Eve "bore" (*yālad*) a child but says only once that she conceived (*hārāh*). Ancient Jewish interpretive tradition saw the text's silence about a second conception as significant: one conception and two births implies that Cain and Abel were twins.[9] In terms of Hebrew idiom, this is entirely possible, though it is not a necessary inference.[10] However, the narrative analogy with the birth of the twins Esau and Jacob (Gen. 25:22–26)—to which we will return—does, on balance, make it likely that Cain and Abel are indeed envisaged as twins.

On Recognizing the Issue That the Text Raises

The characters have been introduced. We now move directly to a brief but decisive moment in their lives.

> [2]Now Abel was a keeper of sheep, and Cain a tiller of the ground. [3]In the course of time Cain brought to the LORD an offering of the fruit of the ground, [4]and Abel for his part brought of the firstlings of his flock, their fat portions. And the LORD had regard for Abel and his offering, [5]but for Cain and his offering he had no regard. (Gen. 4:2–5)

8. The Hebrew of Eve's speech is difficult. An interpretive crux in earlier times was whether or not Adam and Eve had sexual intercourse only outside Eden, since sex is first mentioned here. Cornelius à Lapide, a great Jesuit scholar in the early seventeenth century, followed the church fathers in having a clear take on this: "Some Jewish scholars, together with our heretics, think that Adam had known Eve in Paradise" (*Commentarii in Sacram Scripturam*, 96 [my translation]). This particular debate is best left in the history books, even if its subject matter—sex and God—is of enduring interest.

9. So, e.g., "AND SHE AGAIN BORE implies an additional birth, but not an additional pregnancy" (Midrash Rabbah: Genesis 22:3, in Freedman, *Midrash Rabbah: Genesis I*, 183). Calvin also sees the logic of this silence and proposes that Cain and Abel are most likely twins. But he attributes the significance of this only to the need to populate the earth as soon as possible (*Calvin's Commentaries: Genesis*, 189–90).

10. Elsewhere, Genesis speaks of Zilpah and Leah "bearing" without prior reference to "conceiving" (Gen. 30:10, 12, 21), but in each instance a single child is born, so there is no real parallel to Eve's childbearing. The closest idiomatic parallel is the account of Shua's bearing children to Judah: "She conceived [*hārāh*] and bore [*yālad*] a son; and he [or the textual variant "she"] named him Er. Again she conceived [*hārāh*] and bore [*yālad*] a son whom she named Onan. Yet again she bore [*yāsaph* with *yālad*, as in 4:2] a son, and she named him Shelah" (Gen. 38:3–5). The question is whether the text implies that Shelah is a younger twin to Onan—to which one can only say that it is a natural but not a necessary reading.

Regular patterns of life develop. On the one hand, there is a mixed economy, with a division of labor between animal husbandry and agriculture. On the other hand, the regular religious practice of offering sacrifice to God takes place, with offerings appropriate to the form of labor. So far, all is straightforward. But a surprise comes in the differential response of the LORD to the sacrifices: one is accepted, the other is not. The text shows no interest in how the differential response might have been discerned, though commentators and artists have often depicted it in terms either of fire descending on one sacrifice but not the other, or of smoke ascending from one but not the other. The text's sole concern is to establish that there was a differing response. The surprising puzzle is the text's silence about why the LORD accepted one sacrifice but not the other.

The question for the reader is unavoidable: What are we to make of this? How are we to understand it? The move we make here will determine how we read the story as a whole. The instinctive assumption of the overwhelming majority of readers down the ages has been simple: there must be some reason why the LORD responded thus. They have then sought to discern what that reason might be. One usually looks for some clue in the text to provide that reason. For numerous interpreters today, no less than for Colet and Erasmus at their dinner party, the nature of Cain's unacceptability remains an ongoing challenge to one's ingenuity. Possible options can indeed be wide-ranging.[11] Nonetheless, there is a tendency to focus on the immediately preceding account of the sacrifices offered and to find there the clue. As Iain Provan puts it from a Christian perspective,

> The reason for the disfavour is not explicitly clear, but it is likely that it is because Cain brings to God only "*some of the fruits* of the soil," while Abel brings "*fat portions* from some of the firstborn of his flock." In other words, Abel is careful to bring his very best to God, while Cain fails to do so.[12]

Alternatively, from a Jewish perspective, Nahum Sarna says,

> The reason for God's different reactions may be inferred from the descriptions of the offerings: Abel's is characterized as being "the choicest of the firstlings

11. See, e.g., Spina, "The 'Ground' for Cain's Rejection"; Hayward, "What Did Cain Do Wrong?"

12. Provan, *Discovering Genesis*, 99. In a footnote Provan also cites the fourth-century Ephrem the Syrian, who says, "Abel was very discerning in his choice of offerings, whereas Cain showed no such discernment" (Ephrem, *Commentary on Genesis* 3.2.1 [Louth, *Genesis 1–11*, 104]). An exegetical argument from silence could appeal to a passage such as 2 Chron. 31:5, which tells of an offering of the "first fruits" (*rēʾshīt*) of cereal produce.

> of his flock"; Cain's is simply termed as coming "from the fruit of the soil," without further detail. Abel appears to have demonstrated a quality of heart and mind that Cain did not possess. Cain's purpose was noble, but his act was not ungrudging and openhearted. Thus the narrative conveys the fundamental principle of Judaism that the act of worship must be informed by genuine devotion of the heart.[13]

Indeed, the understanding that there was something problematic about Cain and/or his offering is also found already in the New Testament's handling of the story. Thus, in the list of biblical exemplars of faith in Hebrews 11, we read, "By faith Abel offered to God a more acceptable sacrifice than Cain's. Through this he received approval as righteous, God himself giving approval to his gifts; he died, but through his faith he still speaks" (11:4). Abel's offering *by faith* shows that there was a quality in his sacrificing that Cain lacked, as is confirmed by Abel's being *approved as righteous* by God's acceptance of the offering. Alternatively, in the account of faithful living in 1 John, we read, "For this is the message you have heard from the beginning, that we should love one another. We must not be like Cain who was from the evil one and murdered his brother. And why did he murder him? Because his own deeds were evil and his brother's righteous" (1 John 3:11–12). Here there is a clear contrast between Cain *as evil and acting evilly* over against Abel *as righteous*; Cain's basic orientation was turned away from God.

Although the readings in Hebrews and 1 John could have been derived from the familiar Masoretic Text of Genesis 4, the strong likelihood is that the writers of Hebrews and 1 John would have read the story in its ancient Greek form in the Septuagint. Here, strikingly, a reason for the unacceptability of Cain's offering *is* present. It comes in the divine address to Cain in Genesis 4:7, where the Greek has a wholly different sense than the Hebrew: "If you rightly offer, but do not rightly divide, have you not sinned?"[14] This Greek text apparently indicates a fault in Cain's sacrificial procedure (whatever

13. Sarna, *Genesis*, 32. Such a construal of course has wide biblical resonance; see, e.g., David's famous insistence to Araunah the Jebusite that he will not accept Araunah's threshing floor (where the Jerusalem temple would be built) as a gift but rather will pay for it, because "I will not offer burnt offerings to the LORD my God that cost me nothing" (2 Sam. 24:24).

14. The Greek text is *ouk, ean orthōs prosenengkēs, orthōs de mē dielēs, hēmartes*. In terms of a possible Hebrew *Vorlage*, the difference from the MT might be only one consonant, though with substantial difference in vocalization (see Wevers, *Notes on the Greek Text of Genesis*, 55). However, the rest of Gen. 4:7 in the Greek makes poor sense: *hēsuchason, pros se hē apostrophē autou, kai su arxeis autou*: "Be still; his/its turning away/turning back is towards you, and you will rule over him/it." It is entirely unclear what the antecedent of the pronoun "he/it" is, and so whose is the turning away/back towards Cain, as there is no noun in the Greek of 4:7a. The noun "your face" in 4:6 does not make good sense of it. So perhaps the antecedent is Abel, back

exactly the "dividing" would have entailed, which would seem to be a term more applicable to Abel's animal sacrifice, with its limbs and entrails, than to Cain's cereal sacrifice). Thus, in the form of the story that was familiar to the New Testament writers and the church fathers, there was a fault in what Cain did with his sacrifice. To be sure, a fault in sacrificial procedure does not have the same intensity as the absence of faith or the presence of evil that the New Testament writers ascribe to Cain. But the key point is that, already within the received biblical text, Cain had done something wrong, and so it was natural for interpreters to develop this reading in ways that were appropriate to their own concerns, in line with what they understood to be the tenor of the text.

"Don't offer God second best," "Don't hold back from God," "Respond to God with faith," "Resist evil urges"—these are meaningful moral and spiritual principles for both Jews and Christians alike. The New Testament use of the story has an obvious weight for Christians. The story of Cain and Abel is often used in the catechesis of children, and the moral of the story is consistently seen to be some form of this mode of reading. Spiritual formation along these lines will be good spiritual formation.

But the initial assumption that there *must* be a comprehensible reason why the Lord accepted Abel's sacrifice but not Cain's needs to be revisited. The fact that such an assumption offers a meaningful reading does not mean that it is the only or even the best approach to the text.[15] For there is an antecedent issue that must be considered. To adapt some well-known words: "To rationalize, or not to rationalize; that is the question." Might it be possible—indeed, preferable—to read the story on the basis that there is no explanation, in terms of what counts as a humanly meaningful reason, for the Lord's differential response?[16] This proposal can easily make interpreters nervous, as it seems

---

in 4:4, though this too hardly reads well. It is not easy to surmise how the NT writers might have construed the divine address to Cain as a whole, other than being puzzled by it.

15. A game-changing reading of the story is offered by Jon Levenson in *The Death and Resurrection of the Beloved Son*, 69–81. Levenson persuasively makes the case that rationalizing approaches to the Lord's response to Cain miss the point of the Hebrew text.

16. It is not hard to show that there are drawbacks with the familiar appeal to the wording of Gen. 4:3–4 to explain the Lord's differential response. As Jon Levenson puts it,

> If we are to rationalize the rejection of Cain's offering and the acceptance of Abel's by reference to a word or two in the text and on the basis of an argument from silence, we could just as easily rationalize the reverse result, for whereas Cain brought his sacrifice "to the Lord" (v 3), Abel, on this sort of microscopic over-reading, did not. I have the suspicion that if Cain's sacrifice had been accepted but Abel's rejected, commentators into our own time would be telling us that Cain acted out of religious devotion, but Abel out of mere imitation of his older brother, and on the basis of the same text (4:1–4a)

to imply that God acts arbitrarily. Yet there are two good reasons why one should resist trying to find an explanation here.

The first reason has to do with the inner-biblical narrative analogy between the story of Cain and Abel and the story of Jacob and Esau (which will be developed more fully below). The story of the birth of Jacob and Esau in Genesis 25 is striking:

> [21]Isaac prayed to the LORD for his wife, because she was barren; and the LORD granted his prayer, and his wife Rebekah conceived. [22]The children struggled together within her; and she said, "If it is to be this way, why do I live?" So she went to inquire of the LORD. [23]And the LORD said to her,
>
> "Two nations are in your womb,
> and two peoples born of you shall be divided;
> the one shall be stronger than the other,
> the elder shall serve the younger."
>
> [24]When her time to give birth was at hand, there were twins in her womb. [25]The first came out red, all his body like a hairy mantle; so they named him Esau. [26]Afterward his brother came out, with his hand gripping Esau's heel; so he was named Jacob. (Gen. 25:21–26)

The story starts straightforwardly: first there is a problem, and then there is a resolution at God's behest. All should be well. But soon Rebekah's acutely painful condition makes her apparently despair of life. So she goes "to inquire of the LORD" (a procedure about whose specifics we are disappointingly told nothing), and she receives an answer in poetic form (poetry being considered appropriate for heightened modes of speech on special occasions).[17] The content of the LORD's message is startling, since the idea that two nations were in Rebekah's womb might not have been clear prior to the birth of the twins. But apart from the fact that the wider narrative makes clear that particular persons can embody whole peoples (Jacob is / will be the Israelites, Esau is / will be the Edomites), there is a difference between Jacob and Esau. The younger twin is favored over the older twin: he is both stronger and will receive the other's service.[18] God makes a differential decision that favors Jacob over Esau while they are still in their mother's womb.

The logic of this scenario is precisely pinpointed by Paul:

> [10]Something similar [to God's promise of children to Abraham and Sarah] happened to Rebecca when she had conceived children by one husband, our ancestor

---

that is now often said to testify to Abel's moral superiority to the hapless Cain. (*Death and Resurrection of the Beloved Son*, 72)

17. Compare Exod. 3:15b and my comment on it (ch. 2, p. 63).

18. The Hebrew of Gen. 25:23b is open to more than one reading, but a traditional construal still seems to me best.

> Isaac. [11]Even before they had been born or had done anything good or bad (so that God's purpose of election might continue, [12]not by works but by his call) she was told, "The elder shall serve the younger." (Rom. 9:10–12)

If God's preferential decision is made while children are still in their mother's womb, then they cannot have done anything to deserve it—because they have not yet done anything at all in their pre-birth state. In other words, God's favoring Jacob before his birth necessarily resists rationalization in any recognizable terms. If we read the stories of Cain and Abel and of Jacob and Esau as mutually interpretive of each other, then we have good reason not to rationalize the LORD's favoring of Abel over Cain any more than we should rationalize His favoring of Jacob over Esau.

■ It was an unfortunate moment in the history of Christian theology when St. Augustine focused on Gen. 25:23—the one passage in Scripture where God makes a differential decision between people before their birth—and read it in the light of Paul's discussion of divine election in such a way as to develop an account of salvation and perdition in relation to one's eternal destiny. That is, Gen. 25:23 interpreted through the lens of Rom. 9 became the biblical basis for Augustine's notion of double predestination, some people being predestined for salvation and others for perdition. In the context of Genesis, however, such notions are nowhere in view, and to introduce them goes against—rather than with—the grain of the text. The text's concern is with relative strength and dominion/subjection in the historical existence of Jacob's and Esau's descendants. Further, Paul's point about God's decisions depending on God and not on the doings of people does not entail what Augustine inferred from it, not least because Paul's strong language about God's initiative in Rom. 9 is counterbalanced by equally strong language about the need for human response, with the outcomes contingent on such response, in Rom. 11:11–24.[19] Augustine's reading of Gen. 25:23 must sadly qualify as one of the more serious misreadings of Scripture in the history of the Christian church.[20] ■

The other reason for not rationalizing the LORD's favoring of Abel over Cain can be seen if we stand back from the biblical narrative to reflect more widely on certain features of life. That is, it is an inescapable fact of life that some of the things that matter most to people are unequally distributed.

On the one hand, in a way that has some resonance with the LORD's oracle to Rebekah, important things, especially intelligence and beauty, are differentially distributed in the womb. Of course, good education can help everyone; but the fact remains that some people have greater intellectual ability, and

19. I offer a fuller discussion of the dynamics of divine initiative and human responsiveness, with reference also to Rom. 9–11, in my *Old Testament Theology*, 107–43 (see esp. 139–43 for Rom. 9–11 and a theological summary).

20. A useful introduction to Augustine's reading of Gen. 25:22–23 in the light of Paul is Charry, "Rebekah's Twins."

others less, as something they are born with. Likewise, facial appearance and aspects of body shape are a given. Although modern surgery can enable some alteration of appearance and shape, such alteration is only available to some, not all, and also within limits (the short will never become tall, nor the tall short). Ironically—and irrationally—although we as human beings have no say whatsoever in the intelligence or appearance with which we are born, these are often the very things of which we are most proud or most ashamed. For those of us who feel "unfavored" in terms of what we were born with, who wish we were other than what we are, learning to live well with what we are can be one of life's greatest challenges.

On the other hand, many things happen in the course of life which bear no relation to whether people have done anything to "deserve" them. Some people enjoy robust good health; others do not. One twenty-five-year-old may be successful at sports; another may get, say, multiple sclerosis or cancer, struggle with ill health, and die prematurely. Accidents happen in cars and airplanes. People can be drowned in a tsunami or cheated by those whom they supposed they could trust. And so on. The possible disappointments, accidents, and tragedies of life are too numerous to list. Put differently, many people at some time(s) in their lives find themselves "unfavored" in what happens to them, in ways that bear no relation whatsoever to their personal qualities or anything that they may have done. This is not to deny that people can sometimes bring misfortune and/or tragedy upon themselves by the way they live and by the foolish or corrupt things they do. The point is that, very often, misfortune and/or tragedy is unrelated to how people live and what they do.

In such situations of being "unfavored," either through birth or through the circumstances of life, people sometimes cast about for answers: "What have I/we/you/they done to deserve this?" But such rationalizing questions, which try to find something in the past that might "explain" the situation, have no good answer and lead nowhere, precisely because there is no reason—in terms of what people have done—for what has happened to them. The only questions that are fruitful are not of a backward-looking and rationalizing nature, but rather of a forward-looking and practical nature: "What can I/we/you/they do about this? What can I/we/you/they yet hope for?"

I propose, therefore, that the issue at the heart of the story of Cain and Abel is not the avoidance of being half-hearted or only giving the second best to God, meaningful and important though that is. Rather, the issue is how to handle life in a world where some are more favored than others and, especially, how to cope with being, in one way or another, the one who is unfavored.

Although supposing that Cain did something wrong makes good sense and fits readily with a Christian rule of faith, my proposed reading makes no less sense and should fit no less with a healthy rule of faith. One might look to a significant parallel in John's Gospel, where Jesus on one occasion specifically rejects rationalizing an affliction as the wrong approach and instead points to a forward-looking perspective in terms of what can be made of the situation:

> [1]As [Jesus] walked along, he saw a man blind from birth. [2]His disciples asked him, "Rabbi, who sinned, this man or his parents, that he was born blind?" [3]Jesus answered, "Neither this man nor his parents sinned; he was born blind so that God's works might be revealed in him." (John 9:1–3)

A Christian rule of faith needs to recognize that some things have no explanation, at least in terms of the kinds of "explanations" that people are often inclined to give. Rather, the only potentially fruitful questions are those which look to what may yet be done.

The Lord*'s Guidance and Cain's Response*

If we can see that the point of the story of Cain and Abel may be not to rationalize—"Why has this happened?"—but rather to look forward to "What best might be made of this?" we are well placed to appreciate the tenor and concern of the words of the Lord to Cain that directly follow.

> [5]So Cain was greatly distressed, and his face fell. [6]The Lord said to Cain, "Why are you distressed,[21] and why has your face fallen? [7]If you do well, will not your face be lifted up?[22] But if you do not do well, sin will be a creature lying down at the door and its desire will be for you; but you must master it."[23] (Gen. 4:5–7)

Cain's response to the nonacceptance of his sacrifice is readily understandable. He is angry, and his disappointment and bewilderment are expressed bodily: his expression droops. When something unwelcome, unexpected, and undeserved happens, a bodily reaction is a natural response. So the opening words of the Lord in 4:6 about why Cain's face has fallen are essentially rhetorical, as the cause of Cain's dismay is not in doubt. It is what follows that is all-important.

21. "Distressed" (NJPS) is preferable to "angry" (NRSV) because *ḥārāh lĕ* "expresses despondency or distress, as opposed to *ḥārāh 'af*, which means 'to be angry'" (Sarna, *Genesis*, 33).

22. NRSV: "If you do well, will you not be accepted?"

23. NRSV: "And if you do not do well, sin is lurking at the door; its desire is for you, but you must master it."

Unfortunately, the Hebrew text of the LORD's words in 4:7 is difficult.[24] We have also already noted how greatly the Greek of the Septuagint differs from the Hebrew. It is possible that the text of 4:7 may have been damaged at some very early stage in its transmission. Nonetheless, the Hebrew does make sense, and that sense is fully appropriate to the function of the divine words in their context as guidance to Cain in his dismay. However, the translation and interpretation are more-than-usually interdependent.[25]

The opening words in the Hebrew read, "Is there not, if you do well, a lifting up?" The question is, a lifting up of what? In context it makes most sense to relate this to what has just fallen—that is, Cain's face. The face that has fallen can be lifted up,[26] if Cain does well. That is, if he handles the situation rightly, his dismay can be overcome and his equanimity restored.

■ There is a problem of Hebrew idiom: What is the implied object of the verb "lift up" (*nāśāʾ*)? The verb, here in infinitive construct as a verbal noun, "a lifting up," is commonly used with nouns for sin (*ḥattāʾt*), transgression (*peshaʿ*), or guilt/punishment (*ʿāvōn*), the sense being "forgive"/"accept."[27] Because it is a common idiom, *nāśāʾ* is sometimes used on its own as shorthand for the full phrase *nāśāʾ ḥattāʾt/peshaʿ/ʿāvōn*. A good example is Abraham's engagement with the LORD over whether He will forgive Sodom and Gomorrah (*nāśāʾ*, Gen. 18:24, 26). So some interpreters find this sense of *nāśāʾ* in Gen. 4:7.[28] Alternatively, *nāśāʾ* can be used with "face" (*pānīm*) and have the sense of someone stronger acting graciously and favorably towards someone weaker; thus, the LORD accepts Abraham's intercession over Sodom (Gen. 19:21), David accepts Abigail's intercession over Nabal (1 Sam. 25:35), and Naaman was "in high favor" with the king of Aram (2 Kings 5:1). However, in this idiomatic usage *nāśāʾ* never stands on its own without *pānīm* also being specified. Since *pānīm* is mentioned in Gen. 4:6b, it is possible to see the specific idiom as implicit in 4:7a. It is unclear whether the common translation of *nāśāʾ* here as "be accepted" (thus, e.g., NRSV, NIV, CEB, going back to KJV) is reading the implicit object as "sin" or "face."[29]

24. The text-critical discussion in *BHQ* is far more helpful than the too-brief treatment in *BHS*.

25. Proposed textual emendations are not only conjectural but also necessarily inconclusive, as they vary greatly and generally try to give a more "original" meaning to the whole story, which has, *ex hypothesi*, been obscured or lost in the received Hebrew text. An interesting representative example which gives a good sense of the terrain is Crouch, "*ḥtʾt* as Interpolative Gloss."

26. English does not have an idiom that is the direct opposite of the face falling. Idiomatic expressions might be "Your face lit up" or "Hold your head up."

27. See, e.g., Gen. 50:17a (*peshaʿ* and *ḥattāʾt*); Exod. 10:17; 32:32a (*ḥattāʾt*); Num. 14:18 (*ʿāvōn* and *peshaʿ*); Ps. 32:5b (*ʿāvōn* and *ḥattāʾt*).

28. E.g., Gordon Wenham translates Gen. 4:7a as "Is there not forgiveness if you do well?" and in his comments claims that *nāśāʾ* refers "to God's forgiveness or acceptance of Cain" (*Genesis 1–15*, 93, 105).

29. For fuller philological discussion and bibliography, see Williamson, "On Getting Carried Away with the Infinitive Construct of *nśʾ*."

To find either of these idioms having to do with "acceptance" in the text is likely to be a corollary of seeing the issue at stake as how, in principle, Cain can offer a better, more acceptable sacrifice in the future. But if the issue is how Cain is to handle his existential condition of dismay at the nonacceptance of his sacrifice, then the best sense for *nāsāʾ* is the straightforward lifting up of the face that has fallen, the overcoming of disappointment.[30] ■

The next phrase envisages what will happen if Cain fails to handle his situation well. Dismay at being unfavored or feelings of being wronged can easily grow and develop into deep resentment and bitterness. The text portrays this dramatically. Cain's internal feelings of dismay, which will deepen if the situation is not well handled, are depicted as developing into "sin," which in this context most likely envisages a bitterness which can corrode the self, together with a malice which may aim to hurt the more favored other person. Further, this sin is depicted as an animal lying down, perhaps lying in wait,[31] near to where Cain is. That it lies "at the door" suggests lying patiently with a view to a future opening.[32] If it is "at the door" and "its desire is for you," Cain will face a dangerous and possibly even deadly attack and is likely to have a fight, maybe a life-and-death struggle, on his hands. Failure to handle his dismay in a good way will escalate into danger both for himself and for others.

However, even so, the danger posed by personified sin is not final. Cain will have a fight on his hands, but the outcome is not a foregone conclusion. Cain

30. I can hardly improve on the comment of Ibn Ezra: "According to most commentators, this refers to Cain's sin being 'lifted up' and forgiven. But in my view it refers to being able to hold one's head up high. Remember that Cain's 'face fell' (v. 5) in shame" (Carasik, *Commentators' Bible: Genesis*, 49).

31. The grammar is difficult, in that "sin" (*ḥattāʾt*) is feminine, while the participial verb "lying down" (*rōvēts*) is masculine, as are the two following suffixes. So apparently the participle is being used as a noun, "a recumbent one," as a predicate to "sin" as subject. "A recumbent one" is then the antecedent of "its desire is / will be for you" and "you must master it."

The meaning of *rāvats* is "lie on the ground." The idea of "lying in wait" is context-specific, related to the words ("its desire will be for you") that immediately follow. The context is the reason for other common renderings of *rāvats* here, such as "crouch" or "lurk," which go beyond the regular meaning of the verb.

Many interpreters have noted the Akkadian noun *rābitsu*, which can mean "demon," and have suggested that this may lend background resonance to the notion of personified sin lying in wait with hostile intent in this context. Although this makes good sense, this option is surveyed and a note of caution sounded by R. Gordon, "'Couch' or 'Crouch'?," esp. 196–200.

32. An ancient rabbi observes that sin, like a dog, can lie quietly until it catches its victim off guard: "There are dogs in Rome that know how to deceive men. One goes and sits down before a baker's shop and pretends to be asleep, and when the shopkeeper dozes off he dislodges a loaf near the ground [i.e., scattering the whole pile], and while the onlookers are collecting [the scattered loaves] he succeeds in snatching a loaf and making off" (Genesis Rabbah 22:6, in Freedman, *Midrash Rabbah: Genesis I*, 185).

can still resist: "but you must master it" (*vĕʾattāh timshol-bō*). The precise rendering of this final phrase is open to discussion, as Hebrew is thin on forms indicating mood (e.g., "will," "may," "should," "must"), and the appropriate mood must usually be inferred contextually. This is an issue to which we will return. But "you must master it" is a good rendering.

■ The translators of the NEB and REB reckoned that the logic of the two alternatives being presented to Cain is that of success or failure. They therefore set aside the active vocalization (*timshol*) of the Masoretes and the ancient versions in favor of a passive construal, "you will be mastered by it" (i.e., *timmāshēl*). I'm inclined to think that this is a good example of unimaginative logic trumping a hopeful paradox. At any rate, the point of the text in its received vocalization is that initial failure leads to a struggle, but that this struggle need not become a final failure. ■

These words of God to Cain spell out what lies at the heart of the story. Cain is exposed to great danger through his dismay and disappointment if he does not handle them well; if he allows them to take root, they will become a destructive power. But even if he does initially succumb to this danger, that need not be final, and he can—indeed, must—still resist and overcome it. Andreas Schüle suggestively characterizes God's words here as those of a philosopher or a psychologist; indeed, God speaks "almost in the mode of a spiritual mentor." Or, "to put it in terms of the Old Testament, God is here the *teacher of wisdom* and Cain the student." The concern is to "clarify the emotional situation to Cain. Feelings such as jealousy, anger, and disappointment make people susceptible to the wiles of sin. Strikingly, the dichotomy of good and evil is varied. The good which the human should bring forth is pitted against sin personified. . . . While the good only happens when people 'produce' it, sin has its own, autonomous efficacy."[33]

The trouble is, Cain does not listen well; he is not a responsive student.

> [8]Cain said to his brother Abel, "Let us go out to the field." And when they were in the field, Cain rose up against his brother Abel, and killed him. (Gen. 4:8)

Cain's words could sound like a proposal for a pleasant walk and talk. But his desire to go somewhere away from other people is part of his plan to settle scores with Abel.[34] Cain is so resentful of Abel's being favored over him that he overreacts. He does not just want to do Abel down in some way; instead, he destroys him. In terms of what the LORD has just said to him, Cain is not only "not doing well"; he also has no concern at all to master the hostile beast

33. Schüle, *Theology from the Beginning*, 117, 283.
34. On the text-critical issue and the meaning of "field" (*sādeh*), see above, 127nn3–4.

of resentment. Rather, he welcomes it and allows it fully to have its way; it masters him. His disregard for the LORD's words is complete.

The Consequences for Cain of His Murdering Abel

The remainder of the story is an extended dialogue between the LORD and Cain which probes the consequences of Cain's choice and action.

> [9]Then the LORD said to Cain, "Where is your brother Abel?" He said, "I do not know; am I my brother's keeper?" [10]And the LORD said, "What have you done? Listen; your brother's blood is crying out to me from the ground!" (Gen. 4:9–10)

The LORD's questions are, on one level, genuine questions. But they are akin to the questions of a trial lawyer or a therapist who wants to direct the dialogue in a particular way. Cain answers untruthfully and evasively. As it is a convention of biblical narrative that a person's first words are often strategically indicative of their character,[35] Cain's character is hereby unforgettably captured. However, his attempted shrugging off of accountability comes up against the LORD's confronting him with the knowledge that his brother's blood has been shed in such a way that He cannot but be aware. The LORD then moves on directly to the consequences for Cain of his brutality.

> [11]And now you are cursed from the ground,[36] which has opened its mouth to receive your brother's blood from your hand. [12]When you till the ground, it will no longer yield to you its strength; you will be a restless wanderer on the earth.[37] (Gen. 4:11–12)

35. There is a question as to whether Cain's first quoted words are "Let us go out to the field" in v. 8, since the MT does not include them. But even if the text includes them, they are still devious, masking a desire to murder beneath a seemingly friendly proposal.

36. The expression "cursed from" (*'ārūr min*) is difficult to gauge precisely, as there are three distinct possibilities. First, this could be the *min* of comparison, "more cursed than the ground," with direct cross-reference to Gen. 3:17, "cursed is the ground." Second, the *min* could express the source from which the curse will come—i.e., the ground (which has received Abel's blood) will no longer be fruitful for Cain, even though hitherto he has farmed it (4:2b); this is the point made explicitly in 4:12a. Third, the *min* could have the sense of "away from"—i.e., the curse will take the form of Cain's banishment from the fertile land; this is the point made explicitly in 4:12b. Since the second and third points are specified in the text, they are surely preferable to the sense "more cursed than." Indeed, they belong together, in that Cain's ceaseless wandering is the consequence and corollary of the land ceasing to be fruitful for him. The rendering "cursed from" can contain both consequences set forth in 4:12.

37. A rendering such as "ceaseless wanderer" (NJPS) is preferable to "a fugitive and a wanderer" (NRSV), but I prefer "restless wanderer" (NIV). The Hebrew words *nā' vānād* are most likely a hendiadys in which the initial verb *nūa'*, which expresses regular unsettled movement,

Hitherto, Cain has tilled the ground. Yet because the ground has received his brother's blood, that accustomed mode of life is now permanently closed to him. Instead of being settled on fertile ground, he will wander in an unsettled way and presumably acquire food in a more uncertain, perhaps scavenging, kind of way. Cain is not condemned to death and will still have life, but it will be a different mode of life, lesser and diminished in comparison to what he had previously.

> [13]Cain said to the LORD, "My punishment is greater than I can bear! [14]Today you have driven me away from the soil, and I shall be hidden from your face; I shall be a restless wanderer on the earth, and anyone who meets me may kill me." (Gen. 4:13–14)

Cain does not like his punishment (v. 13); but his language neither expresses remorse ("I have done wrong" or "I can see that I deserve this") nor acknowledges that, unlike Abel, he still has life. He does not raise the issue of how he will find food but, rather, initially expresses the consequence of his banishment from the fertile ground in terms of a distancing from God ("hidden from your face," v. 14a). What precisely this envisages is unclear.[38] However, it is likely a recognition of the expected future consequences of his state as someone who has let sin have its way with him and has shown no signs of wanting to do something about it (i.e., seeking to "master" it); once this dialogue is over, his regular condition will be that of estrangement from God.

A further consequence is that since Cain will be moving about on the edges of settled society, he will have the kind of vulnerability historically associated with "gypsies" or vagrants. He will become a person who can easily be viewed with suspicion and thus victimized, manipulated, and maltreated by settled people.[39]

Significantly, in the text at this point, where the regular conditions of life on earth are envisaged, there is also a certain shift in Cain's identity. Hitherto in the story he has been a single person, the brother and murderer of Abel. But

---

qualifies the nature of the wandering expressed by the second verb, *nōd*. Cain will be the kind of wanderer who will be unable to settle, well captured in English by "restless."

38. Numerous possibilities can be imagined. Is the LORD's presence somehow associated specifically with fertile ground (*'ădāmāh*) as distinct from, say, desert regions (*midbar*)? Or does this envisage a shrine to the LORD, located in the region of fertile ground, from which Cain will be barred? Or could Cain be saying that he would no longer expect to receive God's providential care, as exemplified in the liability to being killed that he immediately goes on to express? My proposed reading continues to make the LORD's words in 4:7 the interpretive key to the story.

39. The content of the next few paragraphs draws on my essay "The Mark of Cain—Revealed at Last?"

now he is implicitly recognized as the ancestor of a people descended from him, just as Jacob and Esau in their mother's womb are said to be "two nations/ peoples" (Gen. 25:23). The Hebrew idiom used in the phrase "anyone who meets me may kill me" most naturally envisages a potential plurality of finders and killers. A single Cain could only be killed once, but a tribe or group of people descended from him would have many members who could be killed.

■ The Hebrew for "anyone who meets me" (*kol mōtsʾī*) uses the regular word for "all" (*kol*) and could be rendered "all who meet me," as in the next verse, where "whoever kills Cain" (*kol hōrēg qayin*) again has *kol* (Gen. 4:15). If a specifically singular subject were envisaged, the participle would be preceded by the definite article, *ha*—i.e., *hammōtsʾī*, *hahōrēg*, "the one who finds/kills." The issue is not entirely straightforward, as *kol* can have an indefinite sense: "whoever," "anyone." Nonetheless, even if the sense is indefinite, a plurality of people finding and/or killing is still the most natural implication of the idiom. ■

> [15]Then the LORD said to him, "Not so![40] Whoever kills Cain will suffer a sevenfold vengeance." So the LORD set this as a mark for Cain,[41] so that no one who came upon him would kill him. [16]Then Cain went away from the presence of the LORD, and settled in the land of Nod [i.e., land of Wandering],[42] east of Eden. (Gen. 4:15–16)

If Cain's anxiety is that he (in the person of his descendants) will be constantly at risk of being murdered, the LORD makes this anxiety unwarranted by giving him a mark/sign to protect him.[43] This is a concession which restricts the potential consequences of Cain's punishment in a particular way.

What is this mark? Whole books have been written on the subject.[44] Proposals about the mark, like proposals about what was wrong with Cain's sacrifice, are many and varied. The usual assumption is that the text does not specify the mark, meaning one must make an intelligent conjecture—or, to be blunt, guess. Such guessing is readily apparent in the midrashic Genesis Rabbah from late antiquity:

> R. Judah said: He caused the orb of the sun to shine on his account. Said R. Nehemiah to him: For that wretch He would cause the orb of the sun to shine!

40. I am happy to stay with the NRSV, which follows the Greek and other ancient versions (which imply a *Vorlage* of *lōʾ kēn*), even though the MT's *lākēn* ("therefore") also makes sense as indicating that the words which follow respond directly to Cain's expressed fear.

41. NRSV: "And the LORD put a mark on Cain."

42. The name of Cain's location, *nōd*, is the same root used to depict Cain's future condition as a wanderer, *nōd*.

43. It may be that "sign" is a slightly better rendering than "mark" for *ʾōt*, if it is understood in the way I propose, but I am happy to retain the time-honored wording "mark of Cain."

44. Ruth Mellinkoff's *The Mark of Cain* is an illuminating read.

> Rather, he caused leprosy to break out on him. . . . Rab said: He gave him a dog. Abba Jose said: He made a horn grow out of him. Rab said: He made him an example to murderers. R. Ḥanin said: He made him an example to penitents. R. Levi said in the name of R. Simeon b. Laḳish: He suspended his judgment until the Flood came and swept him away.[45]

In recent times, conjectures have predominantly envisaged a mark on Cain's body,[46] especially a mark on his forehead, usually by analogy with the protective mark on the forehead described in Ezekiel 9:4.

There are, however, clues in the Hebrew. The preposition used to depict the mark in relation to Cain means "for"—that is, "for his protection"; it does not imply a mark specifically on Cain's body (though it does not preclude the possibility).[47] Moreover, the words which the LORD addresses to Cain, "Whoever kills Cain will suffer a sevenfold vengeance," clearly serve a protective function. Both these points are, of course, well recognized; yet usually they are held apart from each other. As Robert Davidson puts it, "[God] protects him with a solemn threat of vengeance, and places on him a *mark* or sign to indicate that he is a protected person."[48] But why not use Occam's razor to cut the Gordian knot? That is, instead of assuming two distinct things, a saying and a sign, the latter of which needs to be conjectured, one can reduce the two to one by removing the conjecture and thereby solve the problem: the saying, the threat of vengeance, *is* the sign which protects Cain.

The additional clue in the text which supports this possibility is the surprising form of the LORD's words to Cain. In direct address, one would expect the wording to be in the second person: "Whoever kills you." Yet the wording is third person: "Whoever kills Cain." This third-person form represents what other people will say not *to* but *about* Cain. So when the LORD speaks to Cain with these words, He is in effect using common parlance, presumably in the context of the story's formation.[49] A well-known saying serves to protect Cain in the person of his descendants. If those descendants have a reputation for being extremely dangerous because they indulge in murderous

45. Freedman, *Midrash Rabbah: Genesis I*, 191.

46. Thus Hermann Gunkel: "The mark that Yahweh gives Cain was, naturally, on Cain's body" (*Genesis*, 46); or Gerhard von Rad: "Yahweh obviously placed the sign on Cain's body; the narrator appears to be thinking of a tattoo or something similar" (*Genesis*, 107); or, in the most recent commentary of which I am aware, Kathleen O'Connor: "The mark is protective, a tattoo or tribal marking to identify him to others" (*Genesis 1–25A*, 84).

47. The preposition is *lĕ*, "for." The NRSV's "mark on Cain" would really require the preposition *ʿal*, "upon," as in the "sign upon [*ʿal*] your hand/wrist" in Deut. 6:8.

48. Davidson, *Genesis 1–11*, 54.

49. From the perspective of the story itself, the saying will be in use in the future, but, from the perspective of the writer, it presumably already is in use.

overreaction—the killing of one of them will lead to the killing of many others in retaliation[50]—that is a good reason for people generally to leave them well enough alone.

■ The main difficulty for my proposal, I think, is that the Hebrew is not as specific as it might be. My translation, "so the LORD set this as a mark," would ideally render the Hebrew *vayyāsem yhwh zōʾt lĕqayin ʾōt* (or *lĕʾōt*)—but the Hebrew has no "this" (*zōʾt*). It is in keeping with Hebrew idiom to understand the preceding saying as the antecedent and referent of "mark"/"sign"; but the text as it stands does not require it. I have taken the liberty of making it specific in my translation, as I consider it to be the best way of understanding the sense of the text. Of course, if the Hebrew had been more specific, the puzzle about the nature of the mark of Cain would not have arisen in the first place! ■

Who are these descendants? They are usually reckoned to be the Kenites.[51] The difficulty, however, is that the Old Testament does not elsewhere portray the Kenites as notoriously murderous; nor are the descendants of Cain mentioned in Genesis 4:17–24 portrayed as murderous (with the exception of Lamech). So it may be that Cain's descendants should be envisaged less in terms of a particular tribal identity and more in terms of a *type* of person or people.

If Cain, in the person of his descendants, is protected by a reputation for murderous overreaction, that is in keeping with Cain's action towards Abel. Abel was favored over Cain, and Cain was not just disappointed but overreacted with murder; his descendants will overreact to one killing with many killings. Indeed, a little further on in the narrative, Lamech shows himself to be a true descendant of Cain when he boasts not only of murderously overreacting to a hurt but also of doing it to an extent that puts Cain himself in the shade:[52] "I have killed a man for wounding me, / a young man for striking me. / If Cain is avenged sevenfold, / truly Lamech seventy-sevenfold" (Gen. 4:23–24).[53]

But if Cain, in the person of his descendants, is protected by a reputation for unrestrained murderous vengeance, how is the LORD giving such a mark

50. The idiom of "sevenfold" vengeance is not a precise numerical indication but rather expresses an open-ended "many times," as in "The righteous falls seven times, but gets up again" (Prov. 24:16 AT).

51. In Hebrew the linkage between Cain (*qayin*) and Kenite (*qēynī*, or even, once, *qayin*, Judg. 4:11) is more obvious than in English.

52. I wonder if there is a wry irony in the presentation of Lamech as making this boast specifically to his two wives. They could represent a compliant audience who might be inclined, for reasons of self-preservation, to appear to accept his boast at face value rather than challenge him as to whether his deeds really matched his words.

53. The best commentary on this is the words of Jesus, who draws on the language of Lamech's boast so as to replace *revenge* without limits with *forgiveness* without limits (Matt. 18:21–22).

to Cain to be understood? Is the giving of the mark an act of grace, as it is often understood to be? Is the LORD in effect approving mass murder? Or is He doing something else?

I have argued that the portrayal of Cain is of someone who has allowed himself to be consumed by sin in the form of bitter and murderous resentment. He has no apparent concern to heed the LORD's counsel to "master" it, but rather has let sin have its way with him. Thus, Cain and his descendants should likely be seen as in some way negative exemplars—not of murder as such,[54] but rather of a way of life that is heedless of the guidance of the LORD in handling difficulties and that therefore becomes injurious, both to self and to others.[55]

In this sense, they would exemplify something found elsewhere in Genesis. Israel's world is a storied world, in that it has places which bear a certain meaning and have certain resonances because of particular stories that are attached to them. Cain and his descendants would be exemplars of heedlessness of the LORD's way, not dissimilar to Lot's wife, whose permanent presence as a pillar of salt appears to be a known marker that symbolizes careless unconcern for a puzzling divine instruction (Gen. 19:17, 26).[56] Knowing that the entire territory around the Dead Sea was once a desirably well-watered and fertile region that was transformed into barren desert by the LORD's judgment on the egregious sin of its inhabitants (Gen. 13:10–11, 13; 18:16–19:29) makes this a landscape with a meaning, a pictorial depiction of the bleak and barren consequences of heedlessness of the LORD's way.[57] By analogy, Cain and his descendants could be seen as spiritually

54. So, e.g., Gunkel: "Cain has become for all times the paradigm of the murderer pursued by divine vengeance" (*Genesis*, 49).

55. This would be akin to the fool in Proverbs, only in a more destructive mode.

56. It is, of course, easy to rationalize the instruction not to look back into something that prima facie makes better sense. Thus Nahum Sarna thinks in terms of the intrinsic dangers attendant upon an earthquake if one is caught in proximity: "She lingered in flight and was overwhelmed by the spreading devastation" (*Genesis*, 138). Alternatively, S. R. Driver, building on the brief reference to the story by Jesus (Luke 17:32), finds a constructive moral and spiritual lesson: "Lot's wife is the type of those who, in whatever age, 'look back' with regretful longings upon possessions and enjoyments which are inconsistent with the salvation offered to them" (*Book of Genesis*, 202). Such imaginative moves indeed make sense. Nonetheless, I wonder whether the command not to look back—precisely because it goes against the natural instinct to see what is happening and so may easily be disregarded—carries a deeper significance in terms of the symbolic importance of resisting a natural inclination which, at least sometimes, can be disastrous. The mythic resonance with the story of Orpheus and Eurydice might also indicate a meaning along these lines.

57. This symbolic resonance no longer pertains in the twenty-first century, when the expertise of Israeli desert agriculture has transformed the Jordan Valley into a condition more suggestive of the description in Gen. 13.

comparable to the bleak and barren state of that valley region as a whole. In some such way, Genesis 4 enables those who know about Cain and his descendants to see them as exemplifying an attitude towards God and others that is to be avoided—in the idiom of Deuteronomy, "all Israel will hear and be afraid."[58]

The question of how many people in the contexts of the story's composition, tradition history, redaction, and reception within the life of ancient Israel (whenever and wherever these contexts were) had some actual encounter with Cain in the person of his descendants has no clear answer. We simply do not know. What surely matters most is the literary portrayal of a type of human being, preserved in a privileged position at the outset of Genesis, which offers an archetypal picture of a basic existential challenge. If feelings of disappointment at being in some way unfavored are indulged, they can become sinful and destructive of self and others. Abel is murdered, and Cain is mastered by savage resentment. Although Cain's reputation for murderous overreaction may keep him and his descendants alive, their condition in life is not enviable but pitiable. Cain becomes distanced from the LORD, and he "settles" in a land where, ironically, one cannot really settle, as the land is symbolically named "Wandering." It may well be that Cain's restless wandering symbolizes his restless existential state; he is at the mercy of the turmoil of resentment.

Jacob and Esau as a Narrative Analogy to Cain and Abel

I have already noted the likely narrative analogy between Cain and Abel and Jacob and Esau. In each instance there are two brothers—most likely twins—and essentially the first thing that is said about them is that the one who comes out second at birth is favored over the firstborn brother. Esau is in the position of Cain, the unfavored firstborn, while Jacob is favored like Abel. The story of Cain and Abel focuses almost entirely on the unfavored Cain, while the later and much more extensive narrative focuses predominantly on the favored Jacob, although the unfavored Esau also has a significant role.

On the one hand, neither Abel nor Jacob is favored, and neither Cain nor Esau is unfavored, because they have in any way deserved it. On the other hand, however, the story of Jacob and Esau presents a particular difficulty to readers: the favored Jacob seems to be especially *un*deserving.

58. See Deut. 13:12 (ET 11); 17:13; 19:20; 21:21.

In the first episode in which we meet Esau and Jacob as adult figures, neither is an attractive character. Esau, who sells his birthright for a mess of pottage, is uncouth and irresponsible. And Jacob, who will not feed him in his hunger without first extracting his birthright from him, is uncompassionate and manipulative (Gen. 25:29–34).

More developed, and more difficult in almost every way, is the account of Jacob's gaining the blessing that the dying Isaac intended for Esau (Gen. 27:1–45). Jacob deceives Isaac and thereby cheats Esau out of the blessing. The story is enigmatic to the reader of the overall Jacob narrative inasmuch as no reference is made to the oracle that the LORD gave to Rebekah in her pregnancy, the oracle in which Jacob is favored over Esau (25:23). The position of this oracle at the very outset of the story of Jacob and Esau makes it an interpretive key to the whole. Yet the question of how the content of the oracle might have, or should have, affected the thoughts and actions of the characters in Genesis 27 is left entirely to the reader's imagination. Unsurprisingly, this allows for great diversity in how readers reconcile (or not) the LORD's favoring of Jacob with the deceptive actions of Jacob and his mother Rebekah, who instigates the deception. The story raises uncomfortable questions about the possibility of the LORD's purposes being fulfilled through immoral and manipulative actions.

The outline of the story is straightforward. Isaac, anticipating his imminent death, tells Esau to hunt and bring him his favorite savory food "so that I may bless you before I die" (Gen. 27:1–4). Rebekah overhears this and tells Jacob to help her quickly prepare Isaac's favorite food while Esau is out hunting, so that when Jacob takes it to Isaac, he, instead of Esau, will receive Isaac's blessing (27:5–10). When Jacob questions the practicality of this (though not its morality), Rebekah overrules his doubt and makes all the necessary arrangements—not only the food but also an appropriate disguise for Jacob (27:11–17). When Jacob comes to Isaac as though he were Esau, Isaac is suspicious and repeatedly questions whether he really is Esau, but the deception is successful (27:18–27a). The result is that Isaac blesses Jacob with words whose climax resonates not only with the LORD's oracle to Rebekah but also with the LORD's opening words of commission to Abraham (25:23; cf. 12:3a):

> [29] Let peoples serve you,
>   and nations bow down to you.
> Be lord over your brothers,
>   and may your mother's sons bow down to you.
> Cursed be everyone who curses you,
>   and blessed be everyone who blesses you! (Gen. 27:29)

Isaac's blessing irreversibly favors Jacob over Esau.[59] No sooner does the blessed Jacob leave than Esau returns, makes a savory meal, and comes to Isaac for his blessing (27:30–31). The ensuing dialogue between Isaac and Esau, with the one realizing his deception and the other his loss, is given both space and expressive development by the narrator; their pain matters, and the reader needs to be aware of it (27:32–38). Esau eventually receives a quasi-blessing, but the preferential position of Jacob remains (27:39–40).

Esau is now in the unfavored position of Cain. In the important and life-shaping matter of the paternal blessing, he has lost out, through no fault of his own, to his unscrupulous brother. His reaction is strong: Esau is filled with murderous hatred towards Jacob. The only thing that holds him back from immediate vengeance is a concern not to upset his father for as long as he remains alive; so Esau will bide his time for a short while (27:41). This delay, however, gives Rebekah a further opportunity to intervene. She warns Jacob of Esau's murderous intentions and tells him to leave immediately, to go and stay with her brother Laban in Haran. She makes it easier for Jacob to flee in his moment of triumph over his brother by implying that this need not be for long ("Stay with him a while").[60] Indeed, she implausibly suggests that when Esau's anger dies down he will forget "what you have done to him," and so it should not be long before she sends for Jacob to come home (27:42–45). Finally, she deftly presents to Isaac the issue of Jacob's departure as a matter of matrimonial priorities, and the issue of Esau's murderous rage is brushed under the carpet (27:46–28:5).

Jacob thus leaves home. As one favored by the LORD, Jacob in the early stages of his journey sees angels and receives in a dream a promise of land and descendants. His response, however, only takes the form of a vow that if the LORD will protect him, then the LORD will be his God, and he will formalize this at that place, Bethel (28:10–22). He then stays with his uncle, Laban, for many years, and the two take turns in outwitting the other. Over time, Jacob prospers and acquires both wives and wealth. No summons home from his mother ever comes. Eventually, however, Jacob decides that he wants to return home (30:25) and is also told by the LORD to do so (31:3). After a protracted process of disentangling himself from Laban, he sets off (Gen. 30–31).

59. I say "irreversibly" insofar as this is seen as an exercise of a speech act appropriate to the socially recognized occasion of a deathbed pronouncement, somewhat analogous to formal pronouncements in other recognized contexts, such as marriage vows or a presidential oath of office. See Thiselton, "Supposed Power of Words in the Biblical Writings."

60. The best idiomatic parallel for the Hebrew *yāmīm 'ăḥādīm* ("a while") is "Jacob served seven years for Rachel, and they seemed to him but a few days [*yāmīm 'ăḥādīm*] because of the love he had for her" (Gen. 29:20). Spanish has a comparable idiom: *unos dias* ("a few days").

Just as when he left home, at an early stage of the journey Jacob encounters angels, which could be a positive sign (Gen. 32:1–2).[61] However, he knows that the key issue is how his brother will receive him. So he sends ahead messengers to Esau to prepare his way. They are to speak deferentially ("your servant Jacob" to "my lord Esau") and insinuate that Jacob in his wealth has much to offer (pay off?) his brother (32:3–5). Jacob tacitly inverts his favored position in the oracle to Rebekah and in Isaac's blessing, so that he is now the subservient one. When these messengers return, what they say is hardly reassuring: "We came to your brother Esau, and he is coming to meet you, and four hundred men are with him." In addition, they have been given no message of welcome to convey. Four hundred men could constitute a small army,[62] sufficient to wipe out Jacob and all he has. Unsurprisingly, Jacob, who has no military resources, "was greatly afraid and distressed" (32:6–7a). Alongside practical arrangements centering on generous gifts for Esau, Jacob prays—for the first time, in terms of the overall narrative portrayal.[63] In this prayer, deferential language to God surrounds a fearful request: "Deliver me, please, from the hand of my brother, from the hand of Esau, for I am afraid of him; he may come and kill us all, the mothers with the children" (32:11). The closer Jacob comes to Esau, the more fearful he becomes, for he knows that life and death are at stake in their meeting (32:7b–23).

This is the context for the most famous and resonant moment in Jacob's whole story: "Jacob was left alone; and a man wrestled with him until daybreak" (Gen. 32:24). Most key aspects of this mysterious encounter remain enigmatic. With whom does Jacob wrestle? Is it a man (*'īsh*, v. 24)? Is it God (*'ĕlōhīm*, vv. 28, 30)? Is it God in the human form of an angel (*mal'āk*—not specified in the text, but often suggested in the history of interpretation)? And why do they wrestle? The best interpretive clue to the episode is its narrative context, immediately prior to Jacob's meeting with Esau the next morning. In some way this episode mediates between Jacob's fearing for his life because of Esau and the meeting between the brothers that ensues. In some way the one with whom Jacob wrestles would appear to be both God and Esau,[64] and

61. In Gen. 32 the Hebrew versification is one ahead of the English versification. In this paragraph and the next I will give only the English versification.

62. When David, on the run from Saul, gathers a significant fighting force around himself, it is said to number "about four hundred" (1 Sam. 22:2).

63. Jacob's vow at Bethel (Gen. 28:20–22) is only marginally, at most, a prayer. It is the specification of a conditional arrangement which speaks of God in the third person. The final phrase, however, which actually addresses God in the second person, gives the vow a certain element of prayer.

64. This contextual logic is fully recognized in Midrash Rabbah 77:3, where it is proposed that the figure is the guardian angel of Esau; cross-reference is also made to Jacob's words in

Jacob's surviving this encounter is bound up with his surviving the encounter the next morning. Although the morning meeting will be told in the language of regular human encounter, an encounter with God underlies it.

> [1]Now Jacob looked up and what he saw was Esau coming,[65] and four hundred men with him. So he divided the children among Leah and Rachel and the two maids. [2]He put the maids with their children in front, then Leah with her children, and Rachel and Joseph last of all. [3]He himself went on ahead of them, bowing himself to the ground seven times, until he came near his brother. (Gen. 33:1–3)

The moment of truth and reckoning has come. What Jacob initially sees is none other than the threatening scenario previously reported by his messengers: Esau and a small army. Jacob's immediate dispositions of his family reflect his priorities, with those he cares for the most put at the rear so that if Esau attacks, they have the best chance of escape. However, he realizes that it is no use to try to hide behind his family; he must go in front of them to face his brother. If this is to be his final moment, he will face it without cowering or fleeing. He proceeds, though, in a mode of abject obeisance, constantly prostrating himself on the ground.[66]

> [4]But Esau ran to meet him, and embraced him, and fell on his neck and kissed him, and they wept. (Gen. 33:4)

This is one of the memorable moments in the Bible. Esau is Cain, the unfavored brother. Like Cain, Esau's initial response of hatred meant that he had to face the beast of bitter resentment wanting to get hold of him. But unlike Cain, who ignored the LORD's words ("but you must master it"), Esau has, at it were, heeded them. He has mastered the beast of resentment, and he welcomes Jacob in a manner that is apparently wholehearted and unreserved. From a Christian perspective, the best commentary on the manner of his welcome—running, embracing, falling on Jacob's neck, kissing, weeping—is that this appears to be the language of welcome and reconciliation on which

---

Gen. 33:10, where he says that seeing Esau is like seeing God (Freedman, *Midrash Rabbah: Genesis II*, 711).

65. The NRSV's "Jacob looked up and saw" is inaccurate; it omits the particle *hinnēh*, presumably on the assumption that it is no more than a quaint archaism ("lo," "behold") whose omission is no loss. This fails to appreciate its idiomatic usage whereby it shifts the narrative's perspective from the narrator to a character within the text, analogous to the way a movie camera's perspective can shift to look through the eyes of a character within a scene. See also Exod. 3:2 (ch. 2, pp. 54–55) for this same issue.

66. The idiom "seven times" has here the same idiomatic force of "many times," as in Gen. 4:15 (see above, 144n50).

Jesus draws to depict the father's welcome of the prodigal son ("His father . . . ran and put his arms around him [lit., "fell on his neck"] and kissed him," Luke 15:20). Even if, in what follows, Esau and Jacob keep some distance between themselves, the initiative in this distancing comes entirely from Jacob. Everything that Esau says is gracious and accepting.

The only disappointing part for the reader is that we are not told how Esau came to this point. The pathos of his initial dismay and pain at losing Isaac's blessing and his consequent hatred of Jacob are clearly portrayed. Since that point, the narrative has followed Jacob and ignored Esau. We have hints from Jacob's prayer and from his wrestling at the ford of the Jabbok that God has something to do with Esau's forgiveness and generosity; but of what went on in Esau's heart and mind we know nothing. One story, or pair of stories, cannot say everything.

Nonetheless, even if we respect the silence of Genesis and acknowledge that we do not know how Esau got to this point, the significant thing is that he did get there. He realizes the possibility for human life, even when one is unfavored, that the LORD holds out to Cain. He has mastered the beast of resentment. In this regard he is exemplary.

Esau in the History of Interpretation

It is a pity that in the history of interpretation Esau's exemplary moment was mostly either ignored or misread, as it became taken for granted that Esau was a negative figure. In some prophetic literature (e.g., Obadiah; Mal. 1:2–5), Esau/Edom becomes a figure/people who represents betrayal and enmity towards Israel and, as such, is the recipient of the LORD's judgment. These negative prophetic portrayals outweighed the positive portrayal in Genesis and led to its negative rereading.

In an anthology of patristic biblical commentary, Mark Sheridan observes of Genesis 33 that "this chapter does not seem to have inspired much comment in the patristic period." Indeed, the one commentary which Sheridan cites, by Cyril of Alexandria, totally inverts the sense of the text: Jacob takes the initiative in being reconciled with Esau, such that the text prefigures Christ's reconciliation with Israel: "At the end of time our Lord Jesus Christ will be reconciled with Israel, his ancient persecutor, just as Jacob kissed Esau after his return from Haran. . . . See how Jacob . . . came back from Haran and received again Esau into his friendship."[67]

67. Sheridan, *Genesis 12–50*, 225. The text cited is Cyril of Alexandria's *Glaphyra on Genesis* 5:3 (PG 69:261).

In rabbinic and medieval Jewish literature, Esau/Edom becomes a symbol for the Roman Empire and then for Christendom. The sufferings of Jews under these powers played back onto their reading of the biblical text and were allowed to overshadow Esau's exemplary moment of graciousness towards Jacob.

In Genesis 33:4 the Hebrew for "and he kissed him" (*vayyishshāqēhū*) has dots over it. The phenomenon of dots occasionally appearing over words in the Masoretic Text resists clear explanation; it may either indicate some uncertainty about the word in Masoretic tradition or be a pointer to midrashic commentary. In any case, rabbinic commentary on this word tends to diminish Esau's kiss. Rashi, for example, notes that "some explain the dotting as meaning that he did not kiss him with his whole heart"—though he also records the proposal that Esau's kiss was indeed genuine albeit uncharacteristic inasmuch as, despite his known hatred of Jacob, "at that moment his pity was really aroused and he kissed him with his whole heart."[68] (Calvin has a similar suggestion: "It is also possible, that even while cruelty was pent up within, the feeling of humanity may have had a temporary ascendancy.")[69] Genesis Rabbah, however, after noting that the kiss might be genuine, also offers a strongly negative construal: Esau was only pretending to kiss, and really "he wished to bite him" (i.e., this is an imaginative suggestion to think of *nūn-shīn-kaph*, "bite," rather than the text's *nūn-shīn-qōph*, "kiss"), even though Jacob's neck was turned to marble (through God's protective action). The only injury was to Esau's teeth; his subsequent tears were for his pain.[70]

One of the great gains of modern scholarship has been a recovered awareness of the richness and depth of human characterization, and of the surprising nature of divine grace, in biblical narrative.[71]

Some Hermeneutical and Theological Reflections

In chapter 3 I considered the importance of justice in relation to God. I argued that Psalm 82 sees justice as definitional and constitutive of the reality of the true God (and thereby makes explicit what is implicit in much of the

68. Rashi, *Pentateuch*, 161.

69. Calvin, *Calvin's Commentaries: Genesis*, 207.

70. Genesis Rabbah 78:9 (Freedman, *Midrash Rabbah: Genesis II*, 721).

71. The importance of the plain sense of Gen. 33:4 is well recognized in the title of a recent work of Jewish-Christian dialogue: Bayfield, Brichto, and Fisher, *He Kissed Him and They Wept: Towards a Theology of Jewish-Catholic Partnership*.

Old Testament). But how does my reading of Psalm 82 relate to Genesis, with its stories of Cain and Abel and Jacob and Esau and God's differential decisions that favor one over the other? Many readers of Genesis may naturally respond, "It's not fair!" In an obvious sense, that is true: it isn't fair. How, then, can the God who is intrinsically just countenance that which is unfair? If one resists both a knee-jerk reaction of dismissiveness towards the biblical text and a possible too-easy attempt to get round the problem ("There are different and irreconcilable voices in the Bible, and one has to choose between them"), how best may some progress be made?

How Should We Characterize Differential Divine Decisions?

It is not easy to find good theological conceptualities to depict what is going on in these narratives.

Two preliminary points of clarification. First, we are not dealing here with "salvation," as Christians characteristically understand the term. The Old Testament does not address the question of eternal destiny (however much its content may be open to being developed in such terms), but rather is concerned with relationship with God and the purpose of life in this world. Second, Abel's being favored and Cain's being unfavored is directly related to their sacrifices. It does not follow that they are favored or unfavored in everything. After all, Abel is favored in the sacrifice, but he is soon unfavored in the sense that he meets an early and undeserved death.

Jon Levenson, in his groundbreaking *The Death and Resurrection of the Beloved Son*, has argued that divine election, with its corollary of nonelection, is a key issue in Genesis. Just as, elsewhere in the Hebrew Bible, God chooses Israel in a way that He does not choose other nations, so in Genesis God characteristically chooses a younger son over an elder and assigns the status of the firstborn, the beloved son, to the younger son in a way that conflicts with general social norms and expectations.[72] The beloved son is marked for both exaltation and humiliation, the latter in the form of a symbolic death. Moreover, "most of these substitutions [of a younger for an older son] are *genealogical* through and through: their function is to justify the privileged bloodlines." Thus, for example, the result of Isaac's blessing in Genesis 27 is that "from now on, the descendants of Esau, the Edomites, will be seen as collateral members of the family of Abraham. The trunk of the chosen family continues through Jacob and his descendants, the Israelites, or, as

72. "Isaac, Jacob, Joseph, and Ephraim move to the fore in place of Ishmael, Esau, Reuben, and Manasseh, respectively" (Levenson, *Death and Resurrection of the Beloved Son*, 72).

they came later to be called, the Jews."[73] There are two corollaries of this. One is the moral and theological issue, which confronts the reader of the text, of whether "these unpredictable acts of choosing" are "best described as arbitrariness and condemned as unworthy of a God of justice." The other is the existential issue for Cain, within the world of the text, of whether he can "suffer the exaltation of the younger brother at his own expense." These corollaries quickly come together, and Cain comes to represent a fundamental issue in life: "What Cain cannot bear is a world in which distributive justice is not the highest principle and not every inequity is an iniquity."[74]

I am deeply informed by Levenson's reading of Genesis. I want, however, to differentiate my reading of the story of Cain and Abel and its implications from Levenson's thesis, as I am arguing something different. On the one hand, Genesis 4:1–16 has an archetypal "Everyman" character and lacks a genealogical interest, other than with the descendants of Cain, who appear to be more of a type of person than an identifiable ethnic group. On the other hand, there is no concern for the "exaltation" of Abel as a type of the favored son, and Abel's life and narrative presence are fleeting.[75] The narrative's interest is entirely focused on the unfavored Cain.

Nonetheless, I want to retain and use Levenson's memorable epigram that "not every inequity is an iniquity," which well captures a central concern of the biblical text. I am interpreting the specific challenges faced by the paradigmatic figures of Cain and Esau—those inequities for which God's differential decisions are responsible—as representing challenges in principle faced by anyone. The text's perspective is not inequity as injustice or iniquity, but inequity as a life situation in which people have to face how to handle their being unfavored. I infer from the story of Cain and Abel that God's differential decision is not to be "explained," that the center of interest is the unfavored Cain, and that the LORD's guidance on how to handle being unfavored is widely applicable. I infer from the analogous story of Jacob and Esau that (1) things such as beauty and intelligence are differentially given to people from the womb, developing the possible implications of the LORD's

73. Levenson, *Death and Resurrection of the Beloved Son*, 70, 69.

74. Levenson, *Death and Resurrection of the Beloved Son*, 70–71, 74, 75.

75. Levenson of course recognizes that "Abel . . . seems at first glance to break decisively with the paradigm of the beloved son" (*Death and Resurrection of the Beloved Son*, 75); but he argues that the paradigm still pertains. However, his account of how postbiblical Judaism provided an exaltation for Abel does not remedy its absence in the biblical text. And although his interesting argument that "Seth is Abel redivivus" (78) may indeed show that "the death of the beloved son, even when it is not averted, can still be reversed," this reversal (with a Seth who is of no narrative interest) hardly bears comparison with the narrative portrayals of Abraham, Jacob, and Joseph.

oracle to Rebekah about her as-yet-unborn twins; and that (2) deprivations and disasters happen in the course of life, developing the possible implications of Esau's losing the blessing to Jacob through no fault of his own. The stories together pose the existential challenge of how best to respond in situations of being unfavored—that is, whether to be Cain or to be Esau.

On Interpreting Language of Divine Decision and Action

Another related core theological issue in the story of Cain and Abel is how best to understand and speak of divine decision and action in the world.

The language of Genesis 4, where God actively "looks on" one sacrifice and "does not look on" the other, can be puzzling—indeed, off-putting—in more than one way. In relation to the character of God, such language can encourage a sense of God's being arbitrary. Another dimension of the language is the depiction of God's directly interacting with the brothers and their sacrifices so as to bring about the particular difference. How best should this strong language of divine action and interaction be understood?

In the first place, there is a question about the idiom and convention in Hebrew narrative, especially in the early traditions in the Pentateuch, in which God is portrayed as an active character who speaks and acts, by analogy with human speech and action. Christian theology in reflective mode typically qualifies or modifies this by appealing to the notion of divine "accommodation" and the limits of human language. God does not speak and act like a human does as such, but this is nonetheless a meaningful and appropriate way to depict and think of Him and less misleading than the use of impersonal and noninteractive language. Although much Christian theology down the ages has preferred to work in a more abstract and theoretical idiom, the narrative form of so much of the Bible has always been one of its strengths in making its subject matter accessible and engaging to people generally. It is important to enter into the world of the text with full imaginative seriousness.

Alongside this, readers should appreciate the richness and diversity of the Bible's literary genres and recognize that the relationship between text and referent may take many forms. However, as noted in chapter 3,[76] many contemporary readers are happier to recognize a diversity of genres and modes of reference in modern works of literature and film, where they feel generally at home with the cultural conventions, than in the Bible. The problem can be exacerbated when the Bible is seen not only as ancient but also as sacred

76. See p. 120.

literature, which can encourage deferential reverence instead of—rather than as well as—lively exploration and interaction.

In terms of the specific idiom and convention operative in Genesis 4, it is worth briefly returning to the LORD's negative response to Cain's sacrifice, a response whose inflexibility is surely meant to steer the reader. If Cain had gotten wrong some particular aspect of his sacrifice, whether in terms of his intention or his sacrificial technique—as is envisaged in the LXX rendering, "If you rightly offer, but do not rightly divide, have you not sinned?"—then one might expect that, if the story's concern were with the character and responsiveness of God, a just and equity-seeking God would have *less* regard for Cain's sacrifice, but scarcely none at all, as in the binary presentation of the text. In addition, one might expect the dialogue that follows to address the question of what to do better in future sacrifices (e.g., "Be more wholehearted" or "Divide the offering thus"). But it does not. Thus, the LORD's undifferentiated rejection of Cain's sacrifice suggests that the dynamics of divine character and responsiveness ("Is God indeed just?"; "How and why does God differentiate?") are not to the point here. Rather, the text's concern is to describe a situation in which the central issue is proper human response to unexpected and unmerited disappointment in relation to God and others, which is the focus of the dialogue that immediately follows. The operative narrative convention indeed presents the LORD as inscrutable, but the focus is not on that inscrutability in itself but rather on the implications for human life that follow from it—with a tacit further implication that only in the context of right human response will God's inscrutability be rightly (if at all) understood.

A second issue is specifically theological—that is, the question of how best to think of God and of divine action in the world, in terms of both overall divine providence and possible specific actions ("particular providence" in an older terminology).[77] Some Christians have been led by the biblical idiom of divine action to develop strong accounts of divine causality in which everything that happens is to be ascribed to the will of God (even while recognizing that God's will complements, rather than competes with, accounts of causality in recognizable human modes). This, however, leads to well-known difficulties, especially in contexts of evil and suffering. A reflective approach will tend to introduce conceptual distinctions that are not articulated explicitly in Scripture but that seek to extend scriptural language.

For example, one can make distinctions between what God desires, what God permits, and what God knows about. A telling example of this quest for a good theological conceptuality is the words of Jesus in Matthew 10:29: "Are

77. An excellent account of the issues is Wood, *Question of Providence*.

not two sparrows sold for a penny? Yet not one of them falls to the ground *without your Father's will* [RSV] / *without your Father's leave* [NEB] / *without your Father knowing about it already* [CEB]." The Greek text simply has "without your Father [*aneu tou patros humōn*]." The text leaves nonspecific the relationship between God and the dying bird even while making clear that there is a relationship of some sort. Nonetheless, there is a good case for using language that highlights trust in God while simultaneously underlining the limits of human comprehension—for example, "No situation is beyond God's good purposes and His ability to bring something good out of it" or "No one who trusts God ever falls out of God's care."

I propose, therefore, that the Hebrew idiom of the LORD "looking on" Abel and "not looking on" Cain is to be taken seriously without being taken woodenly. It points towards a particular understanding of life in this world as God's world—that is, when this world is understood in relation to God as active creator and sustainer. In God's world, differences between people's characteristics, abilities, situations, and outcomes are part of the way the world is, such that certain kinds of inequity are intrinsic and inevitable. This is the pattern that God has given to His creation. The human challenge is to learn how to live well with God and with other people. This challenge is in many ways sharper and more difficult for those who are in some way "less favored" than for those who are, by comparison, "more favored"—although Jesus memorably warns that "from everyone to whom much has been given, much will be required" (Luke 12:48). Most people, however, in the course of their lives have the experience of being "less favored" in one way or another.

Divine Justice and Divine Inequity

What, then, might be said about the question of justice and inequity in relation to God? As the beginnings of an answer, we should note that it can be misleading to conjure with abstract nouns without regard to the particularities of human life and circumstances.

Since the French Revolution, which arguably marked the birth of modern political culture, "liberty" and "equality" have been high-value terms with wide resonance. There are, of course, many life situations in which concerns of liberty and/or equality rightly come to the fore. For those who live under domineering or totalitarian state control, basic human freedoms, which can be summed up as sociopolitical "liberty," assume moral and political priority. For those who are locked into contexts of social and educational deprivation, greater access to resources to which others also have access, which can be summed up as "equality of opportunity," may similarly be an appropriate moral and political goal. The difficulty with these terms is the ease with which "liberty" and "equality" can be bandied about in a slogan-like way that enables their advocates to claim the moral high ground in relation to their preferred agenda. But the sheer complexity and range of forces that bear upon human life—the particular life situations into which people are born and in which they grow up and by which they are formed; the pressures and expectations of families and friends and employers; the divergent goals of differing sociopolitical agendas; the pressures of contemporary consumer commercialism and the advertising images of "the good life" that lack any serious vision of the common good—necessarily qualify and constrain the meaning and value of "liberty" and "equality" for many people for much of the time.

"Justice" in the Old Testament has a narrower and more specific focus than it does in much modern political parlance. In Psalm 82 "justice" has to do with the needs of the weak, the poor, and the vulnerable in relation to those who would oppress and exploit them: "Give justice to the weak and the orphan; / maintain the right of the lowly and the destitute. / Rescue the weak and the needy; / deliver them from the hand of the wicked" (Ps. 82:3–4). The proposed intertext, Deuteronomy 10:17–19, has a similar emphasis, to which is added an equally characteristic accent on the need to resist corrupting justice through prejudice or venality: "For the Lord your God is . . . the great God . . . who is not partial and takes no bribe, who executes justice for the orphan and the widow, and who loves the immigrants, providing them food and clothing." Since the problem of corruption on the part of those with power is a perennial concern, the specific biblical focus remains fundamental. But this does not mean that one cannot appropriately go beyond the biblical concepts and find other ways of implementing justice.

In short, the recognition of certain inequities as intrinsic to life in God's world is no excuse for being heedless of the need for justice. But this recognition does not in itself offer guidance as to the *specific* forms of equity and justice that humans should appropriately strive for as an instantiation of God's priorities. On any reckoning, to speak of justice and inequity in the abstract, and play them off against each other, will not help one understand how to live better and make life better for others.

Human Free Will and Choice: Two Modern Accounts

The stories of Cain and Abel and Jacob and Esau raise the issue of human choosing—as encapsulated in the words of the Lord to Cain in Genesis 4:7—

as a central aspect of life in God's world. It may be helpful briefly to reflect further on this with the help of two modern classics, one of literature and the other of psychology.

John Steinbeck's East of Eden

John Steinbeck's novel *East of Eden* offers a profound and creative interpretation and use of the biblical story of Cain and Abel.[78] A central thread in Steinbeck's story focuses on two pairs of brothers whose names, like Cain and Abel, begin with *C* and *A*: Charles and Adam Trask, and Cal (Caleb) and Aron Trask. At key moments Charles and Cal act resentfully, without care for life, against Adam and Aron, respectively.[79]

Cyrus Trask, the father of Adam and Charles, favors Adam over Charles for no good reason. Charles, in his resentment, comes close to murdering Adam. Through an accident Charles also acquires a mark on his forehead.

Adam Trask, the father of Cal and Aron, does not have a favorite. But Cal, feeling rejected by his father, who compares him unfavorably with Aron, resentfully acts against Aron. Cal not only wounds Aron deeply but initiates a train of events that lead to his death. When an anxious Adam asks Cal where Aron is (when he has fled from home after Cal's wounding action), Cal responds, "How do I know? Am I supposed to look after him?"

Alongside the story of the Trask family is the story of the Hamilton family, especially Samuel Hamilton (presented as Steinbeck's own maternal grandfather), and the story of Lee, a Chinese American who is a servant to Adam Trask and a friend of Samuel Hamilton. The story of Cain and Abel is first introduced in the context of trying to find names for Adam's twin sons, and Lee says, "I think this is the best-known story in the world because it is everybody's story. I think it is the symbol story of the human soul."[80] Subsequently, Lee tells of how "the story bit deeply into me and I went into it word for word." He is particularly intrigued by the fact that standard translations of the Bible, while mostly agreeing with each other, render the latter part of Genesis 4:7 differently. Lee thus studies Hebrew for two years with four

78. A collection of Steinbeck's letters from the time he wrote *East of Eden* gives an appreciation of how the book, and especially the central characters Samuel and Lee, represents Steinbeck's thinking. See Steinbeck, *Journal of a Novel*.

79. Steinbeck depicts Charles's actions against Adam as the "symbolic killing of brother by brother" (*Journal of a Novel*, 25).

80. *East of Eden*, ch. 22, #4 (p. 268). Steinbeck says of his use of the story of Cain and Abel, "I am glad that I can use the oldest story in the world to be the design of the newest story for me. The lack of change in the world is the thing which astonishes me" (*Journal of a Novel*, 104).

other Chinese scholars.[81] He conveys the result of their study in relation to Genesis 4:7 thus:

> Don't you see? The American Standard translation ["Do thou rule over it"] *orders* men to triumph over sin, and you can call sin ignorance. The King James translation ["Thou shalt rule over him"] makes a promise in "Thou shalt," meaning that men will surely triumph over sin. But the Hebrew word, the word *timshel*[82]—"Thou mayest"—that gives a choice. It might be the most important word in the world.[83]

Hereafter the issue of human choice, as represented by *timshel* (consistently rendered by Steinbeck simply as "thou mayest" rather than the full "thou mayest rule"), is raised at two key moments in the story: in the dying Samuel's challenge to Adam to accept and not be destroyed by the terrible truth about his wife, Cathy, and in the dying Adam's final word to a distraught Cal in relation to the guilt he feels for what he did to Aron.[84]

Steinbeck reads Genesis 4 as an enduring classic about the human condition—and reads it more searchingly than many who read it as Scripture. His translation of *timshel* as "thou mayest rule" is a valid rendering of the Hebrew, though the word does not mean "may" to the exclusion of translations such as "must." And although God is not a point of reference in Steinbeck's story, the importance of human dignity, centered in human free will and choice, is. Steinbeck memorably shows that the human freedom to choose is real and potent precisely because life in the world is inescapably characterized by inequities, dilemmas, and tragedies.

Viktor Frankl's Man's Search for Meaning

Strong modern resonance with the story of Cain and Abel can also be found in the work of Viennese psychiatrist Viktor Frankl. Frankl developed a particular understanding and practice of psychotherapy that he called "logotherapy," which involves learning how to weave the threads of a broken life into a pattern of meaning and responsibility. His classic work is *Man's Search*

81. Steinbeck himself noted intriguing differences in modern translations of Gen. 4:7 and sought advice about the meaning of *timshol*, though without learning Hebrew himself (*Journal of a Novel*, 107–9, 122).

82. For some reason Steinbeck always transliterates the Hebrew as *timshel* rather than the more accurate *timshol*.

83. *East of Eden*, ch. 24, #2 (p. 301). Steinbeck characterizes this significance thus: "Here is individual responsibility and the invention of conscience" (*Journal of a Novel*, 108).

84. *East of Eden*, ch. 24, #3 (pp. 304–6); ch. 55, #3 (pp. 597–601).

for Meaning, which draws on Frankl's time in Nazi concentration camps and has sold widely and enduringly. With regard to his work in general, he says,

> Psychoanalysis has often been blamed for its so-called pan-sexualism. I, for one, doubt whether this reproach has ever been legitimate. However, there is something which seems to me to be an even more erroneous and dangerous assumption, namely, that which I call "pan-determinism." By that I mean the view of man which disregards his capacity to take a stand toward any conditions whatsoever. Man is *not* fully conditioned and determined but rather determines himself whether he gives in to conditions or stands up to them. In other words, man is ultimately self-determining. Man does not simply exist but always decides what his existence will be, what he will become in the next moment.[85]

Frankl relates his general point to the specific horror of life in a concentration camp:

> We who lived in concentration camps can remember the men who walked through the huts comforting others, giving away their last piece of bread. They may have been few in number, but they offer sufficient proof that everything can be taken from a man but one thing: the last of the human freedoms—to choose one's attitude in any given set of circumstances, to choose one's own way.[86]

Frankl was not explicitly religious. Yet by declaring the ability of people to choose how to respond to hardship to be constitutive of human dignity, he clearly draws deeply on his Jewish heritage with its biblical roots and rabbinic developments. In his own way he can be read as a commentator on the LORD's words to Cain in Genesis 4:7.

Conclusion: Towards a Grammar of the Inscrutable God

The fourth facet of "knowing that the LORD is God" is a recognition that the LORD is often inscrutable. God's ways with the world can be not only beyond rational explanation but also difficult to live with. Yet a corollary of this is the recognition that humans have been given a will and an ability to choose, in certain respects, how they live and how they handle the life situation in which they find themselves. Perhaps paradoxically, it is those who handle well their being "unfavored" who most enlarge a vision of what it means to be human.

85. Frankl, *Man's Search for Meaning*, 154.
86. Frankl, *Man's Search for Meaning*, 86.

In certain ways the language of "choice" has become devalued in much contemporary culture. On the one hand, some have trivialized it by implying that choices in life are somewhat like wandering around a supermarket and taking what catches one's fancy off the shelf. On the other hand, some point to biological, sociological, and environmental factors (of which one is often not consciously aware) that can constrain and limit whatever choices one may make; sometimes this becomes a determinist stance that denies that humans have free will or any real ability to choose at all.[87] The most significant uses of "choice," however, relate precisely to those situations in life that are *unchosen* and unwelcome, in which the question of how to respond indeed becomes formative for the self and the future. But if "choice" is overused and easily devalued, it may be that a term such as "creative consent" will be more helpful for some.[88]

Although the core issue of human choice / creative consent is meaningful on its own terms in relation to the stories of Cain and Abel and Jacob and Esau, it is also readily amenable to a certain reframing in an explicitly Christian frame of reference. While writing this chapter I read Erik Varden's *The Shattering of Loneliness*. In this moving reflection on Christian faith, Varden, among other things, draws on the testimony of Maïti Girtanner, a veteran of the French Resistance in the Second World War.[89]

When young, Maïti (born in 1922) wanted to be a pianist, for which she had the gifts and the training. When the German army occupied France in 1940, she worked with a local Resistance network to help people escape into the Free Zone controlled by the Vichy government. She also used her piano recitals for the German elite to gather information and to intercede for arrested comrades. But she came under suspicion and in 1943 was arrested and submitted to punitive torture, supervised by a doctor. Although she survived, she lived in chronic pain for the rest of her life. She was, however, determined

87. For a recent account, written in a thoughtful and engaging way from the perspective of a secular neuroscientist, that leans strongly towards seeing free will as an illusion (albeit generally a necessary one for a smooth-running life or society) but that does not foreclose the complexity of the issues, see Critchlow, *Science of Fate*. Although Critchlow recognizes theological and philosophical dimensions to the issue in an interesting interaction with Rowan Williams (154–57), she leaves their possible implications disappointingly underdeveloped.

88. I borrow this phrase from Thomas Merton, who writes, "Resignation is not enough. God demands of us a creative consent, in our deepest and most hidden self, the self we do not experience every day, and perhaps never experience, though it is always there" (*Conjectures of a Guilty Bystander*, 181).

89. Towards the end of her life she gave a television interview and then had a book-length conversation with Guillaume Tabard, editor in chief of *Le Figaro*. See Girtanner and Tabard, *Résistance et pardon: Maïti Girtanner*; and Girtanner with Tabard, *Même les bourreaux ont une âme*. I will cite Varden's account in *Shattering of Loneliness*, 98–106, 170.

"to make Christian sense of what her life had become" and after the war set a goal for herself: "I shan't make of my life a tragedy."

When asked how she kept herself together during her imprisonment and torture, she said, "I resisted in my mind. . . . As long as I could orient my thoughts, as long as I could pray, I was victorious." The example of Christ's suffering gave her the conviction that providence was operative in her pain. But after the war she had to confront the truth of her new reality:

> Suffering, for me, was not a transitory stage, but a state of being. Such a thing is very hard to admit. We always live in the hope that our wounds will pass. We expect our life's threads to reconnect. In my case, it was otherwise. It was simply a matter of building on new foundations, not of my choice.

She was unable to return to the piano, but she resolved to make a gift of what had been taken from her: "I had not to be nostalgic for what I had been or for what I might have become. Instead I had to love what I was and to seek what I ought to be." Her great concern was to forgive. In 1984 she was contacted by the doctor who had supervised her torture. He was dying and fearful of death and wanted to know if what Maïti had said about eternity, in her words of witness during her torture, was true. He visited her, she gave her pardon, and they were both changed by it. Varden summarizes his account of Maïti Girtanner in terms of "the coherence of her resolve to let Christ's passion be, not just an object of devout meditation, but a pattern for the building of a life."

In the context of the argument of this chapter, I am struck by the seemingly natural convergence between Maïti's recognition of her need to choose to rebuild her life on foundations not of her choice (in essence, the issue faced by Cain and Esau) and the enabling example of the passion of Christ (Maïti's own explicitly Christian framing of her challenge). In principle, the dynamics of the Old and New Testaments are not identical. Genesis offers no explicit clue for making sense of the LORD's stark nonacceptance of Cain and his offering; and it says nothing about the resources available to Cain and Esau for mastering the beast of resentful hatred. There is indeed a mystery about the LORD's actions and words, but it is not an obviously inviting mystery. The grammar of God and divine inscrutability here is austerely challenging. The wider biblical context, however, makes a difference. Already within the Old Testament, emphasis is laid upon the LORD's gracious purposes which, however testing they may be, are always for good.[90] The New

90. See, e.g., Exod. 34:6–7; Deut. 8:2–5, 16. Whatever the respective dates of origin of the content and composition of Gen. 4, Exod. 34, and Deut. 8—questions about the history of

Testament then presents Jesus as the ultimate key to understanding rejection, suffering, and death within the good purposes of God. The difference that is made by the wider biblical context is not that it diminishes the challenge of making choices in—or creatively consenting to—life in terms of making the most of the unwelcome. Rather, the context for understanding and the resources for embracing the unwelcome in terms of God's good purposes and His enabling are amplified.

ideas and the history of literature are distinctly imponderable here—canonical preservation and practices of regular reading encourage the reader to make intertextual linkages between these discrete passages and, in varying ways, to read them in the light of each other.

5

The Only God

Surprising Universality and Particularity in 2 Kings 5

In his satirical novel *Submission*, Michel Houellebecq portrays a dystopian future for France. In the 2022 presidential election the Socialists and the Muslim Brotherhood combine to block the National Front, and for the first time a Muslim takes office as head of state. In education, in particular, there are moves to Islamize institutions: Muslim identity becomes necessary for teaching staff. François, the narrator of the novel, is a middle-aged academic who teaches literature at the University of Paris III–Sorbonne but now finds himself out of a job. Very little that is worthwhile is happening in François's life apart from periodic sex, mainly with his former Jewish girlfriend, Myriam (moments with whom were, in François's judgment, "enough to justify a man's existence");[1] but the political developments mean that she has left France for Israel and shows no signs of returning.

After François has drifted for a while, Robert Rediger, a senior figure at the Sorbonne, attempts to persuade him to rejoin the university. Since this would require François to become a Muslim, Rediger offers him a copy of his bestselling *Ten Questions on Islam*. The chapter that particularly engages François is on polygamy; he has already admired Rediger's own polygamous household (which, in line with his sense of what really matters, he depicts as "a forty-year-old wife to do the cooking, a fifteen-year-old wife for whatever else").[2] François ponders and dithers for a while, but he finds the offer of a

1. Houellebecq, *Submission*, 29.
2. Houellebecq, *Submission*, 218.

tripled salary and more than one wife too much to resist. The book concludes with his envisaging the transition he is about to make. He memorizes and formally recites the Shahadah, the foundational affirmation of Muslim identity: "I testify that there is no God but God, and Muhammad is the messenger of God." His final reflection is that he "has the chance at a second life, with very little connection to the old one. I would have nothing to mourn."[3] *Submission* illustrates how a disenchanted figure can be brought into a new way of living—though what really persuades François is not the truth of Islam, or a fresh appreciation of ultimate values, but the prospect of better money and more sex, in shameless male chauvinist mode.

Houellebecq's novel has its own concerns and is characteristic of his oeuvre, with its "decline and fall" tenor and the simultaneous portrayal of the degeneration of Western civilization and of a particular figure within it. For present purposes I would like the story, with François's formal turning point being the Muslim confession of God, to linger in the background of my reading of a biblical story. My next exploration of "knowing that the LORD is God" considers a story at the heart of which someone from outside Israel comes to make Israel's pivotal confession of faith. I hope Houellebecq's story will help sharpen an appreciation of the distinctive tenor of the biblical text.

A Reading of 2 Kings 5

The story of Naaman is one of the famous stories of the Old Testament. Even though it is more challenging to understand than may initially appear,[4] I propose to plunge straight into a reading and subsequent reflection on it.[5] Its literary context is the cycle of stories about Elisha and his prophetic ministry in the Northern Kingdom of Israel.

> [1]Naaman, commander of the army of the king of Aram, was a great man and in high favor with his master, because by him the LORD had given victory to Aram.[6] The man was a mighty warrior—with a skin disease.[7] (2 Kings 5:1)

3. Houellebecq, *Submission*, 248–49, 250.

4. There are numerous small divergences between the Hebrew and Greek texts of the story, but they make little difference to its interpretation, for which my focus is on the MT.

5. A comprehensive guide to twentieth-century scholarship on the story is Baumgart, *Gott, Prophet und Israel*.

6. Older translations, up to at least the RSV, rendered the Hebrew *ʾărām* with "Syria." Since modern Syria is not coextensive with its ancient antecedent, there can be value in the defamiliarizing "Aram"—even if "Syria" is hardly more misleading than "Israel"!

7. I have changed the NRSV to try to retain the dramatic build-up of the Hebrew as well as to discard its use of "leprosy."

Naaman is portrayed glowingly. He is the chief of staff to the Aramean king and highly esteemed by the king, because his success as military commander had brought victorious peace to the Arameans. Yet the positive picture of Naaman ends on a surprisingly downbeat note: he has an affliction in the form of a skin disease.

■ The term for this affliction—the Hebrew noun *tsāra'at*, together with its related verbal form (as used here)—poses problems for a translator. The time-honored translation, which has a certain "biblical" resonance to it, is "leprosy." However, the Hebrew term covers a range of skin diseases, as depicted in Lev. 13–14 (where even a house can be affected). The condition known to modern medicine as Hansen's disease, which is still common in contexts of poverty and deprivation, would have been only one among many possible referents. The only specific note about the nature of the disease in this particular story—where it seems not to diminish Naaman's abilities or impede normal social interactions—comes at the end, when Gehazi acquires the affliction that Naaman had had, and his condition is said to be "like snow" (2 Kings 5:27b; so also the hand of Moses, Exod. 4:6; and Miriam, Num. 12:10). Such whiteness is not characteristic of leprosy proper, even though skin discoloration is. Modern medicine is not in a position to identify the disease envisaged in 2 Kings 5, even though suggestions such as psoriasis or eczema are common. Modern biblical translations which retain "leprosy" (e.g., NEB, JB, NRSV, NJPS, and some commentators—e.g., John Gray and Marvin Sweeney)[8] usually add a note to clarify that the biblical term envisages a wider range of skin afflictions than "leprosy" in a modern medical sense.

Since the text speaks of a disfiguring skin disease whose precise nature is unknown, I opt for the slightly cumbersome "skin disease" and will change the NRSV accordingly throughout. ■

The other surprising note in this introduction is that Naaman was the human agent by whom "the LORD had given victory to Aram"—an observation which presumably reflects the perspective of the narrator rather than of Naaman himself or his king.[9] The surprise is hardly that the LORD is active beyond Israel,[10] for that is apparent elsewhere in the storyline of Kings (e.g., 1 Kings 17), is deeply rooted in the tradition of the exodus from Egypt, and would be taken for granted by a reader of the canonical text, which begins with the one God as Creator of all. Rather, His giving victory to Aram was apparently *at Israel's expense*, symbolized by the presence of the Israelite slave girl in Naaman's household as mentioned in the next verse.[11] That is, the

8. See Gray, *I & II Kings*, 502, 504; Sweeney, *I & II Kings*, 293, 298.

9. It is possible to read the Hebrew as depicting the king's recognition of the LORD's giving victory by Naaman, even if that is an unlikely construal.

10. Commentators regularly highlight the "universalist" perspective of the story. See, e.g., Alter, *Ancient Israel*, 751, 755; Nelson, *First and Second Kings*, 177; Provan, *1 and 2 Kings*, 191.

11. Interactions between Aram and Israel are recurrent in the cycle of Elisha stories and so become the natural default assumption in a context such as this, where the opponent is not specified. The previous occasion on which Aram featured in the Kings storyline was the Aramean

story makes clear at the outset that, whatever the LORD's special relationship with Israel, He does not necessarily act in accordance with Israel's wishes and preferences; the LORD's actions cannot be presumed upon.

> [2]Now the Arameans on one of their raids had taken a young girl captive from the land of Israel, and she served Naaman's wife. [3]She said to her mistress, "If only my lord were with the prophet who is in Samaria! He would cure him of his skin disease." [4]So Naaman went in and told his lord just what the girl from the land of Israel had said. (2 Kings 5:2–4)

A young girl, probably in her early teens[12] and from somewhere in northern Israel (i.e., presumably not far from Aram), had been captured on an Aramean raid.[13] For her, after this raid, initially life might appear to have ended. To be enslaved and taken into exile could readily feel like a living death. In terms of the archetypal story of Cain and Abel, she is someone unfavored who has to make the most of a situation not of her choosing.[14] She finds herself, however, in what appears to be a good home. Here she wants, and is able, to give good advice. Whatever she may or may not know about prophecy (the prophet as someone sent by God to speak and act for God), she knows of the prophet as someone in whom the power of God might be encountered in a life-giving way. So she speaks confidently along these lines. Both Naaman's wife and Naaman himself are willing to heed her, and Naaman acts on her words.

■ The young woman has only this one brief moment of opportunity (as the narrator tells it) involving nothing more spectacular than a few words, but she nonetheless makes a telling difference. Unsurprisingly, then, she is paradigmatic for many commentators of making the most, under God, of whatever opportunity life brings, however limited it may seem. Gregory Mobley nicely expands a point about "the wisdom of the little people" into a larger concern of Kings overall:

---

victory over Israel at Ramoth-gilead (1 Kings 22). Although the context of the victory of 2 Kings 5:1 is nonspecific, ancient interpretive tradition unsurprisingly linked it with 1 Kings 22. Josephus already has an "Amanos," who is almost certainly "Naaman," as the archer whose arrow struck Ahab in that Aramean victory (*A.J.* 8:414, in *Jewish Antiquities, Books V–VIII*, 794–95).

12. The text is imprecise about her age—assuming that the Hebrew epithet *qāṭōn* does not have its primary sense of "small" but is a reference to age rather than size. However, the subsequent restoration of Naaman's skin to be like that of a "young boy" (*naʿar qāṭōn*, 2 Kings 5:14)—which is a counterpart to the depiction of the "young girl" (*naʿărāh qĕṭannāh*, 5:2)—appears to envisage a time of life when skin is still at its smoothest—i.e., prepubescence.

13. Border raids were endemic in many contexts in the ancient and the medieval worlds. It is one of those facets of premodern life, with its insecurities, that can be hard for many modern readers fully to imagine—even though the modern world is developing its own, different forms of insecurity.

14. See ch. 4 of this book.

This contrast between the clichéd formulaic texture of the accounts about the rote mendacities, petty corruptions, cruel injustices, and bungling statecraft of the big shots, and the vivid, quirky folktales about the little people—lepers, Syrian house slaves, rural juvenile delinquents, family farmers, roving bands of itinerant, undomesticated seers and the informal network of women who fed and sheltered them—may hold theological significance itself. The meek inherited and kept vital the traditional faith of Israel throughout the monarchical era.[15] ■

[5]And the king of Aram said, "Go then, and I will send along a letter [*sēpher*] to the king of Israel." He went, taking with him ten talents of silver, six thousand shekels of gold, and ten sets of garments. [6]He brought the letter to the king of Israel, which read, "When this letter reaches you, know that I have sent to you my servant Naaman, that you may cure him of his skin disease." [7]When the king of Israel read the letter, he tore his clothes and said, "Am I God, to give death or life, that this man sends word to me to cure a man of his skin disease? Just look and see how he is trying to pick a quarrel with me." (2 Kings 5:5–7)

The practicalities of the situation need attending to. Naaman's going to see his king would, one imagines, be primarily to request a leave of absence, but no doubt also to make clear to his master that he wants to travel to neighboring Israel for a good reason (and so is doing nothing underhanded or perhaps even traitorous).

Interestingly, the king of Aram is nowhere named, and neither is the king of Israel when he comes on stage. One can of course conjecture about their identities.[16] But perhaps a tacit point in the story is that the kings—those figures of power who usually give their names to the framing and telling of history[17]—are not the significant figures in this story. They are incidental.

The kings are not only marginal, but they are also uncomprehending, and comically so. The incomprehension appears to begin with the king of Aram when he sends Naaman to the king of Israel with a royal letter. One might expect this to be a letter of recommendation requesting safe passage and any appropriate assistance, with an assurance of peaceful intent. We are told only, however, that it contains a request to the Israelite king to "cure him [Naaman] of his skin disease." This is open to more than one reading. It could be a request for permission to let Naaman find healing somewhere in the land of Israel, under the auspices of its king—in other words, "I am sending him to you so that you will enable him to find the healing that he is seeking." But the apparent lack of any mention of a "prophet in Samaria," as specified by

15. Mobley, "1 and 2 Kings," 123 (see also 136).

16. Jehoram is the generally favored candidate for the king of Israel, for contextual reasons within 2 Kings. Ben-hadad has often been reckoned to be the Aramean king on the same grounds.

17. Ancient societies regularly used regnal years to structure time, as do the books of Kings.

the slave girl, suggests that, if that were the import of the letter, then it was at least poorly worded and that the Aramean king was uncertain how to couch his unusual request. Moreover, the treasure which accompanies the Aramean king's favored general is so vast that it is suggestive not just of a gift or of remuneration for the prophet but also of a symbolic gesture of power meant to impress the king of Israel with the wealth of his northern neighbor and perhaps also serve as a political sweetener.[18] In addition, Naaman travels with a military retinue (as will be noted in vv. 9, 15).

At any rate, the Israelite king reads the letter suspiciously. He sees it as a ludicrous request to perform a healing himself (though it is ironic that his words about God giving death or life, which he utters in uncomprehending irritation, are indeed validated within the story when he is not around). He reckons that the only reason for such a request is that it is a pretext to renew hostilities when he fails to respond positively to the Aramean king's letter and its accompanying bounty. In any case, each king seems ill at ease with the notion of an afflicted man seeking a prophet with a view to healing, and each in one way or another transposes the issue into more familiar (to them) categories of power politics.

> [8]But when Elisha the man of God heard that the king of Israel had torn his clothes, he sent a message to the king, "Why have you torn your clothes? Let him come to me, that he may learn that there is a prophet in Israel." [9]So Naaman came with his horses and chariots, and halted at the entrance of Elisha's house. (2 Kings 5:8–9)

Local news travels fast, and the slave girl's "prophet in Samaria," now identified as none other than Elisha, intervenes. His message to the king is succinct: the king's dismay, symbolized by tearing his clothes, is unwarranted. If the Aramean general will but come to Elisha, he will learn that there is indeed a prophet in Israel; and perhaps, by implication, the king too will learn, or be reminded of, something he ought to have known when he read the letter. At any rate, Naaman with his retinue does go to Elisha, and the scene is set for his encounter with the Israelite prophet.

18. The treasure is so vast that it is natural to wonder whether the numbers may be idiomatically hyperbolic, perhaps akin to saying of someone today that "they've got millions." But there is no way of telling. Determining the precise amount indicated by the talents and the shekels (taken at face value) is unstraightforward, as any standard discussion of weights and measures in the ancient world quickly reveals. Marvin Sweeney puts it this way, with helpful imprecision: "ten talents of silver, equivalent to some 660 to 1,320 pounds of silver, according to common Mesopotamian measures; six thousand shekels of gold, equivalent to some 110 to 220 pounds of gold" (*I & II Kings*, 299).

> [10]Elisha sent a messenger to him, saying, "Go, wash in the Jordan seven times, and your flesh shall be restored and you shall be clean." [11]But Naaman became angry and went away, saying, "See here![19] I thought to myself[20] that he would surely come out, and stand and call on the name of the LORD his God, and would wave his hand over the spot, and cure the skin disease! [12]Are not Abana and Pharpar, the rivers of Damascus, better than all the waters of Israel? Could I not wash in them, and be clean?" He turned and went away in a rage. [13]But his servants approached and said to him, "Father, if the prophet had commanded you to do something difficult, would you not have done it? How much more, when all he said to you was, 'Wash, and be clean'?" [14]So he went down and immersed himself seven times in the Jordan, according to the word of the man of God; his flesh was restored like the flesh of a young boy, and he was clean. (2 Kings 5:10–14)

Elisha acts surprisingly. He ignores conventional courtesies and does not come out to greet his visitor and speak face-to-face. The natural symbolic significance of this is a lack of interest or rejection (or, conceivably, playing hard to get). Yet the sending of a messenger in his place suggests that this is not the meaning of Elisha's (in)action. Rather, the purpose of Elisha's non-appearance could be to challenge and unsettle some of the assumptions that Naaman is likely to have held—as might be inferred both from Naaman's immediate response and from the subsequent exchange in which Elisha refuses any of Naaman's vast treasure.[21] Sending an ordinary person to speak to Naaman might also be symbolically on a par with the surprising message that is conveyed. Washing or bathing in water sounds inadequate for dealing with a skin disease, which would already have proved resistant to the obvious treatment of being washed and wiped. Of course, washing "seven times" indicates that this would not be a regular washing, but one that is symbolically charged (even if the precise symbolic significance of "seven times" is left open);[22] and it would be in a river in Israel, which might perhaps symbolize

19. The NRSV, as usual, omits *hinnēh*. Yet even if *hinnēh* does not here serve the particular function of shifting the perspective within the story, as in Exod. 3:2 and Gen. 33:1 (see above, pp. 54, 150), it is still an idiomatic exclamation which ought to be retained in translation, as all languages have exclamations.

20. This rendering (following Alter, *Ancient Israel*, 753; and, similarly, Sweeney, "I said to myself" [*I & II Kings*, 293]) seems to me the most likely construal of "to me" (*'ēlay*), located directly after "I said/thought" (*'āmartī*), though other construals are possible.

21. As ever, more than one construal is possible when the text is silent. As Gwilym Jones puts it, "Various motives have been found behind Elisha's detachment: he may have been demonstrating that he was not a wonder-worker who expected payment, or else indicating that he wished no political involvement with Syria, or again be deliberately testing Naaman's faith" (*1 and 2 Kings*, 2:416).

22. In this context I imagine that "seven times" means precisely that, rather than being the idiom for "many times" that is common in the OT (see ch. 4, 144n50). Nonetheless, it may also

entry into Israel's world (as in Josh. 3–4). Whatever the case, it is a mundane action that is not in line with what one might expect to be required for a special healing—as Naaman does not hesitate to point out.

Naaman's angry response indicates that in his own way he is as poorly attuned to the prophet in Israel as are the two kings. Of course, on one level, his expectations are entirely reasonable. Invocation of the deity ("call on the name of the LORD") is a primary religious act, especially appropriate at times of heightened significance (one thinks, for example, of Samuel invoking the LORD before Israel fights the Philistines, or of Elijah invoking the LORD on Mount Carmel).[23] A posture of standing in prayer with arms outstretched is well attested (one thinks, for example, of Solomon at the dedication of the temple, or perhaps of Moses with his arms raised as Israel fights Amalek).[24] The exact meaning of "the spot" over which Elisha should wave his hand[25]—whether the space outside the house or Naaman's infected body—is not clear, but the general sense of Naaman's declaration is straightforward: prophetic presence, prayer, and directed action should bring healing. Moreover, if the mundane act of washing is required, why should it be in the Jordan, which (despite its resonant fame down the ages) is not, and probably never was, an impressive river?[26] Naaman also cannot resist the chauvinistic observation that the local rivers around Damascus are "better" than any or all of the waters of Israel;[27] but part of his point may be that washing in a river in the absence of Elisha could just as well be done at home as in Israel. Naaman presumably feels either that he is being mocked by Elisha or that Elisha is a charlatan who is wasting his time.

Naaman's servants respond to him with admirable common sense. As Robert Alter nicely puts it, "They intuit that the ostensibly simple command to

---

be symbolically significant. Gina Hens-Piazza points out two suggestive parallels: the son of the Shunammite woman sneezes seven times as he returns to life (2 Kings 4:35), and sprinkling seven times constitutes complete ritual action (Lev. 14:7, 16, 27, 51) (*1–2 Kings*, 260).

23. See 1 Sam. 7:7–11; 1 Kings 18:36–38.

24. See 1 Kings 8:22; Exod. 17:8–13. The battle with Amalek does not mention prayer, though it is easy to see why Jewish and Christian tradition interpreted Moses' action thus. On any reading of the Amalek episode, there is a linkage between the raising of human hands and the realization of some kind of divine power.

25. The NRSV's "the spot" is nicely equivocal in its rendering of the Hebrew *māqōm* ("place"); it is genuinely unclear whether this refers to the location where they were standing or the diseased area(s) of Naaman's body.

26. The Jordan might have had more water prior to the use of its tributaries for water supply in the modern state of Israel. But the river winds and meanders, and the sight it affords has probably only ever been impressive when it opens out into the lake of Galilee and into the Dead Sea.

27. Damascus enjoys a water supply that no city of biblical Israel enjoyed. The position of Damascus in relation to the mountains means that it can be depicted as a "huge luxuriant oasis" with "a nearly unlimited supply of water" (Baly, *Geography of the Bible*, 111).

dip seven times in the Jordan is actually the direction for a miraculous cure."[28] They gently deflate the note of chauvinistic irritation in their master's words by pointing out that, although he is of course a man accustomed to great undertakings, the performance of a simple task is not demeaning. If there is a simple thing to do, then he should simply do it. Their words are somewhat like the words of Naaman's Israelite slave girl in that nonpowerful people who remain nameless in the story nonetheless play a crucial role within it.[29] Although, of all the Arameans, only Naaman's name is passed down to posterity, his is not a solo performance. These servants get through to their master and restore his own good sense. Naaman now goes to the Jordan and is healed.[30] We are told nothing about what his immersion in the Jordan and the restoration of his skin felt like to him. What matters is that his obedience to the prophet's words realizes the prophet's promise.[31]

> [15]Then he returned to the man of God, he and all his company; he came and stood before him and said, "Now I know that there is no God in all the earth except in Israel; please accept a present from your servant." [16]But he said, "As the LORD lives, whom I serve, I will accept nothing!" He urged him to accept, but he refused. (2 Kings 5:15–16)

Naaman returns to Elisha, presumably both chastened and joyful. His words are momentous, as his view of reality has changed.[32] Here in Israel he has encountered the true God, and there is no true God elsewhere. The

28. Alter, *Ancient Israel*, 753.

29. As Provan puts it, "The humble have once again exhibited more insight than the exalted" (*1 and 2 Kings*, 192).

30. For figural readings of Naaman's washing in the Jordan, see "Further Reflection 4" below, pp. 194–97.

31. Although Naaman's healing in the Jordan is a turning point in the story, the miracle as such receives no emphasis, so it is probably unwise to designate this narrative as a "miracle story" (or its equivalent). In literary terms, the omniscient narrator who can tell of Naaman's healing and Elisha's clairvoyance can also tell of a domestic conversation between Naaman's wife and slave, of where Gehazi puts his spoil, and of Gehazi's instantaneous affliction with a skin disease like Naaman's. This is a story in which the reader is made privy to much that is surprising.

32. Naaman's confession is oddly depicted as the "involuntary confession of the happy convalescent" by James Montgomery and Henry Snyder Gehman (*Books of Kings*, 375). To read Naaman's words as "involuntary" is to introduce a note absent from the text (as is the idea that he was in any significant sense "convalescent"—why would he need to be?) and goes against its flow since his immediate action is to offer a grateful gift to Elisha. Presumably, the reasoning behind such an interpretation is that Naaman already anticipates a problem arising in the temple of Rimmon; and his confession is "involuntary" because he prefers not to put himself into the bind of saying one thing and doing another (i.e., a particular reading of v. 18 plays back into the reading of v. 15). As ever, such a reading cannot be disproved. But I propose that to see a joyful confession followed by an ingenious expedient does better justice to the flow of the story.

universality of the one God is combined with the particularity of the context in which this one God is known. The precise wording and significance of this confession of faith merit fuller scrutiny, and we will return to it.[33] For the present, the significant thing is that Naaman's words align him with Israel's core understanding of God as expressed in the first commandment and the Shema: there are to be "no other gods" alongside the LORD and "the LORD is the one and only" (*'eḥād*).[34] His sharing of Israel's core confession makes him, in a certain sense, part of Israel (and bears obvious resemblance to saying the Shahadah and becoming a Muslim).

What follows from this? Naaman's immediate instinct is to express his gratitude to Elisha with a tangible gift. (Even if some of his vast treasure might have been left with the king of Israel as a strategic goodwill gesture, he would still hardly be short of talents, shekels, and garments.) Reciprocity was a natural and widespread instinct and practice in the ancient world, and Naaman acts accordingly. But Elisha declines, and does so not with a polite "No, thank you" but with an appeal to the God to whom he is accountable. As a matter of principle, he will accept nothing from Naaman. This presumably puzzles Naaman, who perhaps thinks that this is a formal politeness which he needs to push past, so he tries again. But Elisha stands firm.

His refusal is not explained. But even though it can be important to respect a narrator's silence, sometimes it is important to enter imaginatively into the unexpressed thought of a character; and I suggest that we do so here. Most likely, Elisha's concern is to avoid any idea that somehow God's favor can be bought.[35] If Elisha were to accept even a small part of Naaman's treasure, he would become wealthy. The suspicious might suppose that Elisha helped Naaman because he knew how well he would do out of it.[36] Or they might suppose that only those with the kind of riches that Naaman had could expect anything from God or His prophet. A straightforward gift of gratitude on one level might be too open to misinterpretation on another level; so Elisha declines. The issue of not seeking reward will also recur later in the story. Elisha's implicit understanding of the dynamics of the occasion surely merits the Christian shorthand summary term: grace.[37]

33. See "Further Reflection 1" below, pp. 179–82.

34. See Exod. 20:3 // Deut. 5:7; Deut. 6:4.

35. It is, of course, possible to infer otherwise. Marvin Sweeney, for example, comments, "Elisha's refusal to take payment highlights the power relationship between the prophet and Naaman. . . . Elisha doesn't need anything from Naaman, but Naaman needs Elisha" (*I & II Kings*, 301).

36. The complacent acquisition of financial profit on the part of religious leaders is highlighted as a particular problem by Mic. 3:11, discussed below (ch. 6, p. 219).

37. One might perhaps alternatively say that Naaman has "found favor" (*mātsā' ḥēn*) with the LORD, as did Noah and Moses (Gen. 6:8; Exod. 33:12), even if the contexts and the nuance of the idiom differ.

> [17]Then Naaman said, "If not, please let two mule-loads of earth be given to your servant; for your servant will no longer offer burnt offering or sacrifice to other gods but only to the LORD.[38] [18]But may the LORD pardon your servant on one count: when my master goes into the house of Rimmon to worship there, leaning on my arm, and I bow down in the house of Rimmon, when I do bow down in the house of Rimmon, may the LORD pardon your servant on this one count." [19]He said to him, "Go in peace." (2 Kings 5:17–19a)

Naaman goes along with Elisha's refusal of any gift, even though he is disappointed; his "if not" implies that Elisha's acceptance of his gift would have conferred a favor on him. But if that favor cannot be granted, he will ask for a different one instead.[39] This alternative favor relates to a practical problem that Naaman now faces. His recognition of the LORD makes him, in a certain sense, part of Israel. Yet he remains an Aramean, with a family in Damascus and a life that entails responsibilities at the highest level. So he comes up with a proposal whose likely significance in the culture of the ancient world is hard to grasp in the differently configured culture of modernity: he asks for some earth.[40] This will enable him to make a division between what he does for himself, in his own right, and what he does in his public responsibilities as chief of staff to the king. Whatever the precise significance of the earth (which is of sufficient quantity that more than one mule will be needed to carry it),[41] the intent of Naaman's words in verse 17 is clear: his own future actions that express devotion and allegiance will be directed solely to the LORD. He will offer sacrifices on a specially constructed altar, which will either be made from the earth that he wants to take or placed upon such earth.[42] This altar will presumably be located somewhere in the precincts of his home, where he has control over the space. In that way he will express his recognition of the LORD as the true God.

Naaman's responsibilities as chief of staff, however, require him to closely accompany his (most likely) elderly king, who in his growing infirmity needs at times to be physically supported by Naaman.[43] When the king goes to worship

38. The NRSV's "to any god except the LORD" captures the general sense but obscures the fact that Naaman is using the regular OT idiom "other gods" (*'ĕlōhīm 'ăḥērīm*) for what he is rejecting, and is thereby again aligning himself explicitly with the canonical norms of faith.

39. There is a comparable idiomatic use of *vālō'* in Absalom's dialogue with David in 2 Sam. 13:26a.

40. The Greek tradition qualifies the earth as "red" (*purra*), though the significance of this is unclear.

41. For fuller discussion, see "Further Reflection 2" below, pp. 183–89.

42. Altars of both earth and stone are prescribed for Israel in Exod. 20:24–25.

43. The same idiom appears also in 2 Kings 7:2, 17, again probably implying, though not specifying, an elderly king. It is unlikely that the idiom means being a "right-hand man" rather

in the temple of the national deity of Aram,[44] and he is no longer able easily to bow and/or prostrate himself and get up again and so needs Naaman's assistance ("leaning on his arm"), Naaman will need to bow and/or prostrate himself beside his king. The intentionality and directedness of the worship will be the king's and not Naaman's, but Naaman will still need to perform the formal actions as part of his responsibility to the king. Naaman will thus bow down in two contexts: one at home which expresses his intentionality, and another in public which does not express his intentionality and in which he quite literally does no more than "go through the motions." Such a division will enable him both to retain his Aramean responsibilities and to express his Israel-oriented allegiance and worship. His asking for the LORD's pardon is an idiomatic way of asking whether such an arrangement, which could easily be misconstrued, is acceptable: Is this a favor that Elisha can bestow? Elisha apparently does bestow the favor, which is a natural, though not necessary, inference from his "Go in peace."[45] Thus, in effect, Elisha gives Naaman's proposed arrangement his blessing.[46]

> But when Naaman had gone from him a short distance, [20]Gehazi, the servant of Elisha the man of God, thought, "My master has let that Aramean Naaman off too lightly by not accepting from him what he offered. As the LORD lives, I will run after him and get something out of him." [21]So Gehazi went after Naaman. (2 Kings 5:19b–21a)

Elisha's construal of the healing of Naaman as an act of grace that has nothing to do with money is not shared by his servant Gehazi. Gehazi sees a missed opportunity to make the most of their wealthy visitor. "Aramean" on Gehazi's lips in this context seems to carry the slightly contemptuous nuance of the epithet "foreigner," someone of whom a canny Israelite can readily take advantage. He makes this a matter of principle by invoking the LORD (v. 20) in the same way that Elisha had done (v. 16)—though thereby

---

than a physical support, as suggested by Robert L. Cohn ("Form and Perspective in 2 Kings V") and followed by Donald J. Wiseman (*1 and 2 Kings*, 208). This is partly because Naaman's envisaged problem is the need to make physical movements in alignment with his king, and partly because "right-hand man" is an idiom for executive power, which is not at issue in the temple of Rimmon, even if it is on the battlefield.

44. For a survey of what is known about the Aramean deity, here called "Rimmon," see Greenfield, "Aramean God Rammān/Rimmōn."

45. Elisha's mode of speech in the narrative as a whole is somewhat abrupt. It is possible here to imagine an unenthusiastic dismissal along the lines of "You're healed, so you can go. What you do now is up to you. It's not up to me to police what you do."

46. For other possible construals of Naaman's proposal and Elisha's response, see "Further Reflection 3" below, pp. 189–94.

he paradigmatically breaks the third commandment by taking the LORD's name in vain. Whereas Elisha's invocation served to align himself with the LORD's priorities by displaying divine grace and taking nothing for himself, Gehazi seeks to harness the LORD to his priorities and thereby enrich himself.

> When Naaman saw someone running after him, he jumped down from the chariot to meet him and said, "Is everything all right?" [22]He replied, "Yes, but my master has sent me to say, 'Two members of a company of prophets have just come to me from the hill country of Ephraim; please[47] give them a talent of silver and two changes of clothing.'" [23]Naaman said, "Please accept two talents." He urged him, and tied up two talents of silver in two bags, with two changes of clothing, and gave them to two of his servants, who carried them in front of Gehazi. [24]When he came to the citadel, he took the bags from them, and stored them inside; he dismissed the men, and they left. (2 Kings 5:21b–24)

Gehazi easily deceives a still-grateful Naaman, who is anxious that someone running after him may well indicate that something is not right. Gehazi makes his lie more plausible by not attempting to contradict Elisha's implicit message to Naaman that his healing was an act of grace. Although Gehazi himself rejects the propriety of such an understanding, he does not even hint at this to Naaman. Rather, he pitches his request in a low key as a petition concerning an unanticipated need: Could Naaman help Elisha show hospitality to two religiously significant (and likely impoverished)[48] visitors? Naaman is only too willing to help and offers twice as much money as Gehazi had asked for. Gehazi makes a token refusal (Naaman has to "urge" him) but is soon on his way back home with his booty, which is even being carried for him by an honorific escort.

> [25]He went in and stood before his master; and Elisha said to him, "Where have you been, Gehazi?" He answered, "Your servant has not gone anywhere at all." [26]But he said to him, "Did I not go with you in spirit when a man[49] left his chariot to meet you? Is this a time to accept money and to accept clothing, olive orchards and vineyards, sheep and oxen, and male and female slaves? [27]Therefore the skin disease of Naaman shall cling to you, and to your descendants forever." So he left his presence with his skin diseased, as white as snow. (2 Kings 5:25–27)

47. The Hebrew has the particle of entreaty, *nāʾ*, which, as in Exod. 5:3, can sometimes have a force tantamount to "please" in English. See ch. 2, p. 80.

48. Religious communities ("sons of the prophets") would typically need financial assistance, as most likely they did not devote their time and energy towards farming or trading in the way that others did. The story of the widow of a member of a company of prophets in 2 Kings 4:1–7 depicts severe poverty.

49. The NRSV uses the less-specific (gender inclusive?) "someone," but I think it is better to render *ʾîsh* straightforwardly as "a man."

Gehazi's evasive lie to his master receives a startling response. In some way, when Gehazi went after Naaman, Elisha was also there "in spirit."[50] What this means is not explained, any more than is Naaman's healing through immersion in the Jordan, but it clearly refers to a state of awareness that is in some way a corollary of Elisha's proximity to God as a prophet. He knows what would usually be unknowable; he can be clairvoyant.[51] The wording of the text, "when a man left his chariot," in which one might have expected Elisha to mention Naaman by name, is perhaps giving an impression of what it was that Elisha (perhaps somewhat hazily?) saw. Lack of clarity in what he saw might also be implied by his following question—about money, olive orchards, livestock, and slaves—which goes beyond the actual exchange between Gehazi and Naaman. But the import of the question is clear: it is a rebuke to Gehazi for being focused on money and markers of wealth when he should have been rejoicing at a non-Israelite coming to a life-giving recognition of Israel's God.

■ The number of items mentioned is surprising.[52] Two talents of silver would buy a lot of things; but substantial territory ("olive orchards and vineyards"), substantial livestock ("sheep and oxen"), and significant personnel ("male and female slaves") might well cost more than two talents.[53] If so, it could suggest that Elisha does not know exactly how much Gehazi received from Naaman—only that he acquired money and clothing that he should not have acquired. ■

The result is that Gehazi's greed will mark him indelibly,[54] in the form of his getting the skin disease from which Naaman had been healed. The disease that defiles his skin in effect symbolizes the greed that has defiled his heart and mind (though the disease had no such symbolic significance for Naaman).

50. The Hebrew does not use the regular term for "spirit," *rûaḥ*, but rather "heart/mind" (*lēv*), which emphasizes Elisha's awareness of what was going on rather than his presence as such.

51. Even though Elisha mediates a power from God to heal and to see what would usually be unseen, Gehazi, though close to him, is still free to ignore and defy Elisha's priorities. The characteristic biblical tension between the power of God and human freedom is well represented in this story.

52. It is of course possible that the list is conventional, in terms of specifying typical things that the powerful and greedy take from others, as in Samuel's warning about the likely depredations of a king on his people (1 Sam. 8:14–17).

53. The best clue as to the value of two talents of silver is that this was the price Omri paid for the hill of Samaria (1 Kings 16:24). The reference to his "building the hill" (*vayyiven 'et hāhār*, v. 24b) implies that the hill, when purchased, was largely or perhaps wholly uninhabited. Modern excavations have shown that the earliest buildings come from Omri's time in the mid-ninth century; see Avigad, "Samaria (City)." The site is a fine one in a strategic location; but it is possible that such a hill would have cost less than all the things Elisha lists.

54. Rabbinic interpretation envisaged other defects of character in Gehazi, including disbelief in the resurrection of the dead (i.e., by linkage with the preceding story of the Shunammite woman's son, 2 Kings 4:8–37). See Ginzberg, *Legends of the Jews*, 2:1029–30.

■ Elisha's declaration that the disease will affect not only Gehazi but also his descendants "forever" is likely to be read differently by many modern readers than by ancient ones. Today this tends to come across as morally problematic, an unjust penalization of innocent people in years to come. In the ancient context, however, the idiomatic significance is that of the punishment being definitive; the thought is not about generations in the distant future but rather about the thoroughness and finality of punishment for Gehazi in the here and now.[55] Some disciplined historical imagination is needed to keep the idiom in perspective.

Evaluations of this conclusion to the story vary. Curiously, many scholars who write commentaries on Kings say little about Gehazi's affliction and nothing about that of his descendants. Nonetheless, among those who do comment, evaluations differ. On the one hand, Richard Nelson says, "The narrative reaches a satisfying end. . . . Gehazi is deservedly a leper"; though he says nothing about the affliction of Gehazi's descendants.[56] On the other hand, Gregory Mobley says,

> If we read stories such as this with the kind of sober piety we often reserve for the Bible, we cannot help but be shocked at the cold-blooded glee that its composers and original audiences evidently took in the cruel particulars of how the wicked and the foolish eventually received their comeuppance, their just deserts. Better that we read these accounts as folktales from the underclass, from the prophets and their sympathizers who waited through generations for the reign of peace and justice their tradition promised them, and preserved their hopes in the stories and teachings that would grow into our Bible. The pleasures of these impish narratives about poetic justice may escape us, but for our spiritual ancestors in Ephraim . . . the prospect of divine judgment against the high and mighty was one of their few small comforts.[57] ■

What, then, has happened in the course of the story? Everything and nothing. Everything, since grace has been displayed, Naaman has been healed and has come to acknowledge the true God, and routine expectations have been consistently overturned as the ways of God have been encountered. And nothing, since a story that began with the problem of a man suffering from a skin disease ends with a man suffering from a skin disease.

Further Reflection 1: Naaman's Confession of the One God

The possible implications of the story of Naaman for understanding the nature of God and life in God's world merit some further reflection.

Naaman's confession of faith ("Now I know that there is no God in all the earth except in Israel") stands at the heart of the story—and indeed, arguably,

55. Prime intertexts are the second commandment (Exod. 20:5 // Deut. 5:9) and Job 1:18–19, where the death of Job's children serves to heighten the trial that Job himself faces.

56. Nelson, *First and Second Kings*, 180; cf. 176.

57. Mobley, "1 and 2 Kings," 137.

at the heart of the Old Testament. In a certain sense it is also at the heart of this book, insofar as this book is an account of aspects of what it means to "know that the LORD is God."

On Knowing That the LORD *Is God*

Naaman's confession of faith keeps company with other comparable formulations. In Psalm 100, for example, the psalmist calls on "all the earth" to share in Israel's joyful worship of the LORD and issues the summons, "Know that the LORD is God" (vv. 1–3). The LORD's call of Cyrus, who is to carry out His purposes for Jerusalem, will have the goal not only that "you [Cyrus] may know that it is I, the LORD, / the God of Israel, who call you by your name," but also that "they may know, from the rising of the sun / and from the west, that there is no one besides me; / I am the LORD, and there is no other" (Isa. 45:3, 6). The hope that persons and nations beyond Israel will come to recognize and acknowledge Israel's God is recurrent in the Old Testament—though the recognition has to begin with, and be continually renewed within, Israel itself.

The concern to "know that the LORD is God" is particularly important in Deuteronomy and deuteronomically inflected material.[58] Moses says to Israel, in light of the exodus and Sinai traditions,

> To you it was shown so that you would acknowledge [or know] that the LORD is God; there is no other besides him. (Deut. 4:35)

> So acknowledge [or know] today and take to heart that the LORD is God in heaven above and on the earth beneath; there is no other. (Deut. 4:39)

David says to Goliath on the battlefield,

> This very day the LORD will deliver you into my hand . . . so that all the earth may know that there is a God in Israel. (1 Sam. 17:46)

Solomon concludes his prayer at the dedication of the temple with the specific prayer that the LORD provide for Israel

> so that all the peoples of the earth may know that the LORD is God; there is no other. (1 Kings 8:60)

58. There is also extensive use of "know that I am the LORD" in Ezekiel and the Priestly writings, discussed by Walther Zimmerli in his "I Am Yahweh" and "Knowledge of God according to the Book of Ezekiel," in *I Am Yahweh*, 1–28, 29–98; and more recently by John F. Evans in *You Shall Know That I Am Yahweh*.

At the climax of the paradigmatic story of the contest between Elijah and the prophets of Baal on Mount Carmel, Elijah prays,

> [36]O LORD, . . . let it be known this day that you are God in Israel. . . . [37]Answer me, O LORD, answer me, so that this people may know that you, O LORD, are God. (1 Kings 18:36–37)

When the fire of the LORD falls, the people fulfill the prayer:

> [39]They fell on their faces and said, "The LORD indeed is God; the LORD indeed is God." (1 Kings 18:39)

The idiom is less common in Chronicles. Nonetheless, the Chronicler strikingly retells the story of the notorious king Manasseh in a mode somewhat suggestive of the prodigal son. In the extremity of captivity and exile, Manasseh turns repentantly to God, and God restores him and brings him home:

> Then Manasseh knew that the LORD indeed was God. (2 Chron. 33:13)

The cumulative force of these and other passages conveys a core theological vision and theological hope. It is this into which Naaman, like other famous non-Israelites such as Jethro and Rahab (Exod. 18:10–11; Josh. 2:9, 11), paradigmatically enters.

There is a certain sense in which the Hebrew phrase "know that" (*yādaʿ kī*)—which is used in all the passages just cited—is an Old Testament counterpart to the Greek phrase "believe that" (*pisteuein hoti*) in the New Testament.[59] Both terms express epistemic and existential assurance in relation to God. A fuller study of the Old Testament's "know that the LORD is God" could usefully be set alongside key formulations about "believing that Jesus is Lord/ Messiah" by Paul and John in the New Testament. For Paul, the confession that "Jesus Christ is Lord" is perhaps the most succinct shorthand summary of his understanding of Christian faith (Phil. 2:9–11; cf. Rom. 10:9; 1 Cor. 12:3; 2 Cor. 4:5). John's statement of purpose about his Gospel ("These are written so that you may come to believe that Jesus is the Messiah, the Son of God, and that through believing you may have life in his name," John 20:31) plays a comparable summary role. These phrases of the Old and New Testaments—to

59. Although Hebrew has the phrase "believe that" (*heʾĕmīn kī*; e.g., Exod. 4:5), it is not used for weighty theological affirmations, which are rendered by "know that" (*yādaʿ kī*), even though "know that" can also appear in ordinary, everyday usage (e.g., Gen. 12:11; 20:6). I have more fully discussed the OT importance of "know that the LORD is God" in "Knowing God and Knowing about God."

know that the LORD is God and to believe that Jesus is Lord—serve as pithy and memorable formulations of that life-giving goal for humans in relation to God which the surrounding documents amplify more fully and discursively (aspects of which this book is seeking to articulate).

Are Naaman's Words "Monotheistic"?

Modern interpreters regularly use the term "monotheism" to depict Israel's understanding of God, at least from the time of Second Isaiah in the exilic context (whether or not for earlier periods). Naaman's confession is regularly depicted as reflecting a "monotheism" that is perhaps only incipient, though sometimes it is seen as fully formed (depending usually on when the story is dated). "Monotheism," however, is a category whose ability to penetrate the meaning of biblical terminology and thought is more limited than is generally supposed.[60] For the present (the issue will be taken up again in the next Further Reflection), I would simply note a significant recent essay by Benjamin Sommer in relation to Yehezkel Kaufmann's work on biblical "monotheism." Sommer strongly, and surely rightly, commends Kaufmann's basic contention that "monotheism is about the nature of divinity, not about the number of divinities; it is a matter of quality, not quantity"; it is "not a matter of counting; it is a matter of power."[61] Or, in biblical and especially deuteronomic idiom, the acknowledgement of the LORD as "the one and only" (*ʾeḥād*), in relation to whom "there is no other," is a denial of "other gods" (*ʾĕlōhîm ʾăḥērîm*) in terms of their power to help/save and their legitimacy as recipients of allegiance rather than in terms of their ontological status.[62] When Naaman says, "There is no God in all the earth except in Israel," one should not imagine him inferring, as a corollary, "and so I now realize that Rimmon does not exist." Naaman's point is not that "other gods" (*ʾĕlōhîm ʾăḥērîm*) no longer exist; rather, he says that he will offer sacrifices not to them, but only to YHWH (2 Kings 5:17). "Other gods" remain, in one way or another, a permanent challenge to allegiance to the LORD.[63]

60. I have attempted elsewhere to articulate some of the deep problems in the use of the seventeenth-century category "monotheism" for the reading of Israel's scriptures. Pragmatically, I see no good alternative to its continued use, *faute de mieux*, but it is a matter of "handle with care." See my "How Appropriate Is 'Monotheism' as a Category for Biblical Interpretation?"; and my *Old Testament Theology*, esp. 33–40.

61. Sommer, "Kaufmann and Recent Scholarship," 205, 230.

62. See also the discussion of the reality of "other gods" in relation to Ps. 82 in ch. 3 (above, pp. 117, 120).

63. The challenge has less to do with the power of other gods as realities in themselves than it does with their constituting alternative priorities for human identity and allegiance.

Further Reflection 2: Naaman's Request for Israelite Soil

Naaman's Request as a Theological Failure

Naaman's request for Israelite soil, when set alongside his confession of the one God, is regularly seen by commentators to be, in one way or another, problematic. Naaman is often reckoned to be displaying a certain simplemindedness, a failure to grasp what his confession should really entail. Commentators from across the spectrum tend to be in agreement here. For example:

> Naaman was still a slave to the polytheistic superstition that no god could be worshipped in a proper and acceptable manner except in his own land, or upon an altar built of the earth of his own land.[64]

> This striking confession of monotheism [v. 15] . . . is naïvely inconsistent with this request for two mules' burdens of earth so that he might worship Yahweh in Damascus. His reason consented to monotheism but convention bound him practically to monolatry.[65]

> Like any new convert, Naaman's theology is apparently unsophisticated. He properly confesses that "there is no God in all the earth except in Israel," perhaps because that is what he has been taught. He takes the confession literally, however, assuming that the Lord is to be worshipped only on Israelite soil. Hence his proposal to take some of that soil home. . . . Even when Naaman finally confessed the Lord, his theology was simplistic, his notion of God's presence inadequate, his allegiance to God not without distractions.[66]

> Naaman is still very superstitious. His conversion to the true God has not stripped away the beliefs of his background and civilization. He has not become a good theologian. . . . He is still convinced that God is a local God, that he is tied to a particular land.[67]

> Naaman . . . wishes to ensure the future proximity of the God who helped him so tangibly. Since this God resides only in Israel, he wishes to take two muleloads of Israelite earth to Damascus in order to be able to sacrifice to YHWH there (vv. 15a, 17): a splendid earthbound understanding of God, still far removed from the theoretical monotheism of, for instance, Deutero-Isaiah (e.g., Isa. 45:5–6).[68]

64. Keil, *Books of Kings*, 320.
65. Gray, *I & II Kings*, 507.
66. Seow, "First and Second Books of Kings," 195, 198.
67. Ellul, *The Politics of God and the Politics of Man*, 35.
68. Dietrich, "1 and 2 Kings," 251.

I find striking the confidence which these commentators have in the adequacy and appropriateness of modern interpretive categories, especially "monotheism," in relation to which they depict Naaman as naive and simplistic.[69] I propose that it may be worthwhile, even if only as a thought experiment, to do the opposite. That is, we might entertain the possibility that Naaman, given an apparent go-ahead by Elisha, does know what he is doing and that we contemporary interpreters struggle with appropriate conceptualities to understand and appreciate what that is. It is at least possible that certain philosophically formulated conceptions of monotheism may so privilege the universality of the one God that they do not know how to do justice to particular modes of access to that universality.

Put differently, we need to recognize how sheerly difficult it is to interpret Naaman's request for Israelite soil. Judgments about its appropriateness (or otherwise) necessarily depend on judgments about its meaning, yet the story does not offer clarification. This is an issue where the religious and philosophical outlook of the interpreter in the present is likely to loom large in a way that makes self-critical alertness all the more important.

■ It is also possible to read Naaman's request as a coded narrative depiction of a problem facing Israelites of the Northern Kingdom in exile. An ingenious thesis is set out by Alexander Rofé:

> In the present form of the story in the Book of Kings, Elisha does not respond to Naaman's offer to build an altar with the two mule-loads of earth taken from the land of Israel. His silence is in keeping with the Deuteronomistic redaction of Kings, which forbids sacrifice to God anywhere outside Jerusalem, even in the land of Israel, not to mention foreign lands. But, according to all indications, in the original story Elisha explicitly agreed to this initiative. This is clearly the thrust of the story's internal dynamic. Naaman surely would not have required Elisha's permission to carry off some earth from the Holy Land on a pair of mules! It was rather Elisha's agreement to his cultic initiative that he desired. This request, following upon the declarations [the content of 2 Kings 5:15, 17] . . . could not have gone unrequited. The story, in its original form, seems to have sanctioned Naaman's proposal, not because of the needs of some anonymous pagans who wished to serve God, but because of specific historical circumstances, namely the situation of the Israelite exiles, beginning in 731 BCE. Scattered throughout the Assyrian empire, these exiles would be permitted to erect altars and sacrifice to God on foreign soil, following a procedure attributed to Elisha for overcoming the problem of the "unclean land": the altars were to be erected upon earth imported from the Land of Israel.[70]

69. These judgments are also contestable within their own frame of reference. Volkmar Fritz, for example, sees Naaman's confession of God as a "consequent monotheism" that presupposes and is later than Second Isaiah, and sees no theological difficulty in the request for earth (*1 & 2 Kings*, 260).

70. Rofé, *Prophetical Stories*, 131.

Two brief comments. On the one hand, the textual basis for Rofé's thesis is thin. His contention that Elisha "does not respond" to Naaman's proposal about building an altar—with the result that Elisha is aligned with the theological priorities of the deuteronomistic editors—is likely to be missed by most readers. Naaman speaks at length both about the earth and about the temple of Rimmon in a single speech to which Elisha responds with "Go in peace." If there were a break after Naaman's words in v. 17 and a narrative comment such as "And Elisha said nothing in reply / remained silent" (*vĕlōʾ ʿānāh ʾĕlīshāʿ ʾōtō dāvār* or *vayyiddōm ʾĕlīshāʿ*) before Naaman speaks again in v. 18, Rofé's point might have weight. But as the story stands, its most natural reading is that Elisha does respond positively to Naaman's request for earth for an altar.

On the other hand, Rofé's conjecture about what may have given rise to the story is always possible in terms of a putative history of ideas. But his focus on the purported needs of exiled Israelites (the supposed world behind the text), reflected in a coded way in Naaman's request to Elisha, means that the dynamics surrounding an Aramean's worship of the Lord, which is the interest in the world of the text, go out of focus. ■

Towards Rethinking Naaman's Request

In canonical context there is a rich resonance with Naaman's term for soil, *ʾădāmāh*.[71] This is the element out of which humanity, *ʾādām*, is formed (Gen. 2:7), and it is the fertile soil which is identified with home and livelihood (Gen. 4:14).[72] Naaman does not use the term *ʾerets* ("land"). Although he is indeed asking for a piece of the land of Israel, *ʾerets yisrāʾēl*, the term he uses is more elemental than *ʾerets*.

We do not know exactly what Naaman proposed to do with the soil. He may envisage constructing an altar with the earth (akin to the specification in Exod. 20:24, "Make for me an altar of earth"). However, two mule-loads of earth would enable the making of only a rather small altar; the offering of sacrifices, including whole burnt offerings, would be difficult on such a small altar. So it could be that Naaman envisages spreading out the Israelite soil on the ground to provide both a base upon which a regular altar of stone could be built, and a place for himself to stand and/or prostrate himself. For this purpose the envisaged quantity of earth would probably serve well. Despite this uncertainty about precise function, it is clear that Naaman regards the Israelite soil as integral to his future offerings to the Lord.

But can we get any precision in determining what is the soil's likely religious significance? It is possible to downplay its significance in various ways, especially if commentators inhabit a religious tradition that tends to downplay ritual and symbolic dimensions and elements that might loosely be called

71. Unsurprisingly, some commentators who do not think well of Naaman's request translate *ʾădāmāh* pejoratively as "dirt" (so, e.g., House, *1, 2 Kings*, 273).

72. Cain's complaint about loss of the *ʾădāmāh* is eloquent in terms of the value ascribed to it.

"sacramental." The great Puritan commentator Matthew Henry, for example, is unimpressed with Naaman's request:

> It was a happy cure of his leprosy which cured him of his idolatry, a more dangerous disease. But . . . in one instance he over-did it, that he would not only worship the God of Israel, but he would have clods of earth out of the prophet's garden to make an altar of. . . . He that awhile ago had spoken very slightly of the waters of Israel . . . now is in another extreme, and over-values the earth of Israel, supposing that an altar of that earth would be most acceptable to him.[73]

Donald Wiseman comments that Naaman's request for soil shows that "Naaman's knowledge of God was as yet weak."[74] And it may be that T. R. Hobbs deliberately downplays the soil when he suggests that Naaman "asks for a souvenir of Israel," although Hobbs tries to put a positive gloss on this by suggesting that Naaman does so for reasons of "sentiment, rather than superstition."[75]

One possibility is that the logic of Naaman's request is akin to that of those who cherish a garment or keepsake that belongs (or belonged) to a loved one from whom they are separated. This is a logic of the heart more than of the head, in which a deeply felt and strongly meaningful action (holding on to a keepsake) may be hard to explain even to oneself, never mind to someone else. A particular tangible object can focus a love and longing for the person and in some way evoke their presence—or at least what they mean to the one who loves them—even though they are absent. Such a reading of Naaman's request represents a logic of love that essentially resists conventional theological categories—even while the importance of love within the Jewish and Christian faiths would, one hopes, evoke an empathetic rather than a dismissive response.

Terence Fretheim has suggested that Naaman requests the soil "not because he thinks that the Lord is present only on Israelite soil [i.e., a common modern scholarly view]. He wants to build an altar with it, providing a tangible and material tie to the community of faith Elisha represents." Similarly, he construes Naaman's proposed actions in the temple of Rimmon as "not a lapse into syncretism [i.e., a common modern scholarly view], but a recognition that the life of faith must be lived out in ambiguous situations and away from

73. Henry, *Matthew Henry's Commentary*, 406.

74. Wiseman, *1 and 2 Kings*, 208.

75. Hobbs, *2 Kings*, 60, 66. The souvenir suggestion, perhaps by analogy with mementos that pilgrims often bring back from pilgrimages, appears periodically in the literature; see also J. Robinson, *Second Book of Kings*, 55.

the community of faith."[76] Fretheim's reading is a thoughtful attempt to relate the scriptural text to a contemporary context, with its challenges for faithful living. Its possible drawback is that it arguably transposes too easily the issue of soil into the issue of human community, even if soil could meaningfully symbolize absent people (and thus be analogous to a keepsake).

As already noted, it is common among modern interpreters to suppose that Naaman's request instantiates a particular ancient religious mindset in which "Yahwe, the national God of Israel, can only be worshipped aright upon the soil of Israel's land," so that "if he can secure a portion, however small, of the soil of that land, he will with it gain the privilege of sacrificing to the God to whom it belongs."[77] The modern supposition is that, although taking the soil no doubt made sense in that ancient context, such a mindset is rendered unnecessary and indeed improper once one properly grasps the implications of there being only one God, whose scope necessarily extends to the whole earth.

It is striking, however, that there are accounts of Jews and Christians in antiquity and the medieval period who also do something similar to Naaman. Ancient tradition tells of Helena, the mother of Constantine, taking soil (along with other relics) from Jerusalem to Rome.[78] The twelfth-century traveler Rabbi Benjamin of Tudela tells of a place, apparently in Persia, called Shafjathib, "where there is a synagogue, which the Israelites erected with earth and stones brought from Jerusalem, and which they called 'the transplanted [i.e., Shafjathib] of Nehardea.'"[79] Such accounts typically do not reflect on what understandings are embodied and expressed in actions like these. But the accounts are suggestive. While it is of course possible to critique such practices as showing a deficient understanding of the faith in the one God that at those times was formally professed (and examples of deficient understanding and practice are of course all too common in the history of the Jewish and Christian faiths), one should at least ask whether the problem may lie with our interpretive categories.

76. Fretheim, *First and Second Kings*, 153.

77. Burney, *Notes on the Hebrew Text of the Books of Kings*, 280; and Burney, *Outlines of Old Testament Theology*, 35. So too Richard Nelson: "His request in verse 17 is based on the idea that a god was tied to a home territory (Deut. 32:8)" (*First and Second Kings*, 179).

78. The Basilica of the Holy Cross in Jerusalem / Santa Croce in Gerusalemme is a church in Rome. According to tradition, it was founded by Helena and became the resting place for fragments of the True Cross, which she brought from Jerusalem. The church is also reputed to have been set up on a bed of soil which Helena brought from Jerusalem. The tradition is well known (whatever its status), but as yet I have been unable to find an ancient source that specifically mentions the soil, as distinct from the fragments of the cross.

79. Quoted in Wright, *Early Travels in Palestine*, 103.

Thus, I propose a different reading of Naaman's request. The key issue is the possible symbolism of the earth: What does it signify for Naaman? Naaman connects the soil with his henceforth exclusive worship of the LORD. The earth will help clarify Naaman's proposed differentiation between those sacrifices to the LORD that he will offer as his own worship and those sacrifices and/or practices of worship at which he will need to be present in the temple in Damascus. If he recognizes that the only true deity is the LORD, who is specifically the deity of Israel, and that through this recognition (as also through immersion in Israel's river) he has become in some way a part of Israel, then he wants something material and tangible that embodies this specificity.

In a world where the offering of sacrifice was a prime religious act, the specific nature of Israelite soil would strengthen the identification of Naaman's offering of sacrifice as an offering to the LORD, even when in Aram. Put differently, there is no hint that Naaman (any more than the narrator of the story) has any difficulty with envisaging the LORD as present in Aram. The potential difficulty for Naaman relates to the practical maintenance of his own understanding and identity when at a distance from the place where he has come to acknowledge the LORD—that is, when he is in his home culture, whose religious symbolic system centers on Rimmon. How can he offer the LORD's sacrifice in a foreign land? The prospective limitations are not the LORD's but his own. The soil will play a symbolic, quasi-sacramental role in identifying and enabling the authenticity of his sacrifices to the God of all the earth, who is specifically the God of Israel.

It is worth asking what else could have been available to Naaman to take with him. For example, a written document—a *sēpher*, perhaps analogous to the letter (*sēpher*) to the king of Israel in verses 5–7—with content about Israel's knowledge of God could be appropriate to Naaman's need. But such a document is not raised as an option anywhere in the Elijah and Elisha cycles (such an option is for other places and times, when the notion of "scripture" comes into being). Water from the Jordan might have been a possibility (that too has a long later history in the annals of pilgrimage), and it could serve as a symbolic reminder of Naaman's healing; but, if poured out in use, it could not last to enable his future sacrificial worship in the way that the soil could. A carved religious object of wood or stone, an image or idol (*pesel*), would seem natural to many people. But the biblical writers strikingly resist the possible attractions of such objects, and the deuteronomic inflection of Naaman's rejection of the worship of "other gods" tacitly aligns him with such resistance.[80]

80. In a Christian frame of reference, a belief not only in creation but also in God's incarnation in Jesus has led to many Christians finding various artifacts—especially paintings, statues,

A garment might be symbolically significant, as is Elijah's mantle (1 Kings 19:19; 2 Kings 2:13); but it might link Naaman's future worship more with Elisha than with the God whom Elisha serves—or be essentially a keepsake. The lack of good alternatives suggests that Naaman's request for something both elemental and practical, soil, is well directed.

Further Reflection 3: Naaman's Request to Bow in the House of Rimmon and Elisha's Response

The question of how best to understand Naaman's request to bow in the house of Rimmon has, unsurprisingly, divided interpreters. My proposed reading, that he worships the LORD on his altar at home and does no more than go through the motions of worship when he is in the house of Rimmon, is not the only possibility.

Naaman's Request as Sinful

For some, the text presents a clear issue of inappropriate compromise. Matthew Henry, for example, after claiming that Naaman "overdid it" in his request for earth, thinks that here Naaman "underdid it":

> He reserved to himself a liberty to bow in the house of Rimmon. . . . If, in covenanting with God, we make a reservation for any known sin, which we will continue to indulge ourselves in, that reservation is a defeasance of his covenant. We must cast away all our transgressions and not except any house of Rimmon. If we ask for a dispensation to go on in any sin for the future, we mock God, and deceive ourselves.[81]

As moral and spiritual instruction, this is admirable. But how does it fare as a reading of the biblical text? Disappointingly, Henry passes over Elisha's "Go in peace" with no comment whatsoever. Such silence is perhaps unsurprising, given the clear point about sin he wants to make, and may well reflect an unwillingness to criticize the prophet's apparent acquiescence. His overall point may also indicate a somewhat wooden reading of Naaman's asking for

---

and icons—to be of value in enabling worship. Nonetheless, the iconoclast controversy in the Eastern church in the eighth and ninth centuries, and the iconoclastic dimensions of the Reformation in the Western church in the sixteenth century, are reminders that the issues are not straightforward and that worship of the one God can be debased.

81. Henry, *Matthew Henry's Commentary*, 406–7.

pardon, as though it indicates conscious knowledge of sin rather than most likely being a deferential way of asking permission for something unusual and prima facie inconsistent. Unless and until Elisha's tacit permission is argued to be an inappropriate failure on his part, or not permission at all, the kind of reading that Henry offers must surely stand as a misreading.

Naaman's Request as Syncretistic

Another possibility is to construe Naaman's request, together with Elisha's approval, as "effectively syncretism."[82] What this might mean is spelled out in positive form by Richard Briggs (in the context of a fascinating discussion of interpretive charity):

> Elisha's "Go in peace" is in effect demonstrating the appropriate response to one who is seeking a way of honoring Yhwh in a world where the practice of obedience to another god is presupposed. Elisha's evaluation appears to operate on the understanding that, while the worship of other gods is unacceptable in Israel, the options for Naaman, who has worshiped other gods anyway and is now declaring allegiance to Yhwh alone, may (at least in the short term) be different.

Briggs notes the attribution of Naaman's victories to Yhwh in 2 Kings 5:1 and remarks that "it leaves the reader alert to questions of how rightly to attribute claims of divine action to one god rather than another." He then suggests,

> Naaman might say (as indeed perhaps Elisha might say) that the point is that Yhwh can be worshiped even in the house of Rimmon, since he is in fact the only God. Put this way, Elisha's "concession" may be read less as a failure to hold the line and insist on the purity of worship required by monotheism, and more as an affirmation that even in a world (Syria) that looks as though it is dominated by the worship of other gods, Yhwh may still actually be worshiped.[83]

The difficulty with this reading is that it downplays Naaman's clear statement that he will not offer sacrifices to "other gods" (*ʾĕlōhîm ʾăḥērîm*), but only to the Lord. Here we have the language and conceptuality that receives its clearest formulation in Deuteronomy, in terms of exclusive adherence to the Lord and refusal to compromise with that which expresses and enables allegiances other than to the Lord. The logic that would infer from "there is no God in all the earth except in Israel" (2 Kings 5:15) that the worship

82. Thus Antony F. Campbell and Mark A. O'Brien (*Unfolding the Deuteronomistic History*, 445). Unfortunately, they do not elaborate on what they understand by this.

83. R. Briggs, *Virtuous Reader*, 158–59.

of any other supposed deity can really be the worship of Israel's deity, since Israel's deity is the only deity there is, may have its place and time. But it is hardly the logic of Deuteronomy. To find such a sense in the deuteronomically inflected wording of Naaman is surely not to go with its grain.

Elisha's Permission as the Freedom of Faith

A strongly positive construal, at least of Elisha's response to Naaman, is offered by Gerhard von Rad, who observes,

> He [Naaman] knows that when he returns to the heathendom of his home, he will be unable to separate himself from it. Will that be the end of his new-found faith? That is the question. We might formulate it this way: Naaman asks if the command of God will kill him when he goes out there. The sharpness of the conflict that he anticipates will here too become clear only when one comprehends that in Naaman's question a humanity is speaking that does not know about the modern escape, namely the retreat from the world into the inwardness of the heart, where the external circumstances of worship are unimportant. . . .
>
> Elisha's answer is brief as possible and leaves much open, but in its roominess and theological precision [*Bestimmtheit*] it is the product of genuine prophetic intuition. It is theologically precise [*bestimmt*] in invoking no law [*keinerlei Gesetz*] against the man who is setting out for a very threatened existence; i.e., it is in no way casuistic [*kasuistisch*]. Elisha . . . leaves him completely to his new faith [*seinem jungen Glauben*], or better, to God's hand which has sought and found him. When one considers how difficult Elisha made things for Naaman at the beginning, . . . one must be surprised at the almost presumptuous freedom [*die fast verwegene Freiheit*] into which he now directs him.[84]

This is a powerful reading that relates the biblical narrative to enduring issues of life with God. Nonetheless, it is not entirely straightforward.

On the one hand, von Rad arguably downplays the significance of Naaman's desire to build his own altar and there offer worship exclusively to YHWH (5:17). This solemn undertaking by Naaman shows that the issue is indeed not a "retreat from the world into the inwardness of the heart, where the external circumstances of worship are unimportant," inasmuch as he clearly affirms that his worship of the LORD will take the familiar form of the offering of sacrifice known in the Old Testament and its wider world. Naaman's

84. Von Rad, "Naaman: A Critical Retelling," 53–54. The term "retelling" (*Nacherzählung*) in its title links the study with von Rad's overall understanding of the appropriate mode of Christian theological engagement with the OT, which anticipated more recent proposals for literary and canonical readings.

anticipated actions in the temple of Rimmon also do not represent a retreat into inwardness. Rather, he will not be worshiping at all, since he reconceives the nature of the event: he will be performing the actions and movements necessary to help his king, and no more.

On the other hand, one may ask whether Elisha's "Go in peace" reflects the kind of "theological precision" von Rad ascribes to it.[85] Von Rad strikingly depicts this precision in strongly Lutheran categories, which may of course be appropriate, but whose use requires critical cross-examination. In Elisha's words he sees, negatively, the absence of "law" together with its corollary of "casuistry" and, positively, the presence of "faith" together with the enjoyment of "freedom." There may indeed be here a vision of freedom under God from which the religiously timid shrink back. But von Rad is surely construing Elisha's words with categories of subsequent Christian controversy (Protestant over against Catholic) that do not really get to the heart of what is at stake in the biblical text.[86] On most readings of the text, Naaman's request for forgiveness for what he will do in the temple of Rimmon is in some real sense casuistic in relation to his affirmation of YHWH. If it is the case that Naaman will worship YHWH with familiar religious practice, and will not worship Rimmon at all, Elisha is approving such correct worship of YHWH despite its abnormal domestic location. Further, Naaman's corollary request to be permitted merely to go through the motions in the temple of Rimmon is rather strongly casuistic. He is asking whether the exclusive worship of YHWH can tolerate a particular action which is apparently at odds with it. If this is a right reading, it does not diminish the authenticity and freedom of faith that Naaman will enjoy, but it recognizes that authenticity and casuistry may sometimes have to go together.

In short, I judge von Rad's reading—in terms of the freedom of faith—to be fully appropriate in terms of its general tenor, but open to reformulation in terms of which theological categories best capture what is going on in this story.

Faithfulness and Compromise

Christians down the ages have often faced opposition to their faith.[87] Opposition has sometimes developed into persecution. Persecution has sometimes

85. It may be that "precision" does not best capture von Rad's *Bestimmtheit*. It might perhaps be rendered "certitude" or "definiteness" in terms of Elisha's giving a confident and final pronouncement, in von Rad's reading.

86. The point is not the use of postbiblical categories, which is necessary, but their being used too unreflectively in a way that may fail to do justice to the text's own dynamics.

87. I cannot here speak for Jews, whose history of being persecuted is more terrible than that of Christians.

been murderous, especially when sponsored and implemented by hostile state authorities, and has led to martyrdom. Martyrdom early became an important element within Christian history and self-understanding—as did also issues of compromise, vacillation, apostasy, and possible repentance and restoration.[88] But martyrdom is not confined to ancient history. The internecine conflicts of Catholics and Protestants in the sixteenth and seventeenth centuries created many martyrs on both sides. And a modern history of the Orthodox Church observes, “It is by no means impossible that in the thirty years between 1918 and 1948 more Christians died for their faith than in the first 300 years after the Crucifixion.”[89] The twenty-first century has also not started well in this regard.[90]

Any familiarity with the testimonies of Christians facing martyrdom for their faith can readily make believers unsympathetic to Naaman’s request for permission to bow down in the house of Rimmon. It can look like a cowardly failure to live up to the implications of his recognition of the one true God.

But one of the strengths of the biblical narrative is that it can prompt fresh reflection on perennially difficult questions of what constitutes faithfulness or compromise or failure in a world where faith in the one God is contested and the implications of a life of faith are not always self-evident.[91] On the one hand, Naaman’s envisaged situation back home in Aram is not that of Christians (or Jews), as a recognized group, facing hostility. He is someone who has had a life-changing experience in Israel and is seeking to resume his life in Aram, where no one is expecting any problem in his outlook or allegiance. His proposal to offer sacrifices only to the LORD while also going through the necessary motions of supporting his king in the house of Rimmon envisages a particular, pragmatic arrangement of his competing loyalties.[92]

88. Modern literature on the subject has become extensive, ever since Edward Gibbon handled the issue in his own inimitable style and pointed out, among other things, that Christians were as bad as anyone else in practicing persecution (usually of other Christians, considered heretical) when they had opportunity (*Decline and Fall of the Roman Empire*, 2:3–80).

89. Ware, *Orthodox Church*, 20.

90. See Shortt, *Christianophobia*.

91. A prime example in the NT is the question of whether Christians should eat meat that had been offered to idols (1 Cor. 8–10). Differing judgments about the nature of idols are intertwined with differing judgments about what it is appropriate to do.

92. Rabbinic tradition discusses Naaman’s request in terms of a distinction between private and public, which is a not-infrequent move to resolve apparent textual conflicts; see Sanhedrin 74b–75a (Epstein, *Babylonian Talmud: Seder Neziḳin*, 3:505). However, the rabbinic context has to do with non-Jews sanctifying the divine name, and the construal of private and public is entirely different from the reading I am proposing. In this rabbinic construal, what happens in the temple of Rimmon is private because no Jews would be present, and the question is whether Naaman must sanctify the divine name in public—i.e., in the presence of Jews.

On the other hand, one might easily imagine that the bigger challenge for Naaman in the future would be to lead the army of Aram against the army of Israel. Although Naaman has reason not to be starry-eyed about Israel, given his encounter with the king (and perhaps also because of Gehazi, though we are not told whether he ever discovers the truth about Gehazi or his fate), his responsibility to lead in battle against the people of YHWH might well give him pause and be seen as incompatible with his acknowledgment of YHWH. Of course we cannot know. The point of the thought experiment is to remind us that, in life, knowing where to make a stand varies according to circumstance and is, like so much of the story of Naaman, unpredictable.

Further Reflection 4: Christian Figural Reading of Naaman[93]

A figural (or typological) reading of the Old Testament in relation to Jesus Christ and the patterns of Christian faith is an ancient Christian approach to the text which has received some fresh consideration, and also advocacy, in recent scholarship.[94]

Classic Figural Reading

In antiquity, at least from the time of Origen, Naaman's immersion in the Jordan was figurally related to Christian baptism. The assumptions underlying figural reading embodied considerable imaginative range and theological precision. The mere presence of water signified little. Jean Daniélou, for example, notes "the error of certain exegetes [who] try to recognize a type of Baptism wherever water is mentioned in the Old Testament."[95] Rather,

> in the thought of the Fathers, these types are not mere illustrations: the Old Testament figures were meant to authorize Baptism by . . . showing that it has been announced by a whole tradition: they are *testimonia*. . . . And, above all, their purpose is also to explain Baptism, a purpose which still holds good today.[96]

In some places, such as the flood narrative, water symbolizes destruction and thus relates to baptism in terms of conformity to the death of Christ. In

93. In this and the following section I draw on my discussion in "Sacramentality and the Old Testament," esp. 8–13.

94. See, e.g., Dawson, *Christian Figural Reading*; Seitz, *Figured Out*; Radner, *Time and the Word*; Collett, *Figural Reading*.

95. Daniélou, *The Bible and the Liturgy*, 78.

96. Daniélou, *The Bible and the Liturgy*, 71.

other places, such as Israel's crossing the Jordan, the water is seen as purifying and sanctifying—as also is the baptism of Christ in the Jordan.

In ancient readings, the story of Naaman is seen to embody this latter significance. As Daniélou puts it,

> The aspect of baptism which is brought out by the figure of the bath of Naaman is that of purification—as ordinary water washes stains from the body, so the sacred bath purifies us by the power of God. This power, which was exercised on a physical malady with Naaman, acts on the soul in Baptism: "The healing and purifying power which, according to the Biblical narrative, the river Jordan had for Naaman, is the image of the purification produced by the water of baptism."[97]

A Recent Figural Reading

A classic figural reading of Naaman is creatively reformulated in a contemporary context by Peter Leithart, whose commentary on 1–2 Kings is in a series explicitly designed to reconnect biblical interpretation with classic Christian tradition, on the understanding that Christian doctrine should enable and illuminate a reading of Scripture.[98] Leithart says,

> The story of Naaman is the richest Old Testament story of baptism and anticipates Christian baptism in a number of specific ways. For starters, it is an important typological witness because the subject of baptism is a Gentile, an Aramean general. . . . Though dead in leprosy, Naaman is made alive together with Christ.
>
> Naaman's "dipping" in the Jordan is the effective ritual sign of this change of status. Just as the washings of the Levitical system cleanse from various forms of defilement, so Naaman is cleansed and brought near through washing. Because he is a Gentile, Naaman's baptism is a particularly apt sign of Christian baptism, which marks out a new community of worshipers in which the distinction of Jew and Gentile is utterly dissolved (Gal. 3:26–29). Naaman shows an admirable grasp of the implications of his baptism. Having been baptized, he realizes that he is exclusively devoted to Yahweh and promises to worship no other gods (2 Kgs. 5:17). . . .
>
> Like Naaman, some Christians doubt what the New Testament says about the power of baptismal water. . . . How can water do such wonders? Because baptism is not simply water, but water and word, water and promise. God does

97. Daniélou, *The Bible and the Liturgy*, 110. The citation is from Denzinger, *Ritus Orientalium*.

98. Leithart, *1 & 2 Kings*. The series outlook is articulated on pp. 7–12.

> wonders, but he promises to do wonders through water. To say that water can cleanse leprosy, wash away sins, or renew life is an insult to intelligence. Water is just too simple, not to mention too physical and tangible. But that is exactly the point. Baptism is an insult to the wisdom of the world: through the foolishness of water God has chosen to save those who believe. Baptism is a stumbling block for the powerful, who want to do something impressive or at least have something impressive done to them.[99]

Leithart's reading is a fascinating mixture of staying with the text of Kings while simultaneously moving beyond it within the canon of Christian Scripture. Whatever one makes of all the various moves in this interpretation, its rich resonance with the New Testament and Christian baptismal theology makes it a good example of how an ancient figural/typological approach can be reformulated in a contemporary context.

A Problem with Figural Reading

A figural reading may entail loss as well as gain. This, sadly, is well illustrated by the *Revised Common Lectionary*, which provides Old and New Testament readings for worship in contemporary churches. In the readings for Epiphany 6 (Year B), 2 Kings 5:1–14, the story of Naaman up to and including his healing through immersion in the Jordan, is paired with Mark 1:40–45, in which Jesus heals a man suffering from "leprosy" by touching him.[100] By linking these two stories, the lectionary discourages the reader (or hearer) from seeing a baptismal resonance in the story of Naaman. Rather, the figural link has to do with healers who heal people suffering from the same affliction.[101] Elisha the healer prefigures Jesus the healer, as also Naaman with his skin disease prefigures the nameless man in the Gospel whose life is renewed by Jesus. This is a reasonable linkage, though one may wonder why healing a skin disease has become imaginatively more significant than baptism. The trouble is, the lectionary reading stops at 2 Kings 5:14, just when the story reaches its key concern, Naaman's confession of the one God, together with the intriguing implications of his accompanying pledge and request. A life-changing recognition and transformation of identity and allegiance—which are major issues for faith in the contemporary world—disappear from view, as

99. Leithart, *1 & 2 Kings*, 192–95.

100. *Revised Common Lectionary in NRSV*, 337–39. The story of Naaman features nowhere else in the lectionary.

101. The appointed psalm is Ps. 30, with one of the two possible congregational responses specified as: "O Lord my God, I cried out to you, and you restored me to health" (*Revised Common Lectionary in NRSV*, 338).

does Elisha's affirmation of grace, which Gehazi refuses to accept. The overall nature of the story changes, as it becomes solely an account of healing—in which role (despite its memorable narrative build-up) it may well play second fiddle to the healing performed by Jesus in the Gospel. One wonders how the Old Testament can be taken seriously in the life of the church when lectionary compilers, who have a formative role in shaping the contribution of Scripture to worship, diminish it in this way.[102]

Some Hermeneutical Reflections on Reading the Story

The Intrinsic Richness of the Story

The story of Naaman is one of the famous stories of the Old Testament. Its telling evinces high literary craft,[103] and its subject matter is rich and deep. It is, as Robert Cohn well puts it, "an especially apt example of a biblical narrative in which art and theology are symbiotically related."[104] Yet in certain ways the story is somewhat elusive. That is, if one asks, "What is the point, or message, of the story?" it is not easy to give a good answer. So much happens that there is no one obvious point or message. Rather, like many enduring stories or parables, its meaning is rich and resonant in ways that cannot be pinned down to any single concern.

Good uses of the story are likely to be as many and varied as is the scope of disciplined analogical and metaphorical thinking. It is not difficult to think of possible summaries that suggest differing possible readings of the story in whole or in part. For example: The one God is not as people expect. God does not play favorites. God brings not only life but also death. The humble are of more service than the exalted. Obedience requires the swallowing of

102. I recognize that the task of lectionary compilers is thankless, in that they regularly face the charge that they cut out the important part, wherever they stop; and stop they must. In this case, they might appeal to the fact that some scholars have reckoned that the original Naaman story ended at v. 14. But the literary/canonical whole is so much more than the sum of its putative parts, and a lectionary selection that omits what is now the heart of the story shows poor judgment.

103. Although the story reads well as a single unit, it remains possible to postulate complex antecedents in which, in essence, the different phases of the story are taken to be originally independent narrative units or redactional layers. See, e.g., Jones, *1 and 2 Kings*, 412–14. Comparably, G. Hentschel finds many putative layers of "critical" reflection on, and additions to, an original short miracle story (*2 Könige*, 22–26). Such analyses may have value in alerting the reader to varying vocabulary or emphases, but they are usually unattuned to the conventions and nuances of narrative poetics and tend to offer little by way of constructive reflection on the story we actually have.

104. R. Cohn, "Form and Perspective in 2 Kings V," 184.

pride. Faithful service of God should not bring wealth. Exclusive allegiance to the one God brings freedom. Faithfulness can look like hypocrisy to the unsympathetic. God is not mocked, even by the supposedly pious.

Characteristic Modern Approaches to the Meaning of the Story

Modern scholars, while recognizing the richness of the story, have regularly tried to focus and nuance their approach to its meaning in two distinct but related ways. First, when, where, and why was the story composed? Second, why was the story included in the larger history of Kings? But the results of such inquiries are meager because all we have to go on is what stands in the biblical text itself, without further evidence being available; we are restricted to making intelligent conjectures.[105]

In terms of origins, it has often been supposed that the Elisha stories (at least in part) originated among the prophetic groups ("sons of the prophets") with which Elisha is associated in some of the material (though interestingly not in 2 Kings 5 itself). Von Rad could introduce his reading of 2 Kings 5 with the confident claim that we can "define the sociological milieu out of which it arose and for which it was also presumably intended":

> The stories [that cluster around Elisha] reveal a social milieu, one could almost say they make palpable the atmosphere of a group of men in Israel of the ninth century B.C. To be sure, they deal with a very strange stratum of the society in Israel at that time. There was—and the Dead Sea Scrolls suggest that there always were—in Israel . . . a group of religious men that can be included only with difficulty in the usual social categories. The men of that group lived in the vicinity of shrines as though in individual congregations; they listened to the doctrinal lectures of their prophetic masters. We do not know what those prophets spoke about in their lectures, but from all the stories about their leader and master, the prophet Elisha, we feel a breath of their spirit.[106]

He concludes his reading of the story by returning to these "indigent associations of the prophets" and comments, with reference to the content of

105. One recent proposal, which typically selects certain features of the text and constructs a plausible history-of-ideas hypothesis around them, is that of Thomas Römer, "The Strange Conversion of Naaman." Römer focuses on the implicitly positive picture of the Arameans and suggests that the story can "be understood as a late non-Deuteronomistic etiology of an Aramean Yhwh-veneration" (117). He also wonders whether "Naaman serves here also as a 'mirror' for Israelites and Judahites in the diaspora who were perhaps also sometimes in the situation of participating in the cult of other deities" (117–18).

106. Von Rad, "Naaman: A Critical Retelling," 47–48.

2 Kings 5, that "it is moving to see the theological problems with which the men of these circles occupied themselves."[107] In other words, as we read and ponder the story of Naaman we can perhaps recapture something of the theological content of the teaching and discussion in ancient pre-Qumran prophetic groups in the Jordan Valley.

It is a striking scenario. It might even be right. But scholars have become less confident than von Rad was in constructing such scenarios. With regard to what we really know of the story's origins, a certain reticence and agnosticism is, in my judgment, fully appropriate. This need in no way detract from constructive engagement with the story's content.

Similarly, when one asks, "Why was the story included in the larger history of Kings?" there is no clear answer. The story does not pick up themes that have sometimes been proposed as crucial to the so-called Deuteronomistic History, such as hope on the basis of the LORD's promise to the house of David or hope on the basis of repentance.[108] Choon-Leong Seow, for example, observes, "This is no doubt the sort of story that the Israelites, particularly those in exile, liked to tell. Despite the tragedy of defeat and captivity, it seems, greater good may be achieved."[109] Alternatively, Burke Long reflects on the Gehazi episode, with its message that "the power of God is not just restorative [but] . . . also demands righteousness and is a punishment to those who trifle with it," and offers a summary suggestion that "perhaps the narrator saw in this story a metaphor for the history of Israel's kingdoms."[110] Clearly, hopeful and/or admonitory stories can play a role in situations where hope and/or admonition is needed, for people can imaginatively conceive their situation in terms of what happens in the story. It is apparent, however, that general analogical and metaphorical thinking is at work no less in attempts to pinpoint the reason for the story's presence in Kings than in attempts to learn from and appropriate it today.

A particularly interesting example is afforded by some of the closing comments of Peter Leithart. Although his comments are presented as historical observations about Israel in exile (with a rather loose use of "Gentile"), it is hard not to sense a certain overlap in terms of the story's meaning for

107. Von Rad, "Naaman: A Critical Retelling," 55.

108. See von Rad, "Deuteronomic Theology of History in 1 and 2 Kings"; Wolff, "Kerygma of the Deuteronomic Historical Work." There is also the wider issue of understanding the role of the Elijah and Elisha cycles, with their focus on the Northern Kingdom of Israel, in a narrative sequence which overall seems more concerned with the Southern Kingdom of Judah and its capital, Jerusalem.

109. Seow, "First and Second Books of Kings," 193.

110. Long, "2 Kings," 327.

Christians in a contemporary secular culture (even though he only explicitly mentions the church in subsequent remarks):

> Israelites first read this story while in exile, and it instructs them how they are to conduct themselves among the Gentiles. They are to serve Gentiles, directing them, as the little slave-girl does, to Yahweh as the source of cleansing and life. They must not be zealous nationalists who refuse to help the uncircumcised. If they strive to be super-Israel, they will end up not-Israel. To Israel as to Gehazi, the Lord also says: if you lust after Gentile wealth and power, then you will find yourselves going all the way, inheriting also Gentile exclusion and uncleanness.[111]

My own conjecture is that a likely reason for the story's inclusion in Kings is that Naaman recognizes the LORD, the God of Israel, to be the only God and renounces the worship of "other gods" (*ʾĕlōhîm ʾăḥērîm*). Warnings about the worship of "other gods" are something of a leitmotif in Kings.[112] Naaman, who renounces "other gods" because of what happened to him when he became obedient to a prophet, could be exemplary for exiled Judeans who were seeking a way ahead for the future—as also for hope-seeking readers in other places and times.

Conclusion: Towards a Grammar of the Only God

I started this chapter with François's opportunistic embrace of Islam in Houellebecq's novel. Such mixed and murky motives for embracing faith in God are, of course, amply illustrated also within the history of the Christian church, not least in contexts where churches have been aligned with power and the practical benefits have been all too obvious. One of the advantages for churches in a post-Christian culture is that people are less inclined to embrace Christian faith for opportunistic reasons. Yet despite the confession of God being a turning point in both 2 Kings 5 and in Houellebecq's *Submission*, the tenor of each story is of course greatly different. The major difference is that Naaman's confession of the God of Israel is not self-serving or obviously advantageous—indeed, quite the opposite, as the issue of what he will do back home immediately shows.

In terms of our developing further dimensions of what it means to "know that the LORD is God," part of the luminosity of the story of Naaman is that it so clearly illustrates what many (though by no means all) down the ages have

111. Leithart, *1 & 2 Kings*, 196.
112. See Römer, "Form-Critical Problem," esp. 247–48.

recognized: the best reason for believing in the LORD is that one has come to see that the faith is true and that to take such a step becomes the only right thing to do. In Naaman's case this is because an encounter with grace—indeed, in terms of the narrative dynamics, amazing grace—has become a defining moment of opening him to a larger reality which he unreservedly embraces. To "know that the LORD is God" in this context also merits some further concluding reflection on the distinctive nature of "monotheism" in the Bible and in the faiths rooted in it.

The knowledge of the one God, universal in its implications, is accompanied by a strong sense of particularity—that Israel is the place where this knowledge is to be found; if Naaman's worship of the one God, where he has encountered grace, is to be authentic, it needs something specific and concrete to give it its identity (in his case, earth for the altar). In the Old Testament generally, this "monotheism" is also accompanied by a consistent understanding that all people, in principle, have some awareness of God (*ʾĕlōhîm*), although this knowledge is generic and lacks the particular content afforded by Israel's knowledge of God as *yhwh*, the LORD.[113] Biblical "monotheism" is further accompanied by recognition of the problematic presence and persistence of "other gods" both within and beyond Israel.

It is this combination of the universal with the particular, of God and a privileged human context for knowledge of God, that is so distinctive of the Bible. It is foundationally present in the Old Testament, as we have seen. It is equally present in the New Testament: "And this is eternal life, that they may know you, the only true God, and Jesus Christ whom you have sent" (John 17:3). This pattern of understanding is also present in Islam's core affirmation, the Shahadah: "There is no God but God/Allah, and Muhammad is his messenger/prophet."

In recent times, this has led to two different kinds of discussion. On the one hand, an eighteenth-century philosophical "monotheism" that was initially formative of modernity rejected particularity as incompatible with true universality: "natural" religion, expressed as deism, found all "positive" (i.e., humanly posited) religious traditions to be wanting. Arguably, in a contemporary postmodern context this approach is essentially inverted, inasmuch as true particularity now problematizes the universal: "monotheism" is questionable because it entails "violence," since the kind of particularity that is a corollary of a universal belief is seen to entail negative attitudes towards, and constraints upon, those who are "other."

On the other hand, Jews, Christians, and Muslims agree on the combination of the universal and the particular but disagree on the nature and

113. See the discussion of "fear of God" and "fear of the LORD" (ch. 3, pp. 108–9).

location of the content of the particular. Long-standing approaches to interfaith dialogue in terms of seeking common ground, which tend to emphasize the ethical at the expense of the theological (i.e., to prioritize the universal over the particular), have been interestingly complemented in recent times by approaches that encourage interlocutors to inhabit their respective traditions robustly and, through hospitality and attentiveness in dialogue, to make progress by removing misunderstandings and improving the quality of disagreements (i.e., the particular is prioritized over the universal).

Questions as to how best to make progress in all such discussions remain live issues in the twenty-first century. It may be that the Naaman story can offer a fresh perspective. It reminds (would-be) Christian readers of the theological necessity to maintain the tension between the one God and a privileged human point of access, while at the same time showing that the outworking of that tension may take a surprising form that does not neatly fit conventional theological systems.[114]

Finally, one of the recurrent emphases of 2 Kings 5 is the consistently surprising and open-ended nature of what happens. This is, of course, in line with the point that Jesus makes in his reading of the story, in the sole New Testament reference. God's priorities are not necessarily those of His people, and not only in His giving victory to Aram at the expense of Israel. For it is also the case that "there were many in Israel who suffered from skin diseases in the time of the prophet Elisha, and none of them was cleansed except Naaman the Syrian" (Luke 4:27 AT). In the reading of the story offered in this chapter, we see that assumptions and expectations about what the one God does, or should do, and of how people should live before this God are repeatedly overturned.

If the story of Naaman and Elisha is read as Scripture, and thus allowed to play upon the hearts and minds of readers who seek to know God better and to live more truthfully, it offers a richly suggestive vision of at least some aspects of what life in God's world can entail.

114. Those who believe that the truth of God is definitively seen in a judicially murdered man who is then divinely raised into a new mode of existence should surely have a certain intuitive affinity for recognizing that God does not necessarily fit within humanly recognized patterns and precedents, even while patterns and precedents have their place.

6

The Trustworthy God

Assurance and Warning in Psalm 46, Jeremiah 7, and Micah 3

Many years ago I read a study of Old Testament theology (I no longer have any recollection which study or by whom), at an early point in which (I think) the author highlighted Psalm 62:8 (Heb. 9): "Trust in him at all times, O people; / pour out your heart before him; / God is a refuge for us." The accompanying comment was along the lines of "This is the heart of Old Testament theology" or perhaps "This is the basis of Old Testament religion"; again, I have no precise recollection. I am encouraged that the haziness of my memory need not be a problem. For the important thing is that that scholar's insight has stayed with me. There is an obvious sense in which the observation is true, and importantly true. Trust in God is a deep characteristic not only of Israel's scriptures but also of the Jewish and Christian faiths, which are rooted in them.

Of course, "trust" does not say everything that needs to be said about human response to God. I have noted elsewhere that the Old Testament's prime term for appropriate human responsiveness to God is not "trust" (*bāṭaḥ*) but "fear God / the Lord" (*yārēʾ ʾĕlōhîm/yhwh*).[1] Various terms for "obey" (e.g., *shāmaʿ*) also play a prominent role. For example, a notable summary statement on the lips of Moses is: "So now, O Israel, what does the Lord your

In this chapter I build on my *Prophecy and Discernment*, ch. 2; and my "'In God We Trust'? The Challenge of the Prophets."

1. See ch. 3, pp. 108–9.

God require of you? Only to fear the LORD your God, to walk in all his ways, to love him, to serve the LORD your God with all your heart and with all your soul, and to keep the commandments of the LORD your God and his decrees that I am commanding you today, for your own well-being" (Deut. 10:12–13). Other categories, such as wisdom and justice, have also been highlighted in this book. Nonetheless, "trust" captures a particular existential reality that is foundational to faith, as it is to life more generally—not least because those who have no one who is trustworthy, or whom they are able to trust, tend to become diminished as people.

The development and exercise of trust poses basic challenges. First and foremost, it is always necessary to discern whether the recipient of trust is genuinely trustworthy. Trust can be misplaced, sometimes disastrously, and some knowledge of character is necessary to place trust well.[2] In relation to God, if people conceive God to be, say, arbitrary or cruel, they are unlikely to trust Him (though they might be afraid of Him). For those who place trust, there are also questions of which attitudes and modes of behavior appropriately accompany and express the trust, and which attitudes and modes of behavior are incompatible with, and thereby undermine and diminish, that trust. When, for example, does trust become complacency or taking someone for granted?

These preliminary reflections set the scene for our sixth exploration into facets of what it means to "know that the LORD is God." I want to focus on two particular aspects of trust in God in the context of the Old Testament: What understanding of the LORD appropriately underlies and informs trust? What particular attitudes and practices are incompatible with trust and have the capacity to diminish and even nullify it?

This study could well focus on Psalm 62, with which I started. Psalm 62 develops the theme of trust with a number of images of God that express His reliability. In particular, God is a rock and a fortress or shelter, such that those who trust in Him gain stability and will not be "shaken" (*mōt*, vv. 2, 6, 7 [Heb. 3, 7, 8]). Implicitly, those who trust in a God who is firm and immovable acquire at least something of those qualities themselves.[3] This imagery is more fully developed, however, in Psalm 46, and so this psalm will be my focus.

2. In a contemporary context of extensive communication via electronic media, where there may be no face-to-face encounter, problems of determining trustworthiness can be substantial, as the potential for unscrupulous deception of the unwary is even greater than in face-to-face encounter.

3. One might compare, e.g., Isa. 40:28, 31: "The LORD is the everlasting God, . . . / [who] does *not faint or grow weary*. . . . / Those who wait for the LORD shall renew their strength, . . . / they shall run and *not be weary*, / they shall walk *and not faint*" (emphasis added). Those who genuinely engage with the LORD acquire some of His qualities.

A Reading of Psalm 46[4]

Psalm 46 is one of the better-known psalms, not least because of its famous rendering by Martin Luther in his 1529 hymn *Ein feste Burg ist unser Gott*, which is best known in England in the 1831 version of Thomas Carlyle, "A Safe Stronghold Our God Is Still."[5] Luther's hymn extensively and imaginatively links this psalm with other biblical content; indeed, it is somewhat unclear how much Psalm 46 is still in view after the first two lines! Since, however, Luther presented his hymn as a rendering of Psalm 46, that is how it is known.

The psalm's own voice is startlingly evocative.

> **To the leader. Of the Korahites. According to Alamoth. A Song.**[6]
>
> [1] God is our refuge and strength,
> a well-proved help in trouble.[7]
> [2] Therefore we will not fear, though the earth should change,
> though the mountains totter [*mōt*] in the heart of the sea;
> [3] though its waters roar and foam,
> though the mountains tremble with its tumult. (Ps. 46:1–3)

The keynote of the psalm is sounded at the outset: confidence in God. He is a "refuge," a place in which to feel, and be, safe. Indeed, it is likely that "strength" is explicative of "refuge"—in other words, the security of the refuge that is God is underlined by reference to its strength (v. 1a). This does not mean that trouble does not come, but rather that, when it comes, the strong shelter that is God is there too (v. 1b).

Such confidence in God does away with fear, even in the most extreme situation imaginable—the disintegration of the natural world. Mountains/hills in Israel are inland, far from the sea (apart from Mount Carmel); and they are a

4. For the convenience of readers who are not specialists in the OT, I shall present the psalm with the familiar English verse numbering. The Hebrew numbering is one greater, as the psalm title is v. 1 in the MT.

5. Apart from the presence of the hymn in traditional hymnbooks, it can also be found, with notes, in collections such as Watson, *Annotated Anthology of Hymns*, 67–69; and Bradley, *Penguin Book of Hymns*, 5–8. The 1852 version of F. H. Hedge, "A Mighty Fortress Is Our God," is more popular in the US.

6. The notations in the psalm heading present specific interpretive difficulties that are well rehearsed in the commentaries. I have nothing to add; and the content of this heading does not, in my judgment, affect a reading of the psalm.

7. "Well proved" (NRSV margin) more likely captures the idiomatic force of *nimtsāʾ mĕʾōd* than "very present" (NRSV text). The point is that hope for the future is anchored in the past.

natural symbol of stability and strength.[8] So if mountains are tottering—that is, shaking and falling apart—in the waters of the sea, either the mountains have moved to the sea or the sea has come to the mountains. Or if one thinks in terms of ancient cosmological images of the mountains as pillars which uphold the world, then the result of their shaking and falling apart is the end of everything. Either way, the familiar world is utterly overturned.[9] This is symbolic language with mythic resonance that could be used of particular dire situations on earth—just as the eclipse of the sun, moon, and stars is elsewhere used to convey something of the immensity of the overthrow of Babylon (Isa. 13). It conveys that ultimate catastrophe, the end of all that is familiar, can be faced without fear through confidence in God.

> [4] There is a river whose streams make glad the city of God,
> the holy habitation of the Most High.
> [5] God is in the midst of the city; it shall not totter [*mōt*];
> God will help it when the morning dawns.
> [6] The nations are in an uproar, the kingdoms totter [*mōt*];[10]
> he utters his voice, the earth melts.
> [7] The LORD of hosts is with us;
> the God of Jacob is our refuge. (Ps. 46:4–7)

The general scenario of verses 2–3 now becomes specific. By contrast with the shaking mountains and fearful surging sea, there is a river whose waters—implicitly, calm waters—bring joy. That joy is located in a holy place, a city, where a sovereign deity ("the Most High") is specially present. Because God is present in its midst, this city is more firmly established than the mountains: even if the mountains move (v. 2b), this city will not move (v. 5a). That help in trouble which is God (v. 1a) will be realized at the symbolic moment of hope, the dawn of a new day (v. 5b). The picture of nations and kingdoms tottering and falling apart like the mountains into the sea (v. 6a) is a portrayal of instability everywhere apart from God's holy city, though it can also be read as a picture of what happens to nations and kingdoms if they attack that city

8. The Hebrew *har* can mean both "mountain" and "hill," and it is often unclear which English term better captures its sense in context.

9. Scholars sometimes are astonishingly wooden in their handling of poetic imagery. It is hard not to smile (or groan) when reading Charles Briggs's comment on v. 3: "The poet had probably witnessed an earthquake, and seen portions of Mt. Carmel falling into the Mediterranean Sea" (*Book of Psalms*, 1:394).

10. The NRSV is disappointingly insensitive to Hebrew word repetition. The thrice-repeated *mōt* receives a different translation each time ("shake," v. 2; "be moved," v. 5; "totter," v. 6), so the reader of the English is likely to miss the verbal contrast between that which does and does not move (though in Ps. 62:2, 6 [Heb. 3, 7] the repetition of the verb is captured).

(if one reads Ps. 46 in the light of Ps. 48). Either way, the Most High has only to speak—His voice being like a roar from a lion or the blast of a trumpet or a clap of thunder in the sky[11]—and the solid earth melts away (v. 6b). This part of the poem ends with a joyful reaffirmation of the confidence of verse 1, which becomes also a refrain for the poem as a whole.[12] The sovereign God is Israel's God, the LORD of hosts. He is "with us," which means that He is a stronghold, a fortress for His people.

> [8] Come, behold the works of the LORD;
> see what desolations he has brought on the earth.
> [9] He makes wars cease to the end of the earth;
> he breaks the bow, and shatters the spear;
> he burns the shields with fire.[13] (Ps. 46:8–9)

After the picture of the stability of the place where the LORD is present, the psalmist now develops more fully the picture of the sovereignty of the LORD. The idea that the LORD produces "desolations" (v. 8b) may initially be surprising,[14] but it is immediately clarified by what follows. Where previously there was warfare, this is now swept away; the weapons of war being destroyed is what constitutes desolations (v. 9). Implicitly, such desolations are a prerequisite for peace.

> [10] "Be still, and know that I am God!
> I am exalted [*ʾārûm*] among the nations,
> I am exalted [*ʾārûm*] in the earth."
> [11] The LORD of hosts is with us;
> the God of Jacob is our refuge. (Ps. 46:10–11)

The corollary of the vision of weapons being destroyed is a summons to recognize this sovereign God and to respond accordingly (v. 10). The famous and memorable "Be still" is certainly a possible rendering of the Hebrew,

11. The Hebrew idiom *nātan [bĕ]qōlō* is often used of thunder, though it is parallel to the roar of a lion in Amos 1:2, and a trumpet blast is associated with the LORD's presence on Mount Sinai in Exod. 19:16, 19. The point has to do with the overwhelming impact of the divine voice.

12. Noting the presence of the refrain at the end of the third stanza (v. 11 [Heb. 12]), numerous commentators have conjectured that the refrain originally stood also at the end of the first stanza, after v. 3 (Heb. 4), but has dropped out.

13. I am happy to retain the NRSV's "shields," which follows the LXX's *thureous* and provides a closer parallel to bows and spears than does the Hebrew *ʿăgālōt*, which usually means "wagons" but is sometimes rendered here as "chariots" for contextual reasons. Either way, the point that the implements of war are destroyed is unaffected.

14. The LXX reads *terata*, "signs/wonders," which may be a more "proper" rendering.

though its point is not to promote quietism. Rather, in context it means to stop fighting—to let go of the weapons,[15] or perhaps "unclench the warrior's fist,"[16] though idiomatically it can also just mean "Stop!"[17]—because of the realization that such fighting is ultimately futile. Alongside such cessation of futile action belongs the need to make that recognition that stands at the heart of the Old Testament—they are to know that the LORD is indeed God (v. 10a).[18] The LORD, the God of Israel, is also the sovereign God of the whole world (v. 10b). He is "exalted," a vision of height that is symbolic of majesty and transcendence (as people tend to look up in moments of wonder and joy, and look down in moments of confusion and shame).[19] Even if this vision of reality may not always be apparent, it nonetheless remains a vision which implicitly will receive its ultimate realization.[20]

Strikingly, the summons of verse 10 is set on the lips of God Himself. It is tempting to link it with the psalm's other reference to God's speaking, "He utters his voice, the earth melts" (v. 6b).[21] Thus one can imagine verse 10, "Be still, and know that I am God! / I am exalted among the nations, / I am exalted in the earth," as implying that God overturns kingdoms and the regular order of the world: these words are a vision of ultimate reality, in which the God who is above all *is* that reality.[22] Moreover, the nonspecified plural addressees would appear to be everyone, without limit. Both those who already know the LORD and the nations who do not yet know the LORD—all alike need to enter into, or go deeper into, this vision of the sovereign God.

The psalm then concludes by repeating the confident affirmation of verse 7. This sovereign God is none other than the LORD of Hosts, the God of Jacob/

15. The *hiphil* imperative of *rāphāh* often has *yād* ("hand") as an implied object, with the sense "Open your hand"—i.e., "Let go."

16. Thus Alter, *Book of Psalms*, 165.

17. This is the clear force of the idiom in Samuel's response to Saul in 1 Sam. 15:16.

18. See the fuller discussion of "know that the LORD is God" in ch. 5, pp. 180–81.

19. It is difficult to know how best to render the verb *'ārūm*. It has strong resonance with Isaiah's vision, in the Jerusalem temple, of the LORD on His throne as "high and lofty" (*rām vĕnissā'*, Isa. 6:1). I think that the NJPS's "I dominate the nations, I dominate the earth" is infelicitous because it focuses narrowly on power, even if the LORD of hosts is indeed a God of sovereign power. Alter's "I loom among nations, I loom upon earth" is also infelicitous, a surprising lapse of judgment (*Book of Psalms*, 165). Probably the time-honored "exalted" remains best.

20. There is the familiar problem of translating the imperfect/*yiqtol* form *'ārūm*: both "I am exalted" and "I will be exalted" are equally possible. The psalmist is surely affirming an ultimate, and thus in a certain sense future, vision in the present.

21. This linkage is not regularly made by commentators, but it does appear sometimes—e.g., Hossfeld and Zenger, *Die Psalmen 1*, in their comment on v. 10.

22. In a Christian context, there is an obvious resonance with the doxology of the Lord's Prayer, "For the kingdom and the power and the glory are yours forever," a doxology rooted in Jewish thought and practice.

Israel. The title "LORD of hosts" in some Old Testament contexts has specific implications of armies and warfare (e.g., 1 Sam. 17:45), even if elsewhere it looks to have a sense more like "Lord of everything in heaven and on earth" (e.g., Gen. 2:1, where "hosts" appears to mean this). Even if the title does have military overtones, Psalm 46 strikingly sees the LORD's military power as realized in the destruction of the implements of war.[23] This is the God in whom His people can trust unreservedly as the one who is with them and protects them (v. 11).

This preliminary reading of Psalm 46 has left unaddressed two obvious, and related, questions: Who are the "we" who joyfully affirm God's presence and protection? And which and where is the city that, because of God's presence, stands firm even when all else falls apart? The usual answer is that these are Judahite singers located in Jerusalem, Jerusalem being "the holy habitation of the Most High." Thus, the psalm is routinely designated a "Zion psalm."[24] On one level, this appears to be correct within the Psalter as it now stands. Jerusalem with its temple is the place that the LORD protects, and the ancient singers of the psalm would have been expressing their confidence in this.

Yet this should not simply be said without more ado. First, the name "Zion" does not appear in this psalm as it does in all other Zion psalms (e.g., Pss. 2; 48; 76; 84; 87; 110; 132). In traditio-historical terms, it is conceivable that Psalm 46 could have been written for a place other than Jerusalem, even if it was in due course transferred to and appropriated by Jerusalem.[25] Second, the strongly poetic and mythically resonant language throughout the psalm—in which the focus is more on God and the world as a whole than on the city mentioned in the middle stanza—at least raises the question of whether any one actual place on earth should be identified as this "city of God." Or perhaps the question should be *in what sense* or *in what way* a particular place might be thus identified. How might a vision that looks *beyond* the regular order of life on earth be related to a particular place *within* the regular order of life on earth?

23. This point is nicely developed by Martin Klingbeil as the conclusion to his book *Yahweh Fighting from Heaven*, 309–10.

24. So, e.g., Brueggemann and Bellinger: "The Psalm likely came from cultic celebrations of the reign of God and God's choice of Zion as a sacred place of divine presence and hope" (*Psalms*, 216).

25. Possible candidates in the Northern Kingdom of Israel include Shechem, Shiloh, Bethel, and Dan—though the canonical scriptural collection, with its Jerusalem orientation, offers little sense of the mythic resonance of these locations, and one would need to assume the disappearance of much material related to them. The "river" in v. 4 (Heb. 5), if taken to indicate a river as a geographical reality (a distinctly moot point in such a poem), might indicate Dan, located at one of the sources of the Jordan, rather than the other locations.

Overall, the psalm strongly sounds the note of human trust in God, even though the specific verb "trust" (*bāṭaḥ*) is not used. The existential note of not being afraid and of being secure, even *in extremis*, is clear. There is also a holy place to which God gives security, such that, by implication, those who are in that place are secure. Most of the psalm, however, presents a variety of images of God. He is a strong refuge, a sure helper, one whose voice transcends all mundane realities, a destroyer of weapons of destruction, the loftiest glory to which one's eyes can look. It is in response to this vision of God—as ultimate reality, already seen and known to some extent in the here and now—that trust and assurance are humanly appropriate.

But could that trust and assurance become *in*appropriate?

A Reading of Jeremiah's Temple Sermon in Jeremiah 7:1–15[26]

I turn now to a markedly different voice within Israel's scriptures, in which the vision of Zion, the temple in Jerusalem, is not a joy but a problem. The voice is that of the prophet Jeremiah in his famous temple sermon.

Introduction to Jeremiah 7:1–15

For reasons that remain unclear, and do not need probing in this context, Jeremiah's temple sermon appears in two places in the book of Jeremiah: 7:1–15 and 26:1–24.[27] The difference between them is clear.

Jeremiah 7:1–15 gives the content of what Jeremiah says, with minimal narrative framing. In a brief introduction, the LORD instructs Jeremiah as to where to go and whom to address (7:1–2). Then comes the content of Jeremiah's message/sermon, with a challenge to amendment that concludes with a warning that the Jerusalem temple, in which people trust, can be reduced to a ruin like the former temple at Shiloh (7:3–15). There is no subsequent account of response or consequences; the text continues directly with further instructions from the LORD to Jeremiah that are not unrelated but are distinct (7:16–8:3).

Jeremiah 26 starts with a brief account of the LORD's instruction about where Jeremiah is to go and what he is to say (26:1–6). It reads as a summary

26. For convenience I will generally refer to Jer. 7:1–15 simply as Jer. 7 in the discussion of this chapter.

27. One question, raised from time to time, is whether these two passages indeed depict one and the same event. I see no good reason for resisting the natural inference that we are given two presentations of one particularly memorable sermon and occasion.

of 7:1–15, both because of its general content and because of the specific warning about the precedent of Shiloh with which it ends. There is then a vivid and memorable narrative which portrays the varying responses evoked by Jeremiah's words and the consequences for Jeremiah himself. There is a strong initial clamor to put Jeremiah to death, and death is indeed meted out to another prophet, Uriah, who speaks similarly to Jeremiah; yet Jeremiah himself survives to face another day (26:7–24). In short, Jeremiah 7:1–15 gives the content of the sermon, while 26:1–24 tells of its impact and consequences.

■ There are numerous technical discussions about these two passages. One concerns the fact that Jer. 7 is one of the "prose sermons" in the book of Jeremiah. Questions of how these prose sermons relate to the poetic oracles that Jeremiah pronounces elsewhere (e.g., almost the whole of Jer. 2–6, as laid out in the NRSV) tend to be inseparable from questions about the deuteronomically inflected language in the prose sermons, which is not characteristic of the poetic oracles. Complex and extensive discussions of tradition history and of deuteronomistic redaction abound (though there is also a recent pushback against whether this is the best way of posing the question).[28] For present purposes I will focus on the text in its received form. I will take with full imaginative seriousness the literary presentation of Jeremiah as the human voice through whom the LORD speaks, without prejudice to questions about how the portrayal of Jeremiah in the text may or may not relate to the historical figure of Jeremiah in his late seventh-century context. Even if the figure of Jeremiah in the prose sermons is to a greater or lesser extent an interpreted and constructed figure, molded to address contexts subsequent to those that Jeremiah himself faced, that makes no real difference to my argument. My primary thesis is not about religio-political issues in the time of Jeremiah and of those responsible for the book in his name—though I hope to be informed by such discussions and alerted to nuances in the text that might be missed otherwise—but is focused on the subject matter of the text in its own intrinsic implications. ■

A Reading of Jeremiah 7:1–15

[1]The word that came to Jeremiah from the LORD: [2]Stand in the gate of the LORD's house, and proclaim there this word, and say, Hear the word of the LORD, all you people of Judah, you that enter these gates to worship the LORD. (Jer. 7:1–2)

The scene-setting is straightforward. Jeremiah is to stand in the gate of the "house of the LORD," which in this context is clearly the Jerusalem temple. The address to "all" the people of Judah may well imply a feast day, which would be a likely context for the people of Judah in general to come to Jerusalem

28. See Henderson, *Jeremiah under the Shadow of Duhm*.

and the temple. The gate would be a place of maximum exposure, in that people both entering and leaving the temple precincts would hear what Jeremiah was saying.

The LORD's instruction, however, is freighted in a way that is difficult to appreciate today. The symbolic significance of the Jerusalem temple was enormous, in ways that easily escape readers in a largely secularized society, even those who inhabit living traditions of faith rooted in the Bible. Strongly to criticize, never mind to envisage an end of, the temple—as Jeremiah is going to do—was to touch the very heart of Judah's identity.[29]

> [3]Thus says the LORD of hosts, the God of Israel: Amend [*hētīvū*] your ways and your doings, and I will let you dwell in this place. (Jer. 7:3)

Jeremiah's opening words on behalf of the LORD are a direct challenge to the people to "make good" / "get right" (the plain sense of the Hebrew *hētīvū*) their regular way of life. This challenge is presented in summary form and is accompanied by a clause which is simultaneously a promise and a warning: *if* they amend, their life in Jerusalem will be able to continue.

■ I have followed the NRSV's marginal note ("and I will let you dwell," *shākan* [*piel*], which is the vocalization of the MT, attested also in the LXX's *katoikiō*, "I will settle/establish") rather than the NRSV's main text (*shākan* [*qal*], "and let me dwell with you," which is attested in the Vulgate's *habitabo vobiscum*). It is likely that the weighty voice of Wilhelm Rudolph, the author of a major Jeremiah commentary and the editor of Jeremiah in *BHS* (where he indicates a preference for the *qal*), underlies the NRSV's main text. Rudolph's argument in his commentary revolves around the best sense of "in this place" (v. 3b): if it means the land of Judah, then "I will let you dwell" would be appropriate; but since the temple is the central concern of the passage, then the temple (where people would not be dwelling) is the likely referent of "this place," with God's presence there—i.e., "I will dwell with you"—as the key issue.[30] However, it is unwise to distinguish too sharply between temple, city, and land, as they are symbolically interrelated. Moreover, the clear note on which the sermon ends in v. 15 is the warning of exile. An early reference to the possibility of exile in v. 3 would fit well thematically. ■

Jeremiah's words encapsulate various dimensions of his wider message. First, warfare was a regular part of life in the ancient world, and defeat by a significant enemy could lead to the destruction of one's city and deportation

29. In contemporary British terms, the significance of the temple for the people of Judah would be something like the value of the abbey of Westminster for the believer, of the palace of Westminster for the politician, and of Wembley Stadium for the footballer all rolled into one.

30. Rudolph, *Jeremia*, 50.

into exile—which would be the meaning of *not* dwelling "in this place." Second, Jeremiah's preaching elsewhere envisages a growing threat to Judah and Jerusalem "from the north" (1:14–15; 4:6), a threat which in many early passages is nonspecific but which in due course becomes instantiated in the growing power and aggression of Babylon and its king, Nebuchadnezzar (e.g., 21:2).[31] Third, the LORD is sovereign over nations and active within them. He can both bring enemies against Jerusalem to overthrow it, and defend Jerusalem from its enemies and preserve it. If the people of Judah respond appropriately to Jeremiah's words—his summons to amendment—the LORD will respond by preserving Jerusalem (a pattern of interaction and response that is spelled out more fully in 18:7–10). Their future is dependent on their conduct—a core emphasis of biblical prophecy.

> [4]Do not trust in these deceptive [*sheqer*] words: "This is the temple of the LORD, the temple of the LORD, the temple of the LORD."[32] (Jer. 7:4)

Jeremiah continues with a warning. The precise force of the repeated "This is the temple of the LORD," which is said to be "deceptive," is not immediately obvious; but it is clarified by the subsequent citation of what the people are saying—"We are safe [*nitstsalnū*]!" (7:10)—where the verb is regularly used of deliverance from enemies.[33] Thus, the point of "This is the temple of the LORD" appears to be a claim that the presence of the LORD in His temple guarantees that the people of Judah will be saved from their enemies. Its repetition suggests that the claim is being made as some kind of slogan or mantra ("The false doctrine is reinforced by a liturgy"),[34] as is common in times of trouble.

The interesting thing is that what Jeremiah dubs "deceptive"—or "lying" or "false"[35]—is in a certain obvious sense true. The Jerusalem temple *was* the temple of the LORD. The LORD's words on Jeremiah's lips, a little further on

31. "Nebuchadnezzar" is the familiar English form of the name, and a form in which the name commonly occurs in the OT; but the spelling "Nebuchadrezzar" is often used in the book of Jeremiah. On the two forms and their relation to the Babylonian original, see McKane, *Jeremiah*, 496.

32. There is a puzzle in that the Hebrew conveniently rendered as "this" is plural, "these" (*hēmmāh*). The simplest expedient is to take it as referring to the whole complex of temple structures, which makes a summative "this" an appropriate rendering.

33. See, e.g., 2 Kings 18:29, 30, 33, 34; 19:11–12.

34. So McKane, *Jeremiah*, 161.

35. "Lying" is Robert Alter's rendering (*Hebrew Bible: Prophets*, 882), while "false" is that of William McKane (*Jeremiah*, 158, 161). Some translations prefer a single noun for *divrē sheqer*—e.g., "lie" (NEB), "lies" (CEB), or "illusions" (NJPS)—but there is better nuance in a rendering that preserves "words" and depicts their actively misleading character.

in the sermon, refer to the people coming to the temple as coming to "stand before me" (7:10) and depict the temple as "the house which is called by my name" (7:10, 11, 14). So in this sermon the LORD is not denying that the Jerusalem temple is His temple. How, then, can something that is factually true become deceptive and/or false? The question of what makes the true become false is in essence the key concern of Jeremiah's address.

The opening words of 7:3–4, which articulate challenge and warning, are summary keynote concerns of the sermon which are subsequently spelled out more fully: verses 5–7 develop verse 3, and verses 8–11 develop verse 4.

> [5]For if you truly amend your ways and your doings, if you truly act justly one with another, [6]if you do not oppress the immigrant [*gēr*],[36] the orphan, and the widow, or shed innocent blood in this place, and if you do not go after other gods to your own hurt, [7]then I will let you dwell[37] in this place, in the land that I gave of old to your ancestors forever and ever. (Jer. 7:5–7)

The initial challenge to "amend your ways" is now resumed. Jeremiah's emphases here are classic emphases of biblical prophecy. "Amendment" is spelled out in four ways. First and foremost is the need for the people to "act justly" / "practice justice" (*mishpāt*) in their dealings with each other. Consistent integrity is to characterize their shared public life. A tacit implication is that God's people are to be just because God Himself is just;[38] if they are to be His people, then they must demonstrate His priorities and His ways.

■ This tacit implication is made explicit elsewhere in Jeremiah. A rightly famous passage about the nature of God and of human knowledge of Him says,

36. The Hebrew term *gēr* is hard to translate, as there is no precise contemporary equivalent to ancient persons who lived short-term or long-term in a community or tribe other than their own. One common rendering of *gēr* is "alien," as in the NRSV; but in a contemporary culture saturated with science fiction, the resonances of "alien" are more likely to be with the cinematic E.T., or perhaps less friendly extraterrestrials, than with vulnerable human figures (and "resident alien" is hardly better). "Foreigner," "stranger," and "sojourner" are certainly usable. However, I think that there is a good case for adopting the CEB's "immigrant." This term has high contemporary resonance and, allowing for real differences between antiquity and modernity, substantive continuity of meaning with the ancient term. It also works well in reference to both the temporary and the permanent immigrant.

37. As in v. 3, I follow the Masoretic pointing. The NRSV wrongly omits a marginal note to indicate that here, as in v. 3, it is adopting an alternative to the MT.

38. There is natural, strong resonance with the definitional account of God as a God of justice in Ps. 82 (see ch. 3 of this book).

> [23]Thus says the LORD: Do not let the wise boast in their wisdom, do not let the mighty boast in their might, do not let the wealthy boast in their wealth; [24]but let those who boast boast in this, that they understand and know me, that I am the LORD; I act with steadfast love, justice, and righteousness in the earth, for in such people I delight, says the LORD. (Jer. 9:23–24 [Heb. 22–23])

The Hebrew reads simply "in these I delight" (*bĕʾēlleh ḥāphatstī*). Although the NRSV clarifies this as "in these things"—i.e., the just-mentioned qualities of steadfast love and justice—it hardly seems a necessary point to make, for the LORD would not exercise such qualities if He did not delight in them. It makes better sense to see these final words as tying together the thought of the pronouncement as a whole. The referent is best read as those people who boast rightly—i.e., whose boast is not in their might and wealth but in their knowledge of the LORD and their recognition that the practice of steadfast love and justice is what matters most.

Comparably, there is an illuminating denunciation of Jehoiakim, who is compared unfavorably with his father, Josiah:

> [15] Are you a king
> because you compete in cedar?[39]
> Did not your father practice justice and righteousness
> as naturally as eating and drinking?[40]
> Then he was a true king.[41]
> [16] He judged the cause of the poor and needy;
> then kingship was true.[42]
> Is not this to know me? says the LORD. (Jer. 22:15–16 AT)

Here we have an account of "knowing God"—a key term in Jeremiah for a living engagement with God, a term also present in 9:24—explicitly in terms of the practice of justice. The point is that Josiah demonstrated true knowledge of God by living rightly. He demonstrated the qualities and priorities of God in his daily practice of the responsibilities of kingship.

Thus the implication of Jer. 7:5 is that Judah is to practice justice because they are the people of the LORD; to know Him and worship Him means that they should demonstrate the LORD's own priorities in their daily life. ■

39. Jehoiakim is being criticized for a prestige building project dependent on forced labor (Jer. 22:13–14).

40. There are various interpretations of the meaning of the Hebrew "eat and drink and do justice and righteousness" in terms of how the first part relates to the second part. My proposed rendering seems to me to make the best sense.

41. The Hebrew (lit., "then it was good for him") is less likely to be an observation about life going well for Josiah when he practiced justice than it is a point about what qualifies a king to be recognized as a true king. The point in context is the contrast between Jehoiakim's self-serving practice of kingship and Josiah's recognition of what being a king should entail.

42. The Hebrew (lit., "then it was good") is making the same point as in the previous sentence.

Second, the practice of justice is given specific content in characteristic Old Testament manner: "Do not oppress the immigrant [*gēr*], the orphan, and the widow." These are paradigmatically vulnerable people. Immigrants are those who live in the territory of a people not their own. Because they lack the support system that family and clan provide, they are liable to exploitation and oppression. The orphan and the widow are those who have been left bereft by the death of the man in their family and who are without ready means of livelihood and protection. The characteristic Old Testament understanding of justice is that if justice is done for the vulnerable, who are easily manipulated and abused because they may have no one of social standing to speak for them, then it will also be done for others. Get the difficult situation right, and the easier situation should fall into place.

Third, the people are not to "shed innocent blood in this place." This could refer to the unjust condemnation and execution of people who have committed no crime (as in the judicial murder of Naboth in 1 Kings 21), or it could refer to treating undeserving people brutally (as in some of the murders committed by Joab in 2 Samuel). Either way, the concern is with behavior that reduces people to objects who can be treated violently without restraint.

Fourth, "Do not go after other gods [*ʾĕlōhīm ʾăḥērīm*] to your own hurt." This injunction aligns with the core Old Testament understanding, paradigmatically expressed in Deuteronomy, that Israel's/Judah's identity as a people is bound up with their covenantal relationship with the LORD, who is to be the one and only focus of their allegiance. Jeremiah adds to the prohibition the point that such a diminution of allegiance to the LORD would be an act of corporate self-harm. Such a denial of their identity, their raison d'être, would be self-contradictory. It would mean, to a greater or lesser extent, neglecting the commandments that were given to Israel "for [their] good" (Deut. 6:24) and turning from "the fountain of living water" to "cracked cisterns that can hold no water" (Jer. 2:13). The immoral practices just mentioned are thus seen as a corollary of the clouding of their basic identity and vision.

If the people of Judah will amend themselves in these ways, then the LORD will let them "dwell in this place"; He will be with His people as defender and shield when the enemy "from the north" comes against them, so that they will not be defeated and taken into exile. Repentance will bring blessing. There is also a tacit reminder that the LORD's promise to Abraham, Isaac, and Jacob—that He would give the land of Canaan to their descendants in perpetuity—brings with it no guarantee that those descendants will necessarily be able to inhabit and enjoy that land in perpetuity. The absolute gift has certain implicit conditions.

If Jeremiah's sermon were solely about moral corruption and reform, it could, in essence, end here. A core moral vision and challenge, and the wider consequences at stake, have been articulated. But Jeremiah now goes on to amplify the related but distinct issue of the people's corrupt understanding of the temple and of the God who is present there.

> [8]Here you are, trusting in deceptive [*sheqer*] words to no avail. [9]Will you steal, murder, commit adultery, swear falsely, make offerings to Baal, and go after other gods that you have not known, [10]and then come and stand before me in this house, which is called by my name, and say, "We are safe!"—only to go on doing all these abominations? [11]Has this house, which is called by my name, become a den of robbers in your sight? You know, I too am watching, says the LORD. (Jer. 7:8–11)

The deceptive words here are "We are safe!" which, as already noted, clarify the sense of the spurious mantra "This is the temple of the LORD." Jeremiah's basic point is simple. Certain actions and certain words are incompatible, whatever people may suppose: a claim of confidence in God's presence in the temple and in His protection of Jerusalem, which is what the people's words amount to, is rendered null and void by a way of living that is at odds with God's will and ways. The actions listed in verse 9 amount to systematic neglect of, even contempt for, God's ways as expressed in the Ten Commandments, which in Deuteronomy express the very heart of the covenant between the LORD and Israel. The supposition that one can claim God's presence and protection while being careless of God's will and ways—which history suggests is a supposition that comes readily to humans—is mistaken. Or, put the other way round, only those whose way of living embraces God's priorities, so that God's justice is appropriated by them, can legitimately expect the blessing of God's protecting presence.

■ In an intertextual literary reading of the canonical corpus, the actions of v. 9 are clear transgressions of the Decalogue in Exod. 20 and Deut. 5. In terms of tradition history and composition, the actual date of the formulation of the Decalogue is an open question. Many scholars have considered it to be genuinely old, going back to Israel's origins. Others, especially recently, have been inclined to see the Decalogue as a late (post-Jeremiah) summary formulation of Israel's moral insights as developed by prophets and sages. The difficulty—or impossibility—of resolving the question of tradition history and composition need not detract from an imaginatively serious reading of the text in its received form in which the Ten Commandments have become the referent of Jer. 7:9. ■

The image of a den in 7:11 may suggest that the people felt themselves to be both safe and out of sight from any critical perspective. So Jeremiah reminds them that God sees all too clearly what they do, not least in the temple, which is indeed a place of His presence. Not only will they not be safe from their enemies, they will also not be safe from the LORD Himself.

> [12]Go now to my place that was in Shiloh, where I made my name dwell at first, and see what I did to it for the wickedness of my people Israel. [13]And now, because you have done all these things, says the LORD, and when I spoke to you persistently, you did not listen, and when I called you, you did not answer, [14]therefore I will do to the house that is called by my name, in which you trust, and to the place that I gave to you and to your ancestors, just what I did to Shiloh. [15]And I will cast you out of my sight, just as I cast out all your kinsfolk, all the offspring of Ephraim. (Jer. 7:12–15)

The precedent of Shiloh should be a warning to the people of Judah. Once there was an important temple there—its life is depicted in the time of the young Samuel, at the end of the period of the judges (1 Sam. 1–4)—but now it is defunct, presumably a heap of ruins. Why? As a divine response to persistent corruption. Whoever the human agents of Shiloh's destruction were,[43] Jeremiah sees the LORD's hand at work in these human agents, and able to do the same again: "I will do to the house . . . in which you trust . . . just what I did to Shiloh." The corollary of this destruction of the temple, the consequence of Jerusalem being conquered by its enemies, will be that the Southern Kingdom of Judah suffers the same fate as the Northern Kingdom of Israel: exile. Moreover, as in the destruction of the temple, so too in exile—the human agents will in some sense be acting on behalf of the LORD: "I will cast you out of my sight."

It is a hard message, but Jeremiah is unflinching. His initial challenge to amendment of life, with the possibility of continued life in the land, is accompanied by an exposé of corrupt human presumption, a rebuttal of the notion that God's protection can be claimed even while His will is ignored. This leads to the explicit warning that God will not shrink back from having His own sanctuary destroyed and His own people losing everything in exile.

A Reading of Micah's Temple Sermon in Micah 3:9–12[44]

There is a strong parallel to Jeremiah's temple sermon in what might be called Micah's temple sermon in Micah 3:9–12. These words are not said to

43. It is unclear whether Shiloh was destroyed by the Philistines in the context depicted in 1 Sam. 4 or by some other enemy on another occasion.

44. For convenience, in subsequent discussion I will refer to Mic. 3:9–12 simply as Mic. 3.

be delivered in the temple precincts, as Jeremiah's are; there is no narrative introduction which specifies any time or place (other than that at the beginning of the book, Mic. 1:1). But since the passage comprises a moral challenge, a critique of religious presumption, and a warning that focuses on the destruction of the temple—all comparable in content to the words of Jeremiah—there is a case for considering this also to be a temple sermon.

> [9] Hear this, you rulers of the house of Jacob
> and chiefs of the house of Israel,
> who abhor justice [*mishpāt*]
> and pervert all equity,
> [10] who build Zion with bloodshed[45]
> and Jerusalem with wrong!
> [11] Its rulers give judgment for a bribe,
> its priests teach for a price,
> its prophets give oracles for money;
> yet they lean upon the LORD and say,
> "Surely the LORD is in our midst![46]
> No disaster shall come upon us."[47]
> [12] Therefore because of you
> Zion shall be plowed as a field [*sādeh*];
> Jerusalem shall become a heap of ruins,
> and the mountain of the house a wooded height. (Mic. 3:9–12)

This is addressed not to people in general who come to the temple, but rather to the leaders of Israel (v. 9a). The primary charge is their corrupt abandonment of justice (v. 9b). The precise forms that this took cannot be deduced from the poetic rhetoric, beyond the sense that it involved the life-threatening exploitation of laborers (v. 10). The second charge draws in significant religious figures, priests and prophets, alongside the other leaders, and has one point: everything is available for a price; they are thoroughly venal (v. 11a). Yet all these leaders express dependence on, even apparent trust in,[48] the LORD as the one who is "in their midst"—that is, present in the temple. If He is thus

45. The NRSV's "blood" is less accurate, as "bloodshed" is the regular sense of the plural *dāmīm*, as in Gen. 4:10 and 1 Kings 2:5; cf. *GKC* 124n.

46. The NRSV's rendering, "the LORD is with us," conforms the wording here, *bĕqirbēnū*, too quickly to that of Ps. 46:7, 11 (Heb. 8, 12), *ʿimmānū*.

47. The NRSV's "harm" is less precise. The thought is less "We shall not be hurt" than "We shall not be defeated/overthrown." The Hebrew term *rāʿāh* is the regular term for the overthrow of a city by its enemies; cf. Amos 3:6; Jer. 18:8.

48. The *niphal* verb *nishʿan* can express trusting dependence, as in the portrayal of the servant of the LORD in Isa. 50:10, where *nishʿan* ("lean") is parallel to *bātaḥ* ("trust").

present, He is sure to defend His people and preserve them from their enemies (v. 11b). Micah sees such a combination of corruption and presumption as deadly, bringing on the very disaster from which the leaders supposed they were safe: "Therefore because of you . . ." The consequent destruction of Jerusalem and its temple is envisaged as total: no longer a place of settled life ("city," *ʿîr*) but rather open land (*sādeh*, v. 12a), with ruins that mutely testify to what has been lost (v. 12b).[49] The fate of Jerusalem's inhabitants is not mentioned. But if they are not engaged in rebuilding, then the implication is that they are either dead or in exile.

Micah's moral and theological logic is the same as Jeremiah's. In Jeremiah's terminology, what the leaders say in Micah 3:11b is *sheqer*, deceptive or false. Israel and Judah cannot claim God's protection if they ignore God's will. The presence of the LORD in the temple is a morally charged presence, and immoral conduct that is flaunted in His presence cannot expect blessing or even impunity.

■ Strikingly, Micah's words here are cited in the narrative account of Jeremiah's temple sermon (Jer. 26). A moment comes when there is something of an impasse between the clergy (priests and prophets), who are pressing for Jeremiah to be put to death for treason, and the palace officials and the crowd, who are at least somewhat moved by what Jeremiah says. At this point certain "elders" come on the scene and cite Mic. 3:12 verbatim (Jer. 26:16–19). This is not only to show that there is precedent for speaking of the destruction of the temple, as Jeremiah has just done. Although, despite Micah's words, the temple was still standing, this does not mean that Micah "got it wrong." Rather, the elders realize that prophetic pronouncements of judgment are warnings that seek the response of people changing their ways so that the judgment may be averted. They recall that Hezekiah—interestingly not mentioned at all in Micah as the prophet's audience (though he is mentioned in the opening list of kings who set the context for Micah's prophesying [Mic. 1:1])—responded to Micah's words with a renewed turning to the LORD, such that He did not destroy Jerusalem. The elders thus observe that the failure to take seriously the content of Jeremiah's warning—if they continue instead to threaten Jeremiah for speaking in the first place, or even just argue about his right to do so—may mean that they will bring its realization upon themselves. It is a moment in which the essential dynamics of prophecy are illuminatingly highlighted. ■

The voice of Micah 3 is similar to that of Jeremiah 7: Jerusalem with its temple is in imminent danger of being swept away by God. But both are strongly

49. Although "ruin" (*ʿî*) is clear in v. 12b, the translation of the last two words, *bāmôt yāʿar*, is unclear. Should one give weight primarily to the final word and see a picture of trees ("a wooded height," so NRSV)? Or should one find in the penultimate word the implication of some construction still remaining, albeit greatly reduced ("a shrine in the woods," so NJPS; though this depends upon the singular that is present in some of the versions—i.e., *bāmat* rather than the MT's *bāmôt*)? I am inclined to see a picture of trees as expressive of thorough destruction, but the issue only marginally affects the overall tenor of the text.

dissimilar to the voice of Psalm 46: Jerusalem with its temple will assuredly be preserved by God. How best should these distinct voices be heard together?

A Possible Tradition History and History of Ideas

Setting Out an Agenda

Psalm 46 celebrates the LORD's sovereignty and His defense of His city, which is apparently Jerusalem with its temple. Jeremiah 7 and Micah 3 critique unwarranted confidence in the LORD's protection of Jerusalem via His presence in the temple. To read these different voices in conjunction with each other raises certain obvious questions not only about how they interrelate but also about how one should determine that interrelationship.

As noted in the introduction to this book,[50] knowing how best to relate the differing contexts of the biblical material can be one of the most difficult decisions for the interpreter who is interested in Israel's scriptures as Christian Scripture. There is the context of original production, the world behind the text, in which the resonance and significance of the material within its wider Israelite and ancient Near Eastern context is probed. There is also the context of literary preservation, the world within the text, in which particular texts resonate in relation to the portrayal of biblical Israel in the wider literary and theological context of the canonical collection within which they have been preserved and recontextualized. There is also the context of continuing appropriation, the world in front of the text, in which the biblical material is further recontextualized within the ongoing life of Jewish and Christian communities who use the material as part of their self-understanding as the people of God. And there are wider cultural contexts. These differing contexts are not mutually exclusive. Nonetheless, the prioritizing of one context over another can make a difference to the nature and purpose of the interpretive inquiry.

The primary mode of inquiry in modern scholarship has been to examine the biblical content in terms of a history of literature and ideas (the world of the text as a gateway to the world behind the text). So that will be a starting point here.

The Notion of "Zion Theology"

It has become a scholarly consensus that Jeremiah's and Micah's critiques of inappropriate confidence in the protective power of God in the Jerusalem

50. See pp. 7–8.

temple are best understood when they are located within a particular trajectory of religious thought.[51] Why did the people trust in the temple thus? Because they had learned to do so from earlier tradition that was regarded as authoritative. Jeremiah and Micah were critiquing not just the outlook of their contemporaries but a whole stream of religious thought within which they stood. In short, there was a "Zion theology" in Jerusalem and Judah in the period of the Davidic monarchy.

"Zion theology" is a scholarly construct that seeks to gather together, and do justice to, a range of material which is oriented towards Jerusalem and the house of David and which cumulatively appears to represent a particular religio-political outlook of the time.[52] This Zion theology receives notable expression not only in Psalm 46 but also in other psalms, especially Psalms 2, 48, 76, 78, and 132, and in the early (eighth-century) parts of the book of Isaiah.[53] It is closely related to the tradition of God's choice of the house of David in 2 Samuel 7 and in certain psalms, especially Psalms 2, 89, 110, and 132. Scholars reckon that Zion theology gave rise to the confidence of the people of Judah. It was this theology that was the target of Jeremiah's and Micah's critiques. The deuteronomistic inflection of Jeremiah's language in the temple sermon of Jeremiah 7 makes it possible to see the perspectives of the "conditional" Sinai/Horeb covenant being brought to bear on the perspectives of the "unconditional" Davidic covenant and the divine choice of Zion.[54] There was thus a major clash of religious outlooks and traditions in late monarchic Judah, a clash which modern scholarship has brought to light.

The possible history of ideas here has been variously understood and articulated. A typical, succinct expression is that of Thomas Overholt, who says,

> The basis of [the people's] confidence [in Jer. 7] was not just wishful thinking, but a religious conviction mirrored in the words, "This is the temple of Yahweh. . . . We are delivered!" (7:4, 10). This conviction was anchored in the royal ideology: Yahweh had chosen Jerusalem to be his habitation, had founded David's house as the royal line in it. . . . This was not simply a theological dispute. Ideology and foreign policy were intermeshed.[55]

51. The possibly differing dates of Jer. 7 and Mic. 3—on a traditional understanding, the latter is about a century older than the former, but we cannot be sure—do not, I think, substantially affect the issue at stake.

52. An excellent guide is Levenson, "Zion Traditions."

53. According to Gerhard von Rad, for example, Zion is central to Isaiah's message: "The prophet's whole preaching is permeated from its very beginning by the theme of Zion threatened but finally delivered" (*Old Testament Theology*, 2:147–75, esp. 165–66).

54. A putative conflict between Mosaic and Davidic covenants is articulated at length in Bright, *Covenant and Promise*.

55. Overholt, "Jeremiah," 614.

Of course, not everyone brings together Jeremiah 7, Micah 3, and Psalm 46 as I am doing here. However, insofar as Psalm 46 is taken as an expression of Zion theology, and Jeremiah 7 and Micah 3 are taken as critiques of Zion theology, these particular texts would be widely understood to be expressive of ancient theological traditions that were for and against a widely held outlook in late monarchic Jerusalem.

I will try to give a flavor of possible ways of conceiving Zion theology by briefly expounding two significant scholarly accounts.

Jon Levenson's Account of Zion Theology

Jon Levenson offers a memorable account of the significance of Zion, which he suggestively relates to the wider mythic thought-world of the ancient Near East.[56] Not least, he argues for the importance of the notion of Zion as a cosmic mountain with analogies to Zaphon in Ugaritic literature and Olympus in Greek literature:

> The cosmic mountain is a kind of fulcrum for the universe. . . . It is the prime place of communication between transcendent and mundane reality. . . .
>
> The earthly Temple is the world *in nuce*; the world is the Temple *in extenso*. Temple and world do not stand in dialectical tension, but in a relationship characterized by complementarity. . . .
>
> Mount Zion, the Temple on it, and the city around it are a symbol of transcendence, a symbol in Paul Tillich's sense of the word, something "which participates in that to which it points."[57]

In a section entitled "The Meaning of the Cosmic Mountain in Israel," Levenson discusses both Psalm 46 and Jeremiah 7 (along with other related passages). He is clear that there is a "theology of the inviolability of Jerusalem,"[58] but he sees the biblical writers to be using this notion in a variety of ways. The imagery of Psalm 46 is sketched and probed in terms of a striking point: "Jerusalem is *in* ordinary history, the history in which 'kingdoms topple' (Ps. 46:7), but it is not *of* it."[59]

> Nature and politics stand together in their opposition to the one great fact of reality: that YHWH is God. Civilization, like the waters of chaos, can refuse to

56. Levenson, *Sinai and Zion*, esp. 87–184. He offers a careful account of the nature and significance of myth on pp. 102–11. This fuller study underlies Levenson's summary account in "Zion Traditions."

57. Levenson, *Sinai and Zion*, 122, 141, 142. The citation is of Paul Tillich, *Dynamics of Faith*, 42.

58. Levenson, *Sinai and Zion*, 165.

59. Levenson, *Sinai and Zion*, 155.

> accept the given. That refusal takes the form of political deeds, of involvement in nations and kingdoms and wars. In place of this, the psalmist calls upon his listeners simply to "be still."[60]

Levenson looks at Isaiah 7–8 and 29:1–8 and sees a strong yet nuanced account of Zion: "Human folly may compromise, but it cannot nullify the divine protection that envelops the cosmic center."[61]

He introduces his account of Jeremiah 7 in terms of the context of a particular tradition history of ideas:

> In light of Isaiah's counsel at the time of the Syro-Ephraimite War and perhaps also on the occasion of Sennacherib's campaign, we should not be surprised to learn that some in Jerusalem in the days of the Babylonian advance derived confidence from the notion that Mount Zion was invulnerable to any historical onslaught. This becomes clear in the famous "Temple Speech" of Jeremiah (Jer. 7:1–15). The people whom Jeremiah addresses in this oracle stand in the tradition of the Temple mythos.[62]

Nonetheless, Levenson's repeated point is that this mythos had become debased through misunderstanding: "The Temple of YHWH has become a string of nonsense-syllables whose mere repetition is supposed to be effective, a mantra bled of meaning [i.e., Jer. 7:4]. Here we see a denatured form of the old notion of the Temple as the locus of ultimate security."[63] Indeed,

> the fact is that his [Jeremiah's] audience does not adhere to that mythopoetic complex, but to a fragment of it which they have extracted from context. For them, the delicate, highly poetic image of the cosmic mountain has become a matter of doctrine, and the doctrine can be stated in one prosaic sentence: In the Temple one is safe. . . . One cannot imagine a more wooden reading of the mythos of Zion than theirs.[64]

Over against this, Jeremiah "asserts the existence of ethical preconditions for Israel's admittance to the central shrine." Jeremiah's critique is not of the temple as such, but of its misrepresentation:

> The ethical demands which the prophet issues should not be conceived as an alternative to the Temple. What Jeremiah does oppose is the idea that the divine

60. Levenson, *Sinai and Zion*, 153.
61. Levenson, *Sinai and Zion*, 160.
62. Levenson, *Sinai and Zion*, 165–66.
63. Levenson, *Sinai and Zion*, 168.
64. Levenson, *Sinai and Zion*, 168, 169.

> goodness so evident in the Temple is independent of the moral record of those who worship there, in other words, the effort to disengage God's beneficence from man's ethical deeds.[65]

Levenson's conclusion is a nuanced account of Jeremiah's attitude towards Zion theology:

> Whether Jeremiah would have endorsed the full version of the Temple mythos, from which his audience has detached only a piece for their own benefit, is impossible to say with certainty. The analogy he draws with Shiloh would indicate that he would not. But we must not suppose that it is the idea of the cosmic mountain in its fullness which is attacked in the Temple sermon.[66]

Such a picture of mythic and poetic meaning being misunderstood and misappropriated in such a way that Jeremiah needed to speak against it is an attractive account that makes good sense.

However, it remains possible to propose a somewhat different history of thought.

Konrad Schmid's Account of the Rise and Fall of Zion Theology

In the recent study of Konrad Schmid, prime significance for the rise of Zion theology is ascribed to the preservation of Jerusalem in the face of the siege by Sennacherib in 701.[67] In Schmid's reckoning, the actual event at Jerusalem—as distinct from the Assyrian victory over Lachish further south, depicted in famous Assyrian reliefs—was modest:

> King Hezekiah seems only to have been able to raise the Assyrian blockade of Jerusalem through the payment of heavy tribute and the loss of the Shephelah, connected with the fall of Lachish. However, this does not hinder the Hebrew Bible from seeing a powerful act of deliverance by Yhwh in the withdrawal of the Assyrians in 701 BCE.[68]

■ For some reason Schmid passes over in silence the confrontation between the Assyrian Rabshakeh and Hezekiah at the walls of Jerusalem, to which Kings and Isaiah alike give prime space. This encounter is a remarkable and highly ironic moment of theological poker playing, with ultimate deliverance set on an existential edge. It concludes with the angel of the Lord slaying large numbers of the Assyrian army (2 Kings 18:17–19:37; Isa.

65. Levenson, *Sinai and Zion*, 166, 168.
66. Levenson, *Sinai and Zion*, 169.
67. Schmid, *Historical Theology of the Hebrew Bible*, 220–22; cf. 414–18.
68. Schmid, *Historical Theology of the Hebrew Bible*, 220.

36–37). This, for both Kings and Isaiah, is the "powerful act of deliverance by Yhwh." Whatever the relation of the content of this narrative to the historical events of 701, one might have expected its engagement with the LORD's power to deliver Jerusalem to merit inclusion in a discussion of the nature of Zion theology. ■

The modesty of the event was apparently fully compatible with the development of a strong theology of divine presence and protection:

> In the wake of the experience of the deliverance of Jerusalem from the Assyrian blockade in 701 BCE, the theological statement of the safety of Zion as a result of Yhwh's presence received a strong boost. This theological position formed the traditional orthodoxy of monarchal period Jerusalem, the location of Yhwh's temple. The presence of the God of Judah in the temple guaranteed the prosperity of the land as well as its political security. The Zion psalms of Pss 46 and 48 in their original form likely belong to the Assyrian period.[69]

Unfortunately, this Zion theology "loses its plausibility after 587 BCE."[70] The fall of Jerusalem to the Babylonians is something that should not have happened:

> In the destruction of Jerusalem and its temple in 587 BCE, something took place that, according to the traditional orthodoxy of the First Jerusalem Temple expressed in Ps 48, not only could not happen, but—even stronger—was totally unimaginable: Yhwh is the God imagined to be enthroned on Zion, whose divine presence there guarantees Jerusalem and Judah's protection and safety. The cultic recitation of the Psalms served as the ritual reassurance and safeguard of this conception. In the reality that it was confessed in the cult, it was implemented and held to be valid.[71]

The forceful language in Schmid's characterization of Zion theology (as expressed by Pss. 46 and 48) is notable: God "guarantees" the protection of Jerusalem and the temple, whose fall is "totally unimaginable." In all this, Schmid sees the Zion theology from 701 to 587 as having some resonances with recurrent patterns of human thought:

> Speaking anachronistically, the theology of the Jerusalem cult is a classic theology of glory, which describes God as a powerful protective force, sees him as unfailing, and especially as attached to the powerful and strong. Also in this aspect

69. Schmid, *Historical Theology of the Hebrew Bible*, 221.

70. Schmid, *Historical Theology of the Hebrew Bible*, 221. I have corrected the typo "578 BCE."

71. Schmid, *Historical Theology of the Hebrew Bible*, 231.

> it is a classical counterpart to the other ancient Near Eastern religions that essentially think within this matrix.[72]

Moreover, Zion theology exemplifies the human tendency to embrace theological dogma at its rigid and unrealistic worst. Such theology is "by nature not formulated in such a way that it could respond to historically contrary experiences and incorporate these into its framework. It instead attempts to resist and defensively immunizes itself against the conditions of historical experience."[73]

Schmid does not discuss the possible role of Jeremiah 7 in critiquing Zion theology, but points to the harsh reality of Judah's fall to the Babylonians as the decisive factor in overturning Zion theology. To be sure, he sees the renewed high valuation of Zion in the postexilic / early Persian-period Isaiah 60 as "messianic," in that functions and actions once ascribed to the Davidic king are now taken over by Zion.[74] But he does not relate this renewed eschatological role for Zion to the continuing interpretation of a Zion psalm such as Psalm 46.

Towards a Reframing of the Interpretive Questions

There is undoubted value in such history-of-ideas accounts for sharpening one's perception of the biblical text. To think about how the biblical documents might have been understood and used within the life of ancient Israel can almost always enrich a contemporary reader's understanding. Levenson's account, in particular, has highly suggestive resonance. There are, however, limitations to even the best of such work. The paucity of evidence means that any account, no matter how confidently it is articulated, contains a high level of conjecture (which thus readily permits divergent accounts).

First, the origins of Zion theology can be variously construed. Despite Schmid's apparent confidence that it originated in the events of 701, numerous scholars have expressed doubt about any particular linkage with the deliverance of Jerusalem, and some have traced it and its antecedents to an earlier period—even back to pre-Israelite times. Gerhard von Rad, for example, held that "these psalms [46, 48, 76] probably date from before the time of Isaiah: but their date is in fact of little importance; for their tradition of an unsuccessful attack on Jerusalem is quite certainly of a very much earlier origin."[75]

72. Schmid, *Historical Theology of the Hebrew Bible*, 334.
73. Schmid, *Historical Theology of the Hebrew Bible*, 334.
74. Schmid, *Historical Theology of the Hebrew Bible*, 422–23.
75. Von Rad, *Old Testament Theology*, 1:157.

Comparably, Jon Levenson has suggested likely Canaanite and Jebusite origins for what developed into Zion theology.[76] However, a case has also been made for the origins of Zion theology in a Second, rather than First, Temple context.[77]

Second, there is also a possibility that the argument about Jeremiah 7, Micah 3, and Zion theology can become unhelpfully circular. Why do those whom Jeremiah and Micah critique hold misleading expectations of the LORD's protective power? Because of a Zion theology based on Isaiah and Psalms. How do we know that Judahites held a Zion theology on the basis of Isaiah and Psalms? Because otherwise Jeremiah and Micah would not have critiqued them in the way they do.

Third, in such discussions related to the history of ideas in the life of the ancient world, there is the possibility that certain questions relating to the scriptural significance of the material can be diminished (though Levenson notably keeps scriptural concerns alive). Perspectives related to the preservation and recontextualization of the documents within a privileged collection which creates its own interpretive context for understanding God and life with God can easily recede from view. The substantive issue of people having a trusting confidence in the sovereignty of God and His defense of His people can easily become an item in the history of Judahite religio-political thought rather than a possible enduring reality. Existential questions of how and why trust in God might become godless, or how it might be genuine and be appropriately maintained, may not feature on the agenda.

■ Canonical recontextualization can itself be approached from the perspective of a history of literature and ideas, and this too can be fruitful. Likely shifts in meaning within the content of the Psalter, already within the biblical period, readily come to mind and are not greatly controversial. There are psalms which refer to a Davidic king or to the ark, neither of which remained possible contemporary referents after Jerusalem's fall to Babylon in 587. How might such psalms have been understood in the Persian or Hellenistic period? It is natural to reckon either that the material became subject to more metaphorical (sometimes specified as "spiritualized") modes of interpretation, or that the realization of that of which the psalm spoke was projected into the future; indeed, both such moves could be made. Similarly, the addition of psalm titles was most likely to encourage an imaginative rereading of the psalms in relation to the life of David—as depicted in the books of Samuel—as a type of the life of faith, in a way that was not original to the Psalms.[78] Nonetheless, canonical recontextualization also enables different perspectives and questions to come to the fore. ■

76. Levenson, "Zion Traditions," 1100, 1101–2; cf. his *Sinai and Zion*, 94.

77. See Wanke, *Die Zionstheologie der Korachiten*.

78. The argument for this last point was persuasively made by Brevard Childs; see his "Psalm Titles and Midrashic Exegesis."

Towards a Theological Interpretation in Literary and Canonical Context

Interpreting Jeremiah 7 and Micah 3 without a Zion Theology

If an account of Jeremiah 7 and Micah 3 which is aware of, but distinct from, a possible history of ideas is to be offered, an obvious starting point is to take seriously a silence in the texts we have read. That is, neither Jeremiah 7 nor Micah 3 makes reference to any Zion theology as such. They neither cite, nor allude to, the wording of Isaiah or the Psalms in terms of their constituting a basis for confidence in the protection of the LORD via the temple.

The intrinsic logic of both Jeremiah 7 and Micah 3 is similar. In each context people are said (a) to act corruptly, yet (b) to be confident that in time of trouble (implicitly, warfare), Jerusalem and the temple will be kept safe: "This is the temple of the LORD. . . . We are delivered." "Surely the LORD is in our midst! No disaster shall come upon us." Religious complacency is accompanied by moral corruption. Indeed, religious complacency can naturally engender moral corruption, if it is reckoned that there will be no ultimate drawback or loss if people just do what they want to do. This is fully meaningful on its own terms. The ease with which humans assume that God is aligned with their priorities, without their seriously troubling to align themselves with God's priorities, is well attested throughout history.

Within the Old Testament, another passage which raises this issue by sounding a note similar to that of Jeremiah 7 and Micah 3 is the fascinating narrative of the two battles between Israel and the Philistines in 1 Samuel 4:

> [1]In those days the Philistines mustered for war against Israel, and Israel went out to battle against them; they encamped at Ebenezer, and the Philistines encamped at Aphek. [2]The Philistines drew up in line against Israel, and when the battle was joined, Israel was defeated by the Philistines, who killed about four thousand men on the field of battle. (1 Sam. 4:1–2)

In this brief battle account, Israel is defeated. An inquiry naturally follows.

> [3]When the troops came to the camp, the elders of Israel said, "Why has the LORD put us to rout today before the Philistines? Let us bring the ark of the covenant of the LORD here from Shiloh, so that he may come among us and save us from the power of our enemies." [4]So the people sent to Shiloh, and brought from there the ark of the covenant of the LORD of hosts, who is enthroned on the cherubim. The two sons of Eli, Hophni and Phinehas, were there with the ark of the covenant of God. (1 Sam. 4:3–4)

Certain "elders" of Israel come up with a way ahead.[79] They answer their own question "Why?" with a proposal to fetch the ark. They reason that the LORD's presence is closely associated with the ark (as other passages also attest);[80] therefore, if the ark is present in their midst, so will the LORD be also, and He will bestow victory on His people. This proposal is accepted, and the ark is brought to the army from Shiloh.

> [5]When the ark of the covenant of the LORD came into the camp, all Israel gave a mighty shout, so that the earth resounded. [6]When the Philistines heard the noise of the shouting, they said, "What does this great shouting in the camp of the Hebrews mean?" When they learned that the ark of the LORD had come to the camp, [7]the Philistines were afraid . . . (1 Sam. 4:5–7a)

The Israelites greet the coming of the ark with an amazing, presumably triumphal, shout. This the Philistines hear in their camp, where they also learn that the ark is now in the Israelite camp (4:5–6). Their immediate response is fear. The narrator now tells us in detail of the full Philistine response.

> . . . for they said, "Gods [or "God" or "a god"; Heb. *ʾĕlōhîm*] have come into the camp." They also said, "Woe to us! For nothing like this has happened before. [8]Woe to us! Who can deliver us from the power of these mighty gods? These are the gods who struck the Egyptians with every sort of plague in the wilderness. [9]Take courage, and be men, O Philistines, in order not to become slaves to the Hebrews as they have been to you; be men and fight." (1 Sam. 4:7a–9)

Primarily the Philistines are afraid for the straightforward reason that "God / gods / a god has come into the camp." This is an unprecedented disaster for them (4:7), for, implicitly, any fight against a deity is fraught with danger. This deity, however, is not just any deity but rather the deity whose power has already been attested among the Egyptians. The Philistines' prospects are thus poor. However, they resolve to "be men" and fight bravely rather than just fleeing or surrendering (4:9).[81]

79. There is an interesting resonance with Jer. 26:17, where again "elders" intervene with a theological proposal. "Elders" are apparently those within Israel who are supposed to have some theological wisdom and insight with which they can guide others. They do not fall within the regular categories of "prophet" or "priest" or "the wise" (cf. Jer. 18:18).

80. A prime passage is Num. 10:35–36, where the movement of the ark is correlated with the movement of the LORD.

81. There is a fascinatingly mixed portrayal of the Philistines in these words, suggestive of striking narratival sophistication. On the one hand, the Philistines' courage is clear. Yet on the other hand, they speak ignorantly of Israel's *ʾĕlōhîm* with a plural adjective and verb in v. 8,

> [10]So the Philistines fought; Israel was defeated, and they fled, everyone to his home. There was a very great slaughter, for there fell of Israel thirty thousand foot soldiers. [11]The ark of God was captured; and the two sons of Eli, Hophni and Phinehas, died. (1 Sam. 4:10–11)

Despite their fears, when the Philistines fight, they win. Indeed, they do not just win—they utterly overwhelm the Israelites. In the first battle, four thousand Israelite soldiers fell; now thirty thousand, more than seven times as many, fall. Moreover, the ark is captured by the Philistines (and its corrupt accompanying priests also die).

In this story, both sides make the assumption that the presence of God in an army's midst, a presence represented by a prime sacred symbolic object, is a potent power for victory. No particular promise of divine protection is needed, for divine presence alone suffices to create the assumption. The Israelites assume that all that is needed is the ark itself, without reference either to their own disposition and practice or that of the priests who attend the ark. They seek to harness God to their desire for victory in battle. But the point of the story is to show the overturning of the Israelites' assumption that the ark of God (and, implicitly, God Himself) can be regarded and treated thus; further, in the narrative that follows, any Philistine assumption that they too can handle the ark as they wish is also overturned (1 Sam. 5–6).[82] The God of the ark resists human manipulation, and His sovereignty is paradoxically reaffirmed.

In addition to the shared reference to God's presence at Shiloh, there are obvious strong conceptual resonances between Jeremiah 7, Micah 3, and 1 Samuel 4 in terms of mistaken complacency about divine presence and protection. The narrative of 1 Samuel, like the sermons of Jeremiah and Micah, makes the point that the presence of God in a sacred object/place may be positively dangerous for His people if they are heedless of His priorities. Confidence in God, if not accompanied by appropriate responsiveness, becomes dangerous delusion.

■ Alongside my reading of 1 Sam. 4 it is, of course, possible to read the narrative in a history-of-ideas mode, and even to find a Zion theology within it. In the extensive literature, a fascinating example is the work of Benjamin Sommer.[83] Sommer reads the ark narrative in 1 Sam. 4–6 as depicting a conflict between a Priestly theology of divine presence

---

and also appear to be confused about Israel's foundation story in that they muddle what happened in Egypt and in the desert.

82. The nature of the ancient practice of capturing divine images is usefully set out in Cogan, *Imperialism and Religion*, 22–41.

83. Sommer, *Bodies of God*, 80–108, esp. 101–7.

in the ark (a "Zion-Sabaoth theology," according to which God is permanently present in the Jerusalem temple on Mount Zion) and a deuteronomistic critique of that notion in favor of understanding the ark solely as a receptacle of the verbal record of the covenant (a "Name theology," with a restricted concept of divine presence in the temple). He explicitly says of 1 Sam. 4 that "this chapter . . . attacks not only Zion-Sabaoth theology but also the doctrine of Zion's inviolability. In this regard the ark narrative in 1 Samuel resembles Jeremiah 7."[84] If one reads the narrative in terms of the concerns of its writers in relation to the putative religious disputes in which they were engaging in the exilic or postexilic context of the sixth century, this is certainly a possible construal.[85] However, even if it is an accurate account of what may underlie and inform the narrative, it elides a plain-sense reading of the storyline in the world of the text (and in my judgment struggles to capture the story's distinctive thrust). To read the Israelites and Philistines as articulating a Zion theology which is thereby critiqued is not to enter with full imaginative seriousness into the world of the story, which is set prior to David's bringing Jerusalem under Israelite control in 2 Sam. 5. In the story, the issue has to do with mistaken suppositions about divine presence and power in a holy object—mistaken because of presumption on the part of the Israelites and ignorance on the part of the Philistines. ■

In concluding this section I would like to return to the point noted earlier, that the words which Jeremiah labels as "deceptive"/"false" are in an obvious sense true, for the Jerusalem temple *was* "the temple of the LORD." This tension embodies a characteristic biblical understanding of the nature of language. Depictions of God, and claims about life in God's world, should not be understood or evaluated in the abstract, but always in relation to how they are used. Promises and assurances from God are not like lottery jackpots, to do with as one likes. Their intrinsic nature, which is to engender relationship, seeks to create in their recipients a trust that will be expressed in ways that enhance the relationship—as is the case also with marriage vows. The absence of such responsiveness can reduce the words to mere words. Self-serving attitudes in particular can empty correctly formulated and right-sounding words of their truth content. Questions of truth about God in the Bible are not just factual, evidential, or epistemological; they are also moral, existential, and relational.

Interpreting Psalm 46 in Scriptural Context

The danger that people who in some way trust God can become complacent, and thereby morally careless or perhaps corrupt, is undoubtedly

84. Sommer, *Bodies of God*, 106.

85. In a not-dissimilar way, Klaas Smelik sees the ark narrative as retrojecting the theological message of Jeremiah's critique of the temple into the past: "The capture of the Ark by the Philistines is actually an allusion to the pillage and destruction of the Temple of Jerusalem, the Ark being comparable with the holy vessels and the Philistines with the Babylonians" (*Converting the Past*, 53–58).

heightened by words of assurance and promises of protection that do not also specify practices which would display right responsiveness to those words. This can be part of the problem posed by a psalm such as Psalm 46.

But how should the psalm function in its canonical context? Most of it is poetically descriptive, and it paints a series of startling images of God's sovereignty and dependability. It does, however, have two double imperatives specifying what people are to do. The first, "Come, see" (v. 8), invokes a vision, essentially imaginative (though perhaps once symbolically acted out in a ceremonial context), of God's power to destroy those implements on which humans usually rely to gain power and security. The second, "Be still and know" (v. 10), invokes a vision of God's sovereignty over everyone and everything. Implicitly, to "be still" means to relinquish those implements whose destruction and ultimate futility have just been depicted, in favor of a different kind of security found in God Himself—in knowing that the LORD is the one eternal God. Both pairs of imperatives relate to grasping the vision of God which the psalm sets out. The psalm does not specify moral priorities in the manner of, say, Psalms 15 and 24.[86] Nonetheless, the imperative to drop all implements and trappings of war is rich in ethical implication: it envisages peace-oriented qualities, even if not concrete practices—a willingness to relinquish the notion that security ultimately depends on weapons—though there is openness as to the fuller specification of what this may entail.

This is where the question of the context for reading can make a difference. If the sovereign God, whose power and presence is celebrated, is specifically the LORD of hosts, the God of Jacob, this undoubtedly presupposes the particular story of Israel as the context for the use of the psalm. In terms of a history of ideas, it is an open question how much of that story could have been presupposed and would have been known in the psalm's possible context of origin. If one dates the psalm to a time in the early monarchic period prior to much of the content of Torah—which is a feasible historical-critical scenario—then arguably only a rather thin story of Israel might be envisaged. If, however, one interprets the psalm within the literary-cum-canonical context in which it has been preserved, then the psalm is set in the thick context of the full portrayal of God's call of, and commandments to, Israel. Of course, this thick context can still be read and understood in poor and self-serving ways. Yet it offers richer contextual resources for understanding and appropriating the psalm than does a history-of-ideas contextualization. One may no longer be hearing the psalm

86. Interestingly, the final note of Ps. 15, with its extensive rehearsal of the moral qualities appropriate to presence in the temple, is "Those who do these things shall never be moved [*lōʾ yimmōt lĕʿōlām*]." There is the same note of stability, with the same Hebrew term, as in Pss. 46 and 62.

as it was "originally" heard (whatever that might mean);[87] but one can hear the psalm in the context in which it was considered suitable for preservation, and in which the majority of its users throughout history have heard it.

Although the early singers and hearers of the poem that has been preserved as Psalm 46 would, one imagines, have been located in the precincts of the Jerusalem temple in the First and/or Second Temple period, the vast majority of its users, both Jewish and Christian, have used it in other contexts. They have done so with the knowledge that the Jerusalem temple was destroyed by the Romans in 70 AD/CE/↑[88] and has never been rebuilt. Yet if they use the psalm meaningfully, they are still confidently affirming that this sovereign God, the LORD of hosts, the God of Israel/Jacob, "is with us" and "is our refuge," and that it is appropriate to celebrate the security of His city. This of course requires various kinds of metaphorical and analogical readings of the text. It is possible, nonetheless, for such moves still to take seriously the poetry and mythic resonance of the psalm.

In this regard I would like to consider a famous hymn of John Newton (1725–1807), "Glorious Things of Thee Are Spoken." Newton did not intend it as a paraphrase of Psalm 46 in the mode of Luther's *Ein feste Burg*, for Newton accompanied it (in the 1779 *Olney Hymns* in which it first appeared) with a reference to Isaiah 33:20–21. Moreover, the opening line is taken from Psalm 87:3 (KJV), "Glorious things are spoken of thee, O city of God." Nonetheless, the hymn has a strong resonance with the imagery of Psalm 46 in terms of God's giving security to Zion, even in the face of possible opposition, and in terms of the image of the life-giving waters and of the confidence of those who inhabit Zion.

> Glorious things of thee are spoken,
> Zion, City of our God!
> He, whose word cannot be broken,
> Form'd thee for his own abode:
> On the rock of ages founded,
> What can shake thy sure repose?
> With salvation's walls surrounded
> Thou may'st smile at all thy foes.

87. The scare quotes are used since we do not in fact know the date of composition of the psalm or its initial availability. Nor do we have any record of how it would have been understood, either by temple worshipers in general or by temple personnel such as Levites (assuming it was first used in the Jerusalem temple). It is thus hard to give content to the notion of an "original" hearing other than in terms of our best guess as to how its language might have functioned.

88. I discuss the limitations of CE as an alternative to AD, and propose an alternative, in my *The Bible in a Disenchanted Age*, 74–77.

See! the streams of living waters,
Springing from eternal love,
Well supply thy sons and daughters,
And all fear of want remove:
Who can faint while such a river
Ever flows their thirst t'assuage?
Grace, which like the Lord, the Giver,
Never fails from age to age.

Round each habitation hov'ring,
See the cloud and fire appear!
For a glory and a cov'ring,
Shewing that the Lord is near:
Thus deriving from their banner
Light by night, and shade by day;
Safe they feed upon the Manna
Which he gives them when they pray.[89]

Saviour, if of Zion's city
I, through grace, a member am,
Let the world deride or pity,
I will glory in thy name:
Fading is the worldling's pleasure,
All his boasted pomp and show;
Solid joys and lasting treasure
None but Zion's children know.[90]

Newton's poetic imagery stays for the most part with the imagery of the Old Testament, even though it is refracted through the New Testament and Christian tradition. In particular, "Zion, city of our God" has become a metaphor for the church as the home of the people of God, which is itself a symbol of God's heavenly city.[91] This metaphorical language has acquired rich resonance through Jesus' words of promise and assurance to Peter, "On this rock I will build my church, and the gates of Hades will not prevail against it" (Matt. 16:18); through John's vision of the new Jerusalem (Rev. 21); through Augustine's weighty *City of God*; and doubtless through other Christian influences as well.

89. In most contemporary hymnbooks, the fifth line of this verse is modified to "Thus they march, the pillar leading," and the seventh to "Daily on the manna feeding."

90. The text is taken from Watson, *Annotated Anthology of Hymns*, 216–17. I have omitted the fourth verse.

91. It is unlikely that Newton gave much, if any, thought to the historic city of Jerusalem, which during his lifetime was a not particularly significant part of the Ottoman Empire.

Overall, Newton's vision of Zion has a poetic and imaginative range surely comparable to that of Psalm 46. This Zion of "sure repose" relates to particular Christian churches rather as the Zion that "shall not totter / fall apart / be moved" relates to the specific city of Jerusalem; in each case there is a vision of a reality that is greater than particular embodiments. Newton's repeated imperative "See" summons the imagination in a way analogous to the "Come, see" of Psalm 46:8 (Heb. 9), so that in each poem people are invited to enter more fully into the picture which the poet paints. Newton's hymn exudes a confidence that is based not on any qualities of Newton himself or of the church but in the nature of God and His word.[92] The security and assurance of each poem is rooted in a vision of God whose truth will not readily be negated by various kinds of opposition, scorn, or denial, precisely because the vision is of an ultimate reality that transcends specific events and places and times.

Conclusion: Towards a Grammar of a Trustworthy God

I have structured this chapter's discussion in terms of how best to hear differing scriptural voices, that of Psalm 46 in relation to those of Jeremiah 7 and Micah 3. This has been with a view to clarifying the role of trust in relation to "knowing that the LORD is God," and to highlighting the interdependent nature of trust and obedience in the knowledge of God.

I conclude with some further reflections on what is involved in a way of life that is framed by an ultimate vision of reality. Initially, it must be acknowledged that in a certain sense I have not been comparing like with like. Psalm 46 sets out a God-centered vision of an ultimate reality which is already partially seen and realized in the here and now. Jeremiah 7 and Micah 3 do not offer a comparable competing vision. Rather, they critique a way of living and thinking in relation to God which is deluded because it is self-serving. In that sense, their role is intrinsically a corrective of something gone wrong rather than a vision of what is ultimately right. Yet both perspectives are necessary.

Psalm 46 is important for the way in which it portrays trust in God—trust, not as an abstract principle but as a concrete picture, in which there is no loss

92. There has been much discussion of the "if" in the first line of the last verse, in terms of what it implies: lack of certainty? humility? I think it is best taken as definitional, as in the words of the Johannine Jesus, "If you love me, you will keep my commandments" and "You are my friends if you do what I command you" (John 14:15; 15:14)—where the point is that obedience is constitutive of what loving or being a friend means. So too, glorying in God's name and having solid joys, even in the face of dismissiveness and scorn, shows what being a member of Zion's city means.

of hope even *in extremis*. When all else crumbles, God's city stands secure. In place of warfare, God brings peace. In place of weaponry and warfare to try to secure safety, people are to look to the God who is above all and learn a different way of living. Human stability derives from the stability of God.

Of course, visions can be illusions and/or delusions. There is, to be sure, an obvious sense in which any vision of ultimate reality must be self-authenticating inasmuch as, if it is ultimate, there is nothing above or beyond it to justify it. A vision of God as sovereignly trustworthy and enabling human stability is akin to the confidence that ultimately good will triumph over evil, whatever the extensive evidence that suggests otherwise. Nonetheless, we need to understand what the vision properly entails, as well as reasons to embrace it. That makes it all the more important to look at the vision's wider context and frame of reference.

In terms of the thesis of this chapter, I am proposing that Jeremiah 7 and Micah 3 may be well read as part of that wider canonical context which offers guidelines for understanding and using Psalm 46 in relation to "knowing that the LORD is God," or, in this psalm's particular wording, "knowing that I [the LORD] am God." If a vision of God is to be valid, what must accompany it? Meaningful words about trust in God's presence and protection necessarily imply a wider portrayal of God's character and purposes, which fill out what obedience to the psalm's imperatives to "come and see" and "be still and know" entails. The imperative to "be still and know" does not mean that human activity is not needed, but rather that it needs a particular, peace-oriented shaping if it is to be fruitful in serving the vision of God's exaltation. A meaningful vision of God's sovereignty and a life-enhancing trust in Him are not separable from obedience to His will. A searing vision of desolation and the loss of God's city, as in Jeremiah 7 and Micah 3, can appropriately be held alongside an ultimate vision of the preservation of God's city, as in Psalm 46, as a necessary imaginative stimulus to resist complacency.

Believers have to learn how to hold together divine promise and divine warning, assurance and critical self-awareness, both individually and communally. The scriptural text sounds necessary complementary notes: against anxiety, reassurance; against presumption, judgment. Knowledge of the God to whom Scripture bears witness is indeed challenging, but it is intrinsically both spacious and secure.

Epilogue

In recent theological scholarship there has been an important renewal of interest in a trinitarian understanding of God. I welcome and share this interest. Nonetheless, the richness of the Christian understanding of God is such that an explicitly trinitarian focus cannot be the sole approach to theology. I am in full agreement with Katherine Sonderegger, who says, "Christology cannot be the sole measure, ground, and matter of the doctrine of God; there is more, infinitely more to the One, Eternal God."[1] To use the terms of classic theological discussion, it is necessary to consider both the one God (*de Deo uno*) and the triune God (*de Deo trino*). This book is primarily a contribution to understanding the former.

A Summary Account of the Book's Content

What is the book about? In the introduction I set out as my thesis that the entire book is to be read as an exposition of the phrase "know that the LORD is God" (Ps. 100:3), in at least some of its facets. Moreover, an intrinsic corollary of "knowing that the LORD is God" has been argued to be—as might be expressed with further words from the Psalter—"The earth is the LORD's and all that is in it" (Ps. 24:1). Although explicit forms of the key biblical phrase have only featured in chapters 5 and 6, I have presented all the chapters in such a way that I hope that this indicative key has been heuristically helpful throughout for appreciating at least some dimensions of a multidimensional reality.

1. Sonderegger, *Systematic Theology*, 1:157. The context of Sonderegger's affirmation is a critique of the theology of Jürgen Moltmann. Her book fascinatingly focuses on the Old Testament.

It may be helpful to offer a summary account of the chapters, along with some reflective comment, so that a clearer overview of the book as a whole may be gained.

Chapter 1: The Wise God

My first chapter begins at the beginning (in a sense) with creation. The most famous and memorable depiction of creation in the Old Testament is, of course, Genesis 1. Numerous other passages, however, articulate different facets of what God's work as Creator entails; Proverbs 8, in particular, relates God's creative work to wisdom. Biblical accounts of creation, as also of eschatology (for the beginning and the end mirror each other), always have implications for life in the here and now. That is, the key issue in understanding these accounts is not speculation about something that happened a long time ago, or something that will happen in the distant future, but discovering what it means to know ourselves and the world as creatures in relation to God as Creator. Although much recent interest in creation in the Old Testament has tended to focus on ecological issues (because of obvious, pressing concerns for the environment in a contemporary context), Proverbs 8 reminds us that creation has other implications also. Wisdom's presence and agency in creation expresses the understanding that for humans to attain wisdom is to become in tune with reality, with the way things really are in God's purposes (notwithstanding the presence of folly and evil in the world). This core insight is common ground for Jews and Christians, however much its further dimensions may be spelled out differently in each tradition; for Christian faith, the wisdom within reality is supremely given a human face in Jesus Christ. To speak of God as Creator, with wisdom as His agent, is not to speak of some abstract idea removed from the specifics of everyday life, but precisely to locate the possibility of living wisely and well *in* everyday life with an appropriate responsiveness to an ultimate reality which is personal, moral, and relational.

The scientifically and technologically oriented culture of the contemporary world struggles not only to make this recognition but even to allow for its possibility in the first place. Nonetheless, part of the problem may be a matter of looking for the wrong thing in the wrong place—all too often, as though God were some kind of a large, invisible being somewhere in outer space who supposedly intervenes intermittently and inconsequentially, somewhat in the mode of a UFO. Rather, divine reality is recognized as and when people respond appropriately to its presence in the world and thereby begin to instantiate the nature of that reality in what they say and do. What it means to affirm God as Creator is inseparable from learning to live wisely in responsive attunement to the world.

If this is so, then it also fits with the classic sense of theology as the articulations that arise from right responsiveness to God, as humans enter more deeply into life in God's world. Whatever long-term patterns of life and thought develop, and whatever the technical and detailed issues to which they may give rise, the heart of theology remains speech about God that is rooted in engagement with God—the creature responding to the Creator.

Chapter 2: The Mysterious God

The second chapter explores the nature of God in terms of mystery, which I argue to be the central concern of the divine self-revelation in Exodus 3. On the one hand, God is appropriately symbolized by fire, which simultaneously attracts and repels and also intrinsically resists human manipulation and control (however much this symbolism may become somewhat muted in a technologically sophisticated culture). On the other hand, the tautological "I AM WHO/AS I AM" opens potentially limitless vistas for understanding God while simultaneously resisting precise definition. The nondestroying fire and the words mutually interpret each other.

If this portrayal of God is rightly expressed in terms of "the more you know, the more you know you don't know," then the limits to the knowledge of God arise specifically within the very act of attaining it. Put differently, the unknowing that arises from knowing God is entirely different from the unknowing that says agnostically, "If there is a God, God is the kind of reality about which one cannot really know anything." Such agnosticism can be essentially passive, hardly more than thoughts in an armchair.[2] In the biblical account, it is not accidental that Moses receives God's name, together with what God says about His nature, in the context of dialogue, a to-and-fro between personal agents (however much this is a literary convention, it is a convention that reflects a particular understanding of reality). Moreover, the overall dialogue is oriented to Moses' existential questions about how, as a prophet, he can speak and act for God in the way that God requires of him, when Israel needs deliverance from oppression. The theological articulation of the name and nature of God in Exodus 3 is not abstract but closely tied to engagement with God in the context of a mission to bring new life and

2. There can also be a different kind of agnosticism which arises as an expression of disappointment and disillusion. That existential dimension usually makes the core issue to be something other than epistemic.

hope. The unknowing that is intrinsic to the nature of God is a corollary of a knowing engagement with this God.

The fact that God is beyond human knowing entails a certain humility on the part of those who do know Him. In the context of the Exodus narrative, Moses' knowledge of God as the LORD leads directly into conflict with a human sovereign power, the pharaoh, who denies Him and resists His will to deliver His people from slavery. This conflict is prolonged; although the LORD's will eventually prevails over the Egyptians, one would not have expected that the will of a sovereign God would take so long to be realized (whatever its appropriateness in terms of narrative drama)—and be realized with the symbolism of blood and death, which is to be commemorated by a particular mode of eating. The ways of God are not self-evident, and however much Jewish and Christian thought and practice seek to accustom themselves to the biblical vision, the recognition that there are limits to human understanding—even if wisdom is attained—remains.

Chapter 3: The Just God

In the third chapter I argue that Psalm 82, which initially may appear to be a testimony to polytheistic mythology, is in fact an imaginative depiction of the meaning of the generic term *ʾĕlōhîm*, a grammatically plural term which Jews and Christians, following the biblical lead, consistently render with the singular "God." As elsewhere, the biblical theological vision is not expressed in an abstract mode of argument. Rather, the poet depicts the specific scenario of a divine assembly in which a sovereign deity pronounces a sentence of death on the other deities present, who thereby cease to be divine. A lack of justice, with its consequence of the dissolution of the fabric of life on earth, is the issue which exposes these other deities as not what they appeared to be. Thereby justice is seen to be definitional of the true nature of God (*ʾĕlōhîm*).

The depiction of the Creator God in Proverbs 8 as working with wisdom already implies the moral nature of Israel's God. But God's moral nature is affirmed with particular emphasis in Psalm 82, where justice becomes constitutive of the divine nature. That which the psalmist affirms here is also at the heart of large swaths of prophetic and legal material in the Old Testament. It is not just that humans should practice justice because God commands it. Rather, the human practice of justice reveals and displays on earth the nature and priorities of the Creator God. Again, the theological affirmation about God has intrinsic implications for human life and what it means to live well.

This biblical vision of the one God who is intrinsically just has frequently been depicted as "ethical monotheism." In modernity, "ethical monotheism" has often been seen as an enduring contribution to human knowledge from the Bible and from the Jewish and Christian faiths (often characterized as "the Judeo-Christian tradition"). But the steady dissolution of biblically oriented faith and theology in the public life of Western culture means, I suspect, that no shorthand such as "ethical monotheism" can still capture the biblical vision. The biblical vision entails a rediscovery that belief in God simultaneously affirms deep human intuitions about the fundamental importance of justice (even on the part of those who do not recognize justice as a witness to God) and critiques the ready tendency for people to align justice with their own desires and priorities. Apart from its core and unswerving affirmation of care for the poor and the vulnerable, the biblical vision of justice is in important ways open and underdetermined, especially when the changing nature of human society is taken into account. Thus, the prayer which concludes Psalm 82—"Rise up, O God, judge the earth"—becomes part of a never-ending quest to discover and realize in practice what genuinely constitutes justice. As elsewhere, human priorities, as expressed in the desire for justice, are affirmed, enlarged, and critiqued by being relocated within an understanding of justice that expresses the nature and priorities of the one God.

Chapter 4: The Inscrutable God

Chapter 4 focuses on one particular problem that naturally arises if God is seen as intrinsically just: How are we to understand God in a world in which so much seems arbitrary and unfair?

My reading of Genesis 4 proposes that the figures of Abel and Cain do not just represent two lines within humanity that will in due course become Israel and other nations. They also represent different conditions of humanity: those who are favored and unfavored, in one way or another, for no apparent reason in terms of what they have done. The Genesis text shows a particular interest in how the unfavored, specifically Cain and Esau, handle the situation in which they find themselves. The key point in these stories is to resist rationalizing the situation in terms of human deserving and instead to focus on the choice that one has in resolving what to do—whether to succumb to destructive resentment in the mode of Cain, or to seek what may yet be made out of the unchosen situation.

That inequities in life should be ascribed to the inscrutable purposes of God is not a notion that readily plays well in contemporary culture. It is easy to set justice over against inequity and to be dismissive of any role for God: either God is not really just or, more likely, blind chance rules. Yet inequities in life remain an inescapable fact, in terms both of what we are born with and of what happens to us in life. Recognizing that human dignity requires the exercise of one's choice in responding well to that which is unwelcome and difficult—as a corollary of the inscrutability of God—may in reality be salutary and life-giving. Notions of life as a time of testing/proving, where learning to live well is a continuing intrinsic challenge—notions once common yet now largely disregarded, even among believers—may yet have an unexpected wisdom. If one has had the privilege of knowing someone who has overcome deep affliction with graciousness and generosity, it is not uncommon to feel that one has been granted a fuller vision of what it means to be human, a vision which tends not to be found in the straightforwardly prosperous or successful. Thus, even if this chapter may be in certain ways the least palatable in the book, the subject matter of Genesis 4 remains important.

In certain ways the imponderable, seemingly arbitrary, nature of divine action in Genesis 4 has affinities with divine mystery in Exodus 3. But the accent in Genesis 4 is not on wonder and humility before a reality that is always greater and deeper. Rather, it is on the need to deal with likely resentment and bitterness when one's hand in life feels badly dealt. Playing the hand well may in due course lead to wonder at divine mystery, but that is a possible goal and not a starting point.

Finally, however, the challenge of responding well to that which is unchosen and unwelcome should resonate with Christians, who are called to discipleship in the way of the cross. When disappointment and affliction are set in this context, there can be a renewed sense of the mystery of God's ways with the world—seen supremely in the death and resurrection of Jesus—as that which can give meaning and hope even to that which seems futile and pointless.

Chapter 5: The Only God

This chapter's reading of the Naaman story in 2 Kings 5 has at its heart the distinctive Old Testament affirmation that the one true God is in and with Israel in a way that is not the same elsewhere. Other gods (*ʾĕlōhīm ʾăḥērīm*) there may be. But their significance pales in light of the vision of the God who, for Israel, is the "one and only" (*eḥād*), in relation to whom other deities are set aside. This distinctive Israelite affirmation is made by a non-Israelite who through an experience of grace realizes a hope that is not infrequently expressed in Israel's scriptures: that other nations also will come to "know that the Lord is God" and to recognize that "God is with Israel."

That God is with Israel does not mean therefore that everything is straightforward for Israel. The Naaman story depicts the Lord giving victory to Aram at Israel's expense. The king of Israel appears to be singularly uninformed about how to help an Aramean who seeks healing from Israel's God. Gehazi, despite his proximity to the prophet Elisha, still succumbs to greed and deception and is lastingly blighted. Naaman's allegiance to the LORD in his home situation will not be expressed with formal consistency. On the whole, natural-seeming human expectations about what it ought to mean for God to be specially present with a particular people are consistently overturned in this story (as regularly elsewhere in the biblical canon also). The God symbolized by fire and cloud eludes human management and requires humans to remain open and alert.

Nonetheless, the story well displays the characteristic biblical understanding that true knowledge of the one God has a particularity of content that is tied to a particular people. This does not deny that God—or the divine wisdom that is immanent within creation—is in some way accessible to people everywhere. Rather, it affirms an infinite reality in the context of a specific, gracious self-revelation that needs to be recognized and entered into. Challenges remain in terms of finding appropriate contemporary conceptualities to articulate this. Within a Christian context, the particularity of the knowledge of God in Jesus Christ is no longer identical to the particularity of the knowledge of God in Israel's scriptures. Yet the one grows out of, and stands in continuity with, the other, and Israel's witness to the dynamics of its knowledge of God should still inform its Christian understanding and appropriation.

Chapter 6: The Trustworthy God

The final chapter considers trust as a constitutive element in Israel's knowledge of God. The mode of portrayal in Psalm 46, as in Psalm 82, is an imaginative poetic picture rather than a more abstract formulation. On the one hand, a vision of God's city standing firm even when the natural elements of the world disintegrate can appeal powerfully to the imagination. On the other hand, such a vision necessarily leaves open and unresolved numerous questions that can be put to it. Part of the function of the canonical collection is to provide a thick context in which those questions can be handled with some literacy.

The prime focus of this chapter's discussion is the relationship of trust to ways of living that appropriately express that trust. This is approached via negative examples of ways of living that do not express, and are incompatible with, trust. Jeremiah 7 and Micah 3 set out scathing critiques of claims of confident trust in God's protection. These claims are seen to be false and delusional precisely because they have become detached from attention to the character of God. Concern for God's will and priorities should be expressed by seeking justice for the vulnerable and needy (Jer. 7) and by *not* seeking personal gain on the part of political and religious leaders in their dealings with others (Mic. 3). The absence of such priorities in life empties language about trust in God of its content. Indeed, that which is factually true—the Jerusalem temple was indeed the temple of the LORD—can become deceptive and untrue, if it is used self-servingly. Language can be self-involving in demanding ways. Trust is a relational reality that must take account of the character of the one trusted—supremely when the recipient of trust is God.

Other great celebrations of trust and confidence in God, such as Luther's *Ein feste Burg* and Newton's "Glorious Things of Thee Are Spoken," share with Psalm 46 a disinclination to spell out the wider corollaries of that trust. But that means no more than that psalms and hymns alike do not stand alone, apart from the whole scriptural context and living tradition of which they are a part. The poetry and metaphor in the vision of these Christian hymns, as in Psalm 46, are also a reminder that the mundane realization of the vision of the city of God can take many surprising forms. The existential imagination of (would-be) believers needs to remain alert.

On What Has and Has Not Been Discussed

These six chapters taken together do not, of course, constitute all that can be said about what it means to "know that the LORD is God." It will always be possible to suggest other topics and/or texts and/or sequences of thought. And no doubt the particular selection made is indicative of my particular Christian identity and priorities. But that is just to recognize that any selective account of the content of the Old Testament will always be open to various kinds of "But what about/if . . . ?" questions. My core contention is that all the aspects of God and human life that have been discussed are (a) elements of a basic "grammar" of God within Israel's scriptures; (b) understandings of God that are common to Jews and Christians, even though they develop them differently within their respective traditions; and (c) understandings of God in which implications for the nature and practice of human life are integral and inseparable.

My prime regret is that I have not found space for what is said about the name and nature of God as gracious and merciful in Exodus 32–34, especially Exodus 34:6–7. Within the book of Exodus this is an essential complement and counterpart to Exodus 3. In my teaching I have often lamented that Christian tradition has attended far more to Exodus 3 than to Exodus 34; yet there is an obvious sense in which I am continuing that imbalance here. Jewish tradition has been much more attentive to Exodus 34:6–7, finding in it, to borrow the classic medieval formulation, the Thirteen Attributes of God.[3] My first book (my revised doctoral dissertation) was on Exodus 32–34,[4] and I had hoped to revisit and develop my early career work in late career. But, because of certain constraints of time and practicability, this has unfortunately not proved possible.[5]

Jesus and the Old Testament

One question which has regularly been put to me over the years, in one way or another, is "Where is Jesus in your reading of the Old Testament?" Insofar as I attend to the meaning of Israel's scriptures as ancient and pre-Christian compositions, I say little about Jesus unless and until I move into a New Testament frame of reference. This may seem puzzling to some, since it may well look as if either I am not really doing anything different from conventional, historically oriented interpretation, or I am not really reading Israel's scriptures as Christian Scripture in the way that I claim. Some brief comment is therefore in order here. Any fuller answer would for the most part involve amplifying the points about "reading as Scripture" that were made in the introduction.[6]

A first consideration is that, for most Christians, Jesus is the reason for being interested in Israel's scriptures in the first place. He is the one who, in the terminology of Matthew's Gospel, "fulfills" them (though such fulfillment is variously understood) and leads to their becoming the Old Testament of Christian faith. Thus, the Christian point of access to Israel's scriptures lies outside them. However much it may be appropriate for Christians imaginatively to bracket Jesus in their reading of Israel's scriptures, and to ask what the material meant before the coming of Jesus, it remains important to recognize that without Jesus' realization and enactment of Israel's scriptures there

3. This book is not an attempt to articulate the Six Attributes of God!

4. Moberly, *At the Mountain of God: Story and Theology in Exodus 32–34*.

5. I have discussed Exod. 34:6–7 in the context of considering Jonah's moaning citation of it in Jon. 4:2 (see "Educating Jonah," in my *Old Testament Theology*, 181–210). I also offered some preliminary further thoughts in "How May We Speak of God?"

6. Although there is some bibliography on the specific question of Jesus in the OT, it is not as extensive or as helpful as it might be. Significant treatments by leading biblical scholars in recent years include, e.g., Childs, "Does the Old Testament Witness to Jesus Christ?"; and Witte, *Jesus Christus im Alten Testament*. Childs and Witte come at the issue in markedly different ways, in relation to their own specific concerns. Witte's orientation is to the history of ideas, while Childs's is to contemporary hermeneutics. Disappointingly, neither scholar even mentions, let alone utilizes, the concerns of the other. A proper analysis of these and other discussions must await another context.

would be no contemporary believers seeking to read those scriptures and to understand them as Christian Scripture. In the absence of this rationale, or a Jewish identity, it is difficult to see how Israel's scriptures can be read other than as ancient history or cultural/literary classic.

Second, if Christian faith indeed involves engagement with the wisdom and truth of reality (in the terms of Prov. 8 and John 1), then it should, over time, lead to a more open and clear-eyed vision of the world and all that is in it. To see what is before our eyes in the world is always complex and demanding. Educational formation, in the many contexts in which it takes place, makes a difference to how people see what they see. For a Christian, Jesus is not only the light at which to look but also the light by which to see. To learn what seeing in the light of Christ means takes time and is not self-evident. With specific reference to Israel's scriptures as the Christian Old Testament, it arguably prescribes nothing in advance other than a commitment to the importance of the material and a sense of its congruence with what is important for faith in Christ. This can then be developed in dialogue with at least some of the immeasurable interpretive resources that have become available over the last two thousand years. Through such seeking, one may grow in knowledge and love.

It follows, third, that part of what seeing in the light of Christ involves is the utilizing of a rule of faith in the reading of Scripture. As already indicated, I understand a rule of faith to be a complex, interlocking set of judgments about how things go and what makes sense in a Christian frame of reference (with variations in differing Christian traditions)—which involves certain practices, in terms of discipleship, as well as intellectual understandings.[7] Insofar as the Old and New Testaments are read together as the two-Testament canon of Christian faith, readers may not make of the material whatever they will, for Christian faith provides certain guidelines. These guidelines are not incorrigible. For example, in the light of the philological and historical understandings that have become available in recent centuries, it has been necessary to rethink the nature of "the messiah" in the Old Testament,[8] as well as the ways in which one should best understand the Old Testament

7. See p. 9.

8. Although various royal and priestly figures are said to be "the LORD's anointed" (*mĕshiaḥ yhwh* or comparable formulations), the notion of a particular coming figure, "the messiah" (*hammāshiaḥ*), is not as such present in the OT. A combination of biblical passages that express various future-oriented hopes led to the formulation of messianic expectations in ancient Jewish and Christian interpretations. This is an interesting example of how an understanding that is rooted in the biblical text can go beyond what the texts themselves say. There is perhaps an analogy here to the way in which an understanding of God as triune is rooted in, yet goes beyond, what the NT itself says.

to "look towards" Jesus as the one who realizes its meaning and hopes. Or, insofar as the Apostles' and Nicene Creeds—which can be taken as expressions of a Christian rule of faith—are silent about God's call of Abraham and Israel, their content may need to be at least informally supplemented in a contemporary context. But the creedal affirmation that the God of the Old Testament is not other than the God of the New Testament—that the God of Israel is the God and Father of our Lord Jesus Christ—remains fundamental to Christian faith. More generally, I have tried in this book to articulate a vision of God and humanity in the Old Testament with which Christian thought and practice stands in substantive continuity—"continuity," rather than "identity," being the appropriate term for the relationship.

Finally, to read Israel's scriptures as the Old Testament in the light of Christ requires alertness to the importance of recontextualization and an ability to hold together synthetically more than one interpretive context. For a Christian, God is the triune God for all eternity. Yet, historically speaking, the biblical writers did not conceive God as triune. Thus, when I read of God as intrinsically mysterious in Exodus 3 or as intrinsically just in Psalm 82, I now understand this to be the triune God, even though the biblical writers themselves did not thus understand Him; and in my own historical imagination I seek to approximate the outlook of the biblical writers. Yet in my theological imagination I readily appropriate the patristic notion of Old Testament theophanies as christological or as appearances of the preincarnate Word—a notion that follows the lead of John's Gospel, especially John 12:37–41. Methodologically, one can combine, though one should not confuse or conflate, different perspectives and approaches. Substantively, believers down the ages alike hope to see the one God. But although there is continuity in the seeing, there is also difference.

Conclusion: On Formulating a Grammar of God from the Old Testament

In this book I have attempted to articulate certain key facets of a grammar of God in the Old Testament. Or, to put it in the Old Testament's own terminology, I have tried to articulate certain aspects of what it means to "know that the LORD is God." In doing so I have sought to attend to the particularities of the ancient pre-Christian text in what it says about YHWH, the God of Abraham and of Israel, while simultaneously working with the perspective whereby the LORD, the God of Israel, is not only the eternal Creator God of all that is but is also supremely known in Jesus Christ. From a Christian perspective, "knowing that the LORD is God" is accompanied by "confessing that Jesus is Lord" and "believing that Jesus is the Christ, the Son of God." Nonetheless, my primary focus has been the nature and meaning of the Old Testament's own voices in their particular witness to their God, in their affirmation that Israel has been given the amazing gift of knowing that their deity, YHWH / the LORD, who has called them to be His people, is the one and only God. Inseparable from Israel's knowing that the LORD is God is a vision of what it means to be human, in modes that are of enduring existential significance.

Central to my purpose in writing is a hope to enhance and extend the terms of thought and discussion about the nature of faith in God in today's world, especially by highlighting the potential contribution of the Old Testament.[9] All too often there is a dismaying narrowness of focus. One fashionable concern, for example, is the relationship between monotheism and violence: Does not belief in one God, the fount of truth, mean that believers either behave exclusively and repressively towards those who do not share their faith, or else relate to them in a proselytizing mode that demeans their values and priorities? Alternatively, countless discussions about the Bible in relation to faith center on whether one should "take the text literally" and how far its content is or is not "historically reliable." There are indeed legitimate concerns in these debates,[10] as also in heated debates about sex and gender. But so many of the important realities of faith and life fall out of sight when such arguments take center stage.

In terms of the use of Scripture, I have emphasized that there is no one way to read biblical texts, since how we read depends on why we read and on the context in which we are located. Recognition of the hermeneutical fruitfulness of the plurality of contexts in which both texts and readers are situated is all-important. To be sure, much biblical content is in certain ways underdetermined, in the sense that differing construals can be possible even when interpreters share common aims and interests. Nonetheless, I have tried to show how the biblical writers characteristically articulate theology in concrete modes that exploit the potential of diverse literary forms, especially poetry and narrative. I have also consistently offered "strong" readings of my selected passages, not so as to close down interpretation ("This is the only right way to read the text") but rather to open it up ("See how rich and full of implication the text is").

My reason for being a professional biblical scholar is my abiding sense of the richness, the breadth and depth, of the content of the Old Testament.

9. The challenges here are, of course, many and great. A fresh and suggestive angle of vision is offered by Brent Strawn in *The Old Testament Is Dying*.

10. I discuss monotheism and violence in my *Old Testament Theology*, 41–74, and evidentialist approaches to the Bible in my *The Bible in a Disenchanted Age*.

How much there is that can enlarge and enrich an understanding of God and life in the world. How indispensable is its content for coming to understand Jesus in his life, death, and resurrection. How great is the debt of Christian faith to the Jewish faith that preceded, and still accompanies, it. How fruitfully the Old Testament can still nourish a life of faith and discipleship in the world of the twenty-first century. I am endlessly intrigued by the history of the ancient world. But I am even more interested in, and astonished by, the fact that the small—and by most conventional counts, insignificant—people of Israel came to believe (or in its own terminology, to know) that its deity, YHWH, was the only God, and was able to preserve its mature and tested witness to this knowledge in its scriptures. These scriptures have been treasured and privileged by Jews and Christians down the centuries until today; they have been, and still are, instrumental in millions of people entering into that ancient faith (in modes not identical but continuous) and finding it to be true and life-giving.

Of course, most of the content of the Old Testament has not been discussed here at all. And there are parts of it which I still struggle to understand. Nonetheless, I hope that the few passages that have been discussed show something of how enriching a study of God, in the context of Israel's scriptures as Christian Scripture, can be.

Bibliography

Alexander, Philip. "'In the Beginning': Rabbinic and Patristic Exegesis of Genesis 1:1." In *The Exegetical Encounter between Jews and Christians in Late Antiquity*, edited by Emmanouela Grypeou and Helen Spurling, 1–29. Jewish and Christian Perspectives 18. Leiden: Brill, 2009.

Alt, Albrecht. "The God of the Fathers." In *Essays on Old Testament History and Religion*, 1–77. Translated by R. A. Wilson. Oxford: Blackwell, 1966.

Alter, Robert. *Ancient Israel: The Former Prophets: Joshua, Judges, Samuel, and Kings*. New York: Norton, 2013.

———. *The Art of Bible Translation*. Princeton: Princeton University Press, 2019.

———. *The Book of Psalms*. New York: Norton, 2007.

———. *The Hebrew Bible*. Vol. 2, *Prophets*. New York: Norton, 2019.

Anderson, A. A. *Psalms*. 2 vols. NCB. London: Marshall, Morgan & Scott, 1972.

Assmann, Jan. *The Invention of Religion: Faith and Covenant in the Book of Exodus*. Princeton: Princeton University Press, 2018.

Auerbach, Erich. *Mimesis: The Representation of Reality in Western Literature*. Princeton: Princeton University Press, 1953, 1968.

Avigad, Nahman. "Samaria (City)." In *NEAEHL* 4:1300–1310.

Baly, Denis. *The Geography of the Bible*. London: Lutterworth, 1957.

Barr, James. *The Concept of Biblical Theology: An Old Testament Perspective*. London: SCM, 1999.

Bartelmus, Rüdiger. *HYH: Bedeutung und Funktion eines hebräischen "Allerweltswortes."* ATSAT. St. Ottilien: EOS Verlag, 1982.

Barton, John. *Ethics in Ancient Israel*. Oxford: Oxford University Press, 2014.

Bauckham, Richard. "Where Is Wisdom to Be Found? Colossians 1.15–20 (2)." In *Reading Texts, Seeking Wisdom*, edited by David F. Ford and Graham Stanton, 129–38. London: SCM, 2003.

Baumgart, Norbert Clemens. *Gott, Prophet und Israel: Eine synchrone und diachrone Auslegung der Naamanerzählung und ihrer Gehasiepisode (2 Kön 5)*. ETS 68. Göttingen: Benno, 1994.

Bayfield, Tony, Sidney Brichto, and Eugene Fisher. *He Kissed Him and They Wept: Towards a Theology of Jewish-Catholic Partnership*. London: SCM, 2012.

Bell, Matthew. *Ruled Reading and Biblical Criticism*. JTIS 18. University Park, PA: Eisenbrauns, 2019.

Bellarmine, Robert. *Commentarii in Scripturam Sacram*. Vol. 7. Paris: Pelagaud, 1863.

Blenkinsopp, Joseph. "The Midianite-Kenite Hypothesis Revisited and the Origins of Judah." *JSOT* 33 (2008): 131–53.

Bradley, Ian, ed. *The Penguin Book of Hymns*. London: Penguin, 1990.

Briggs, Charles. *The Book of Psalms*. 2 vols. ICC. Edinburgh: T&T Clark, 1906–7.

Briggs, Richard S. *The Virtuous Reader: Old Testament Narrative and Interpretive Virtue*. STI. Grand Rapids: Baker Academic, 2010.

Bright, John. *Covenant and Promise*. London: SCM, 1977.

Bromiley, Geoffrey W., trans. and ed. *Karl Barth / Rudolf Bultmann: Letters, 1922–1966*. Edinburgh: T&T Clark, 1982.

Brueggemann, Walter. *Theology of the Old Testament: Testimony, Dispute, Advocacy*. Minneapolis: Fortress, 1997.

Brueggemann, Walter, and William H. Bellinger Jr. *Psalms*. NCamBC. New York: Cambridge University Press, 2014.

Brueggemann, Walter, and Hans Walter Wolff, eds. *The Vitality of Old Testament Traditions*. 2nd ed. Atlanta: John Knox, 1982.

Buckley, Michael. *At the Origins of Modern Atheism*. New Haven: Yale University Press, 1987.

Budde, K. "Ps. 82 6f." *JBL* 40 (1921): 39–42.

Bultmann, Rudolf. "Is Exegesis without Presuppositions Possible?" In *New Testament and Mythology and Other Basic Writings*, edited and translated by Schubert M. Ogden, 145–53. London: SCM, 1985.

Burney, C. F. "Christ as the *Archē* of Creation." *JTS* 27 (1926): 160–77.

———. *Notes on the Hebrew Text of the Books of Kings*. Oxford: Clarendon, 1903.

———. *Outlines of Old Testament Theology*. London: Rivingtons, 1899.

Buttenweiser, Moses. *The Psalms*. LBS. New York: Ktav, 1969.

Calvin, John. *Calvin's Commentaries*. Vol. 1, *Genesis*. Translated by John King. CTS. Grand Rapids: Baker Books, 2005.

———. *Commentary on the Book of Psalms*. Vol. 3. Translated by James Anderson for the Calvin Translation Society. Grand Rapids: Baker Books, 2005.

Camp, Claudia V. *Wisdom and the Feminine in the Book of Proverbs*. Sheffield: Almond Press, 1985.

Campbell, Antony F., and Mark A. O'Brien. *Unfolding the Deuteronomistic History: Origins, Upgrades, Present Text*. Minneapolis: Fortress, 2000.

Caputo, John D. *Hermeneutics: Facts and Interpretation in the Age of Information*. New York: Pelican, 2018.

Carasik, Michael, ed. *The Commentators' Bible: Exodus*. Philadelphia: Jewish Publication Society, 2005.

———. *The Commentators' Bible: Genesis*. Philadelphia: Jewish Publication Society, 2018.

Carroll, Robert P. "Strange Fire: Abstract of Presence Absent in the Text; Meditations on Exodus 3." *JSOT* 61 (1994): 39–58.

———. *Wolf in the Sheepfold: The Bible as a Problem for Christianity*. London: SPCK, 1991.

Chapman, Stephen B. *The Law and the Prophets*. FAT 27. Tübingen: Mohr Siebeck, 2000.

Charry, Ellen. "Rebekah's Twins: Augustine on Election in Genesis." In *Genesis and Christian Theology*, edited by Nathan MacDonald, Mark W. Elliott, and Grant Macaskill, 267–86. Grand Rapids: Eerdmans, 2012.

Childs, Brevard S. "Does the Old Testament Witness to Jesus Christ?" In *Evangelium, Schriftauslegung, Kirche: Festschrift für Peter Stuhlmacher zum 65. Geburtstag*, edited by J. Ådna et al., 57–64. Göttingen: Vandenhoeck & Ruprecht, 1997.

———. "Psalm Titles and Midrashic Exegesis." *JSS* 16 (1971): 137–50.

Clément, Olivier. *The Roots of Christian Mysticism: Texts from the Patristic Era with Commentary*. Translated by Theodore Berkeley and Jeremy Hummerstone. London: New City, 1993.

Clines, David J. A., ed. *Dictionary of Classical Hebrew*. 8 vols. Sheffield: Sheffield Academic Press, 1993–2016.

Cogan, Morton. *Imperialism and Religion: Assyria, Judah, and Israel in the Eighth and Seventh Centuries B.C.E.* SBLMS 19. Missoula, MT: Society of Biblical Literature, 1974.

Cohen, Naomi. *Philo's Scriptures: Citations from the Prophets and Writings*. SJSJ 123. Leiden: Brill, 2007.

Cohn, Haim H. "Justice." In *Contemporary Jewish Religious Thought: Original Essays on Critical Concepts, Movements, and Beliefs*, edited by Arthur A. Cohen and Paul Mendes-Flohr, 515–20. New York: Macmillan, 1987.

Cohn, Robert L. "Form and Perspective in 2 Kings V." *VT* 33, no. 2 (1983): 171–84.

Collett, Donald. *Figural Reading and the Old Testament: Theology and Practice*. Grand Rapids: Baker Academic, 2020.

———. "A Place to Stand: Proverbs 8 and the Construction of Ecclesial Space." *SJT* 70, no. 2 (2017): 166–83.

Cornelius, Izak. "The Visual Representations of the World in the Ancient Near East and the Hebrew Bible." *JNSL* 20 (1994): 193–218.

Cox, Dermot. "Fear or Conscience? *Yir'at YHWH* in Proverbs 1–9." *Studia Hierosolymitana* 3 (1982): 83–90.

Critchlow, Hannah. *The Science of Fate: Why Your Future Is More Predictable Than You Think*. London: Hodder & Stoughton, 2019.

Crossan, John Dominic. *The Birth of Christianity: Discovering What Happened in the Years Immediately after the Execution of Jesus*. San Francisco: HarperSanFrancisco, 1998.

Crouch, C. L. "*ḥt't* as Interpolative Gloss: A Solution to Gen 4,7." *ZAW* 123 (2011): 250–58.

Daniélou, Jean. *The Bible and the Liturgy*. London: Darton, Longman & Todd, 1960.

Davidson, Robert. *Genesis 1–11*. CBC. Cambridge: Cambridge University Press, 1973.

Davies, Graham I. *Exodus 1–18*. Vol. 1. ICC. London: T&T Clark, 2020.

Dawson, John David. *Christian Figural Reading and the Fashioning of Identity*. Berkeley: University of California Press, 2002.

Dell, Katharine. "Didactic Intertextuality: Proverbial Wisdom as Illustrated in Ruth." In *Reading Proverbs Intertextually*, edited by Katharine Dell and Will Kynes, 103–14. LHBOTS 629. London: T&T Clark, 2019.

Denzinger, Heinrich. *Ritus Orientalium*. Würzburg: Typis et sumptibus Stahelianis, 1863.

Dietrich, Walter. "1 and 2 Kings." In *The Oxford Bible Commentary*, edited by John Barton and John Muddiman, 232–66. Oxford: Oxford University Press, 2001.

Dohmen, Christoph. *Exodus 1–18*. HTKAT. Freiburg: Herder, 2015.

Driver, S. R. *The Book of Genesis*. London: Methuen, 1904.

———. *Notes on the Hebrew Text and the Topography of the Books of Samuel*. Oxford: Clarendon, 1913.

Durham, John I. *Exodus*. WBC 3. Waco: Word, 1987.

Ehrlich, Arnold B. *Die Psalmen*. Berlin: Poppelauer, 1905.

Eising, H. "*Chayil*." In *TDOT* 4:348–55.

Ellul, Jacques. *The Politics of God and the Politics of Man*. Translated by Geoffrey W. Bromiley. Grand Rapids: Eerdmans, 1972.

Epstein, I., ed. *The Babylonian Talmud: Seder Neziḳin*. Vol. 3. London: Soncino, 1935.

Erasmus. "Letter 116: 'To Johannes Sixtinus.'" In *The Correspondence of Erasmus: Letters 1–141, 1484 to 1500*, 229–33. Translated by R. A. B. Mynors and D. F. S. Thomson. Toronto: University of Toronto Press, 1974.

Evagrius. *On Prayer: 153 Texts*. In *The Philokalia*, edited by G. E. H. Palmer, Philip Sherrard, and Kallistos Ware, 1:55–71. London: Faber & Faber, 1979.

Evans, John F. *You Shall Know That I Am Yahweh: An Inner-Biblical Interpretation of Ezekiel's Recognition Formula*. BBRS 25. University Park, PA: Eisenbrauns, 2019.

Falk, Z. W. "Exodus XXI:6." *VT* 9 (1959): 86–88.

Fischer, Georg. *Jahwe unser Gott: Sprache, Aufbau und Erzähltechnik in der Berufung des Mose (Ex 3–4)*. OBO 91. Göttingen: Vandenhoeck & Ruprecht, 1989.

Fox, Michael V. *Proverbs 1–9*. AB 18A. New York: Doubleday, 2000.

Frankl, Viktor E. *Man's Search for Meaning*. New York: Simon & Schuster, 1985. Revised and enlarged edition of *Ein Psycholog erlebt das Konzentrationslager*, 1946.

Freedman, H., trans. and ed. *Midrash Rabbah: Genesis I*. London: Soncino, 1951.

———. *Midrash Rabbah: Genesis II*. London: Soncino, 1939.

Fretheim, Terence E. *Exodus*. IBCTP. Louisville: John Knox, 1991.

———. *First and Second Kings*. Westminster Bible Companion. Louisville: Westminster John Knox, 1999.

Fritz, Volkmar. *1 & 2 Kings*. Translated by Anselm Hagedorn. CC. Minneapolis: Fortress, 2003.

Gers-Uphaus, Christian. "Gott als wahrer *elohim* und Retter der Armen—Psalm 82 im Korpus der Asafpsalmen." *BZ* 63 (2019): 30–48.

———. *Sterbliche Götter—göttliche Menschen: Psalm 82 und seine frühchristlichen Deutungen*. SB 240. Stuttgart: Katholisches Bibelwerk, 2019.

Gibbon, Edward. *The Decline and Fall of the Roman Empire*. Vol. 2. London: Everyman, 1993.

Ginzberg, Louis. *The Legends of the Jews*. Vol. 2. Philadelphia: Jewish Publication Society, 2003.

Girtanner, Maïti, and Guillaume Tabard. *Résistance et pardon: Maïti Girtanner*. Produced by Michael Farin. Paris: La Procure, 2005. DVD.

Girtanner, Maïti, with Guillaume Tabard. *Même les bourreaux ont une âme*. Paris: CLD, 2006.

Goldingay, John. *Old Testament Theology*. Vol. 2, *Israel's Faith*. Downers Grove, IL: IVP Academic, 2006.

———. *Psalms 42–89*. BCOTWP. Grand Rapids: Baker Academic, 2007.

Gordon, Cyrus H. "*ʾlhym* in Its Reputed Meaning of *Rulers, Judges*." *JBL* 54 (1935): 139–44.

Gordon, Robert. "'Couch' or 'Crouch'? Genesis 4:7 and the Temptation of Cain." In *On Stone and Scroll: Essays in Honour of Graham Ivor Davies*, edited by James K.

Aitken, Katharine J. Dell, and Brian A. Mastin, 195–209. BZAW 420. Berlin: de Gruyter, 2011.

Gray, John. *I & II Kings*. 3rd ed. OTL. London: SCM, 1977.

Gray, John. *The Soul of the Marionette: A Short Enquiry into Human Freedom*. New York: Penguin Random House, 2016.

Greenfield, Jonas C. "The Aramean God Rammān/Rimmōn." *IEJ* 26, no. 4 (1976): 195–98.

Gregory of Nyssa. *Oration on the Deity of the Son and the Holy Spirit*. In PG 46:554–76.

Guelzo, Allen C. *Abraham Lincoln: Redeemer President*. Grand Rapids: Eerdmans, 1999.

Gunkel, Hermann. *Genesis*. Translated by Mark Biddle. Mercer Library of Biblical Studies. Macon, GA: Mercer University Press, 1997.

Gurtner, Daniel. *Exodus: A Commentary on the Greek Text of Codex Vaticanus*. SCS. Leiden: Brill, 2013.

Harrison, Peter. *The Territories of Science and Religion*. Chicago: University of Chicago Press, 2015.

Hartenstein, Friedhelm. "The Beginnings of YHWH and 'Longing for the Origin': A Historico-Hermeneutical Query." In *The Origins of Yahwism*, edited by Jürgen van Oorschot and Markus Witte, 283–307. BZAW 484. Berlin: de Gruyter, 2017.

Hayward, Robert. "What Did Cain Do Wrong? Jewish and Christian Exegesis of Genesis 4:3–6." In *The Exegetical Encounter between Jews and Christians in Late Antiquity*, edited by Emmanouela Grypeou and Helen Spurling, 101–23. Jewish and Christian Perspectives 18. Leiden: Brill, 2009.

Held, Shai. *The Heart of Torah*. Vol. 1, *Essays on the Weekly Torah Portion: Genesis and Exodus*. Philadelphia: Jewish Publication Society, 2017.

Henderson, Joseph M. *Jeremiah under the Shadow of Duhm: A Critique of Poetic Form as a Criterion of Authenticity*. London: T&T Clark, 2019.

Henry, Matthew. *Matthew Henry's Commentary on the Whole Bible*. Edited by Leslie F. Church. London: Marshall, Morgan & Scott, 1960.

Hens-Piazza, Gina. *1–2 Kings*. AOTC. Nashville: Abingdon, 2006.

Hentschel, G. *2 Könige*. DNEB. Würzburg: Echter Verlag, 1985.

Hilary of Poitiers (Hilaire de Poitiers). *La Trinité I*. SC 443. Paris: Cerf, 1999.

Hobbs, T. R. *2 Kings*. WBC 13. Waco: Word, 1985.

Hossfeld, Frank-Lothar, and Erich Zenger. *A Commentary on Psalms 51–100*. Translated by Linda M. Maloney. Hermeneia. Minneapolis: Fortress, 2005.

———. *Die Psalmen 1: Psalm 1–50*. Würzburg: Echter Verlag, 1993.

Houellebecq, Michel. *Submission*. Translated by Lorin Stein. London: Vintage, 2016.

House, Paul R. *1, 2 Kings*. TNAC 8. Nashville: Broadman & Holman, 1995.

Houtman, Cornelis. *Exodus*. Vol. 1. Translated by Johan Rebel and Sierd Woudstra. HCOT. Kampen: Kok, 1993.

Hugo, Victor. *Les Misérables*. Translated by Norman Denny. London: Penguin, 2012.

Huizinga, Johan. *Erasmus and the Age of Reformation*. 1924. Reprint, London: Phoenix, 2002.

Hunter, Alastair. *Psalms*. OTR. London: Routledge, 1999.

Jacob, Benno. *The Second Book of the Bible: Exodus*. Translated by Walter Jacob. Hoboken, NJ: Ktav, 1992.

Janzen, J. Gerald. ". . . and the Bush Was Not Consumed." In *When Prayer Takes Place: Forays into a Biblical World*, edited by Brent Strawn and Patrick Miller, 17–23. Cambridge: James Clarke, 2017.

Johnson, Elizabeth A. *She Who Is: The Mystery of God in Feminist Theological Discourse*. New York: Crossroad, 1994.

Jones, Gwilym H. *1 and 2 Kings*. 2 vols. NCBC. Grand Rapids: Eerdmans, 1984.

Josephus. *Jewish Antiquities, Books V–VIII*. Translated by H. St. J. Thackeray and Ralph Marcus. LCL. Cambridge, MA: Harvard University Press, 1988.

Kadushin, Max. *The Rabbinic Mind*. 3rd ed. New York: Bloch, 1972.

Keel, Othmar. *Die Weisheit spielt vor Gott: Ein ikonographischer Beitrag zur Deutung des* mesahäqät *in Spr. 8,30f*. Göttingen: Vandenhoeck & Ruprecht, 1974.

Keil, C. F. *The Books of Kings*. Translated by James Martin. 2nd ed. Edinburgh: T&T Clark, 1857.

Klingbeil, Martin. *Yahweh Fighting from Heaven: God as Warrior and as God of Heaven in the Hebrew Psalter and Ancient Near Eastern Iconography*. OBO 169. Göttingen: Vandenhoeck & Ruprecht, 1999.

Kraus, Hans-Joachim. *Psalms 60–150*. Translated by Hilton C. Oswald. CC. Minneapolis: Augsburg, 1989.

Kugel, James L. *The Bible as It Was*. Cambridge, MA: Harvard University Press, 1997.

———. *The Idea of Biblical Poetry: Parallelism and Its History*. New Haven: Yale University Press, 1981.

LaCocque, André, and Paul Ricoeur. *Thinking Biblically: Exegetical and Hermeneutical Studies*. Translated by David Pellauer. Chicago: University of Chicago Press, 1998.

Langston, Scott M. *Exodus through the Centuries*. BBC. Oxford: Blackwell, 2006.

Lapide, Cornelius à. *Commentarii in Sacram Scripturam*. Vol. 1. Paris: Pelagaud, 1865. First published 1616.

Lash, Nicholas. *The Beginning and the End of 'Religion.'* Cambridge: Cambridge University Press, 1996.

———. "What Might Martyrdom Mean?" In *Suffering and Martyrdom in the New Testament*, edited by William Horbury and Brian McNeil, 183–98. Cambridge: Cambridge University Press, 1981. Reprinted in his *Theology on the Way to Emmaus*, 75–92. London: SCM, 1986.

Legaspi, Michael C. *Wisdom in Classical and Biblical Tradition*. New York: Oxford University Press, 2018.

Leithart, Peter J. *1 & 2 Kings*. BTCB. Grand Rapids: Brazos, 2006.

Lenzi, Alan. "Proverbs 8:22–31: Three Perspectives on Its Composition." *JBL* 125, no. 4 (2006): 687–714.

Levenson, Jon D. *Creation and the Persistence of Evil: The Jewish Drama of Divine Omnipotence*. Princeton: Princeton University Press, 1988.

———. *The Death and Resurrection of the Beloved Son: The Transformation of Child Sacrifice in Judaism and Christianity*. New Haven: Yale University Press, 1993.

———. "Genesis." In *The Jewish Study Bible*, edited by Adele Berlin and Marc Zvi Brettler, 7–94. 2nd ed. New York: Oxford University Press, 2014.

———. "Is There a Counterpart in the Hebrew Bible to New Testament Anti-Semitism?" *JEC* 22 (1985): 242–60.

———. *Sinai and Zion: An Entry into the Jewish Bible*. Minneapolis: Winston Press, 1985.

———. "Zion Traditions." In *ABD* 6:1098–1102.

Levine, Etan. *The Burning Bush: Jewish Symbolism and Mysticism*. New York: Sepher-Hermon Press, 1981.

Lloyd-Jones, Hugh. *The Justice of Zeus*. Berkeley: University of California Press, 1971.

Loader, James A. *Proverbs 1–9*. HCOT. Leuven: Peeters, 2014.

Long, Burke O. "2 Kings." In *Harper's Bible Commentary*, edited by James L. Mays, 323–41. San Francisco: Harper & Row, 1988.

Louth, Andrew, ed. *Genesis 1–11*. ACCSOT 1. Downers Grove, IL: InterVarsity, 2001.

Luther, Martin. *Selected Psalms II*. Vol. 13 of *Luther's Works*. Edited by Jaroslav Pelikan. Translated by C. M. Jacobs. St. Louis: Concordia, 1956.

Macaskill, Grant. "Name Christology, Divine Aseity, and the I Am Sayings in the Fourth Gospel." *JTI* 12, no. 2 (2018): 217–41.

Machinist, Peter. "How Gods Die, Biblically and Otherwise: A Problem of Cosmic Restructuring." In *Reconsidering the Concept of Revolutionary Monotheism*, edited by Beate Pongratz-Leisten, 189–240. Winona Lake, IN: Eisenbrauns, 2011.

Maier, Christl, Grant Macaskill, and Joachim Schaper. *Congress Volume Aberdeen 2019*. VTSup. Leiden: Brill, 2021.

Maimonides. *The Guide of the Perplexed*. Translated by Shlomo Pines. Chicago: University of Chicago Press, 1963.

Martin, Dale B. *Biblical Truths: The Meaning of Scripture in the Twenty-First Century*. New Haven: Yale University Press, 2017.

McCann, J. Clinton, Jr. "The Single Most Important Text in the Entire Bible: Toward a Theology of the Psalms." In *Soundings in the Theology of the Psalms: Perspectives and Methods in Contemporary Scholarship*, edited by Rolf A. Jacobson, 63–75. Minneapolis: Fortress, 2011.

McKane, William. *Jeremiah*. Vol. 1. ICC. Edinburgh: T&T Clark, 1986.

McNeile, A. H. *The Book of Exodus*. 3rd ed. London: Methuen, 1931.

Meessen, Yves. "Penser le verbe 'être' autrement: Lecture d'Exode 3,14 par Paul Ricoeur." *NRT* 130 (2008): 760–74.

Mellinkoff, Ruth. *The Mark of Cain*. Berkeley: University of California Press, 1981.

Merton, Thomas. *Conjectures of a Guilty Bystander*. London: Sheldon, 1977.

Miller, Patrick D. "God and the Gods." In *Israelite Religion and Biblical Theology*, 365–96. JSOTSS 267. Sheffield: Sheffield Academic, 2000.

———. "The Old Testament and Christian Faith." In *Israelite Religion and Biblical Theology*, 648–57. JSOTSS 267. Sheffield: Sheffield Academic, 2000.

Moberly, R. W. L. *At the Mountain of God: Story and Theology in Exodus 32–34*. JSOTSS 22. Sheffield: JSOT Press, 1983.

———. *The Bible in a Disenchanted Age: The Enduring Possibility of Christian Faith*. Grand Rapids: Baker Academic, 2018.

———. "Does God Lie to His Prophets? The Story of Micaiah ben Imlah as a Test Case." *HTR* 96, no. 1 (2003): 1–23.

———. "Election and the Transformation of *Ḥērem*." In *The Call of Abraham: Essays on the Election of Israel in Honor of Jon D. Levenson*, edited by Gary A. Anderson and Joel S. Kaminsky, 67–89. Notre Dame: University of Notre Dame Press, 2013.

———. "Exemplars of Faith in Hebrews 11: Abel." In *The Epistle to the Hebrews and Christian Theology*, edited by Richard Bauckham, Daniel R. Driver, Trevor A. Hart, and Nathan MacDonald, 353–63. Grand Rapids: Eerdmans, 2009.

———. "How Appropriate Is 'Monotheism' as a Category for Biblical Interpretation?" In *Early Jewish and Christian Monotheism*, edited by Loren T. Stuckenbruck and Wendy E. S. North, 216–34. JSNTSS 263. London: T&T Clark, 2004.

———. "How May We Speak of God? A Reconsideration of the Nature of Biblical Theology." *TynBul* 53, no. 2 (2002): 177–202.

———. "'In God We Trust'? The Challenge of the Prophets." *Ex Auditu* 24 (2008): 18–33.

———. "Is Monotheism Bad for You? Some Reflections on God, the Bible, and Life in the Light of Regina Schwartz's *The Curse of Cain*." In *The God of Israel*, edited by Robert P. Gordon, 94–112. UCOP 64. Cambridge: Cambridge University Press, 2007.

———. "Justice and the Recognition of the True God: A Reading of Psalm 82." *RB* 127 (2020): 215–36.

———. "Knowing God and Knowing about God: Martin Buber's *Two Types of Faith* Revisited." *SJT* 65, no. 4 (2012): 402–20.

———. "The Mark of Cain—Revealed at Last?" *HTR* 100, no. 1 (2007): 11–28.

———. *The Old Testament of the Old Testament: Patriarchal Narratives and Mosaic Yahwism*. 1992. Reprint, Eugene, OR: Wipf & Stock, 2001.

———. *Old Testament Theology: Reading the Hebrew Bible as Christian Scripture*. Grand Rapids: Baker Academic, 2013.

———. *Prophecy and Discernment*. CSCD. Cambridge: Cambridge University Press, 2006.

———. "Sacramentality and the Old Testament." In *The Oxford Handbook of Sacramental Theology*, edited by Hans Boersma and Matthew Levering, 7–21. Oxford: Oxford University Press, 2015.

———. "Theological Approaches to the Old Testament." In *The Hebrew Bible: A Critical Companion*, edited by John Barton, 481–506. Princeton: Princeton University Press, 2016.

———. "Theological Interpretation, Second Naiveté, and the Rediscovery of the Old Testament." *ATR* 99, no. 4 (2017): 651–70.

———. *The Theology of the Book of Genesis*. OTT. Cambridge: Cambridge University Press, 2009.

Mobley, Gregory. "1 and 2 Kings." In *Theological Bible Commentary*, edited by Gail R. O'Day and David L. Petersen, 119–43. Louisville: Westminster John Knox, 2009.

Montgomery, James A., and Henry Snyder Gehman. *The Books of Kings*. ICC. Edinburgh: T&T Clark, 1951.

Mosser, Carl. "The Earliest Patristic Interpretations of Psalm 82, Jewish Antecedents, and the Origins of Christian Deification." *JTS* 56, no. 1 (2005): 30–74.

Nagel, Thomas. *Mind and Cosmos: Why the Materialist Neo-Darwinian Conception of Nature Is Almost Certainly False*. Oxford: Oxford University Press, 2012.

———. "Secular Philosophy and the Religious Temperament." In *Secular Philosophy and the Religious Temperament: Essays, 2002–2008*, 3–18. Oxford: Oxford University Press, 2010.

Nelson, Richard. *First and Second Kings*. IBCTP. Atlanta: John Knox, 1987.

Noth, Martin. *Exodus*. Translated by J. S. Bowden. OTL. London: SCM, 1962.

O'Connor, Kathleen. *Genesis 1–25A*. SHBC. Macon, GA: Smyth & Helwys, 2018.

———. "Wisdom Literature and Experience of the Divine." In *Biblical Theology: Problems and Perspectives; In Honor of J. Christiaan Beker*, edited by Steven J. Kraftchick, Charles D. Myers Jr., and Ben C. Ollenburger, 183–95. Nashville: Abingdon, 1995.

Otto, Rudolf. *The Idea of the Holy*. Translated by John Harvey. Oxford: Oxford University Press, 1924.

Overholt, Thomas. "Jeremiah." In *Harper's Bible Commentary*, edited by James L. Mays, 597–645. San Francisco: Harper & Row, 1988.

Polak, Frank H. "Storytelling and Redaction: Varieties of Linguistic Usage in the Exodus Narrative." In *The Formation of the Pentateuch: Bridging the Academic*

Cultures of Europe, Israel, and North America, edited by Jan C. Gertz, Bernard M. Levinson, Dalit Rom-Shiloni, and Konrad Schmid, 443–75. FAT 111. Tübingen: Mohr Siebeck, 2016.

Popkin, Richard H., ed. *Pascal: Selections*. New York: Macmillan, 1989.

Provan, Iain. *Discovering Genesis: Content, Interpretation, Reception*. London: SPCK, 2015.

———. *1 and 2 Kings*. NIBC. Peabody, MA: Hendrickson, 1995.

Radner, Ephraim. *Time and the Word: Figural Reading of the Christian Scriptures*. Grand Rapids: Eerdmans, 2016.

Rashi. *The Pentateuch with the Commentary of Rashi*. Translated and edited by M. Rosenbaum and A. M. Silbermann. Jerusalem: Silbermann, 1972.

Revised Common Lectionary in NRSV. London: Mowbray, 1998.

Ricoeur, Paul. *The Symbolism of Evil*. Boston: Beacon, 1969.

Robinson, J. *The Second Book of Kings*. CBC. Cambridge: Cambridge University Press, 1976.

Robinson, Marilynne. *What Are We Doing Here? Essays*. London: Virago, 2018.

Rofé, Alexander. *The Prophetical Stories: The Narratives about the Prophets in the Hebrew Bible, Their Literary Types, and History*. Jerusalem: Magnes, 1988.

Römer, Thomas. "The Form-Critical Problem of the So-Called Deuteronomistic History." In *The Changing Face of Form Criticism for the Twenty-First Century*, edited by Marvin Sweeney and Ehud Ben Zvi, 240–52. Grand Rapids: Eerdmans, 2003.

———. "The Revelation of the Divine Name to Moses and the Construction of a Memory about the Origins of the Encounter between Yhwh and Israel." In *Israel's Exodus in Transdisciplinary Perspective: Text, Archaeology, Culture, and Geoscience*, edited by Thomas E. Levy, Thomas Schneider, and William H. C. Propp, 305–15. Cham, Switzerland: Springer, 2015.

———. "The Strange Conversion of Naaman, Chief of the Aramean Army." In *Research on Israel and Aram*, edited by Angelika Berlejung and Aren Maier, 105–19. Tübingen: Mohr Siebeck, 2019.

Ross, W. D., ed. *Aristotle's Metaphysics*. Vol. 1. Oxford: Clarendon, 1924.

Rowley, H. H. *From Joseph to Joshua: Biblical Traditions in the Light of Archaeology*. Oxford: Oxford University Press, 1950.

Ruden, Sarah. *The Face of Water: A Translator on Beauty and Meaning in the Bible*. New York: Vintage, 2018.

Rudolph, Wilhelm. *Jeremia*. 3rd ed. HAT 12. Tübingen: Mohr Siebeck, 1968.

Sacks, Jonathan. *Faith in the Future*. London: Darton, Longman & Todd, 1995.

———. *Future Tense: A Vision for Jews and Judaism in the Global Culture*. London: Hodder & Stoughton, 2009.

Saebø, Magne. "God's Name in Exodus 3.13–15: An Expression of Revelation or Veiling?" In *On the Way to Canon: Creative Tradition History in the Old Testament*, 78–92. JSOTSS 191. Sheffield: Sheffield Academic, 1988.

Sandmel, Samuel. "The Haggada within Scripture." *JBL* 80, no. 2 (1961): 105–22.

———. "Parallelomania." In *Presidential Voices: The Society of Biblical Literature in the Twentieth Century*, edited by Harold W. Attridge and James C. VanderKam, 107–18. Atlanta: Society of Biblical Literature, 2006.

Sarna, Nahum. *Exploring Exodus: The Heritage of Biblical Israel*. New York: Schocken, 1987.

———. *The JPS Torah Commentary: Genesis*. Philadelphia: Jewish Publication Society, 1989.

Schaefer, Konrad. *Psalms*. Berit Olam. Collegeville, MN: Liturgical Press, 2001.

Schmid, Konrad. "Gibt es 'Reste hebräischen Heidentums' im Alten Testament? Methodische Überlegungen anhand von Dtn 32,8f. und Ps 82." In *Primäre und sekundäre Religion als Kategorie der Religionsgeschichte der Alten Testaments*, edited by Andreas Wagner, 105–20. BZAW 364. Berlin: de Gruyter, 2006.

———. *A Historical Theology of the Hebrew Bible*. Translated by Peter Altmann. Grand Rapids: Eerdmans, 2019.

Schüle, Andreas. *Theology from the Beginning: Essays on the Primeval History and Its Canonical Context*. FAT 113. Tübingen: Mohr Siebeck, 2017.

Schwab, Zoltan. "Is Fear of the Lord the Source of Wisdom or Vice Versa?" *VT* 63 (2013): 652–62.

Seitz, Christopher R. *The Elder Testament: Canon, Theology, Trinity*. Waco: Baylor University Press, 2018.

———. *Figured Out: Typology and Providence in Christian Scripture*. Louisville: Westminster John Knox, 2001.

Seow, Choon-Leong. "The First and Second Books of Kings." In *NIB* 3:1–295.

Sheridan, Mark, ed. *Genesis 12–50*. ACCSOT 2. Downers Grove, IL: InterVarsity, 2002.

Shortt, Rupert. *Christianophobia: A Faith under Attack*. London: Rider, 2012.

Shulman, Ahouva. "The Particle *nā'* in Biblical Hebrew Prose." *Hebrew Studies* 40 (1999): 57–82.

Smelik, Klaas A. D. *Converting the Past: Studies in Ancient Israelite and Moabite Historiography*. OTS 28. Leiden: Brill, 1992.

Smith, Mark S. *The Origins of Biblical Monotheism: Israel's Polytheistic Background and the Ugaritic Texts*. Oxford: Oxford University Press, 2001.

Sommer, Benjamin D. *The Bodies of God and the World of Ancient Israel*. New York: Cambridge University Press, 2009.

———. "Kaufmann and Recent Scholarship: Toward a Richer Discourse of Monotheism." In *Yehezkel Kaufmann and the Reinvention of Jewish Biblical Scholarship*, edited by Job Y. Jindo, Benjamin D. Sommer, and Thomas Staubli, 204–39. OBO 283. Fribourg: Academic Press; Göttingen: Vandenhoeck & Ruprecht, 2017.

Sonderegger, Katherine. *Systematic Theology*. Vol. 1, *The Doctrine of God*. Minneapolis: Fortress, 2015.

Sonnet, Jean-Pierre. "*Ehyeh asher Ehyeh* (Exodus 3:14): God's 'Narrative Identity' among Suspense, Curiosity, and Surprise." *Poetics Today* 31, no. 2 (2010): 331–51.

Sperber, Alexander. *The Bible in Aramaic*. Vol. 1, *The Pentateuch according to Targum Onkelos*. Leiden: Brill, 1992.

Spina, Frank Anthony. "The 'Ground' for Cain's Rejection (Gen 4): *ʾădāmāh* in the Context of Gen 1–11." *ZAW* 104 (1992): 319–32.

Spurgeon, Charles H. *The Treasury of David*. Vol. 4. London: Passmore & Alabaster, 1876.

Steinbeck, John. *East of Eden*. John Steinbeck Centennial Edition. New York: Viking, 2003.

———. *Journal of a Novel: The "East of Eden" Letters*. New York: Penguin, 2001.

Stewart, Anne W. *Poetic Ethics in Proverbs: Wisdom Literature and the Shaping of the Moral Self*. Cambridge: Cambridge University Press, 2016.

Strawn, Brent A. *The Old Testament Is Dying: A Diagnosis and Recommended Treatment*. Grand Rapids: Baker Academic, 2017.

———. "The Poetics of Psalm 82: Three Critical Notes along with a Plea for the Poetic." *RB* 121, no. 1 (2014): 21–46.

———. "Psalm 82." In *Psalms for Preaching and Worship: A Lectionary Commentary*, edited by Roger E. Van Harn and Brent A. Strawn, 215–20. Grand Rapids: Eerdmans, 2009.

Sweeney, Marvin A. *I & II Kings*. OTL. Louisville: Westminster John Knox, 2007.

Sykora, Josef. *The Unfavored: Judah and Saul in the Narratives of Genesis and 1 Samuel*. Siphrut 25. University Park, PA: Eisenbrauns, 2018.

Tate, Marvin E. *Psalms 51–100*. WBC 20. Dallas: Word, 1990.

Terrien, Samuel. *The Psalms: Strophic Structure and Theological Commentary*. Grand Rapids: Eerdmans, 2003.

Thiselton, Anthony C. "The Supposed Power of Words in the Biblical Writings." *JTS* 25 (1974): 283–99. Reprinted, with minor editorial modification, in *Thiselton on Hermeneutics*, 53–67. Aldershot, UK: Ashgate, 2006.

Tigay, Jeffrey. "Exodus." In *The Jewish Study Bible*, edited by Adele Berlin and Marc Zvi Brettler, 95–192. 2nd ed. New York: Oxford University Press, 2014.

———. *The JPS Torah Commentary: Deuteronomy*. Philadelphia: Jewish Publication Society, 1996.

Tillich, Paul. *Dynamics of Faith*. New York: Harper & Row, 1958.

Treier, Daniel J. *Proverbs and Ecclesiastes*. BTCB. Grand Rapids: Brazos, 2011.

Trotter, James M. "Death of the *ʾlhym* in Psalm 82." *JBL* 131, no. 2 (2012): 221–39.

Tsevat, Matitiahu. "God and the Gods in Assembly: An Interpretation of Psalm 82." *HUCA* 40 (1969): 123–37. Reprinted in *The Meaning of the Book of Job and Other Biblical Studies*, 131–47. New York: Ktav, 1980.

van Oorschot, Jürgen, and Markus Witte, eds. *The Origins of Yahwism*. BZAW 484. Berlin: de Gruyter, 2017.

Varden, Erik. *The Shattering of Loneliness: On Christian Remembrance*. London: Bloomsbury Continuum, 2018.

von Rad, Gerhard. "The Deuteronomic Theology of History in 1 and 2 Kings." In *From Genesis to Chronicles: Explorations in Old Testament Theology*, 154–66. Edited by K. C. Hanson. Translated by E. W. Trueman Dicken. Minneapolis: Fortress, 2005.

———. *Genesis*. Translated by John H. Marks. 3rd ed. London: SCM, 1972.

———. *Moses*. Translated by Stephen Neill. Edited and revised by K. C. Hanson. Cambridge: James Clarke, 2011.

———. "Naaman: A Critical Retelling." In *God at Work in Israel*, 47–57. Translated by John H. Marks. Nashville: Abingdon, 1980.

———. *Old Testament Theology*. Translated by D. M. G. Stalker. 2 vols. London: SCM, 1975.

———. *Wisdom in Israel*. Translated by James D. Martin. London: SCM, 1970.

Wanke, Gunther. *Die Zionstheologie der Korachiten in ihrem traditionsgeschichtlichen Zusammenhang*. BZAW 97. Berlin: de Gruyter, 1966.

Ware, Kallistos. *The Orthodox Church*. Harmondsworth, UK: Penguin, 1985.

Watson, J. R., ed. *An Annotated Anthology of Hymns*. Oxford: Oxford University Press, 2002.

Weeks, Stuart. "The Context and Meaning of Proverbs 8:30a." *JBL* 125, no. 3 (2006): 433–42.

———. *Early Israelite Wisdom*. OTM. Oxford: Oxford University Press, 1994.

———. *Instruction and Imagery in Proverbs 1–9*. Oxford: Oxford University Press, 2007.

Weinfeld, Moshe. *Deuteronomy and the Deuteronomistic School*. Oxford: Clarendon, 1972.

———. *Social Justice in Ancient Israel and in the Ancient Near East*. Minneapolis: Fortress, 1995.

Wells, Samuel. *Learning to Dream Again: Rediscovering the Heart of God*. Grand Rapids: Eerdmans, 2013.

Wenham, Gordon J. *Genesis 1–15*. WBC 1. Waco: Word, 1987.

———. "Sanctuary Symbolism in the Garden of Eden Story." In *Proceedings of the Ninth World Congress of Jewish Studies*, 19–25. Jerusalem: World Union of Jewish Studies, 1986.

Wesselschmidt, Quentin F., ed. *Psalms 51–150*. ACCSOT 8. Downers Grove, IL: InterVarsity, 2007.

West, Martin L. "Towards Monotheism." In *Pagan Monotheism in Late Antiquity*, edited by Polymnia Athanassiadi and Michael Frede, 21–40. Oxford: Clarendon, 1999.

Wevers, John W. *Notes on the Greek Text of Exodus*. SBLSCS 30. Atlanta: Scholars Press, 1990.

———. *Notes on the Greek Text of Genesis*. SBLSCS 35. Atlanta: Scholars Press, 1993.

Williams, Catrin H. *I Am He: The Interpretation of 'Anî Hû' in Jewish and Early Christian Literature*. WUNT 2/113. Tübingen: Mohr Siebeck, 2000.

Williams, Rowan. *Christ on Trial: How the Gospel Unsettles Our Judgement*. London: Fount, 2000.

Williamson, H. G. M. "On Getting Carried Away with the Infinitive Construct of *nś'*." In *Shai le-Sara Japhet: Studies in the Bible, Its Exegesis and Its Language*, edited by Moshe Bar-Asher et al., 357–67. Jerusalem: Bialik Institute, 2007.

Wiseman, Donald J. *1 and 2 Kings*. TOTC. Leicester, UK: Inter-Varsity, 1993.

Witte, Markus. *Jesus Christus im Alten Testament: Eine biblisch-theologische Skizze*. SEThV 4. Münster: Lit Verlag, 2013.

Wolff, Hans Walter. "The Kerygma of the Deuteronomic Historical Work." In *The Vitality of Old Testament Traditions*, edited by Walter Brueggemann and Hans Walter Wolff, 83–100. Atlanta: John Knox, 1975.

Wood, Charles M. *The Question of Providence*. Louisville: Westminster John Knox, 2008.

Wright, Thomas, ed. *Early Travels in Palestine*. London: Bohn, 1848.

Yoder, Christine Roy. *Wisdom as a Woman of Substance: A Socioeconomic Reading of Proverbs 1–9 and 31:10–31*. BZAW 304. Berlin: de Gruyter, 2014.

Young, Frances. "Proverbs 8 in Interpretation (2): Wisdom Personified." In *Reading Texts, Seeking Wisdom*, edited by David Ford and Graham Stanton, 102–15. London: SCM, 2003.

Zevit, Ziony. *The Religions of Ancient Israel: A Synthesis of Parallactic Approaches*. London: Continuum, 2001.

Zimmerli, Walther. *I Am Yahweh*. Translated by Douglas Stott. Edited with an introduction by Walter Brueggemann. Atlanta: John Knox, 1982.

Index of Authors

Index of Subjects

Index of Scripture and Other Ancient Writings

Old Testament

Genesis

Exodus

Leviticus

Numbers

Deuteronomy

Psalms

Proverbs